The Perfect Servant

THE PERFECT SERVANT

Eunuchs and the Social Construction of Gender in Byzantium

Kathryn M. Ringrose

The University of Chicago Press
Chicago and London

Kathryn M. Ringrose is lecturer in history at the University of California, San Diego.

The University of Chicago Press, Chicago 60637
The University of Chicago Press, Ltd., London

Printed in the United States of America

12 11 10 09 08 07 06 05 04 03 1 2 3 4 5
ISBN: 0-226-72015-2 (cloth)

Library of Congress Cataloging-in-Publication Data

Ringrose, Kathryn M.
The perfect servant: eunuchs and the social construction of gender in Byzantium / Kathryn M. Ringrose.
p. cm.
Includes bibliographical references and index.
ISBN 0-226-72015-2 (cloth : alk. paper)
1. Eunuchs—Byzantine Empire. 2. Sex role—Byzantine Empire. 3. Byzantine Empire—Civilization. I. Title.
HQ449 .R56 2003
305.3′09495—dc21

200214105

♾ The paper used in this publication meets the minimum requirements of the American National Standard for Information Sciences—Permanence of Paper for Printed Library Materials, ANSI Z39.48-1992.

For David: scholar, teacher, dearest friend, and lifelong companion

CONTENTS

ILLUSTRATIONS

SPELLING CONVENTIONS FOR GREEK NAMES

This manuscript contains many Greek names and titles. Recent years have brought greater consistency in the use of spellings and an effort to use spellings that reflect Greek roots. Whenever possible, I have followed the spellings in the *Oxford Dictionary of Byzantium (ODB).* The reader will note some inconsistencies. Most personal names have been spelled as transliterated Greek following the *ODB;* some have been left in their familiar English form. They are either names that are familiar (e.g., Constantine, Basil, Theodore) or names spelled in the English form by recent translators (e.g., Andrew, Candace). Most of the new spellings are easily recognizable, but a few can cause confusion and have been listed in the appendix.

The most frequent inconsistency in the use of Greek, Latin, and English spellings involves the words *cubiculum* and *koubikoularios.* The *ODB* (s.v. "koiton," "koitonities") translates Latin *cubiculum* as Greek *koiton* (κοιτών) but draws a distinction between the servants (koitonites, κοιτωνίτης) of the imperial bedchamber (the *koiton*) and the servants of the *cubiculum.* The *ODB* refers to the latter as the "corps of eunuchs of the palace," using the Greek word *koubikoularioi.* This is "a general term to designate palace eunuchs who waited upon the emperor, the servants of the *sacrum cubiculum*" (*ODB* ii, 1154). Since my concern is with the palace as a whole, I have used the Latin *cubiculum* and the Greek term *koubikoularios,* hopefully avoiding confusion with the more intimate terms *koiton* and *koitonites.*

ACKNOWLEDGMENTS

This book has been in progress for many years and I owe its completion to a wide range of friends, colleagues, and family members. I have been privileged to have financial support from the American Council for Learned Studies, the National Endowment for the Humanities, and the American Philosophical Society. I am indebted to the library staffs at the University of California, San Diego; Dumbarton Oaks; and the Institute for Advanced Studies in Princeton for consistently answering my pleas for obscure materials. I remember with pleasure a year in Princeton where scholars both at the university and at the Institute for Advanced Studies helped me to formulate this project. I owe special thanks to Peter Brown, Giles Constable, Patrick Geary, Judith Herrin, Philip Rousseau, and Joan Scott for suggesting new avenues of research about eunuchs and pointing me toward rewarding theoretical and primary materials. That year in their company provided me with a wealth of intellectual riches.

I am indebted to many other friends and colleagues. Gilbert Herdt early on invited me to contribute to one of his publications. He provided a valuable critique of what became an early framework for many of the ideas in this book. I am indebted to Matina McGrath, who meticulously checked my Greek translations, and to my colleague Alden Mosshammer, who acted as a referee when Matina and I could not agree. Claudia Rapp and Aline Hornaday critiqued early drafts of the manuscript, and Chuck Allen helped me make the manuscript accessible for a general audience. David Goodblatt helped with Hebrew sources, and David Noel Freedman kept encouraging me, always with that mischievous twinkle in his eye.

My thanks to the University of Chicago Press and to Doug Mitchell my ever-patient editor and to the two anonymous press readers. I will never be able to suffciently thank "reader number two" who read the manuscript at least twice and offered a detailed critique that saved me from a number of serious errors. I owe a similar debt to Maia Rigas, whose painstaking editing improved the effectiveness of this book. Any remaining errors or omissions in the manuscript are, of course, my own.

In the winter of 2000–2001, as the manuscript was nearing completion, I began to lose my sight. During the following year, while the skilled surgeons at the Shiley Eye Clinic of the University of California, San Diego, repaired my eyes, my husband, David, put aside his own historical scholarship, finished entering my revisions to the manuscript, and prepared the footnotes and bibliography. He became my eyes and acted as my secretary. Without his help the manuscript would never have been finished.

Finally, I offer a note of encouragement to the many other part-time and temporary faculty, the "lecturers," who also labor in the undergraduate trenches, teaching too many students for too little pay and no benefits at institutions like the University of California. Organizations such as Independent Scholars and granting agencies like the National Endowment for the Humanities have recognized that we are serious scholars with good training and scholarly potential. Their support has made this book possible.

INTRODUCTION

Eunuchs of Byzantium: Context and Definition

Like most Byzantine historians I love to visit Constantinople, the great Byzantine capital. Today it stands empty, robed in the modern buildings of Istanbul, peopled only by tourists. I can only see the real dwellers in this city in my imagination, an imagination honed by years of reading Byzantine texts. The tenth-century city bustles with men of all social ranks, and the markets are full of lower-class women. Upper-class women, if seen at all, are heavily veiled and carefully escorted. And then there are the eunuchs. We find them in the streets, carrying messages, escorting wealthy women, guarding young children. They are beardless, carefully groomed, well dressed in expensive clothing, for they are the costly, elite agents and servants, the elegant adornments of a wealthy, urban aristocracy. Those who are still young might be mistaken for adolescent boys, albeit slightly unusual adolescent boys, with fine, fair skin, faces that are just a bit broad, and tall thin bodies with narrow shoulders and graceful carriage. Older eunuchs often show the signs of poor health. Their faces are prematurely lined, and youthful fairness has become pallor. Their bodies are stooped from osteoporosis. Even so, they sport a thick, luxuriant head of hair and present themselves as wealthy, cultured gentlemen. The most successful of these distinctive people live in the grand houses that surround the palace.

The great palace complex next to the hippodrome is now mostly gone, buried deep beneath the modern city. If we could enter the imperial palace of the tenth century, however, we would find it controlled by eunuchs. They guard the doorways, supervise access to the emperor, manage the servants who see to the everyday needs of the imperial family—the cooks, the bakers, and cleaning staff. Eunuchs serve as barbers, dressers, and doctors. They manage the imperial finances and record keeping. They guard and control the imperial regalia, packing crowns carefully in storage boxes, selecting ceremonial garments, and helping the emperor keep track of his daily round of ceremonial obligations. Eunuchs of the household serve in the imperial choir of singers. In the apartments of the empress a similar corps of eunuchs serves and guards her well-being. Each of the imperial heirs has his own staff of eunuchs, servants who will loyally serve him throughout his life. This pattern is repeated around the city in the mansions of the great aristocratic families.

The great church, Hagia Sophia, still remains. In the tenth century we would find many eunuchs there as well. Alongside "whole" or "bearded" men, eunuchs serve as priests, bishops, and even patriarchs, and are celebrated for their perfect celibacy. Such churchmen also have households staffed with eunuch servants and singers. As we move about the city we find eunuch monks and holy hermits. We encounter luxurious monasteries reserved especially for eunuchs, elite places of retirement or incarceration for powerful eunuchs who have grown too old or too bold in the imperial service. Eunuchs serve in hospitals and orphanages and convents; they dispense largess to widows, orphans, and the poor.

As we leave the elegant core of the city and move into its seamier neighborhoods we find eunuch entertainers, actors, and singers. We also find eunuch prostitutes, castrated children destined to serve men's pleasures for their entire lives, and young men who have had themselves castrated as adults in order to enjoy a life of uncomplicated sexual pleasure with both men and women. As we wander through the city, we gradually develop a perception of these individuals. They are distinctive in physical appearance, dress, and manner and often perform tasks that upper-class men and women are constrained from doing. This distinctiveness includes an element of ambiguity. Among the upper classes and in the centers of government power, the eunuch is a perfect servant of God or of his secular master, one from whom lifelong loyalty is expected. This master-servant relationship borders on the spiritual. Simultaneously, in the urban districts dedicated to sensory pleasures, the eunuch represents the material world; a world devoted to the pleasures of the flesh.

Eunuchs and Gender

This book is a study of the place of eunuchs in Byzantine society and culture, a study of an institution that was both very ancient and quite varied in its makeup.

It asks about Byzantine society's conscious perceptions of eunuchs, about its unconscious assumptions regarding eunuchs, and about the variety of gender subcategories that were encompassed by the term *eunuch*. It suggests that Byzantine society classed eunuchs as what modern analysis defines as a separate gender category, one that was neither male nor female, and that the nature of this gender category changed significantly over a thousand years of Late Antique and Byzantine history. In doing this, the book will explore the construction and perception of gender in the Byzantine world between the sixth and twelfth centuries. The analysis is based on the premise that Byzantine culture incorporated more than two well-defined gender categories as part of normal life in Byzantium, at least among the urban, courtly elite. The eunuchs of Byzantium thus offer an important example of an alternative gender category and of the need to understand how such categories function in society, past and present. Any phenomenon that is so different from modern sexual and gender norms and also so durable is worthy of closer examination and may challenge the assumptions of modern historians of gender.

Accepted for centuries as a functionally legitimate group, eunuchs were a feature of Byzantine society throughout its history, a history that traditionally extends more than a thousand years from the founding of Constantinople in 324 to its capture by the Turks in 1453. Within that long history, eunuchs were particularly prominent both at court and in the church from about 600 to 1100. Although their political influence was seriously curtailed by the Komnenos dynasty in the twelfth century, the eunuchs of Byzantium constituted an institution that persisted and, in the social sense, reproduced itself, for an entire millennium. This distinctively gendered group of individuals flourished despite the fact that Roman and Byzantine law prohibited the making of eunuchs within the empire and that ecclesiastical traditions frowned on bodily mutilation. Eunuchism[1] could not have persisted unless castration was in some way condoned by Byzantine culture. This paradox calls out for closer investigation.

To those of us who have been raised in a Western tradition and reflexively find intermediate gender categories "abnormal" and "unnatural," Byzantine society offers an opportunity to look at a very different culture. It is a culture in which certain individuals were intentionally changed into something that was neither male nor female as defined in Western culture. If, as I believe, gender was constructed in Byzantium in a way that differed significantly from its construction in modern Western society, this study will help us understand the social history of Byzantium.

Before we can begin to explore the topic of eunuchs, however, we must first clarify what we mean by the words *sex* and *gender*. In this book the term *sex* will be used to refer to the biological determinants that establish the difference between what modern society refers to as the male and the female. In the period covered by this book, sex is determined by the nature of the reproductive organs. In modern times, sex is also determined by the nature of the chromosomal structure of the individual. Nevertheless, in Byzantium, even though eunuchs' genital organs had been removed and their physiology significantly altered, they were still considered to be men. After Late Antiquity there is little indication that eunuchs were believed to constitute a "third sex."

The term *gender* refers to the patterns of behavior assumed to be appropriate to a gender group. As we will see, Byzantine society tolerated alternative gender groups that were acculturated into patterns of behavior considered to be appropriate to that group. Thus, eunuchs constituted a third gender within Byzantium. They were men, but a differently acculturated kind of men. In this context, the phrase "to gender" refers to a pattern in which eunuchs were consciously reared and trained to present themselves and act in ways considered appropriate for eunuchs.

In the past ten years a number of scholars concerned with gender theory have suggested that we look at the structure of gender in ancient Greece and Rome in new ways.[2] Perhaps these cultures, so basic to our own, did not perceive sexuality and gender in the same way that we do. Perhaps, for example, sexual object choice was not the salient determinant of gender category as it is in modern society.

This book relies heavily on the theoretical assumption that gender is a socially constructed category, and it is hoped that the following discussion will help to strengthen that proposition. Modern scholars who explore gender theory tend to separate male and female based either on biological differences or "gendered" attributes. Biological differences between men and women are assumed to be inherited, physiologically determined qualities and are reflected in genitalia, biological function in reproduction, and physical appearance as determined by hormonal function. There is also an ongoing discussion as to whether sexual object choice is genetically determined. It is often assumed that none of the above biological elements of the human body are subject to change, yet in fact many of them are subject to cultural construction in which medical or psychological intervention is deemed necessary to help an individual achieve a culturally defined "normality." For example children born with both male and female genitalia are labeled "abnormal" and are reconstructed, usually as males. Male children who are deficient in male hormones are given medication so that they will develop into "normal" males. An adult may conclude that his/her inner being does not concur with the physiology of his/her body and arrange to undergo surgery to change the physiology of his/her genitalia. Our Western culture is so wedded to a bipolar biological structure that we will go to great extremes to preserve the differences between male and female sexual categories and avoid intermediary categories.

In contrast, Byzantine society reared children born with ambiguous sexual organs as "natural eunuchs," individuals especially honored by God because freed from sexual desire and offered them an honored place within society. It also castrated male children in order to create eunuchs, individuals who were also physiologically ambiguous. There is no question that, although these individuals were biologically different from men, this biological difference was socially constructed. Thus Byzantine society routinely gendered young eunuchs into patterns of behavior considered to be "normal" for what it determined would be their gender category. As we will see, this resulted in the creation of a group of individuals that had all the attributes of a third gender.[3]

The phase "social construction" implies that gender is made up of several building blocks, some of them consciously imposed and maintained by society, some of them deep-seated assumptions about individuals that are rarely challenged or even perceived. The image of construction also implies something like a foundation—some feature of the construct that is basic and around which the rest of the edifice is constructed. In Byzantium the basic aspects of maleness and femaleness seem pretty straightforward: men procreate, head households, and manage worldly affairs; women bear children, care for dependents, and manage affairs within the household. As we will see, the worlds inside and outside the household are sharply separate domains (a distinction that should not be confused with modern concepts of public and private). Furthermore, Byzantine society included many sharply defined boundaries between social categories and genders.

I maintain that the fundamental features around which a gender was constructed for eunuchs were the separation of eunuchs from reproduction and family obligations and the aptness of eunuchs for what I will call "perfect service." The idea of "perfect service" as a focal point for the social construction of gender is not something I have found in other studies of the topic. Eunuchs existed outside of the dominant social values and institutions of family, offspring, and procreation. This made them ideally suited to serve as servants, agents, and proxies for their masters or employers, male or female. They moved freely across social and gender barriers and were not precluded from a wide range of roles often deemed unsuitable for the persons whom they served. Moreover, because they were generally castrated at a young age, eunuchs developed distinctive physiological traits, some of which were then combined with learned behaviors such as body language, speech patterns, dress, and affect, resulting in individuals who were readily identifiable to their contemporaries.

This "otherness," together with the ability to transcend important barriers, was combined with de facto celibacy. In a culture that saw celibacy, asceticism, and holiness as related and desirable traits and that firmly believed in spiritual realms that were not accessible to most men and women, people readily assumed that eunuchs had access to spiritual realms that were otherwise inaccessible. Before we look at specific aspects of this process of cultural construction, it will be useful to review some of the dimensions of this question of gender; both as seen from our perspective and as conceptualized in the Byzantine world.

The Byzantine world constructed a gender framework for eunuchs that involved two significant elements: eunuchs as a generalized social category with a range of assigned attributes and eunuchs as identifiable individuals who made the general patterns concrete and who played important historical roles in Byzantine life. These two elements are the topics of parts 1 and 2 of this book. As modern historians, we are able to trace the gradual change in the language, status, and perception of eunuchs over the course of several centuries of Byzantine history. This modern analysis provides a third major theme that runs through this book.

Modern gender theory distinguishes biological markers from gender markers. Gender markers include such elements as dress, body language, patterns of speech, and roles and types of activities that society allots to men and women. They extend to positions of subordination and dominance in social hierarchies, assumptions about physiological characteristics such as strength and intelligence, and assumptions about moral character and integrity. Such markers also include spatial constraints within the family and household and in the exercise of spiritual and secular office. These markers are socially constructed and imposed on men and women, publicly establishing them as members of a particular gender group. Until recently the complexity and strength of these constraints, the degree to which they were considered to be normal, also reflected the degree to which Western society has been wedded to a bipolar model for the organization of both sex and gender.

Assuming that the category "eunuch" and its later subcategories were socially constructed, what is the nature of this construction and how does it relate to other constructed categories that specifically reference men and women? Of particular interest here is the fact that all of the negative attributes in the category "eunuch" are derived from ones ascribed to women. Conversely, most positive attributes are shared with men. This offers insight into how gender categories were socially constructed in the Byzantine world and suggests that careful analysis of Byzantine assumptions about gender attributes may also offer insights into theoretical issues surrounding today's gender constructs.

Surely eunuchs were the ultimate constructed gender category. Society changed the eunuch's physiology and outward physical appearance, then reared him in a special environment and trained him for very specific roles. Eunuchs were easily recognizable in public as a result of their distinctive voices and beardless faces. Some even adopted particular mannerisms that identified them as members of this group. The "thirdness" of the eunuch is an important part of his gender construct.

Given both modern assumptions and the persistent ambiguity associated with eunuchs in our sources, it is hardly surprising that the question has been raised as to whether and, if so, in what ways, Byzantine eunuchs were marginal members of their society. In the course of this discussion three terms—*liminality, marginality,* and *gender*—tend to surface and interact. Eunuchs were certainly liminal if we use this term in its most literal sense, since they operated across thresholds or boundaries. In the course of this study we will see eunuchs cross social, spiritual, and gender boundaries. I would suggest, however, that despite first impressions, eunuchs were not marginal to society in economic, spiritual, or political terms. Rather, they were marginal in the sense that they did not fit easily into a bipolar gender structure. Their existence forced people to talk about them using a language that lacked a convenient vocabulary. They made their contemporaries uneasy because they were seen to move too readily between the worlds of men and women, between earthly sensuality and heavenly spirituality, between imperial presence and ordinary space, and between the church and the secular world.

Yet, despite this apparent marginality, eunuchs constituted a remarkably stable, durable institution in the eastern Mediterranean for more than a thousand years. Their ambiguous gender status allowed them to fill liminal roles, and it placed them in a marginal situation, in part because it was assumed that they did not (or ought not) hold power in their own right. Nevertheless, eunuchs were both powerful and offensive to political rivals. In a society that was working out the relationship between male reproductive organs, intellectual powers, and the "seat" of moral values, a society caught between a very old Eastern Mediterranean value system based on kin and family and a newer Christian one that emphasized asexual spirituality, eunuchs defied all attempts at conventional gender categorization. Their ambiguity allowed them to be identified simultaneously with the grossest of sexual excess and with the angels.

This study has two important dimensions. On a general and theoretical level, it examines the possibility that a culture does not necessarily have to be organized around the bipolar gender model of the modern West. On a more particular historiographical plane, this book focuses on eunuchs because the surviving Byzantine sources seldom speak to issues of gender except in connection with eunuchs. In doing so, however, these sources provide insights into the larger gender patterns of the culture, both as structural patterns and as dynamic, evolving phenomena.

The obvious questions concerning the study of the Byzantine eunuch are, Why did this institution persist, and why was it so important? This question has been asked by many scholars, most recently by the late Alexander Kazhdan, who observed: "It is not clear why eunuchs were so important in the Byzantine administration."[4] What was it that made eunuchs so integral and even essential to the workings of Byzantine society? What rendered this specially gendered category so integral to the life of Byzantium that its social behavior persistently contradicted its own formal strictures by allowing castration and by placing castrated men at the top of its most important administrative hierarchies?

Historical Context

While the primary emphasis in this book is on Byzantine eunuchs from the eighth to the twelfth centuries, the world of that era cannot be understood without a discussion of earlier and broader contexts. Historically, eunuchs can be found throughout much of the Old World. They can be divided into three categories. Often they were men castrated as adults, either as a punishment for crimes or as prisoners of war. This was often the source of court eunuchs. Many eunuchs were castrated as adults willingly to serve in priestly cults. Finally, some eunuchs were castrated as young slaves or as prepubescent boys by their own families in order to prepare them for careers as servants in royal courts and aristocratic homes or as prostitutes.

By the height of the Byzantine Empire in A.D. 1000, eunuchs had been a feature of Middle Eastern and Asian court life for at least three millennia. They appear as court servants in Mesopotamian texts from 2000 B.C.,[5] in Egyptian texts from the nineteenth dynasty (ca. 1300 B.C.),[6] and in Chinese texts from 1100 B.C.[7] Eunuchs played a very visible role in Chinese history and could be found in China, usually in association with the imperial court, until the revolution of the twentieth century. We know that castration was practiced as a punishment in China and that some eunuchs at court achieved great power; we are less informed about the way eunuchs fitted into Chinese society. We also have evidence, admittedly disputed by some scholars, that eunuchs served as courtiers in the Neo-Assyrian Empire (934–610 B.C.) and that their roles at court were analogous to those of later Byzantine court eunuchs.[8] There were certainly eunuchs in the Persian Empire.[9] The practice of having eunuchs was continued by Hellenistic and Roman rulers, by the Byzantines, and by the Muslims.[10] In the Islamic world and those parts of North Africa, Spain, and Italy controlled by Islam, eunuchs served both at court and as servants at important religious shrines.[11]

The category of men who castrate themselves in order to serve in priestly cults has been studied extensively, and the practice still survives in modern society.[12] Castrated priests served the mother goddess Cybele, a very old cult the Greeks adopted from the Phrygians about 700 B.C. We do not know whether castration was originally a part of the cult, since the texts that refer to castrated priests and to the castrated god Attis date from the fourth and fifth centuries B.C. In this context, castration was sought by adult men who were called to the priesthood. The cult flourished in "holy cities" like Hierapolis in Asia Minor, where it had shrines guarded by eunuch priests. In 204 B.C. the cult was brought to Rome, along with its eunuch priests, who were called *galli.*[13] The cult has died out, but cultic castration reappears periodically. The Skoptsy, a radical Christian sect that practiced castration as a mark of special holiness, emerged in eighteenth-century Russia and was not suppressed until the twentieth century.[14] Voluntary male castration appeared again with the Heaven's Gate cult in the 1990s.

A superficially similar cult known as the *hijras* has been known in India since the second century B.C. This is a group of self-castrated devotees of the goddess Kali who perform dances and songs at weddings.[15] This group continues to exist in modern India; in fact, a recent article in the *Wall Street Journal* featured a *hijra* who was planning to run for political office.[16] As with the *galli,* but unlike many Byzantine eunuchs, the *hijras* are castrated voluntarily as adults. The durability of such communities of castrated religious servants is suggested by the fact that, as of 1990, thirty-one elderly eunuch tomb guards from Mecca and Medina were still alive.[17]

Thus the practice of making eunuchs who then filled established roles in society existed long before Byzantium. Eunuchs could be found throughout the eastern and southern Mediterranean and across the Middle East, India, and China. It is an institution with a long history, one that extends even to the present day. In a certain sense this deep-seated cultural reality suggests that, instead of asking Why eunuchs? we should ask Why not eunuchs?—a question more logically directed toward Western Europe. That is a discussion for another book, but it remains that eunuchism was a time-honored feature of eastern Mediterranean life, not a debilitating, "oriental" intrusion. If we go beyond the situation created by castration, we find that pre-Columbian America also included intermediate gendering in the form of the berdache. As Richard Trexler defines it, "a berdache is a biological male who dressed, gestured, and spoke as an 'effeminate,' that is, as individual cultures said women did and expected women or effeminates to act . . ." These gender intermediates were found from the lands of the Delaware

Indians to the Aztec and Inca Empires.[18] As foreign as eunuchism may appear to us, it is important to remember that for millennia eunuchs and other intermediate gender categories, like the berdache of North America, could be found in all urbanized regions of the world except northwest Europe and the British Isles.

Societies traditionally arrange sexual and gender groups in some sort of order. Modern U.S. society tends to take the position that such groups are arranged on a horizontal bipolar continuum. Men lie at one end of this continuum, and women, at the other; any deviation from this is highly suspect. Male infants eventually become men, molded into a form predetermined by society. The same is true of girls. Until recent advances in the study of sexuality and sexual orientation we have assumed that this was how the world was constructed and that this was the way it had always been perceived. Since much of the legal and cultural tradition of the United States and the British Commonwealth stems from northwest Europe and England, it is not surprising that those scholars from the English-speaking world who are firmly rooted in a bipolar sexual and gender framework find eunuchism offensive, "oriental," and a cultural tradition that epitomizes an "other." Even as we become more comfortable with the idea that gays and lesbians might, by biological destiny or by choice, occupy alternative gender categories, we still are repelled by the idea of deliberate human castration.

Eunuchs and Christian Byzantium

By the reign of Constantine I (r. 324–337), the symbolic beginning of Byzantium, eunuchs were a normal feature of the eastern Mediterranean.[19] Constantine himself had eunuchs at his palace, and the number and importance of eunuchs both at court and in aristocratic society continued to grow throughout the Byzantine era. As noted above, the power, though not the number, of eunuchs did not decline until the coming of the later Komnenoi in the middle of the twelfth century.

Eunuchs, like servants and slaves in many societies, were people without past or family. We shall see that as time went on in Byzantium, this topos of institutionalized "otherness" was often contradicted by reality. In Late Antiquity and early Byzantium, eunuchs appear to have been actual slaves, often selected for their beauty and drawn from tribal peoples located along the coast of the Black Sea and in the Caucasus Mountains. The most frequently mentioned source for these eunuchs was Abchasia, on the east coast of the Black Sea.[20] Prokopios of Caesarea tells us that the ruler of the Abchasians selected beautiful boys to be castrated and sold to the Romans and then killed their fathers to avoid subsequent repercussions. The emperor Justinian the Great supposedly sent one of his own most trusted eunuchs, an Abchasian by birth, to the Abchasian people in hopes of convincing them to end the trade.[21] Prokopios implies that Justinian's intervention ended the practice, yet over the centuries the number of eunuchs at court continued to increase. Although the convention that eunuchs came from outside the empire persisted, we will see that they were drawn from a growing number of sources that included freeborn citizens of the empire who had been intentionally castrated by their own parents.

The geographic origins of specific eunuchs are rarely mentioned in our sources. This silence is a basic part of their gender construct, which assumed separation from place of birth and family. This lack of perceptible or acknowledged social background facilitated a kind of personal anonymity that allowed a new personal self-definition based on the *oikos* of their patrons and reinforced the ethos of perfect service.[22] As we will see in chapter 9, by the ninth century the reality of this tradition of societal alienation and reintegration was fading, allowing us to glimpse the backgrounds and families of some eunuchs.

As Byzantium became a Christian society, the widespread presence of eunuchs was confronted by developing Christian attitudes about celibacy, reproduction, sexual pleasure, and bodily function.[23] One facet of this study examines the way in which Christianity came to terms with eunuchism in the course of several centuries of Byzantine history. Christianity, or rather the Judaic tradition within Christianity, emphasizes the integrity of the physical body and is uncomfortable with bodily mutilation and its results. Jewish traditions exhibit a rigidly bipolar conception of gender, one that has little tolerance for intermediate categories and gender ambiguities. These traditions were continued in early Christian writings regarding the nature of eunuchs and castration. The male body must be preserved in its "natural" state, and castration gravely altered that state.

At the same time, however, the Christianity of Late Antiquity increasingly rejected sexuality and honored the celibate man. A man who could successfully suppress his own sexuality was a man particularly favored by God. This created an ambiguity regarding holiness where eunuchs were concerned. One tradition associated eunuchs with sexual license, lust and erotic behavior for its own sake, not for the sake of procreation. Another, the tradition of the perfect servant, assumed celibacy as a requirement for perfect service. Many eunuchs, and especially those castrated at a young age, lacked sexual desires and found it easy to remain celibate. Yet, in the eyes of the church, perhaps their sanctity came too easily—they "cheated" on the way to the ascetic life. Eventually a compromise was worked out. Intentional, self-inflicted removal of the genitalia and its attendant physiological changes were believed to be an insult to God's creation. At the same time, according to the canons of the early church, a man who was castrated accidentally or by another person could still achieve holiness as a priest, bishop, or cleric. Only those who castrated themselves or achieved celibacy with the aid of the surgeon's knife, were considered to be "homicides, hateful to God and unsuitable for church office."[24]

The Late Antique and Byzantine worlds also inherited Roman patriarchal ideas that gave favored status to adult male heads of households and emphasized procreation and family formation. As a part of this self-presentation, the Romans passed serious legislation designed to protect the genitalia of the Roman citizen.[25] Traditional Roman society also insisted upon a rigid code of behavior intended to ensure that its male citizens were reared and conditioned to present themselves in accordance with a fixed model for masculinity. Men and women were assumed to differ morally, mentally, and physically.[26] Independent men of substance, if properly trained and nurtured, were believed to rise above the level of women and children to become fully masculine heads of households. Laws protecting male genitalia were enshrined in legal, rhetorical and other writings, offering models that were adopted by pagan intellectuals and early church fathers alike in their writings about proper male appearance and behavior.[27] For these authors the appearance and behavior of eunuchs represented the antithesis of appropriate male behavior. The eunuch was scorned as shameful, neither man nor woman, a monstrosity, an outsider, and pitifully womanlike.

In the context of these cultural currents, we will see that Byzantine attitudes about eunuchs were also influenced by the increasing importance of monasticism and the celibate life in the Byzantine world. As eunuchs gained status they became increasingly integral to Byzantine society. Perceptions of eunuchs as a distinct gender group also reflected societal ideas about the literal nature of the flesh and, more specifically, the nature of the flesh of prepubescent boys and men. This is important because the traditional thought patterns of Mediterranean culture emphasized external appearances. The appearance of an individual's body informed the viewer of the quality of his soul and his moral integrity. A corrupt soul would eventually be revealed in a corrupt body. Similarly, the physical body, especially in the castrated individual, was believed to affect his personality and his inner being.

These "imported" Roman and Christian traditions were at odds with the realities of the structure of gender in the eastern Mediterranean and Middle Eastern world of Antiquity and Late Antiquity. The "indigenous" attitude accepted the existence of eunuchs as essential to the operation of aristocratic households and royal courts. Within this cultural framework, the eunuch's alternative gender status could be readily accommodated, sometimes with what seem to be glaring contradictions between formal constraints and actual practice.

It appears that for men of Late Antiquity castration was one of the markers that divided the civilized from the "barbarian" world. Thus the late Roman and Byzantine legal codes repeat earlier Roman injunctions against castration. Under the civil code those who practiced or arranged for castrations were to be punished with death, confiscation, exile, or fines. The law is very clear—in the Christian world no one was supposed to be made a eunuch. It was permissible, however, for barbarians to make each other into eunuchs who could then be sold in the empire.[28] Ecclesiastical law from the time of the first council of Nicaea (325) echoes these regulations, observing that churchmen who castrate themselves or aid in the castration of others are to be deposed unless good medical reasons can be found for the surgery.[29]

As this passage implies, certain kinds of medical problems became a subterfuge that legalized castrations.[30] Despite the censure of Jewish, Roman, and Christian tradition, therefore, Late Antique and Byzantine emperors and wealthy aristocrats continued to have eunuchs in their palaces. Many of these eunuchs came from territories outside the jurisdiction of Roman law, but as we move into the later Byzantine period there are signs that men were willing to wink at legislation that attempted to prevent castration.[31]

In Late Antiquity actual practice seems to have had a rough correspondence with formal legal strictures. Prepubescent boys were usually castrated for economic reasons. They generally came from the outer reaches of the empire or beyond, were castrated, and were sent to Constantinople for sale in the slave markets. In the later Byzantine world, however, freeborn boys were often castrated to ensure their celibacy, save them from the snares of the devil, and permit them access to high positions in the administrations of both church and state. The rhetoric of official disapproval and outsider origins remained, but the growing reality illustrates the fluidity of cultural constructs surrounding the issue of castration.

Eunuch: Defining the Term

While the preceding pages appear to assume a fairly clear-cut meaning for the term *eunuch,* it is in fact a very comprehensive word, at least in contrast to our modern usage. From the perspective of modern gender definitions, the range of people included in this category is remarkably wide, especially during the earlier centuries covered in this study. At one extreme was the "doubly castrated" boy (all of whose genitalia were removed) who was a deliberately created and marketed sex object. At the other were celibate monks who had not been castrated but were referred to as eunuchs, and even nuns whose celibacy caused some authors to describe them as "eunuchs" in a complimentary way.[32] Greek sources of

Late Antiquity, at least in polite prose, used the term *eunuch* to encompass a diverse class of individuals without reference to the extent or nature of their castration, the age at which they were castrated, or their social or civil status. By the second century A.D., the term could refer to any nonreproductive man, whether he was castrated, born without adequate reproductive organs, or had suffered injury that rendered him sterile. Thus we encounter, for example, eunuchs "from birth" and eunuchs "by force" or "by necessity." The word was also a blanket term covering a variety of genital mutilations, ranging from the cutting of the vas deferens (as in a modern vasectomy) to the removal of one or both testicles to the total removal of all male sexual organs. Although other terms came into use that referenced specific kinds of mutilation, *eunuch* remained the general or omnibus term and was rarely further modified based on the appearance of the eunuch's genitalia.

This offers a deep-seated definitional problem to the modern West. If modern Western culture were to define eunuch in the way that the Byzantines did, it would have to consider as eunuchs all men who have had vasectomies, men who have undergone testicular ablation as part of treatment for cancer or other diseases, men born without fully developed sexual organs, and men being treated for prostate cancer with drugs that destroy testosterone. This is something that it would never consider. The reason for this is that the term *eunuch* carries a powerful psychological charge in our society, just as it often did in the ancient and medieval world. It implies far more than sterility. It implies loss of masculine affect, effeminacy, transit from the masculine gender model to the feminine. Even more frightening from the point of view of Western culture is the assumption that in some times and places this transition is involuntary. Whether as punishment for a crime, something perpetrated on a child by a parent, revenge on prisoners of war or political enemies, or imposed by a master on a slave, it registers as a violation of an individual's body that is today considered cruel and unusual punishment, a barbaric act.

What stands out in the way that the term *eunuch* is used in a Byzantine context is that the underlying meaning embedded in the word is an association with the presence or absence of the generative function. In the Late Antique and Byzantine worlds procreation was of central importance in defining gender. Byzantine society, like Roman society from which it grew, was patriarchal in structure. The maintenance of the family was central to this society, and loss of the generative function placed an individual outside of the logic of conventional, family-derived social categories. All of our texts acknowledge this and set eunuchs apart from this patriarchal schema, citing eunuchs' lack of procreative ability and their origins outside of the boundaries of aristocratic society. As will be discussed in chapter 9, eunuchs may have come to be considered "special" in part because they were thought to exist outside of earthly time and space. As a group, they also devised techniques for family advancement, a kind of procreation.

This relationship to procreation, rather than physical appearance or the specifics of genital mutilation, is another key observation about the eunuch viewed as a gender category. Within that generalization other terms appeared to supplement or replace the term when referring to specific groups of nonreproductive men. These included *galli*, an early term used for the eunuch priests of the Magna Mater, and "cut men" (τομιάς) or "cut out men" (ἐκτομίας), which referred to the technique of removing the testicles from the scrotum. These terms appear throughout the period covered here but seem to have become more common toward the end. In the eleventh century, Skylitzes, for example, uses "eunuch" (εὐνοῦχος) and "cut man" (ἐκτομίας) almost interchangeably. A related Latin term *praecisus* appears in Latin sources. The term *crushed* (θλιβίας) referred to eunuchs whose testicles had been crushed intentionally when they were still very small children. The term *spado* (σπάδων) appears occasionally. Athanasios uses *eunuch* and *spado* in the same sentence without distinction. *Spado* was usually used in legal texts to refer to "natural eunuchs," males who were born without well-formed genitalia or who, presumably for physiological reasons, lacked sexual desire.[33] In the tenth century, when doubly castrated eunuchs who lacked both testicles and penis were scarce and valuable in Constantinople, a specific term, *curzinasus,* appears. This term, which enters late Greek as κυρζινάους, comes from the name Khwarizm, which refers to a region in Central Asia where physicians knew how to perform this complex and risky surgery.[34]

By the twelfth century, although the Byzantines still often lumped all nonreproductive men under the single descriptive term, eunuch, they also used these other terms to make important distinctions. Understanding these distinctions will help sort out the seemingly contradictory good eunuch/bad eunuch language of the sources. Society distinguished between eunuchs castrated before puberty and men castrated as adults of their own volition. The first group was honored, and the obvious "otherness" of its members was often held in awe. The second was looked down upon. Prepubescent sexual and reproductive potential could readily be sacrificed to create an individual who was constructed by society to fulfill a particular set of social or religious needs. After puberty this option for creating a eunuch was far less acceptable.

Thus, the term *eunuch* was a very broad one that covered a wide range of individuals. Moreover, its definition developed and changed from the third to the twelfth centuries, and many of its variants became more specific. One important sign of its shifting content is the fact that the Byzantines changed their explanation for the etymological roots of the very word eunuch. Its original etymology reflects the oldest traditional role that eunuchs played in aristocratic society, that of guardians of the bedchamber (ὁ τὴν εὐνὴν ἔχων) and derives from the Greek word for bed (ἐυνή).[35] By the twelfth century Byzantine authors claimed that the term *eunuch* came from the term well- or high-minded (εὔνοος). This newer assumption about the derivation of the term *eunuch*, though mistaken, reflected the very different place that eunuchs occupied in later Byzantine society. By the twelfth century eunuchs were perceived to be perfect servants of God or of aristocratic men, highly educated and well trained. An etymology derived from terms like well-minded or high-minded seemed logical.

Biology, Reproduction, Sexuality, Asceticism

In the Late Antique and Byzantine world, the specific nature of a eunuch's biological loss, mutilation, or abnormality was rarely mentioned. Instead, a man was classed as a eunuch because he could not procreate. This fact excluded him from fatherhood within the traditional patriarchal world of the extended family. Yet that very exclusion allowed him to serve other important, integral roles within the cultural system, and the importance of these roles was recognized and even honored. We will see that in the Byzantine period eunuchs, especially eunuchs castrated before puberty whose physical attributes and acculturation publicly identified them as eunuchs, were assumed to possess distinctive and inherent attributes that were in fact constructed by society. These ranged from beauty and heightened sexual desirability to spirituality, special intellectual abilities, and even "magical" powers.

Eunuchs who were castrated before puberty had certain physical characteristics that were associated with eunuchism. They were beardless and developed distinctive stature, musculature, distribution of fat deposits, facial appearance, skin texture, and voice range. The degree to which these physical changes took place was, of course, affected by the age at which castration took place. These physical changes were important gender markers for eunuchs.

Aristotle, whose scientific ideas remained influential well into the Byzantine period, says that eunuchs are changed into women, or as he puts it, into a female state. He lacks the vocabulary to discuss eunuchs as a separate third category. Galen occasionally entertains the hypothesis that male or female animals, with the removal of the reproductive organs, might be changed into a third type of being that is neither male nor female and is different from either one.[36] In chapter 2, we will see that later Byzantine medical writers followed Aristotle and Galen in discussing eunuchs, using language that reflected sexual bipolarity while classifying eunuchs with women and children in a more nuanced hierarchy of human flesh.

All this suggests one important preliminary observation: modern society distinguishes, linguistically and in other ways, between men who are voluntarily celibate, men who are accidentally or naturally impotent, men who have had vasectomies, and men who have had all of their sexual organs removed. It does not, however, lump all of these categories into one large group or suggest that they have somehow moved outside of their classification as males. Late Antique and Byzantine society does not seem preoccupied with these same physiological distinctions. This may reflect a reluctance to discuss the physiological side of male sexuality. It is more likely, however, that it reflects a tendency to separate men from eunuchs in terms of generative function. This distinction and its gender implications, rather than the physical appearance of the genitals or causal circumstances surrounding castration, became a defining characteristic for eunuchs. This clearly allows the implication that the ability to continue the family line was more important than the ability to engage in what we consider normal sexuality or maintain the appearance of physical perfection.

At the same time there is reason to suggest that Byzantine society did not make a eunuch's sexual activity or his choice of sexual object a salient feature of the construct "eunuch." Thus eunuchs could not procreate, but some eunuchs could be sexually active. Eunuchs are portrayed as engaging in sexual activity with both men and women. They replaced either men or women as partners in the sex act, but partners devoid of procreative potential. Since procreation, rather than sexual activity, was the critical component of gender in this culture, the sexuality of eunuchs was a secondary factor in the social construction of their gender category.

Medical writers, following a classical, pre-Christian tradition, tended to define eunuchs in terms of the quality of their physical bodies. In contrast, as Late Antiquity absorbed Christianity, the philosophers and church fathers often classified men, women, and eunuchs in accordance with their generative powers. For Clement of Alexandria (born A.D. 150), for example, eunuchs encompassed a wide-ranging group of individuals, from men who were sterile or castrated to celibate whole men.[37] Fertility, like life, was essential to the definition of manliness; therefore, eunuchs were not fully men.

The early church admired men who could save their seed and avoid sexual temptation. This allowed such men to turn their vital life forces to more important things. Yet the early church did not admire eunuchs, since it considered that their control over their own sexuality was too ambiguous. On the one hand, they could preserve their vital fluids and maintain an ascetic life style too easily. After all, the drama here lies in man's battle with his physical passions. On the other, a eunuch was suspected of being able to use his condition to facilitate a life of secular debauchery. Thus, while eunuchs could not procreate, some of them were thought to be sexually active and while the church tolerated sexual activity for the sake of procreation, it was reluctant to condone sex for the sake of pleasure. Churchmen also engaged in deep soul-searching about whether celibate eunuchs could achieve holiness. Since the eunuch's celibacy could not be tested, they were skeptical of his mastery of his own body and thus his claim to celibacy. What we see here are several intellectual traditions evolving side by side. In subsequent chapters we will look at these traditions and explore the ways they were accommodated into the long-term reality of eunuchs within Byzantine society.

Within the ecclesiastical and philosophical worlds of Late Antiquity, one finds a great variety of opinions about eunuchs and the degree to which they are men, women, or some sort of "other." Children, because they do not procreate, constituted an anomaly similar to that of eunuchs. For children, however, this condition was not permanent, and with proper societal conditioning boys became men and girls became women. Thus, while preadolescent boys were often seen as magically or spiritually distinct from adult men, at maturity they could be accommodated into the system and developed into full-fledged, sexually active males. Ultimately, the language and logic of polarity that was derived from procreation left eunuchs in limbo.

Byzantine Counterparts to Modern Gender Theory

Before we can understand who and what eunuchs were we need to look briefly at the Byzantine counterparts to modern gender theory. Since our sources were written by individuals reared in the mental universe of medieval Byzantium, whatever they have to say is shaped and filtered by their own culture. Obviously, that is much of what this book is about, but before we can examine the topic in a serious way, it will be useful to sort through some of the definitions and characterizations that Byzantine authors themselves used when they talked about eunuchs.

Byzantine authors observed and commented on topics that we define as gender categories, though they did not identify them as such. These observations were recorded in written texts and in visual imagery that were absorbed into artistic traditions and into literary descriptions. The category of eunuch is particularly interesting because, while eunuchs were prominent in the empire for a thousand years, surviving references to them often carry a heavy load of negative rhetorical tradition. It can be very challenging to separate the substance of the socially constructed category from the negative rhetoric that surrounds it at any given time. The very process of sorting through the variety of ways in which this gender category was presented offers interesting insights into Byzantine society itself. We must remember, however, that everything we find in the sources is part of a social construction that was a dynamic and ongoing process. Since this society's discourse regarding eunuchs evolved over time, we can trace changes in social attitudes about eunuchs and about gender construction in general.

The Byzantine world had a rather different concept of the arrangement of biological and gender groups than does the modern West. In the first place, these two classifications, biology and gender, were considered to be one. The biological nature of the physical body was assumed to be directly linked with a variety of other elements within the individual, elements that had little to do with either sex or gender: strength, courage, moral character, intelligence, to name only a few. Much of this structure of sexual and gender classifications in the Late Antique and Byzantine worlds was conditioned by earlier Greek medical beliefs about the composition of the body. While this is examined more carefully in chapter 2, a few points are worth introducing here.

Aristotle and Galen, while taking for granted that men and women constituted polar opposites, were inclined to see both sexuality and gender in terms of ascending ladders leading toward perfection. The rungs of these ladders, some of which were "biological" while others were socially determined, were based on the theory of humors prevalent in the medical thought of the Ancient World.[38] This ladder image also relied on culturally determined ideal norms for the education and acculturation of young men and women, on ideas about appropriate social behavior for the sexes, and on unquestioned assumptions about the intellectual and moral potential of men and women.

At the bottom of the ladder were women and girls, who were associated with coolness and dampness. Partway up the ladder were boys and adolescent males who, having left the socialization of childhood in the women's quarters, were learning to be complete or active men. At the top of the ladder were those men who possessed the ultimate masculine attributes: heat, dryness, activity, fertility, and training in male behavior. As they matured and were acculturated into appropriate male behavior, young males gradually moved up the ladder.[39] In this model, males who were castrated before puberty were "stuck" in a kind of arrested development. They were more manly than women or young male children, but they could never reach the status of sexually mature men and thus could never attain the culturally defined attributes of full masculinity. As the engendering process evolved, they were placed on a different gender path altogether.

The ladder image implies both a hierarchy of gender and a polarity between male and female. Thomas Laqueur argues in favor of a single sex model for antiquity in which gender was more important than biological sexuality; according to this model the female body was constructed relative to a male reference point.[40] This argument has many merits, but in the Byzantine case it has to be reconciled with the fact that Byzantine society had a separate classification of individual, the eunuch, born male but then culturally and physiologically constituted into an individual who was referenced positively toward men and negatively toward women. When Byzantine sources wanted to speak well of eunuchs they did so in terms of positive attributes traditionally ascribed to men. When they wanted to be critical of eunuchs they did so in terms of negative values traditionally ascribed to women.

These definitional issues must also be seen within the hierarchically organized Byzantine society. Human beings—men, women, and children—were undefined, imperfect creatures until molded and perfected by society. Men were believed to be more suited, by nature, to perfection than women. Thus, out of the great mass of humanity, only physically whole men could achieve the highest peaks of physical and moral perfection. In an increasingly Christian world attracted to asceticism, these men fell into two gendered groups. One was made up of active, worldly men who lived, procreated, and often were the leaders of the material world. The other consisted of contemplative men who consciously rejected their sexual natures. Both worldly, procreative men of affairs and ascetic men were biologically or physiologically "male," but they were perceived as distinctive gender groups because of their different relationships to sexuality and reproduction.

The ideal type of the ascetic male was the physically whole male who struggled to achieve holiness through denial of sexual urges and denial of the body. This type of holiness is presented as a trope in a variety of hagiographical sources and in cults associated with figures like St. Symeon the Stylite the Younger. This trope is important to an understanding of the Byzantine reconfiguration of such important Biblical figures as the prophet Daniel, a process that is examined more closely in chapter 5. The category of voluntarily celibate holy man, however, is distinct from the category of the castrated eunuch who served at court or in the church even though the individuals in all of these categories were sometimes referred to as eunuchs.

Individual eunuchs often shared gendered roles and attributes that were characteristic of either active men of family and public life or ascetics. Nevertheless, because of eunuchs' mutilation and their inability to procreate, they remained part of a group that had been assigned a distinctive gender identity. They could not achieve the status of aristocratic men and were long denied the heights of ascetic achievement because of the presumption that they did not have to fight their own sexuality. As physiologically and biologically incomplete men, eunuchs also shared many of the attributes of prepubescent boys who were perceived to be in a state in which their gender status was still ambivalent. If we look at the Byzantine gender construct in this way, we see that eunuchs were not necessarily effeminate; rather, they lacked full masculine status. The standards for achieving perfection within one's gender group were not based on opposing standards of masculinity and femininity but on aristocratic masculine standards alone. The perception of eunuchs as something like a third sex or third gender is fairly constant throughout Late Antiquity and the Byzantine world, but a shift in that perception is central to this book.

One recurrent theme raised in this context was the issue of whether eunuchs were perceived as artificially created beings and, if so, who was assumed to be responsible for their creation. This question is closely tied to society's perception of nature. In Late Antiquity castration was regularly condemned as "against nature," and the eunuch himself was condemned as a creature whose very existence was "against nature." Yet by the tenth century some authors had shifted the focus from "against nature" to "beyond nature." This subtle change brings the implication of access to a world beyond the natural world, a significant shift in a profoundly religious society.

Another indicator of the complexity of the subject is the fact that, by the twelfth century, Byzantine sources used several terms to refer to eunuchs, and these terms referred specifically to the nature of each eunuch's mutilation. This increasing specificity of definition and tendency to identify individuals by the nature of their mutilation reflects a subtle hierarchy evolving among several subgroups encompassed by the general term *eunuch*.

One of the more complicated topics that arises here is the question of the sexual preference of eunuchs. While Byzantine culture often saw eunuchs as involuntary celibates, it also assumed that some eunuchs were sexually active, but not in ways that were central to their gender construct. As eunuchs have become an increasingly acceptable subject of study, some scholars are making the assumption that eunuchs can be equated with modern male homosexuals and that eunuchs preferred men as sexual partners, playing a passive role in same-sex relationships. This idea probably grows out of studies of the *galli* in the ancient world and anthropological studies of the modern *hijra* in India.[41] Among groups like the modern *hijra,* gender preference has been established prior to castration. In Byzantium, where it appears that castration was commonly done to children rather than to adult men, it took place before personal gender preference could possibly have been determined.

This brings us to thorny issues that modern biology is even now trying to deal with. Is what we call homosexual behavior an inherited trait, or is it learned behavior? Our Byzantine sources often tell us that eunuchs were passive partners in same-sex relationships, yet these same authors pity eunuchs for desiring women and for being unable to act on their desires.

As Michel Foucault has so ably shown, we must not assume that other societies operate using our categories, no matter how obvious and basic they might appear to us.[42] We must avoid the tendency to ascribe reflexively to the medieval world our modern assumptions about sexual categories and behaviors that seem familiar at first glance, or to make quick assumptions about the sexual nature of a society in a world that was very different from ours. Thus it would be anachronistic and illogical to assume that the Byzantine category of eunuch was in any way analogous to the modern category "gay," despite the pejorative traditions shared by both. It is true that some Byzantine sources do refer to a category of eunuchs who are "eunuchs by nature."[43] For example, in the tenth-century Vita of St. Andrew the Fool we find that such a eunuch befriends the saint's disciple, Epiphanios. This eunuch is young, and the saint accuses him of being a sodomite.[44] In the Vita of St. Basil the Younger there is a long diatribe against the powerful court eunuch, Samonas. He is called a "eunuch by nature" (φύσει ὁ Σαμωνᾶς εὐνοῦχος), and accused of engaging in acts of sodomy.[45] In the Vita of St. Niphon of Constantiana, probably written some time after the tenth century, we find the demons debating over the soul of a eunuch who is called a sodomite. He too is a "eunuch by nature" (φύσει εὐνοῦχος, both in "spirit" (ψυχή) and in "body" (σῶμα). In this case the saint saves the eunuch's soul. Yet in the same vita we are told of another eunuch, a "eunuch by nature" (τῇ φύσει εὐνοῦχος), who loved money and beat his servants; even the Virgin could not save him.[46]

Byzantine sources are likely to assume that eunuchs acted as passive partners in same-sex relationships without presenting it as a matter of personal sexual preference. In fact, the official lecture on duties that the chief court eunuch gave to eunuchs being inaugurated into service in the imperial private quarters states that a eunuch must not be friendly with or associate with "men of bad reputation or those who are innovative." Notice that sexual behavior that we would label homosexual is not forbidden, or even mentioned. This is not what is being prohibited. Instead, the eunuch is being told to be careful with whom he has any kind of associations. I suspect that "eunuch by nature" may be a code phrase sometimes used to refer to those castrated men who actively seek out sexual relations with other men.[47] While such references allude to sexual acts that we associate with male homosexuality, there is nothing to suggest that the gender construct for eunuchs can be usefully compared with modern concepts of homosexuality.

In a more general sense, there is little evidence that individuals in the Byzantine world were placed in gender categories primarily because of sexual preference of any sort, an important way of assigning gender in some societies. The presence or absence of genitalia also does not elicit much comment in our Byzantine sources. In Byzantine society, gender categories were determined in ways that remind one of some American Indian societies in the nineteenth century, in which the primary determinants of gender were social roles and conventions dictating external appearances, physical mannerisms, facial expressions, and manner of dress.[48] While their inability to procreate was part of the construct, their sexual preferences, although sometimes discussed by innuendo, were not.

As with many of the generalizations that will emerge as we go along, it is important to remember that everything we find in the sources is part of a social construction that is a dynamic process. After the eighth century, when new eunuchs were increasingly drawn from free members of Byzantine society, they could no longer be classified as outsiders. In later chapters we will see that Byzantine society regularly reflected on eunuchs as a group, discussing the morality of castration, reviling eunuchs, honoring them, inventing roles and attributes for them, and even creating "historical" eunuchs and setting them in a fictional past that was an invention of the present.

Many of the attributes of eunuchs that we would consider socially assigned aspects of gender were considered by our Late Antique and Byzantine sources to be inherent and, in their minds, biological. For example, eunuchs were criticized because they cried easily. A modern observer might suggest that this was probably related to the way they were reared. A Byzantine observer, however, would say that eunuchs cried because they had lost the inherent masculine quality of emotional self-control, a loss that was assumed to be a biological or inherent consequence of the loss of the testicles.

The Filter of Language

The very longevity and evolution of the gender construct of Byzantine eunuchs often confuses our perceptions of it. The rhetorical repertoire available to Byzantine authors, who often had their own agendas, resulted in highly contradictory characterizations of eunuchs, even in the work of a given author. Inevitably, therefore, this book is also a study of the use of language. We know Byzantium only dimly, through incomplete documents written by people whose own rhetorical intentions are often veiled. One methodological premise of this book is that a close study of language can identify attitudes, cultural structures, and gender assumptions that are never stated overtly. In the case of eunuchs, these linguistic structures reflect a society that long tolerated ambiguities in gender assignment. In practice, eunuchs were consistently perceived to be ambiguous, at least in relationship to modern-day conventional male/female gender categories. As a result, their presence fostered the use of language and elicited comments in the sources that are remarkably revealing in ways their authors never anticipated.

While we saw above that the Byzantine gender construct for eunuchs is hierarchical and is referenced to an ideal masculinity—either that of the active secular man or the ascetic man—it is important to note that our Late Antique and Byzantine sources attempt to express the construct in language that reflects a bipolar, male/female, tradition. The structure of the Greek language identifies individuals as either masculine or feminine. Eunuchs were invariably treated grammatically as being of the masculine gender and were never associated with feminine or neuter grammatical forms. Thus the language reflexively placed individuals in fixed masculine or feminine categories and did not readily allow for a definition of individuals belonging to alternative or intermediate sexual categories. Whether the Byzantine conceptualization of gender was bipolar or single-sex in orientation, it remained difficult to articulate definitions of individuals who neither conformed to accepted polarities nor progressed along the ladder that led to the male ideal. Nevertheless, Byzantine culture developed a variety of ways of talking about eunuchs. As we will see in chapter 1, the language that evolved was often a language of ambiguity and negation.

After the ninth century, however, we find that many Byzantine sources move beyond earlier bipolar linguistic traditions and acknowledge this hierarchical arrangement of gender groups by defining eunuchs in terms of those masculine qualities they lacked rather than in terms of those feminine qualities they were perceived to possess. Increasingly, those desirable qualities that eunuchs lacked were exactly those qualities that define ideal masculinity, such as strength and courage. Yet despite the tidiness of this single-sex structure, it is clear that a bipolar model is also lurking in the language available to our sources.

We see elements of a bipolar model in the way that the bipolarity of the Greek language prevented the medical and scientific community from adequately expressing gender diversity even though its own tradition supported a vertical continuum that explained physiological differences between men, women, children, and eunuchs as a progression toward ideal masculinity. This medical tradition also offered a similar explanation for old age—elderly men moved down the physiological ladder in the direction of eunuchs, women, and children. Of course, all these interpretive problems are further compounded when we try to translate Greek into English.[49]

The Nature of the Sources

The primary sources for this study are, like most Byzantine sources, scattered and thin. Useful references can be found throughout the corpus of primary sources, often in asides and linguistic or rhetorical devices used without conscious reflection by the author. Finding data is further complicated by the fact that eunuchs, and especially "good" eunuchs, often are not even identified as eunuchs. The collection of data has been made difficult by generations of editors who, until recently, often employed euphemisms or repressed references to eunuchs in texts and sometimes did not even include the term *eunuch* in indices.

Both Byzantine and modern medical sources yield valuable information about eunuchs. The teachings of Aristotle, Galen, and Hippocrates formed the basis for medical attitudes about eunuchs. Byzantine physicians like Paul of Aegina and Theophilos Protospatharios tend to rely on Galen, though their variants on Galenic teachings are often of great interest. Byzantine discussions of nutrition tend to be gender-specific and yield important information about gendered categories for types of flesh and its makeup and the way in which foods of different kinds reinforce gender categories. Recipes for ointments and medicines are often gendered, suggesting different kinds of treatments for different gender groups. These kinds of medical sources tend to be quite fixed in their vocabulary, even over a long time span.

In Byzantine historical narratives, with some exceptions that will be discussed, eunuchs frequently are objects of derision and are treated as scapegoats for imperial failures. Such narratives were almost inevitably written with a political agenda or were designed to justify particular outcomes. Authors who were wedded to a worldview in which masculine strength and values were dominant stressed the effeminacy of eunuchs and ascribed to them a whole set of negative stereotypes derived from those attributed to women. Ecclesiastical histories are less severe, probably because a great many high church officials, monks, and holy men were eunuchs. In these sources, eunuchs are often praised and valued for their celibacy.

Sermon literature has yielded little material. The only sermon I have found that directly deals with eunuchs is the first of St. John Chrysostom's famous vanity of vanities sermons, which tradition says was delivered over the great eunuch Eutropios as he cowered under the altar in Hagia Sophia. John Chrysostom never tells us that the subject of his sermon is a eunuch.[50] He doesn't need to, for the sermon is filled with "eunuch speak"—specialized language routinely used to describe eunuchs. Random, interesting pieces of information have also been culled from sermons that deal with the eunuch of Queen Candace in the Book of Acts and with the "eunuchs for the kingdom of heaven" passage in Matthew. In general churchmen seem to have been reluctant to address the issue of eunuchs directly, for reasons that will be discussed later in this book. Sermon literature does, however, yield a rich collection of materials regarding angels. As we will see, the connections between eunuchs and angels are numerous and intriguing, and the sermon literature has proved most useful in this regard.

Byzantine law codes sometimes discuss eunuchs, and the gradual improvement in the status of the eunuch can be traced in these documents. At the same time, legal codes are immensely conservative, and new laws did not necessarily cancel out older ones. Thus law codes often reiterated older, traditional legislation even though it was out of date. As a result, the law codes are seldom reliable guides about what constituted current practice. We get a hint of contemporary awareness of this phenomenon in the eleventh century. Theophylaktos of Ohrid observed that the old legislation of Justinian regarding the making of eunuchs was still on the books, but as far as Theophylaktos was concerned, these laws, both ecclesiastical and civil, "should be thrown away like the rotten soles of shoes, known to be useless and clearly unfit for service in either your monastic institutions or the church of God."[51]

There is an especially rich body of epistolary writings from the tenth century. Most of these letters focus on members of the court and other elite figures of Constantinople, many of whom were eunuchs. While some of the letters malign eunuchs in the usual way, others reflect a warm relationship between members of the elite and well-placed court eunuchs.

The hagiographical corpus, that is, the stories of the lives of the saints of the period, with its much wider range of stories and topoi, yields a surprising volume of interesting material about eunuchs. Again, some authors use traditional vindictive language, casting eunuchs as symbols of the material world and its evils, and even as tools of the devil. A surprising number of authors, however, present eunuchs as holy and righteous men. A single hagiographer will people his text with both bad and good eunuchs, further reflecting the ambivalence with which eunuchs were regarded. This kind of source provides many portrayals of the roles that eunuchs played in everyday life and especially of their important role as cultural and sometimes spiritual intermediaries.

The ninth and tenth centuries in Byzantium produced a number of *taktika* or lists of officeholders and rules for protocol. These are extremely important for determining the offices and titles that eunuchs held within the state bureaucracy and their rank within the structure of government. This source has been extensively used in previous studies of eunuchs, most notably by Rodolphe Guilland.[52] Thanks to his work we can effectively exploit information on the roles of eunuchs at court as displayed in the writings of Constantine VII Porphyrogennetos, most notably in his *De ceremoniis.*

Eunuchs also appear in a number of miscellaneous sources. They are referred to in a number of monastic foundation documents (*typikon*), appear in travelers' tales, are found in the *Timarion*, that wonderful romp through Hades,[53] and in the *oneirokritika* or dream books. Changing attitudes about eunuchs and their role in society can also be found in evolving folk traditions about the city of Constantinople and its founder, the emperor Constantine, the legends surrounding the emperor Justinian, and in society's changing perceptions of the prophet Daniel. Artistic imagery yields interesting insights into discussions of eunuchs. To a limited extent this material will be used, though it will remain the task of an art historian to fully analyze its importance.

Finally, one of the most compelling texts used in this study is the *Defense of Eunuchs* of the eleventh-century bishop Theophylaktos of Ohrid. Composed by the author for his brother, a high-ranking eunuch on the episcopal staff of Hagia Sophia, it is written in the classical dialectical tradition and features a debate, which Theophylaktos claims to have heard as he hid behind a curtain, between a bearded monk and a eunuch over the merits of the recent castration of the eunuch's young nephew. This setting allows Theophylaktos to lay out common perceptions, both good and bad, about eunuchs.

Theophylaktos's treatise is unique in that it offers a systematic compendium of negative and positive observations about eunuchs and castration, and there is no other discussion of this kind in the corpus of Byzantine sources. It was written for important personal reasons, and thus its positive attitude may not reflect general attitudes in Theophylaktos's world. Yet it is an enormously rich work, and its acceptance and humanity touches the reader.

Unfortunately we have almost no written works that can be securely attributed to eunuchs themselves. As a result, they have no voice of their own.[54] If we could securely identify him as a eunuch, St. Symeon the New Theologian might provide us with such a voice, and his use of language might offer insights into a eunuch's voice.[55] The nearest approximation, and obviously a debatable one, is found in a number of passages in which authors speak as or for eunuchs.

The secondary literature on eunuchs in the Byzantine Empire is not large and tends to be based on an institutional approach to history. The topic of eunuchs has long fascinated historians, and scholars of the eighteenth and nineteenth centuries saw it as an "oriental" element in Christian Byzantine culture and as an affront to Graeco-Roman classical traditions. This tradition persisted until recently and caused historians to treat the topic in a tentative fashion. Only in the 1950s did Rodolphe Guilland condense and publish his series of articles on eunuchs into a single volume.[56] He was primarily interested in the study of the imperial administrative system and focused mainly on the eunuchs who held positions at the imperial court and the nature of their offices and honors.

In 1978, Keith Hopkins devoted two chapters of his book *Conquerors and Slaves* to a sociological analysis of the eunuchs of the Byzantine court.[57] His thoughtful analysis suggests that eunuchs exercised real power and were not simply scapegoats for incompetent emperors and hostile commentators. He dismisses the pejorative language used about eunuchs as "what we might expect," and notes the obvious comparison between Byzantine court eunuchs and court Jews in the German states in the seventeenth and eighteenth centuries: both were reviled yet well rewarded and powerful. He points out the critical role that eunuchs played in mediating between ordinary people and an increasingly unapproachable emperor and between the aristocracy and a growing bureaucratic structure.

In the last few years several important studies that deal with eunuchs have appeared. In *Eternal Victory* Michael McCormick shows the ways in which the power of the eunuchs was illustrated in court ritual.[58] More recently, Peter Brown has discussed eunuchs as part of his study of the body in early Christian society.[59] The best introduction and survey of the roles of eunuchs in Late Antique aristocratic households, including the imperial household, is found in Peter Guyot, *Eunuchen als Sklaven und Freigelassene in der griechisch-römischen Antike.*[60] In the 1990s, Shaun Marmon published an excellent book entitled *Eunuchs and Sacred Boundaries in Islamic Society,* which covers the twelfth to the fourteenth centuries.[61] Marmon offers some useful ideas about eunuchs as beings who existed in part outside of normal space and time. More recently, Piotr Scholz has offered a sweeping but superficial essay on eunuchs that ranges from the Ancient Near East to China and the Vatican but says little about Byzantium.[62] An excellent new study of eunuchs in the Late Antique and medieval West has recently been written by Mathew Kuefler, *The Manly Eunuch: Masculinity, Gender Ambiguity, and Christian Ideology in Late Antiquity.*

Conclusion

The Byzantine world did not have a single or necessarily negative perception of eunuchs. In some periods and in the eyes of some authors, eunuchs were hated and reviled; in other periods, as seen by other authors, eunuchs were honored and respected. Our sources are filled with ambivalence about eunuchs, about what sort of individuals they were, and about how they "fit" within the human race and the spiritual world. Whether eunuchs were placed in sexual or gender categories, these categories were fluid and, reflecting societal change, evolved over the centuries.

Part 1 of this book approaches the issue in terms of generalized problems of language and categorical perceptions, particularly the filter and framework of language, medical lore, and prevailing assumptions about physiology and routine forms of acculturation. Part 2 shifts the focus and analyzes the topic in terms of the depictions, careers, legends, and narratives that in one way or another talk about eunuchs as individuals or protagonists. These are not necessarily "historical" sources in the sense of "real-world" narratives about actual people. These sources often describe eunuchs that appear in dreams, miraculous visions, hagiographical tales, and foundation legends. These accounts of imagined eunuchs thus supplement the almost two hundred documented eunuchs who appear in chronicles and other narratives of the period. These individuals, real or imagined, show us both how eunuchs fit into Byzantine society and what sorts of functions and unique characteristics society assigned to them.

The conclusion addresses the most important issue that has emerged from this work: the basic function of eunuchs as a group in Byzantium, a function important enough for the institution to endure for a millennium just in this society. There is little question that in the Byzantine world eunuchs represented a distinct gender category, one that was defined by dress, assumed sexual behavior, work, physical appearance, quality of voice, and for some eunuchs, personal affect. It is clear that we are dealing with a culture that socially constructed a gender category with the aid of a form of physical mutilation that led to physiological change. Furthermore, if we look at this society in terms of our modern models for the organization of the categories of sex and gender, it is quickly apparent that both of these categories were fluid and socially dependent. The next step is to examine some of the conscious and unconscious patterns of language, medical thought, and cultural normalization that permeate our sources.

PART I

Gender as Social Construct

Byzantine society regularly expressed a wide range of both conscious and unconscious assumptions about eunuchs. Part I of this book uses modern models that describe the social construction of gender to analyze four ways in which perceptions about eunuchs were culturally rooted in Byzantine society. Eunuchs were discussed using a very specific language. They were assumed to display both physiological and psychological traits that were the result of castration. They were acculturated to fulfill particular societal roles and expectations. By the tenth century the gender model built around eunuchs was so much a part of society that authors found it necessary to rewrite historical narratives and give eunuchs a historical past.

These materials also suggest that Byzantine society was not wedded to a rigid bipolar gender structure of the sort long assumed to be "normal" in today's Western societies, but rather was comfortable with alternative, intermediate gender categories. These categories filled important niches in the fabric of society, and their very existence encouraged the creation of the specialized individuals who filled them.

The material in part I both outlines the structure of these gender models and supports my contention that gender is a fluid concept, one that is capable of change over an extended period of time.

CHAPTER I

The Language of Gender

The first barrier we encounter when trying to understand a concept as basic as gender is the very language that is used about the topic. This chapter looks at the ways in which Byzantine culture talked about eunuchs. While this is, in part, a problem of vocabulary, it is also one of linguistic allusions, negative language, and descriptive tropes. The language through which an author expresses himself, consciously or inadvertently, is itself important evidence in determining how gender was constructed in the author's own world. Thus it is with good reason that Averil Cameron has urged Byzantine scholars to investigate the ways that language itself structures gender categories within a society.[1]

I suggest that, in the case of eunuchs, the reverse is also true. Since Byzantium accommodated gender constructs that went beyond the conventional bipolarity of male/female, its people often had to improvise ways of expressing this fact using a language that lacked a convenient vocabulary for the purpose. This resulted in more than a few circumlocutions, seeming contradictions, and coded references to eunuchs and the gender construct assigned to them.

Classical Greek is a highly inflected language, especially in its written form. Despite centuries of Roman domination of the Greek-speaking territories, a simplified form of Greek continued to be the language of communication in these regions. Latin, however, remained the language of law and administration until the early sixth century. From the sixth century onward, Greek was the dominant written and spoken language of the Byzantine Empire. Some Byzantine authors wrote in a language that was far simpler than classical Greek and far more dependent on word order for meaning. Others wrote in a very elaborate, convoluted style reminiscent of the language of classical Athens.

Both Greek and Latin are gendered languages in the sense that inanimate objects are assigned genders: masculine, feminine, and neuter. In Greek, trees, for example, have different botanical names, and some are classed as masculine; others, feminine; and still others, neuter. One might expect that Greek would use the neuter gender form to discuss eunuchs, even as it uses the neuter gender for children, but this is not the case. Eunuchs were masculine.

Although Greek as a language was organized into three genders, only two, the masculine and the feminine, were used in reference to adult human beings. This linguistic limitation made it difficult for Byzantine authors to talk directly about third gender categories, much less qualify them in their own terms. In effect, Byzantine society was constructed to accommodate a third gender category yet could not effectively discuss individuals that belonged to this category. This difficulty was complicated by the changing nature of the eunuch as a gender structure and by the persistence of older, pejorative language and imagery in the rhetorical repertoire of later authors.

The language used in connection with eunuchs in Late Antiquity, the period from the second to the eighth centuries, was heavily negative.[2] At that time eunuchs were usually slaves who were servants in the imperial household and in the households of the aristocracy. The authors of that period, both lay and ecclesiastical, were usually hostile to eunuchs. Laymen resented their access to power while churchmen resented the apparent ease with which eunuchs could achieve celibacy and associated them with sexual temptation. This contradiction between high status and hostility is in part explained by the variety of types of and reasons for mutilation encompassed by the category of "eunuch." It was in this early period in Byzantine history that eunuchs were most often classified by their contemporaries as a distinct "third" sex, a term that does not carry the same meaning as gender in this context.[3] As we move into the period from the eighth to the twelfth centuries, however, eunuchs became increasingly important at court and they began to fill roles unique to them. Under these circumstances the language associated with eunuchs moved away from its earlier negative tone.

In the second half of the twelfth century, however, the eunuchs at the court were politically marginalized under the Komnenos dynasty. While eunuchs continued to exist and fill important social roles in Byzantium, they no longer held important government posts.[4] From that time on, the status of court eunuchs declined and the older, negative language became more evident.

In the course of analyzing scores of texts I have found intriguing patterns within the language used to describe eunuchs. There are clear ways in which an author's choice of vocabulary, word form, and innuendo reveal underlying assumptions about eunuchs, about the language itself, and about Byzantine society. In the course of almost a thousand years of Byzantine history these patterns changed remarkably little despite regular changes in the status of eunuchs themselves.

The discussion of this problem falls into two parts. The first focuses on words, language, and specific modes of expression. I have identified at least five specific patterns of expression, patterns that helped to apply available language to eunuchs. First, as expected, eunuchs are frequently associated with language that reflects feminine characteristics. Second, they are often described using a language of ambiguity or lack of stability. Third, eunuchs are almost always defined or described with a language of negation that speaks in terms of what they are not rather than what they are. Fourth, in a seeming contradiction, they are also described in a language of competence, which relates to the idea of perfect service. Finally, eunuchs seem to have been recognized as artificially created beings, and the language associated with them often reflects this. They are referred to in various ways as created beings, outside of nature, or beyond nature.

The second focus for my examination of the way language expresses the gender structure of eunuchs is the language ascribed to eunuchs themselves. This, however, is problematic. With the possible exception of the writings of St. Symeon the New Theologian, there are virtually no sources authored by eunuchs.[5] Thus we have no way of verifying the language they may have used about themselves or others. Nevertheless, I have found a small number of passages in which the author, a whole (or, as the late Byzantines would say, a "testiculated") man, presents what purport to be words actually spoken by a eunuch. Despite inherent problems, it can be revealing to explore the vocabulary and language chosen by authors who, in a literal sense, put words into eunuchs' mouths. When an author presents a eunuch as a participant in a narrative, what attitudes and assumptions about eunuchs does he express? How does such an author choose his language, and what inferences can be drawn from his choices?

Words, Language, and Modes of Expression

The Language of Feminine Traits

It will come as no surprise that authors frequently claimed that eunuchs were womanlike or womanish (γυναικώδης).[6] Saint Basil says that eunuchs are womanlike (θηλυδρώδης), a pejorative description,[7] as does the eleventh-century historian, Skylitzes,[8] when he says that the eunuch general sent to fight the Saracens in Crete was an effeminate man (θηλυδρίας). The chronicler Leo the Deacon, who disliked the powerful court eunuch Joseph Bringas (d. 965), refers to him as a little woman (γυναικάριον).[9] He also puts the phrase "little woman" (γύναιον) into the mouth of a Rus' general who is disparaging his opponent, a eunuch general in the Byzantine army.[10] Interestingly, the term *catamite* (κίναιδος), which in English is used for a young male passive partner in a same-sex relationship with an older man, is rarely used in association with eunuchs. Symeon Metaphrastes, in the Vita of St. John Chrysostom, offers one of the rare examples of this usage when he says that the eunuch Victor was openly a catamite (προφανῶς κίναιδος).[11]

Authors are far more likely to associate eunuchs with negative feminine traits than to say directly that they are women. In the Byzantine world women were assumed to lack the ability to control their physical, emotional, or sexual appetites. Thus, like women, eunuchs are assumed to be inclined to abuse both food and drink.[12] St. Basil says that eunuchs are "mad for women" (γυναικομανής), an accusation of sexual excess.[13] Eunuchs are described as having soft white flesh (μαλακόσαρκος, λευκὸς τῷ σώματι ὡσεὶ χιών).[14] They smell of musk.[15] They weave webs (περιπλέκω) and ensnare (περισπειράω). These are all traits associated with women.[16]

After the fourth century sexual excess is rarely charged against eunuchs. Yet charges that eunuchs lacked self-control in other areas continue throughout the history of the empire. Eunuchs are regularly accused of being unable to curb their acquisitiveness, whether for power or for treasure. St. Basil finds them "mad for gold" (χρυσομανής).[17] John of Antioch says that they are grasping (ἁρπάζω).[18] This is echoed by Eunapios of Sardis,[19] and later, by Leo the Deacon.[20] Like women, eunuchs cannot control their emotions. They are quick to anger (ὀξύθυμος)[21] and fly into rages (λυσσώδης).[22] They can become depressed and weep into their food (κλαυσιδείπνον).[23] Their voices are high and shrill, like those of women (ὀξύφωνος).[24] The longevity of these attitudes is reflected in Theophylaktos of Ohrid's eleventh-century *Defense of Eunuchs* when the critic of eunuchs says that eunuchs are weak (ἀσθενής),[25] small-minded (μικρόψυχος),[26] and greedy (φιλοκερδής).[27] As a result of castration, he says, they become morally weak (εὐένδοτος)[28] and are easily angered by trifles (μικρολυπία).[29]

Eunuchs are sometimes described with clusters of words that create images that the classical world associated with women. For example, both John of Damascus and Eunapios of Sardis develop snake imagery when talking about eunuchs. Eunapios says that the eunuch Eutropios's wicked lies are dragged out, like a snake's trail.[30] Eutropios (d. 399) is described as a great and thousand-twisted snake[31] who binds everyone tightly in his coils[32] and is always whispering (from ψιθυρίζω).[33]

Both Leo the Deacon and Skylitzes regularly refer to eunuchs as reared in the shade (from σκιατραφέω).[34] This clearly refers to the assumption that proper men are reared out of doors, where they engage in athletic and military activities. Eunuchs, along with women, however, are reared indoors or "in the shade."

At the same time, it is suggestive that eunuchs are never defined in terms of positive female attributes. For example, although eunuchs often played important roles in nurturing, feeding and protecting the young and helpless, these traditionally positive female attributes do not become a part of the linguistic matrix used to discuss eunuchs.

Authors of the early period—Lucian, a second-century satirist, and St. Basil, who lived in the fourth century, for example—tend to emphasize the ways in which eunuchs are like women, but none of them ever suggest that eunuchs actually are women. These early sources generally treat eunuchs as an intermediary or third sex. By the twelfth century, however, there is no question about what eunuchs are. They are men, although men specially configured and gendered to serve special purposes. They are, in some ways, less than whole men, but they are still men.

Language of Ambiguity

Byzantine society, like earlier classical Greek society, valued emotional and physical stability. The physiognomic literature displays this ideal well: when you look at a person, you should be able to see exactly who and what he is. Proper men display in their appearance, bearing, speech, and manner their masculine attributes. Thus an important characteristic of eunuchs—and one related to their incomplete masculinity—is their ambiguity. Eunuchs are therefore described regularly in ways that suggest that they have an ambiguous or unstable nature. Lucian expresses this when he says that eunuchs are ambiguous (ἀμφίβολος)[35] and are something compounded (τι σύνθετον καὶ μικτὸν).[36] Gregory of Nazianzos continues in this same vein when he says that eunuchs are of an ambivalent nature (ἀμφιβόλους μὲν γένος).[37] Similarly, Leo the Deacon says that the eunuch Joseph is ambiguous (ἀμφίβολος).[38] Photios, admittedly in an angry letter, says that the eunuch John (latest date 873) is an androgyne (ἀνδρόγυνος).[39]

This sense of physical instability can also be applied to a eunuch's personality. Michael Psellos says that John the Orphanotrophos (d. 1043) is ever changing (ποικίλος).[40] Here he is referring to John's moods, but this particular term, which is also used for richly embroidered fabrics, silk that changes color depending on the light, and marble veined in many colors, is frequently associated both with eunuchs and with magicians.

Even the names of two popular fictional eunuchs who appear in the hagiographical corpus, Hyacinth and Proteos, imply sexual and physical ambiguity and change. Hyacinth would remind readers of the beautiful boy whom Apollo loved yet accidentally killed and then changed into a flower that bore the sign of his grief. Proteos is probably named for the shape-shifting sea god.[41]

While Byzantine culture generally frowned upon ambiguity, some authors suggest that it could be a positive attribute. Leo the Deacon tells us that Polyeuctos, the revered eunuch patriarch (d. 970), was able to say whatever he wished and that he had gained this freedom because he was a eunuch.[42] Agathias says that the eunuch Narses (d. 574) was a successful leader because he was flexible, quickly able to adjust to things however they fell out.[43] Skylitzes says that the great court eunuch Basil the Nothos (latest date 985) was successful because he knew how to adapt wisely to difficult situations.[44] The continuator of Skylitzes, in a laudatory passage, says that the eunuch John, bishop of Sidon, was ambidextrous (ἀμφιδέξιος), here perhaps meaning that he was ambiguous but in a good way.[45]

The Byzantine world was clearly uncomfortable with eunuchs because they did not fit into well-defined categories. Nevertheless, it recognized that ambiguous appearance and behavior, which would not have been tolerated in a whole man, facilitated the successful playing out of the social roles to which eunuchs were assigned.

There is an even more tantalizing issue inherent in the positively charged attribute of changeableness and flexibility ascribed to eunuchs. In this culture, the same sort of ambiguity is also very characteristic of descriptions of angels, magicians, and demons. Angels change their faces, their appearances, their natures, and they, too, are asexual beings.[46] It is no accident that eunuchs are frequently confused with angels in Byzantine literary sources after about the fourth century. There are also hints that some writers associated eunuchs with bad fortune and with magical powers. Niketas Choniates, for example, tells us that the bishop Niketas, a eunuch, could foretell the future,[47] while the continuator of Skylitzes says that the eunuch Nikephoritzes (d. 1078) was "on the left" (σκαιός), meaning he was ill-omened.[48] Theophylaktos of Ohrid also tells us that some people considered eunuchs to be omens (οἰωνίζομαι).[49]

Language of Negation

Eunuchs are regularly described with a rather extensive language of negation that defines them in terms of what they are not. These adjectives of negation are readily apparent in Greek because they all begin with the alpha privative prefix. Eunuchs are beardless (ἀγένειος),[50] low-born (ἀγεννής),[51] fruitless or unable to bear fruit (ἄκαρπος),[52] unmanly (ἄνανδρος),[53] ignorant of war (ἀπειροπόλεμος),[54] not working (ἀργός or ἀεργός),[55] sickly (ἀσθενής),[56] unsuckled or unweaned (ἄθηλος),[57] unwilling to share (ἀμετάδοτος),[58] not gentle, cruel (ἀπηνής),[59] insatiable (ἀπροσκορής),[60] dishonored (ἄτιμος),[61] unworthy (ἄχρηστος).[62] Theophylaktos of Ohrid is aware of this negative rhetoric and specifically lists negative charges leveled against eunuchs. They are labeled as ill-omened (ἀπαίσιος οἰωνός),[63] disorderly (ἄκοσμος),[64] undignified (ἄσεμνος),[65] and unsociable (ἀκοινώνητος).[66]

Any one of these words on its own is unremarkable, but when we bring them together in a list we discover negations of everything that defines an active, fully masculine man of affairs in Byzantine culture. He is bearded, wellborn, fruitful, manly, a good fighter, generous, intelligent, mentally stable, actively engaged, healthy, a part of a family, kind, content with what he has, and honorable. He knows how to dress and how to behave, and he deals openly and honorably with his fellow men.

Language of Competence and Service

Thus the language associated with descriptions of eunuchs characterizes them as ambiguous, associates them with the negative attributes stereotypically associated with women, and presents them as incomplete "men" who lack the attributes of men who have been reared to the status of full-fledged, active males. Such an extensive language of negation raises questions about the underlying capacity of classical Greek to define individuals outside traditional gender categories. It raises a parallel question as well: Are there any positive attributes or categories that apply directly to eunuchs?

In fact, eunuchs are said to possess two positive attributes. Eunuchs are "well-minded" (εὔνοος). As mentioned in chapter 1, by the twelfth century our sources even suggest that this is the etymological root of the term *eunuch*.[67] This is not the case, but what is important here is not modern accuracy but instead what individuals at that time believed to be true. The sources not only reiterate this characteristic but also highlight a second positive trait: eunuchs are perfect servants. Eunuchs are thus intelligent and capable of learning complex tasks and function as extensions of their masters. In Byzantine culture neither of these characteristics was particularly valued among active men. The aristocratic master looked for such traits in those who served him, but not in his peers. Indeed, service was a mark of unmanliness.

Thus eunuchs like Narses, Basil the Nothos, and John are praised for being intelligent and learned (ἄνδρα φρενήρη, ἐχέφρων [ἔχων φρήν], λόγιος, εὐπαιδευτότατος),[68] sensible (ἔμφρων),[69] and vigorous (δραστήριος).[70] Skylitzes says that the eunuch John accomplished his tasks easily (κατειργάσατο ῥᾳδίως).[71] Tasks that eunuchs traditionally undertook required intelligence and a high level of training that was beyond the reach of most men.

It is probable that the Byzantines believed that this kind of developed mental acuity was possible in eunuchs because they were not troubled by sexual desires. The eunuchs' asexual nature is here a very important and positive part of their role as servants. Asexuality is also an important characteristic of perfect servants, and evidence indicates that the Byzantines believed that only asexual men could achieve perfection in this role. One can speculate about why this should be the case, but it is so thoroughly assumed that it is rarely if ever directly discussed.[72]

The eunuch as perfect servant is reflected in other language used in connection with eunuchs. Symeon Magistros says that the eunuch Basil the Nothos served the emperor rightly and fittingly.[73] Skylitzes tells us that the eunuch John the Philosopher was trustworthy.[74] Prokopios says that the great eunuch Narses was "clothed in great power [by the emperor]",[75] while Leo the Deacon tells us that Basil the Nothos was "most vigorous and shrewd, cleverly adjusting himself to the situation of things."[76] Skylitzes says that the eunuch Nikephoros was "faithful to the emperor,"[77] while Theophylaktos assures us that eunuchs are good imperial servants because they are not subjugated. Unlike slaves, eunuchs are gifted with freedom of thought, making them free to serve as frank advisers.[78] By the fifth century, for some eunuchs, the idea of perfect service was focused on God. This is reflected in the increasing number of church officials, holy men, and patriarchs who were eunuchs.

These positive attributes assigned to eunuchs—intelligence and effectiveness as servants—are, however, completely overshadowed by the pervasiveness of the language of negation mentioned above. Why might this be so? In modern society, this kind of negative linguistic definition is regularly applied to groups that lack status in the community. They are defined in terms of what they are not, on a scale established and defined by the dominant group. Another possibility is that we are here encountering an irresistible rhetorical flourish, the rhythm of those long lists of words beginning with alpha.

Perhaps. But in Byzantine culture essentially the same language of negation is also used in connection with angels, Christ, and God. These are categories that are defined by what they are not, and they certainly do not define low-status groups within the society. Thus angels are described as "ageless" (ἀγηράτων), which is why they are youths; "immortal" (ἀθάνατα); "unbroken" (ἀθραύστων), another way in which they resemble youths; "unspotted" (ἀκηλίδωτος); "intangible" (ἀναψηλάφητα); "uncorrupted" (ἀνόλεθρα); "unsuffering" (ἀπαθές); "insubstantial" (ἀπαχῆ); "unstained" (ἄρρυτον or ἄσπιλον); "incorporeal" (ἀσώματα); "incorruptible" (ἄφθαρτα).[79]

This use of language is characteristic of the strain of apophatic or negative theology in Byzantine theological writings. It reflects the idea that God is beyond description using human words or thoughts. He can only be understood through the elimination of those things that He is not. Thus God, Christ, and angels can only be described in terms of what they are not, since humans cannot comprehend what they really are.[80]

This prompts us to pose the question as to why this same apophatic language was applied to eunuchs. At a linguistic level, it may reflect the fact that the language did not have ways of easily or directly describing persons who were not identified with the conventional man/woman gender categories. At the same time, however, it reinforces the proposition that eunuchs were seen as sharing in some measure the transcendent qualities attributed to angels. This is an important aspect of the Byzantine engendering of eunuchs, which will be treated in chapter 8.

Language of Artificial Creation

Finally, there is a linguistic tradition that supports the idea that eunuchs were perceived as an artificial creation that belonged to the realm of culture rather than to the realm of nature. This idea is apparent in the second-century writings of Lucian, who says that eunuchs are composite or contrived (τι σύνθετον),[81] that they are wonders, marvels, portents, prodigies (τερατῶδες)[82] and that they exist outside of human nature (ἔξω τῆς ἀνθρωπείας φύσεως).[83] Later, Leo the Deacon informs us that Joseph the eunuch is an artificial woman (γυναίου τεχνητοῦ).[84] Almost all of the early sources that discuss eunuchs do so in terms of nature. The condition of the eunuch is "against nature." He exists "outside of nature."

My belief is that eunuchs were perceived by their contemporaries as invented beings, modified by humans to fill specific roles in a highly cultured and stratified society and thus outside the realm of nature. We will see that by the eleventh century this concept has shifted subtly and some authors say that castration allows eunuchs to live "beyond nature," conveying the implication that their condition had spiritual justification and approval.

Since eunuchs were almost always associated with large and powerful institutions like the court or the church, one might speculate that they were perceived to have been created by these institutions. As we will see in chapters 3 and 9, eunuchs were often castrated before puberty. In a cultural sense eunuchs were most certainly "invented"—in our own vocabulary, they were "culturally constructed." The process of social construction was not obvious at the time because Byzantine culture assumed that many of the things we view as external or acquired traits were part of one's inherent or physiological makeup.

Thus there was a distinct, consistent language that was used to discuss eunuchs. This should come as no surprise, but the frequency and power of the invective used against eunuchs is a reflection of their status not just as officials at court but as individuals within their culture. The ambiguity used in the language about eunuchs also suggests that the rest of society had mentally placed them within an ambiguous realm, one that straddled the earthly and the preternatural. This possibility is discussed in chapter 7. Finally, linguistic assumptions about eunuchs offer important insights into the gender constructs of both men and women in this society.

Speaking as a Eunuch . . .

Today there are no surviving published sources in which eunuchs actually speak for themselves. The most we can do is explore the language that whole men used when they wrote passages they attributed to eunuchs. When an author creates an imaginary dialogue between a whole man and a eunuch, what does he think that a eunuch ought to say? Passages like this are few and far between. I have culled a few from different genres and found them quite suggestive.

The first is from a traditional historical source and would have been written for an audience of whole men. In it, the historian Theophanes describes a meeting in 667–668 between Sergios, a representative of the Armenian Saborios, who has rebelled against the Byzantine Empire, and the eunuch Andrew, an emissary of the Byzantine emperor. The two meet first in Damascus, before the Arab ruler Mu'āwiya,[85] whose followers have been conducting frequent campaigns against the eastern frontier of the empire. The rebel Saborios, a general in command of the forces of Byzantium's Armeniac theme, has sent Sergios, his general, to Mu'āwiya to ask for aid against the Byzantines.

> When Andrew had reached Damascus, he found that Sergius had anticipated him; as for Mauias, he pretended to be sympathetic to the emperor. Sergius was sitting in front of Mauias, and when Andrew entered, Sergius, on seeing him, got up. Mauias upbraided Sergius, saying, "Why were you afraid?" Sergius excused himself, saying he had done so out of habit.

In the early part of this dialogue we see the eunuch Andrew, who, even though he is a eunuch, is an extension or representative of the emperor. Therefore it was customary for Sergios, who was technically a Byzantine officer, to stand in his presence. For Sergios to refuse to do so was a significant insult to Andrew and, by extension, to the emperor.

> Turning to Andrew, Mauias asked, "What are you seeking?" He replied, "That you should give help against the rebel." The other said, "Both of you are my enemies. To the one that gives me more I will give help." Then Andrew said to him, "Be not in doubt, O Emir: a few great things from an emperor are more advantageous to you than a great many from a rebel. However, do as you please." Having said these things, Andrew fell silent. Mauias said, "I am thinking it over"; and he bade both of them go out. Then Mauias summoned Sergius in private and said to him, "You will no longer do obeisance to Andrew, since by so doing you will achieve nothing."

As the passage continues, Andrew, at Mu'āwiya's instigation, will no longer be treated by Sergios as a surrogate of the emperor but rather as an individual, a eunuch, and someone to be sneered at. Sergios has seen Andrew through another's eyes.

> The next day Sergius anticipated Andrew and was seated in front of Mauias. When Andrew entered, he did not arise as on the previous day. Looking around at Sergius, Andrew cursed him mightily and threatened him, saying, "If I remain alive, I will show you who I am." Sergius replied, "I am not getting up for you because you are neither a man nor a woman."

Sergios has refused to make *proskynesis* (a formal acknowledgment of Andrew's superior state, often a bow or genuflection) to Andrew. Notice that Andrew's reaction is to glare, be terribly insulted and threatening. This is a classic description of the powerful court eunuch. He intimidates through his affect, since he is assumed to have no other way to intimidate. He is easily insulted, a part of his gender construct—he is perceived to be too sensitive, a trait he shares with women. Andrew tells Sergios that if he [Andrew] lives he will show Sergios what sort of a man he is. He may not be a whole man, but he has the power of the empire and its allies behind him and has resources well beyond those of Sergios. The message is: "Do not belittle me. I am a person even if you don't think so, and in my own way I am powerful." Sergios then delivers the ultimate insult, "You are neither a man nor a woman."

> Mauias stopped both of them and said to Andrew, "Undertake to give me as much as Sergius is giving me."—"And how much is that?" asked Andrew. Mauias replied, "To give to the Arabs the tax revenue." Andrew said, "Bless my soul,[86] O Mauias! You are advising me to give you the body and keep the shadow. Make any agreement you wish with Sergius; for I will do no such thing. However, disregarding you, we shall have recourse to God, who has more power than you to defend the Romans, and we shall place our hopes in Him." After these words he said to Mauias, "Farewell."

Mu'āwiya recognizes that things have gone too far and shifts the conversation to a negotiation for support from Andrew. He says that Sergios has offered to give him the public revenues from the district he hopes to conquer. Andrew replies, "Babai." This is a difficult term to translate and the phrase "Bless my soul" does not really capture the sense of the Greek. In the Greek sources this expression is used by individuals who are not measured in their speech but rather are extravagant in their modes of expression, a tendency attributed to eunuchs. Then Andrew says to Mu'āwiya, "You counsel me to give away the body and keep its shadow." Of course, the body is the district revenues, the shadow is larger imperial authority, but is this perhaps also a veiled reference to his own perceived physical condition? "For I cannot agree to this. Unless you yield, we will take refuge in God who is far more powerful than you and is very fond of the Romans and put our hope in Him." Notice that Andrew does not overtly saber rattle. He rests his position on the moral authority of larger power structures ruled by God. This is not a man who is likely to suggest individual combat or small scale skirmishes.

> And he departed from Damascus in the direction of Melitene along the road that Sergius, too, was about to travel because the rebel dwelt in those parts. When he had reached Arabissos, he [Andrew] met the commander of the pass, who had not joined the rebel, and ordered him to be on the look-out for Sergius when the latter would be returning, so as to hand him over to him. And he himself proceeded to Amnesia to await Sergius and reported to the emperor what had taken place. Now Sergius, after making a covenant with Mauias as he saw fit, took along the Arab general Phadalas with a force of barbarians to fight on the side of Saborios. Sergius was traveling in front of Phadalas and, as he was proceeding joyfully to meet Saborios, he fell into Andrew's trap in the passes. They seized him and brought him prisoner to Andrew. When Sergius saw Andrew, he fell at his feet, begging him to spare his life. But Andrew said to him, "Are you the Sergius who took pride in his private parts in front of Mauias and called me effeminate? Behold, from now on your private parts will be of no benefit to you.

> Nay, they will cause your death." Having said this, he ordered that Sergius' private parts should be cut off, and he hanged him on a gibbet.[87]

Andrew then leaves Damascus but sets a trap for Sergios. This kind of a secret, behind-your-back ambush would have been considered characteristic of a clever eunuch. Sergios is captured, humbled, and brought to Andrew. He begs for mercy, and Andrew explains the situation. He points out that Sergios did not deal with him as the emperor's surrogate. Rather, he treated him as an incomplete, castrated man and called him effeminate. As far as Andrew is concerned, Sergios had demeaned both Andrew and the imperial authority by reducing their interaction to a matter of masculine physical attributes. Thus it was appropriate that Sergios's pride in his own genitals should lead to his death.

The awkwardness of the last sentence in the passage quoted above is no accident. It is Sergios's genitals that are cut off, while the man that remained was hung on a stake. The author is giving us an individual, Andrew, who is proud yet acutely aware of his mutilation. The character is created within the parameters of the assumed gender configuration of eunuchs, yet the author also makes important assumptions about the psychological profile of this eunuch. Andrew is assumed to be sensitive about his condition and to wish that he, too, were a whole man. This is a standard assumption made in all of the sources.[88]

The hagiographical sources have not yielded such a complex passage. Perhaps this is because they are generally more positive about eunuchs than secular sources. One of the best is a story found in the Vita of St. Andrew the Fool, in which one chapter involves a eunuch who becomes the subject of a great deal of criticism. The saint in question is one of the genre of saints who are "fools for Christ." He rarely wears clothes and often indulges in outrageous behavior, yet he always speaks the truth and can see into men's hearts.[89]

In this vignette the saint is sitting in front of the gate to his disciple Epiphanios's house.

> As he sat on the ground in front of the gateway there came a young eunuch who was the chamberlain of one of the nobles.[90] His face was like a rose, the skin of his body white as snow, he was well shaped, fair-haired, possessing an unusual softness, and smelling of musk from afar. As Epiphanios had been brought up together with him and was his friend they loved each other dearly. Now this eunuch carried with him dates, about thirty in number. When he saw the naked body of the holy man he was alarmed and asked Epiphanios, "My dearest and beloved Epiphanios, who is this man and why does he go naked, although it is winter and unbearably cold, being like those who have suffered shipwreck at sea?" Epiphanios answered, "My dearest brother, I do not know what I shall say about

> his appearance, since his mind has been taken prisoner by the Evil One and he wanderers about like one possessed and confused. All such people tear their clothes and run about without feeling anything." This he said because he did not want to reveal the holy man's virtue. When the eunuch heard this he fell silent and, having pity on the blessed man as on one of the poor, gave him all his dates. "Take these just for now," he said, "for I have nothing else with me." But the holy man, who with the eyes of his spirit already knew the works of his soul, looked at him sternly and said, "Fools do not eat a gift of *colophonia*!"[91]
>
> The eunuch, who did not understand what he said, replied, "You truly crazy man, when you see dates, do you think they are fruit from Colophon?'" The blessed man said to him, "You deceiver (δόλιε), go into your master's bedchamber and perform with him the sick practice of the sodomites, that he may give you other dates too. You wretch, who do not see the rays of the kingdom of heaven, who do not know the cruelty and bitterness of hell, do you not even feel shame before the angel who accompanies you as a Christian? What should be done with you, impure that you are, because you frequent the corners and do what should not be done, things which neither dogs nor swine, nor reptiles nor serpents do? You accursed fellow, why do you do this? Woe to your youth, which Satan has wounded and thrown down headlong into the terrible depth of hell with vehemence and boundless vigor! See that you do not go further, lest the Godhead treat you as you deserve, here burning you whole with flashes of lightning, there with the hell of fire." When the eunuch heard this he trembled with fear, his face turned red like fire and his shame was great. Epiphanios said, "Sir, what happened to you? Why were you ashamed? Did I not tell you that he is crazy and says whatever occurs to him? However, my dear friend in the Lord, if you are aware that you are guilty of something of what he said to you, go at once and reform yourself and do not be angry with him for his words! You are young, dear friend, and Satan is wicked, deceiving us to commit sin for no other reason than to have us too for a consolation in the fire of hell."

Most of the dialogue is, admittedly, spoken by a saint. The eunuch serves both as a foil for the saint's words and as an exemplum. The eunuch is presented as beautiful, desirable, urbane, cultured. The saint is naked, cold, like the naked survivors of a shipwreck. His is the world of harsh realities and asceticism. The eunuch's words are considerate, measured, and polite. The saint's are harsh. The real point of the story is to show how easily a eunuch, castrated at a young age, can be destroyed by the Devil and drawn into worldly society. There he will enjoy rich food, fine clothes, and sexual pleasures, as exemplified by the dates. All these things, which are evil for the holy man, are represented by the eunuch. The saint's language, featuring dark corners, shameful acts, dogs, serpents, and pigs, typifies the hostility that many authors express toward eunuchs.

> When the eunuch heard this he went away, whereas the honorable Epiphanios helped the holy man to his feet and showed him to his room. There they found a table ready laid and sat down, enjoying the gifts of God. After they had finished their feast Epiphanios said to the blessed man, "Venerable sir, why did you rebuke my friend so bluntly?" The blessed man answered, "Because he is dear to you and beloved, for this reason did I give him this lecture, for had he not been your friend, he would not have heard a single word from me. This is not my vocation, to rebuke sinners, but to run the straight road which leads to a better life." Epiphanios said again, "I know that too, you servant of God, but this young man is a slave, and when he is forced by his master what can he do?" The holy man replied, "Yes I know, I am not ignorant of that. However, a slave should serve the man who bought him with regard to his physical needs, not with regard to the works of the devil, specially not when it comes to this cursed and disgusting abnormality in which not even animals engage." Epiphanios said, "If a master enjoins his slave to minister to his needs, be they physical, spiritual or sinful, and the slave fails to obey, you surely know, my Lord, how much he will suffer, being maltreated, beaten, threatened and receiving all sorts of punishments." The holy man answered, "This, my son, is the martyrdom of Jesus Christ at which he hinted when he said, 'Blessed are those who are persecuted for righteousness' sake, for theirs is the kingdom of heaven.' Thus if the slaves do not bow to the abominable sodomitic passion of their masters they are blessed and thrice blessed, for thanks to the torments you mention they will be reckoned with the martyrs."[92]

Offering something of a contrast, the Vita of St. John the Almsgiver presents a rather different hagiographical image of the eunuch.[93] In this story a handsome young monk arrives in town accompanied by a beautiful young woman. The community is scandalized, as is St. John, and the young monk is beaten and thrown into prison. That night the young monk appears to St. John in a dream, showing him his beaten body and saying, "Do these things please you, lord? Regarding this one [monk/eunuch], you are deceived, being a man yourself.[94]

St. John asks that the monk be brought to him and asks him to remove his clothing so he can see his wounds. He realizes that he is the same monk who had visited him in his dream and that he is a eunuch. The monk then tells his story.

> Blessed be the Lord, God my master, I do not lie. For not many days ago I was in Gaza and from there I was hastening to worship [at the church of] Sts. Cyrus and

> John, and this girl stopped me in the evening and threw herself at my feet begging to accompany me on my journey because she wished to be a Christian, for she was a Hebrew. I, indeed, fearing the judgment of God who said we should not despise even the smallest being, and [therefore] allowed her to be my companion on the journey. Besides, I thought that since my members were so afflicted it would not be easy for the enemy to lead me into temptation. Once I arrived there and prayed, I arranged it so that she was instructed in [the Christian religion] and baptized. And from that point I wandered about with a simple heart, and fed her by begging, eager, if I were able, to establish her in a convent of virgins.[95]

John offers profound apologies, then tries to give the monk money. The monk says, "If a monk has faith he does not have need of money. If he desires money, he lacks faith entirely." Here we see a eunuch who is the model of Christian monasticism. He recognizes his duty to minister to this woman. He knows that because of his physical mutilation he cannot sin with her. He rises above "appearances," which originally influenced John in his incorrect response to the situation.

In this story the eunuch emerges as the perfect ascetic, more so even than St. John. Notice, however, that the eunuch, in the words of the author, says that he is not a man. Yet he also is never presented as a woman. Nor does he specifically identify himself as a eunuch. He is content to be a monk and stand outside of any other categories of either gender or sex. He is the ultimate ambiguous figure, relying on God and his faith.

Finally, our best example of an author putting words into a eunuch's mouth comes from Theophylaktos of Ohrid. An individual who is acting as the protagonist is a whole man and a monk. He begins the discussion with a long list of all the traditional charges brought against eunuchs. The eunuch then makes this rebuttal:

> It seems to me that you are making reference to eunuchs [here he uses the term *cut man* (ἐκτομίας), a technical term that distinguishes surgically altered eunuchs from other men who are born as eunuchs] who live among the Persians or Arabs or elsewhere, so that in heaping these charges upon us you might squash us under their weight, so that we are unable to look back at you and deny the charge, as if we didn't have among us the archbishops of Thessalonica, Pydna, Petra, Edessa in Bulgaria, and many others in different occupations and social classes. But you might as well bring up the proverbs about the goat and the knife and Bellerophon and the letter when you mention these men.[96] For one is deceived in a foreign land and you hasten, like cupping glasses,[97] to gather up that which is worst.

Don't do that, most worthy of men. Don't mislead a friend and especially not on trivial matters in order to show him to be an enemy of God and a lawless man hostile to all that is dear because he made provision against every passion.

If I, in your opinion, am at variance with the Creator, why isn't he also at variance who has elected to remain celibate and guard his condition with God's help? Marriage includes the procreation which results from it. Consequently if one does not wish to use the sexual organs for the purpose for which they had been made, he would oppose the Creator's plan and argue against the art of wisdom since, indeed, the power of reason has neither formed us in vain nor in an artless way, but skillfully and with a certain useful purpose; but you, yourself [the person to whom the eunuch is speaking, who is a monk committed to celibacy], consider the begetting of children to be superfluous. So it follows that one must not blame a man who has been castrated. In the same way the master of the house rightly cuts down a fig tree that does not fulfill the purpose for which it was planted. So also we do not charge those who remove a sixth finger. You cannot say that the one who does this does so against nature. And you, who have changed the nature of your genitals, even though the natural task of the testicles is to produce sperm for the sake of producing offspring, say that you bewail the sowing of sperm because of your desire for fair virginity. If then also you were fully logical and anticipated that you would not use your genitals for procreation and thus accepted their removal when the time was right, then the decision would not have been worthy of criticism. Do you not waste away your body by fasting and not bathing and all sorts of spiritual practice? As a result, instead of being well fleshed, now your body is languishing; instead of a ruddy complexion, now it appears pallid and you have made your body sickly instead of being strong. What if we said that this change in your body violated the laws of God, since having been made healthy by him you have changed yourself to the opposite? If you censure me for the removal of testicles, I censure you for the destruction of the flesh, so that either you stop judging, or be judged together with me. The words from your own lips are a powerful snare for you and the eagle is captured by his own wings that hastens to the divine light, raising himself above the others. A pagan would criticize such things, for he puts nothing ahead of nature and believes that to live his whole life according to nature and its laws is the goal of the present life. But to you, who have chosen a life beyond nature, who exert yourself and practice it and are successful in it, justice will not ever allow you to open your lips and speak against eunuchs.[98]

Throughout the *Defense of Eunuchs* Theophylaktos makes an impassioned plea for the humanity of eunuchs. Each individual should be judged for his own moral character. He argues that the presence or absence of functioning genitalia has little to do with a man's character. Body and soul are separate entities, and the condition of the body does not reflect the condition of the soul. The eunuch has a place in God's plan for mankind. His mutilated body is no different from that of a holy man who starves his body in order to make it holy. The repeated references to "nature" in this passage echo the language of most of our sources that discuss eunuchs. Eunuch and φύσις (nature) regularly appear together in discussions about eunuchs. We are repeatedly told that castration is "against" or "outside of" nature and that those who have been castrated belong in a world other than the world of nature. Just what world they belong in, that of the holy or the damned, depends on the point of view of the text.

Conclusion

This chapter has shown that language in and of itself contributes to the categories that we use to define social groups. In the case of eunuchs, the language used about them associates them with negative feminine traits and finds them physically and psychologically ambiguous. It references them negatively to the active male standard adopted by the Byzantine elite and suggests that they are an artificial creation that exists outside of nature. The passages in which "whole" authors give eunuchs words to speak are filled with this kind of gendered language, perhaps suggesting that whole men felt that eunuchs understood and acquiesced in their status.

Thus language routinely sets eunuchs outside the norms of male or female gender. At the same time, Byzantine society does not set eunuchs outside its culture and its conceptual framework. Rather, they are associated with other forces that are part of Byzantine thinking but are similarly hard to define—God, angels, magicians, and demons. The result is a "constructed" but stable frame of reference that, somewhat paradoxically, defines eunuchs by not directly defining them. This is one of several facets of Byzantine culture that allows us to think of eunuchs as a separate gender group within society.

This perception is reinforced by other general patterns in the culture. One such pattern is that of scientific and medical ideas. Given that castration did make eunuchs physiologically and visibly distinctive, it is hardly surprising that they are discussed in the medical sources. These sources are instructive in that they discuss some of the "differentness" of eunuchs and explore their physiology, at least as far as the medical categories of the era permitted. At the same time, Greek and Byzantine medical sources often ascribed to the physical body appearances and behaviors that we attribute to learned behavior and cultural conditioning. These themes will be discussed in chapter 2.

CHAPTER 2

Byzantine Medical Lore and the Gendering of Eunuchs

In chapter 1, we saw how Byzantine culture built up a complex language of negation and ambiguity in order to talk about eunuchs. This culture clearly recognized eunuchs as physically distinct from men, women, and children, and this distinctiveness encouraged assumptions about their inherent personality traits and gender characteristics. Modern Western culture believes it can distinguish between acquired personal traits and physiologically or biologically inherent ones. Byzantine culture perceived such matters very differently.

The Byzantines did not make the same distinctions we do and their distinctions, like ours, were culturally determined. If we are to understand the engendering process we must recognize that Byzantine society assumed that traits that we consider learned behavioral attributes were inherent in the *physical* being of the individual. As a result, while this chapter is primarily about medicine and physiology, inevitably it refers to assumptions about the physiology of eunuchs that we recognize as cultural assignments within the gender construct. Because Byzantine society assumed that basic moral and behavioral traits were part of the inherent physical nature of an individual, the boundary between inherent and acquired characteristics that emerges is quite different from ours.

Byzantium had a rich tradition of medical lore to draw upon, and this argument begins with a discussion of some of the basic assumptions made by the medical communities of the classical and Byzantine worlds. We will never know what kind of an impact these medical beliefs had on general perceptions of gender or how much they influenced popular thought. It would be surprising, however, if they did not reflect popular belief in some degree.[1]

Most of the medical lore and practice of the Byzantine world was based on the teachings of Aristotle, Hippocrates, and Galen, with a smattering of ideas from the Methodist school.[2] What we now call the Hippocratic corpus is a collection of various texts written by medical practitioners in the fifth and fourth centuries B.C. These came into the Byzantine world through the teachings of Galen (A.D. 129–210), the best known and most popular medical authority in the Byzantine world. In fact, a sizeable share of our Byzantine medical texts simply reproduce Galen's teachings. Despite the popularity of Galen's teachings, however, Byzantine medical authorities were also familiar with the writings of Aristotle, writings of the fourth century B.C. that were reworked throughout Late Antiquity and beyond.[3]

These medical models were critical in influencing the way Byzantine society thought about the nature of the human body, the composition of the flesh, and the relationship between the body, the soul, and the soul's moral character. These older medical models established norms for these relationships and directly shaped attitudes about eunuchs.[4]

The Hippocratic writings stressed the importance of balance and harmony in the human body. A body that was properly balanced and harmonious was a healthy body. Nothing should be done in excess. Nothing should be allowed to disturb the perfect balance that became the hallmark of the ideal masculine body. This theme, as we will see later, had important gendered elements and reflected assumptions about male perfection. The mature man of affairs must always be completely in control of himself, with a measured stride and melodious voice. This sense of control, balance, and harmony was generally contrasted with women's lack of control—the assumption that women became upset and cried easily, proving that they were emotionally unstable.

As we have seen, these "unmanly" traits were also assumed to be characteristic of eunuchs. Like women, they were assumed to be unable to maintain the focus of either the mind or the body. They lacked balance and harmony in body, mind, and behavior. As a result eunuchs, like women, were believed to be unable to control their desires for food, drink, and physical pleasure. This was clearly a thought system based on men and women as polar opposites, one in which eunuchs occupied an ambiguous position somewhere between the two.

Aristotle acknowledged the importance of balance and moderation in the human body but tended to look at gender in terms of hierarchical structures, not polar opposites. For Aristotle the difference between men and women was largely defined in terms of heat. Men were warm, women were cool. In discussing the determination of sex in the offspring of humans, Aristotle claimed that a man's bodily heat acted in the formation of sperm. In the presence of sufficient heat the sperm formed properly, and the resulting offspring would be male. But, if a man was too cool, his sperm did not develop properly and a female offspring resulted from this "lesser" seed. Aristotle illustrated this with a rare reference to eunuchs. "The mutilation of just one vital part [the testicles] results in a great alteration of their old semblance, and in close approximation to the appearance of the female."[5]

Aristotle believed that vital heat was produced by the heart, but he also argued that it was retained by the sperm and stored in the sexual organs. Sperm was the product of unused nourishment: the male body used heat to change this nourishment first into blood and then into the whitened foamy substance recognized as sperm. Stored sperm then acted as a reservoir and source of heat for the male body, a source that should never be wasted. Women, because they lacked heat, could not make sperm or store heat. Since eunuchs lacked sperm they, like women, also lacked heat. Although they might still be considered men, eunuchs were imperfect men because of their sterility and cool temperature. Their coolness made them passive, like women. Further, because women were believed to produce no seed, eunuchs also resembled them in their sterility.

Here Aristotle presents a hierarchy of sexuality and gender. He has little difficulty locating eunuchs on what Peter Brown calls that "slippery slope" of gender anxiety that was part of status definition for men of the ancient world and Late Antiquity, a downward slope toward a feminized physical state.[6] When sexuality and gender are conceptualized in this hierarchical way, we are being presented with a perfect masculinity with all its positive attributes that rises above an "other" that is peopled with prepubescent boys and girls, women, elderly men, and eunuchs. Each exhibits attributes that are negative mirrors of perfect masculinity.

But Aristotle could also conceptualize men and women as polar opposites. In such cases his descriptive language focuses on masculine attributes as positive principles and feminine attributes as negative and opposing principles. For example, he describes men as possessing a generative principle that women lack, saying that men have an "ability;" women, an "inability." Reproduction depends on the man planting his "spirit" in the fertile matter of the woman's body. He will pass his soul on to his son or daughter, while the woman will provide the material for the child's physical formation.

The strength and longevity of these classical formulations are seen in a discussion of gonorrhea found in Aretaeus of Cappadocia, a Greek medical writer of the second century A.D. and a contemporary of Galen. Aretaeus suggests that when the generative organs of the mature male are no longer able to function because of disease, the victim suffers "lethargy, weakness, faintheartedness, hesitation in his actions, poor hearing, and lack of strength. His limbs are withered; he is idle and very pale. He is womanlike, has no appetite, is barren, has poor circulation, and his body is cold." "In contrast," Aretaeus says, "a man with healthy semen is warm, his joints work well, he is hairy, he has a good voice and agreeable manner, is strong, intelligent, and active, and is clearly recognized as a man. Because he has strong seed, he is strong, courageous and mighty as a wild beast, a model for athletes." The validity of this observation is established for Aretaeus when he compares the healthy man with the eunuch who, because he lacks semen, is "weak, lethargic, high-voiced, hairless, sterile, and womanlike."[7]

Notice that only a few of the elements that mark the gender construct of eunuchs and males are actually based on male hormones or lack thereof: fertility or sterility, patterns of body hair, pitch of voice, and patterns of placement of fatty tissues. The majority of the elements that distinguish a man who is "healthy" (because he produces semen) from one who is "unhealthy" (because he does not) are constructed, assumed elements of an ideal male gender structure. These include strength, courage, fighting ability, athletic skill, good hearing, a hearty appetite, a warm body, intelligence, and a pleasant, "balanced" manner. A masculine man is "active," as opposed to passive, in his dealings with others.

Aristotle rarely talks about eunuchs. Perhaps he perceived them as created beings and therefore not a part of the natural world that he was trying to describe. He does, however, occasionally use eunuchs to help make a point about something else. In the course of explaining the importance of heat and cold, he tells us that during sexual intercourse blood and its attendant warmth is withdrawn from the male brain and concentrated in the genital region. As a result the brain, which tends to be cool in any case, is chilled. The long-term result of this chilling of the brain and scalp is that the hair follicles of the scalp die, resulting in baldness. Children and eunuchs do not have intercourse, and as a result they have full heads of hair. Aristotle also observes that eunuchs, if castrated while still children, never grow beards and have patterns of body hair that resemble those of women rather than men. This provides evidence for him that the removal of the genitalia, the male creative principle, creates creatures that resemble women and prepubescent children.[8]

Galen disagrees with Aristotle in some ways while supporting him in others. For example, Galen echoes Hippocratic rather than Aristotelian teachings when he says that women have the same genitals as men, just inside the body instead of outside, and that women produce seed that joins with the male seed in the production of a new individual. Yet, like Aristotle, he sets up opposing categories in his discussion of the body. Men are warm; women, cold. Men have strong, hard flesh, which is less subject to illness than that of individuals whose flesh is soft and sensitive. This second group includes women, children, eunuchs, and men with white skin, especially those who live in cold places. Truly strong and healthy men can be found in hot places like Egypt and Arabia where they are made strong because their bodies are hot and dry.[9]

Galen taught that "the bodies of eunuchs, women, and children are similar in that, because of their nature or habit they are soft and moist, not hard and dry. When a doctor stretches the limb of a eunuch, woman, or child in order to set a bone or treat a dislocation he is more likely to injure these individuals than is the case in the setting of a man's bone."[10] Regarding the differences in temperature between men, women, and eunuchs Galen says, "As is the case among women, the flesh of eunuchs is cold."[11] Thus, in the Galenic universe, women are soft-fleshed, cool, and moist, while men were hard-fleshed, warm, and dry. Eunuchs, like prepubescent boys, lie somewhere on a continuum between the masculine and feminine.

These ideas persisted. In the sixth century A.D., Alexander of Tralles says that the flesh of eunuchs is like that of young boys, women, and children. Therefore, they should be given gentle medicines. Men, however, can be given much stronger medicines. In the writings of Aetios of Amida, while the medical treatments prescribed for eunuchs, women, and boys are similar, they are different from those prescribed for mature men.[12]

The Galenic system regarded animals in the same way. The flesh of castrated and young animals was moist, soft, and tender. The flesh of male animals was dry, hard (tough), and muscular.[13] For Galen, the flesh of male animals, and especially the part surrounding the genital region, was considered to be unappetizing because of its strong smell and unhealthy because it was difficult to digest.[14]

Galenic teachings elaborated on Hippocratic teachings about the four humors (heat, cold, moisture or phlegm, and dryness). Hippocrates taught that the foods used to nourish an individual had to be suited to the humors of that individual's body. Later Byzantine medical writers who followed the Galenic tradition warned that women, boys, and eunuchs should be careful of consuming "phlegm producing" foods, since phlegm can upset the humors in these "cool" individuals. They provided detailed lists of foods that were dry, warm, moist, and cool. These categories were comparable to those used to describe the gendered bodies of men, women, children, and eunuchs. These concepts were embodied in the mental universe of the society, which assumed the logic of "gendered" eating habits: feeding each individual foods that reinforced and nourished his or her particular physical makeup.

In the Byzantine period we find the anonymous *De alimentia* listing foods that make phlegm. They included meat, internal organs, and shellfish. This same source categorizes vegetable foods into traditional Galenic boxes. Bread and good wine are perfectly balanced foods. Lentils, pulse, cabbage, radishes, turnips, mustard, and vetch are dry foods. Grain, dates, some fruits, cannabis seeds, parsley, cabbage, turnips, mustard, cardamom, carrots, garlic, onions, leeks, cured cheese, sweet wine, green wine, and aged wine are warm foods. Barley, cooked grains, cooked gourds, ripe fruit, cucumbers, berries, tart fruits, lettuce, endive, water, watered wine, acidic wines, and vinegar are cool foods. The foods that are cool, with the addition of fresh walnuts, plums, mulberries, poppy seeds, and beans, are all moist foods.[15] This tradition continued in the Byzantine world as seen in the work of the eleventh-century author Symeon Seth. He assesses the qualities of a variety of foods from pears to wheat to beef to lamb and categorizes them according to their effects on the heat, cold, moisture, and dryness of the human body.[16]

For the Byzantines, foods were definitely gendered. Men were encouraged to eat those foods that corresponded to their warm, dry flesh; women, those that corresponded to their cool, moist flesh. Ascetic men and women were expected to avoid those foods that might incite them to sexual activity since specific foods could heighten or reduce sexual desire.[17] This gender structuring of food is very complex and yet so thoroughly assumed within the culture that it is rarely discussed.

Thus the eunuch's body was assumed to be soft, cool, moist, and fragile and was categorized by doctors with the bodies of women and children.[18] The eunuch boy was reared among women, and he probably ate a bland diet of the kind recommended for women and children, a diet considered appropriate to his body humors. His beard did not grow, and his skin remained fine-grained and soft, allowing him to retain an adolescent loveliness that both men and women considered attractive. Like an aristocratic woman, he was expected to stay indoors and avoid sun tanning and the darkening of his complexion. As he aged he retained his hair, a trait traditionally associated with eunuchs.

Galen also sets up categories of tension and slackness in his efforts to explain the human body. An ideal man's body is in a state of perfect balance and tension. Here Galen offers Aristotle's analogy to the upright loom. The testicles are loom weights that keep a perfect tension on the veins and arteries that go up and over the shoulders and keep a perfect, balanced, tension on the heart. When these weights are removed the body is "sprung," as Galen claims to be able to prove through the dissection of eunuchs. The castrated body is no longer physically the same. Its veins become slack and small, like those of aged people or women.[19]

It would be interesting to know to what extent Galen and Aristotle were implicitly commenting here on the supposed moral and psychological changes that castration brought to men. The moral imagery that centers on the loom and the perfectly woven cloth as the representation of a perfectly lived life was familiar throughout the ancient world and almost certainly registered on Aristotle and

Galen. A weaver could not possibly weave a piece of fine, even fabric on a loom without loom weights.

This discussion of the loom and its analogy to the body brings Galen to a serious discussion of castration. He begins by saying that among the castrated—and here he uses the term "cut out" (ἐκτέμνω) which refers to the ablation of the testicles—the penis "suffers nothing." But with the loss of the testicles one loses the ability to "sow seeds," a refuge, he says, for those who wish to escape sexuality. With the loss of the testicles, masculinity and virility are also lost.[20]

Galen continues with an illuminating discussion about serious athletes. Since, he says, it is known that chaste living is good for an athlete, why don't they have themselves castrated? Why not just cut the seed pathway? This would be foolish, he says, because healthy testicles are necessary to a healthy body. They are needed in order to preserve masculinity and strength. Those who have lost their testicles become cold and weak, like old people. Their veins are pale and no longer work well. They lose their body hair even as their bodies lose strength. Their flesh is soft and pleasing to the touch, in contrast to the flesh of the whole man, which is heavy and manly and feels and smells like the testicles themselves. From all of this Galen concludes that the testicles, not the heart as Aristotle thought, are the real source of heat and strength in the body. Semen is made and stored in the testicles where it is "enjoyed" by the body for its qualities of heat and strength. When too much is stored the sperm moves into the spermatic passages where it makes a man warm and strong.[21]

When we look at the writings of physicians and physiognomists of the Late Antique and Byzantine periods we find that there is little modification of Galen and Aristotle's constructs regarding eunuchs. Later authors, influenced by the *De physiognomia* of Polemo, a second-century orator and writer, attributed eunuchs' psychological characteristics directly to their castration and even claimed that castration caused a sudden and noticeable change in personality, behavior, and moral stance. This is expressed in the *Physiognomonica* of Adamantius Judaeus, a work that predates the fourth century A.D. and is based on the physiognomic text of Polemo.

> Therefore I have known eunuchs to be an evil tribe: they are greedy and replete with tendencies to dissipation. You should be aware, moreover, that castrated eunuchs undergo a change in the general appearance, complexion, and physique that they had before castration.[22]

Theophilos Protospatharios, an author of Byzantine medical texts of uncertain date,[23] explains that eunuchs, if castrated before fourteen years of age, are, like women, lacking in wisdom teeth.[24] This is an old idea dating from the writings of Aristotle and Pliny, and it leads one to wonder whether these commentators ever bothered to open a woman or eunuch's mouth and count the teeth. In any case, the assumption is that individuals who lack masculine force also will lack wisdom teeth. What this society meant by "wisdom" is of interest here since, as we shall see later, the fact that eunuchs could be trained to high levels of skill in certain specific tasks is a part of their gender construct. Skill in keeping books, supplying an army, or running the protocol of an imperial household is clearly not classed as "wisdom" in Byzantine culture.

Theophilos also puts a great deal of credence on the idea that the left side of the body is morally bad and the right side, good. The right side, of course, had long been assumed to be the side that produced male offspring; the left side, female offspring. The right side was strong; the left side, weak. Theophilos elaborates on these older ideas, suggesting that if the right testicle should be damaged the left testicle would become stronger and better able to produce seed and that seed would result in a male offspring.[25] Later we will see that eunuchs are assumed to be "on the left," that is, to behave in a manner that is characteristic of the "left" or female side. Some authors also associate the "left" with magic and evildoing, traits that are also sometimes attributed to eunuchs.

Theophilos also attempts to answer a long-debated question that was raised briefly in the introduction: Can eunuchs experience sexual pleasure?[26] The concepts of love and sex do appear in writings about eunuchs. This is seen in a selection from Philostratos in which the philosopher, Apollonios, saves the life of a eunuch accused of having an emotional involvement with a lady of the harem. He does so by suggesting that the eunuch should be allowed to live, since living with a love that cannot be fulfilled is the cruelest punishment of all.[27]

In general, medieval authors concluded that if a child were made a eunuch before his fourteenth year he would not be able to experience sexual pleasure, though he might engage in passive sexual behavior. Those castrated later in life, however, might be able to experience sexual pleasure though they could not procreate.

> Eunuchs do not experience sexual desire because both passages for the seed are destroyed. For the seed gets to the testes through them [i.e., the passages]. When these passages are rubbed out, the route for the seed is fenced off. The sinews become harsh and dull and do not stretch or secrete fluids. Some eunuchs secrete semen, which they can do because semen is not just made in the testicles and supergeminals [the part above the testicles] but also in various other parts of the body and in the genital parts; because of this it [the semen] is useless and infertile. Boys do not have sexual desire for the following reason: their veins are narrow and full [or engorged] and cannot ejaculate the seed, and irritation [or stimula-

> tion] similarly does not happen. For this reason neither is the fluid agitated in the body in response to the seed.[28]

Like Galen, Theophilos assumes that the semen enters the penis and is ejaculated using a kind of inner system of fluid dynamics. For this system to work, the veins within the testicles must be large and flexible, a condition that only comes with puberty. Thus maturation, along with manly heat, is what allows the semen to be mixed with moisture, agitated, and then expelled.

Depending on the age at which a eunuch was castrated and the technique used, lack of testosterone often caused his body to elongate as he matured.[29] This produced an individual with unusually long, slender limbs and hands, a strikingly tall stature, light musculature, and a distinctive gait. While Byzantine physicians had not progressed much beyond Galen in understanding how the human reproductive system works, most of these early medical authors were good observers. They realized that men castrated before puberty developed a greatly altered physical appearance as they matured and that they lacked sexual desire. Yet, without knowledge of male sex hormones, they had to explain the changes as well as they could. They also tended to distance themselves from the existence of eunuchs within their practical medical world, explaining eunuchs' distinct appearance only when it helped explain the physiology of whole men, women, and children. In the eyes of the Byzantine medical community, eunuchs were neither fully male nor fully female, and it is probable that these physicians, like Aristotle, believed that eunuchs were culturally created individuals, not members of the world of nature.

Ancient and medieval physicians also seem to have had a view of puberty and sexual maturation that was different from that of modern society. A modern physician looks at a prepubescent male and assumes that he will mature into a man and that this maturation process is a natural and expected phenomenon. Thus the immature generative organs are male generative organs in an immature form. Similarly, for a modern physician the prepubescent male body is an adult male body that simply has to mature and grow. For the physician of the Late Antique or Byzantine world, the prepubescent male seems to have been as different from the mature male as was a woman. These observers did not emphasize the gradual and inevitable maturation of the child into the adult but rather the sudden and radical change from the boy to the man.

Given this mindset, castration was simply a method of retaining those qualities that made a prepubescent boy desirable; his beauty, his lack of sexuality, his lack of aggressive behavior, his willingness to serve. Castration offered an opportunity to restructure a prepubescent boy into an individual whose physical and psychological properties were perceived to be distinct from those of a mature man and to preserve elements of prepubescence that were valued by society. Attitudes about prepubertal castration among these physicians may have resembled more closely those of the modern veterinarian than those of the modern physician.

The actual techniques for castrating human males are discussed in detail in the writings on surgery of Paul of Aegina, a seventh-century physician whose techniques are taken almost directly from Galen. Three of his discussions of surgical techniques are of interest here, both for their content and for the way they are contextualized. In chapter 46 of his treatise, Paul of Aegina talks about the surgical removal of excessive male breast tissue—in modern terms, a breast reduction.[30] He explains that men who suffer from overdeveloped breasts will undergo this surgery because their condition makes them appear effeminate and they are ashamed of their appearance. In chapter 57, he discusses the treatment of a diseased foreskin and glans penis. He stresses the importance of preserving the appearance of the penis and foreskin, since in this culture they are important markers of beauty and manliness. He also tells us that in the event that the head of the penis is very diseased and has to be removed, the function of the urethra can be preserved by inserting a small lead pipe into what remains of the penis.[31]

All three of these treatments are found in a part of Paul's book in which he discusses cures for serious ailments of the body. Notice that in these cases this author assumes that surgery is necessary, both for the health of the body and to preserve an appropriately masculine appearance in the body. The two rationales are both presented as medical necessities. For a man, breast reduction is not, as it would be in our culture, "elective surgery."

Elsewhere, in a different section of his work, Paul discusses what we would consider "elective" surgeries, among them castration.[32] He says that he does not like to do castrations, but powerful men sometimes insist that he must.[33] He then tells us that castrations in young children are done in one of two ways, and he suggests that the second is the safer of the two. In the first the child is soaked in a hot bath until the genital parts are completely relaxed. Then the testicles are seized and crushed between the fingers. They remain within the scrotal sack, but are no longer attached to the body. That such castrations were actually done is reinforced by a remark in the writings of the early second-century physician Soranos who, in a discussion of child rearing, cautions nurses to handle a male child's genitals carefully lest "they be damaged."[34] This continued to be a way of making eunuchs well into the Byzantine period and is documented in a remark by Michael Psellos in his collection of legal definitions.[35] In his definition of a eunuch he includes an individual whose testicles were "crushed" by his mother or nursemaid when he was very young. Paul of Aegina's second and preferred technique for castration involves a simple incision and the removal of the testicles from the scrotal sack. He did not consider this to be a difficult or particularly dangerous operation so long as the child had not yet reached puberty.

None of these physicians, either in their discussions of the physiology of eunuchs or in their discussions of castration, suggest that in the Byzantine world castration involved anything more than the removal of the testicles, their separation from the surrounding flesh, or the cutting of the vas deferens. I have found no evidence that eunuchs in the Byzantine world suffered the removal of all of their generative organs, a practice designed to give them the appearance of women. The only eunuchs of this type specifically described in our sources were brought to Constantinople as a gift and had been purchased in the West.[36] Paul of Aegina certainly was aware of the techniques used to reconstruct the urethra using a lead tube. This procedure was associated with the removal of the penis when making eunuchs in China, but Paul mentions this procedure only in connection with reconstructing a diseased penis, never in the context of making eunuchs.

It would be useful to have more systematic information about the typical age at which castration took place. While sources reveal the names of many castrated men, the context of their castration is seldom specified and the actual details of their surgery are never discussed. Thus it is unusual for a source, no matter how detailed, to tell us about a eunuch's place of birth, castration, or death. Only 25 of the 196 examples I have examined so far give any kind of detail about the context of castration. I suspect that the importance of these earthly details was overshadowed by the eunuch's transcendental quality. Sources do, however, sometimes make clear the age at which specific castrations took place, reinforcing the suspicion that the Byzantine world made a distinction between pre- and post-pubertal castrates in favor of the former. Of the few detailed accounts depicting the castration of individuals, nearly all indicate that the subject had the surgery before puberty, some as early as seven years old. There are also scattered references to the castration of infants and very young children.[37]

The contexts and rationales for castration are quite diverse. Three specific cases illustrate this diversity. Eutropios, the great eunuch villain of the fourth century, was castrated as a child, supposedly with the intent that he be sold into prostitution. This is not improbable, but we must remember that almost everything we have that discusses Eutropios is hostile in intent.[38] Solomon, a eunuch general of the sixth century, was inadvertently castrated by a nurse as an infant.[39] Mamas, another sixth-century eunuch, was injured as a youth and castrated for medical reasons.[40]

Castrations were sometimes done for dynastic reasons. In such cases, it ensured that a mature man with a potential claim to the imperial throne would be permanently excluded from the succession. In Byzantium the emperor had to be complete and perfect in body to hold the imperial office. Individuals castrated for dynastic reasons sometimes appeared later as eunuchs in a courtly or religious context. The patriarch Ignatios (d. 877) was the son of Michael Rangabe and was castrated at age fourteen for dynastic reasons,[41] as was Basil Lekapenos while still a child.[42] Romanos, son of Peter of Bulgaria and Maria Lekapenos, was also apparently castrated as a child for political reasons by the powerful eunuch Joseph Bringas, perhaps while Romanos was a hostage in Constantinople.[43]

The emperor Michael V (r. 1041–1042), after the fall of his uncle and patron, the eunuch John the Orphanotrophos, had all of the adult men in John's family castrated. Michael Psellos, an eyewitness observer, expresses his shock that this might have been done to mature men, "in the prime of adult life, having achieved full stature and already bearded, who had become fathers." Psellos considers that these men were condemned to a "life that was half a death."[44] While the above might be considered "punishment," it was almost certainly done for dynastic reasons. Psellos says as much: "The truth is, he [Michael V] was ashamed to kill them openly: he preferred to compass their destruction by mutilation," a punishment apparently less severe.[45] Aside from such dynastic situations, there is little evidence that adult castration was practiced as a criminal punishment, especially after the tenth century.

References to childhood castration are common. As a child Polyeuktos the future patriarch was castrated by his parents in order to advance his career in the church.[46] John the Orphanotrophos, who was a Paphlagonian eunuch, was castrated along with two of his brothers to advance the fortunes of his family.[47] The eunuch Constantine came from similar circumstances, according to the vita of his father, Saint Metrios.[48] The same is said of Nikephoros, bishop of Miletos, who also was castrated as a child by his parents in order to ensure his professional advancement.[49] We have the same story, with slightly more detail about the patrician (*patrikios*) Niketas. A Paphlagonian eunuch, he was castrated by his parents, reared and educated, then sent to Constantinople at age seventeen.[50] The brother of Theophylaktos of Ohrid was probably castrated as a child by his family, following the pattern of the recently castrated child evoked in Theophylaktos's treatise.[51] The assumption of childhood castration is also supported less directly by stories such as that of a seven-year-old girl who was admitted into a monastery under the assumption that she was a eunuch,[52] and another involving a young eunuch monk, seen in chapter 2, who was assumed to be a prepubescent youth.[53] Aside from a few prominent examples of adult castration, the preponderance of the evidence points to the conclusion that most Byzantine eunuchs were castrated as children, usually through the crushing, surgical removal, or tying off of the testicles.

Modern medicine can offer interesting insights into the physiology of eunuchs. Studies of current populations indicate that ten percent of male children have undescended testicles at birth; in two percent of these cases the testicles have still not descended at puberty. The surgeons of the ancient world do not seem to have dealt with this particular problem as such. If the percentage of male children afflicted with this problem was as high in ancient times as today, this may account for some of the surgical efforts that physicians like Paul of Aegina label as "hernia surgery," as well as for sources that suggest that young male children suffering from painful "hernia" were sent to the castrator.[54] It may also account for decisions made by some parents regarding their children's careers. In the Byzantine period boys born with unformed or undescended testicles were judged to be specially favored by God who had relieved them of the burden of fighting sexual desires and marked them for the holy life. There is fairly clear evidence that adult men with undescended testicles were classified as eunuchs in the Late Antique world and as natural eunuchs, or *spadones,* in the Byzantine world.[55]

Individuals whose testicles have not descended properly produce greatly reduced amounts of testosterone and therefore may exhibit some of the physiological characteristics of eunuchism. These characteristics are rarely seen in modern society, in which testosterone therapy is used to treat individuals who suffer from failure of the androgens, or male sex hormones. Modern research into these hormones can give us an accurate idea of how they affect the male body. Prepubescent boys who suffer from lack of androgens cannot pass through puberty successfully without hormone replacement therapy. They will be small for their age, lack a beard, and retain an elevated voice. Since androgens affect nitrogen metabolism, these individuals will lack strength and muscular development and will lag behind in social and psychological maturation.[56]

Here, of course, the problem of evaluating cultural influences arises. Fat deposits in these individuals will follow a female rather than a male pattern, and the penis will remain small. The long bones of the body, especially those of the arms, legs, and hands, will continue to grow. The result is a very tall, slender individual with narrow shoulders and proportionally broad hips. The face will not mature into a "normal" strong-featured male face but rather will retain the delicate features of a boy, with a general broadening of the facial structure. This characteristic appearance may not appeal to members of societies whose taste is based on clearly defined male/female stereotypes. Nevertheless, it seems to have been accepted, even admired, in Byzantium.

Late Antique and Byzantine sources often mention the way eunuchs, while beautiful as boys, "fade" like roses at a relatively young age. Modern studies of testosterone indicate that loss of testosterone triggers the aging process, suggesting that eunuchs age prematurely, get wrinkled skin early, suffer from osteoporosis, and die young.

Perhaps most interesting (and most speculative) is evidence, based on preliminary studies of the brain, that suggests that at puberty the male brain and its thought processes are significantly reorganized. This may be triggered by the action of male hormones released at puberty. If this is the case, it suggests that it is possible that observers in the Late Antique world were correct when they said that eunuchs (and here we could only be referring to individuals castrated before puberty) had personalities and thought processes subtly different from those of testiculated men.[57]

As should be apparent by now, the public perception of eunuchs, both modern and classical, has some basis in medical fact or medical assumption. These medical facts indicate that the physical appearance of a eunuch, especially a eunuch castrated before puberty, was different from that of a normal man and that, in some cultures, this distinctive appearance was suggestive of the physical characteristics of women and boys.

While modern culture does not automatically connect personality with physical appearance, it is evident from the preceding discussion that this connection was made in the Byzantine mind. In that context, physiology, morality, and personal characteristics were inseparable from the physical changes brought about by castration. Thus the clear physical differences shown by most eunuchs allowed commentaries about them to spill over into personal invective with great ease. When our Byzantine authors aimed pejorative rhetoric at eunuchs, this rhetoric usually went beyond physical characteristics as we would define them and included behavioral traits, often ones which their culture associated with women.

This medieval rhetoric has conditioned modern attitudes about eunuchs. They are assumed to be soft and effeminate in appearance, two-faced, greedy, gluttonous, and homosexual. Note that among these attributes only those that deal with physical appearance can be directly attributed to the medical consequences of castration. These physical attributes would have been readily recognizable to most people of the Byzantine period. The rest of the assumed eunuch attributes have been developed out of a package of prevailing beliefs about eunuchs that had been present in the region for a long time and were well established by the Late Antique and Byzantine periods. While Byzantine critics may have thought of these attributes as inherent, what we see is that they actually were enshrined in a language of invective used rhetorically to assault the masculinity of men and denigrate women.[58]

Many eunuchs, and especially prepubertal castrates, were physically identifiable, especially as they aged. As a result, it was easy to classify them into a distinctive group, even though, as we have seen, they varied in the nature of their mutilation. Our sources refer to them as a "tribe" (φῦλον).[59] To be identified as a member of the "tribe of eunuchs" meant that certain assumptions were immediately made about the person in question.

It is important at this point to reiterate that the Byzantine world did not draw the same distinctions between physiological phenomena (as we use the phrase) and psychological or characterological ones. Thus what we have so far presented as a physiological ambiguity was, in that context, intimately connected with social, spiritual, and sexual ambiguity. This is inevitable given the contemporary assumption that an individual's external appearance was directly linked to their inherent internal traits. This complex form of ambiguity was potentially very powerful and was the source of both awe and suspicion. This helps explain how Byzantine writers could continue to stereotype eunuchs with pejorative language while also demonstrating respect for their unique capabilities. The power of their ambiguity is well illustrated by two examples.

One case comes from the Vita of St. John the Almsgiver. In this story, which has already been mentioned, a eunuch-monk was imprisoned and beaten for improperly consorting with a woman. Subsequently a dream revealed to St. John that the monk was a eunuch. Since the monk had not revealed that he was a eunuch, special "magical" intervention was needed to reveal this fact to the saint. The power of the eunuch's ambiguity is seen here in the fact that the situation produced one of the very few stories in which a saint is compelled to apologize. In this case the saint admits that he was wrong but does suggest that in the future the monk ought to be more open about his status, especially if he plans to travel with a young woman.[60] This story illustrates the power that can result from a eunuch's sexual ambiguity.

The potential of this physiological/characterological ambiguity is also illustrated in the example of the patriarch Methodios, who reveals himself to be a eunuch in order to counter a false charge of sexual assault.[61] It also appears in the many stories of women who pretended to be eunuchs in order to enjoy some of the freedom of choice reserved for men. In doing so, they capitalized on society's assumption that they were eunuchs rather than women when they took on roles attributed to either men or eunuchs.[62] The complex ambiguity associated with eunuchs thus allowed them to transcend conventional categories and normative codes for behavior.

The significance of such transcendent ambiguity is heightened when we realize that traditional Graeco-Roman society was most comfortable with order. It favored an ordering of the world that allowed individuals to be "read"; perhaps where one could assume from appearances what sort of individual one was dealing with and where he or she fit into the established social structure. While Byzantine society made a place for eunuchs and acknowledged that they were essential to society, contemporaries were not comfortable with eunuchs.

While the ambiguity associated with eunuchs, an extension of their physiological differences, left society uncomfortable with them and sustained the long-lived pejorative tropes around them, it also empowered them. It allowed them to act as liminal figures operating across boundaries in a society that believed in spiritual realms unattainable by ordinary men. Chapter 3 will take us from this discussion of physiology and assumed inherent traits to what the modern observer would characterize as the process of acculturation. We examine acquired characteristics that, at the time, were thought of as inherent, even though we perceive them as acculturated patterns of "appropriate" behavior.

CHAPTER 3

Gender Construction as Acculturation

As we have seen, both Late Antique and Byzantine cultures believed that castration caused basic changes in the physiology, psychology, and moral character of the eunuch. It was assumed that the adult eunuch's manner and personal affect were the result of the loss of his testicles and of some sort of "male force" within his body. Yet many elements in the eunuch's perceived or actual nature were elements that today's Western culture defines as traits produced by upbringing and training, that is, acculturation.

Even though eunuchs had achieved a higher degree of acceptance by the tenth century, their acculturation reflects an underlying discomfort. This discomfort was often expressed in the rhetoric of those who attacked eunuchs who were involved in political controversy or transgressed the gender role that society had assigned to them. The discomfort derived from the physiological ambiguity of eunuchs, which was "read" by contemporaries as a broader phenomenon than it appears to us. Biological and medical lore treated eunuchs as neither fully male nor fully female, and they lacked procreative powers, an important gender marker for whole men in this society. This lack limited eunuchs' ability to achieve power through family contacts and through their children, a traditional pattern in an aristocratic society. At the same time, in the Late Antique and Byzantine contexts, men who gave up their reproductive powers were thought to acquire expanded spiritual and intellectual powers as a kind of compensation. Consequently, eunuchs, and especially those castrated in childhood, were often thought to have access to realms outside mundane space and time. As we will see, they were sometimes depicted as able to penetrate heavenly realms and, less often, found to be in league with the Devil and his evil forces. In his ambiguity, the eunuch challenged the church's definition of humanity. This is especially true of those eunuchs who had themselves castrated for secular reasons or those men who tried to achieve holiness yet were unable to conquer their own sexuality and turned to castration as a solution.

The ambiguity associated with eunuchs also challenged the integrity of God's creation. Eunuchs were created as whole men yet were reconfigured into something quite different. For the Byzantine world, the fundamental dilemma posed by the ambiguity of eunuchs was this: were eunuchs a creation of God and a part of the natural world or were they a cultural artifact, created "against nature" and destined to live outside of God's plan for mankind? In the latter instance, perhaps they were not human at all. Yet how could this suggestion be reconciled with Biblical teachings which clearly acknowledged their humanity?

Despite such ambiguities and doubts, many eunuchs—and these are the ones that are most apparent in our sources—lived out their lives in powerful positions. They were acculturated (as we would see it) into a manner of self-presentation characteristic of the court eunuch. In the process, they developed traits that we see as acquired but that their contemporaries perceived as inherent. They could readily be identified by their physical appearance, their carriage, patterns of speech, ceremonial costumes, and occupations—occupations that only they were thought capable of performing. Yet they were neither menial servants nor authentic aristocratic nobles. They were something else—ideal agents and perfect servants, often for persons in high places.

Clearly, castration is the ultimate act of gender construction. Given the ambiguities and negative rhetoric attached to eunuchs, it is fascinating to observe that Byzantine society normalized the castration of children by their parents and the creation of these distinctive individuals. The Byzantine world did not normally practice castration as punishment or as a way of asserting authority over its enemies.[1] Nor did it alter men and boys physically so that they became sex objects—artificial women without women's liabilities. Instead, it shaped eunuchs into individuals conditioned to function as perfect servants while preserving the asexuality and spirituality of adolescent boys. With rigorous training these eunuchs, freed from the ties of family and sexual desire, could concentrate on performing perfect service.

As our earlier definition of the term eunuch implies, early Byzantine society tended to look at eunuchs as a homogeneous group whose members were united in their lack of viable sexual organs. Group metaphors about eunuchs are common in the sources. Eunuchs flock, hover, and swarm. They act together as groups, each group loyal to its particular household or to a single individual.[2] This group identity was sustained by the development of cultural traditions that assumed that all eunuchs shared a common personal affect, usually associated with the manifestation of feminine and other negative traits and with the occupation of social roles identified with eunuchs.[3]

For the modern student of gender, much of the personal affect of eunuchs that is reported in our sources was the result of cultural conditioning and not a consequence of the physiological changes brought about by castration. That is, eunuchs were consciously and subliminally molded to fit their assigned roles through *acculturation.* This term includes the more or less systematic rearing of eunuchs so that they end up acquiring personal traits and skills that are seen as their appropriate destiny. To the outside observer, the logic of the process has a circular quality: eunuchs have always done certain things, so therefore they should be trained to do those things, which in turn verifies that this is what eunuchs do. Alongside such purposeful acculturation is a more reflexive, almost subconscious form of acculturation. This involves unspoken assumptions, expectations, and reflexive admonitions that reinforce certain kinds of behavior as "appropriate" as the individual grows up. Speech patterns, body language, and personal demeanor are shaped in part through this kind of acculturation. Finally, adult eunuchs were self-conscious individuals capable of fashioning to some degree their own personae, deliberately minimizing or accentuating selected aspects of general stereotypes.

Our understanding of the acculturation that shaped eunuchs and placed them in their society is complicated by an additional issue. Most of the descriptions we have of the personal affect and self-presentation of Byzantine eunuchs come from hostile sources that recycle the rhetorical traditions of Late Antiquity. In the first part of this chapter I examine these traditions and present what little unbiased material we have regarding this topic. The second part of the chapter looks at the social roles occupied by eunuchs. Here we are on more solid ground, since even hostile commentators are usually accurate about the function and office of a eunuch. At this distance, and with our scattered sources, it is not always easy to document the interconnected processes of acculturation. As always, we must remember that the acculturation process is rendered even more complex by its interaction with assumptions about physiology, the changing nature of the gender construct itself, and changing attitudes toward eunuchs as part of the social order.

Perception, Formation, and Self-Presentation

Eunuchs were acculturated into forms of behavior and social roles that were considered appropriate to their gender construct. The assumption that behavior, demeanor, and even moral character are physiological matters is embedded in Theophylaktos of Ohrid's eleventh-century dialogue, *The Defense of Eunuchs.* Here Theophylaktos reviews the charges leveled against eunuchs by those who are openly hostile to them. After claiming that castration spoils a child's character because it produces moral weakness, Theophylaktos's hostile commentator proceeds to the familiar litany of the faults attributed to eunuchs.

Theophylaktos then provides a modern-sounding refutation of these charges. He suggests that there are many kinds of eunuchs and that their moral and personality traits are as variable as those of whole men. Each man, castrated or not, should be judged on his own merits. Speaking in the voice of the eunuch who states the case in favor of eunuchs, Theophylaktos says,

> If you suggest to me that those [the eunuchs] employed in the palace are the sum total of evil and especially, among these, the ones who are chosen to serve the empresses, I would not hesitate to show you also empresses who are most reverend, filled with the [Divine] word and guided by it, no less than the many of those entrusted with this task. For if they [the eunuchs] were to model themselves after their mistresses, they might draw themselves in the glory of the divine image and become a likeness of the Divine word and propriety, as of course I have heard of many such persons and am convinced of this [their character as described above].[4]

Theophylaktos is clearly trying to counter the assumption that castration, and especially prepubertal castration, changes both the body and soul of a eunuch, "spoiling" him as an individual. Yet Theophylaktos does not question the fact that eunuchs were systematically acculturated. Indeed, he assumes that they will be acculturated by their masters, whether for better or for worse.

We have few descriptions of the training and self-presentation of eunuchs. Therefore, when Theophylaktos's opponent of eunuchism talks about eunuchs who are raised by women and thus acquire the negative traits associated with women, it is difficult to tell how much of this is truth and how much is a recitation of traditional rhetoric. We are required to build our understanding of the gender construct of eunuchs from widely scattered sources.

Assuming that the personal affect presented by Byzantine eunuchs might have its roots in Late Antiquity, we can start with the physiognomic literature of that period. This consists of popular handbooks that offered instruction about the ways in which the external appearance and affect of an individual reflected his inner moral character. The purpose of these books was to answer such questions as, "Would you want to do business with this man?" This literature has been used extensively by Maud Gleason, who studies in detail the self-presentation of the second-century eunuch orator, Favorinus. Following Gleason's reasoning, we can assume that Late Antique society expected eunuchs to exhibit certain behavioral traits that the dominant culture identified as unmasculine and that at least one famous eunuch self-consciously developed a persona based on some of these traits.[5] Late Antiquity ascribed the following characteristics to eunuchs: a soft body lacking muscles; an effeminate voice; proficiency in the use of magic, poisons, and love charms;[6] eyebrows that arched above the eyes; a weak chin; a weepy shrill voice; the habit of holding the head tilted to one side; soft and unstable knees; fleshy hips; a fluid gait in which all of the body seemed in motion; a limp-wristed gesture with the hands upturned; a shifty gaze; and an interest in feminine grooming habits such as various sorts of hair removal.[7] Eunuchs were also thought to be eager to please others, a trait that was considered an unmasculine behavior in this society.[8]

Such a description must be seen in context. Gleason suggests that Late Antique society included an urban elite that was very genteel and affected customs of grooming, eating, and manners that others considered unmasculine. Thus this sort of self-presentation was common in the urbanized part of the eastern Mediterranean and not unique to eunuchs.[9]

Gleason concludes by indicating that some orators, and here she is specifically thinking of the eunuch Favorinus, "adopted characteristics of the 'other' and adopted mannerisms of self-presentation—languid gestures, a high-pitched voice, and a mincing walk." She suggests that orators did this because it was effective with an audience and that "in Favorinus' culture gender roles were constructed by the interplay of individual effort and social expectations."[10] In short she argues convincingly that in Late Antiquity at least some eunuchs carefully cultivated unmasculine behavior as a way of presenting themselves and that they did this because it was what society expected of them.

One aspect of acculturation involves origins and relationship to family. In Late Antiquity and early Byzantium, almost all eunuchs came from servile backgrounds and were foreign born. This remained an assumed part of their gender construct even after the realities of origin changed, and it contributes to their "otherness." Tradition held that they were either prisoners or slaves castrated outside the boundaries of the Roman Empire and brought in subsequently. This idea was reinforced by referencing long-standing, though rarely enforced, legislation that forbade the making of eunuchs within the boundaries of the empire.[11] Even here we can see an easing of the prescriptive penalties thought appropriate for those who broke the laws against castration.[12] As we will see, this and other evidence makes it clear that by the tenth century castrations were taking place within the empire and that many eunuchs were born in the Byzantine empire, not foreigners. Old legislation thus stayed on the books in modified form but was not enforced.

Eunuchs entering the court or aristocratic households conventionally identified themselves with their master's *oikos.* These eunuchs had given up reproduction, family, and extended familial ties in order to become perfect servants. They were trained and shaped by their master to suit his needs. Such gender markers identified eunuchs in the Late Antique and early Byzantine periods, but as we move into the ninth and tenth centuries, we find that there are other characteristics that also define the gender category "eunuch." Moreover, these changes point to divisions within the category itself, illustrating how a socially constructed category might change and develop over time.

Historical texts seldom refer to the "acculturation" process among the palace eunuchs, but Michael Psellos, a courtier writing in the middle of the eleventh century, provides a rare exception as he talks about the rearing of the eunuchs of Constantine VIII (r. 1025–1028).

> They were his friends most of all whom in their infancy he had castrated and whom afterwards he used as chamberlains and private servants. These men were not of noble birth nor freeborn. Actually, they were barbarians and heathens, but they owed their education to the emperor, and because they modeled their own conduct on him, they were accounted worthy of greater respect and honor than others. Their physical degradation was obscured by an adroit and liberal distribution of largess, by their eagerness to confer benefits, and by their display of other gentlemanly qualities.[13]

Psellos's words are as interesting for what they do not say as for what they do say. Notice that he specifically points out that Constantine VIII selected "barbarians" and "heathens" for his personal servants, not nobles or freeborn men. The specificity of this observation allows the inference that by Psellos's day barbarians and foreigners were no longer the rule among eunuch servants in the palace. Constantine VIII selected his eunuchs personally, and they were educated by the emperor and "modeled their own conduct on him." Although castrated and suffering from "physical degradation," Constantine VIII's eunuchs reportedly learned to speak and act like gentlemen and were lavish in their philanthropy. The account suggests that within certain parameters the gender structure of the eunuch was flexible and that court eunuchs and those who served in noble households were molded to suit their masters' desires.

Psellos was aware of the kind of physiognomic traditions discussed by Gleason. Furthermore, he was an orator and very much a public person. He understood the importance of self-presentation and describes various individuals in terms derived from physiognomic traditions. In his description of the emperor Basil II, taken from an earlier author and elaborated, Psellos tells us that Basil had arched eyebrows, a reflection of his pride. They were not overhanging or growing in a straight line as suited a woman. In a later passage that was clearly intended to be a flattering description of Constantine, the infant son of Michael VII, Psellos notes that the child's eyebrows made a perfectly straight line across his face and that this was a mark of beauty.[14]

Successful acculturation required that eunuchs be trained from a young age. A number of our texts indicate that eunuchs were brought to the palace as children or young adults. There they were acculturated into specific roles within the imperial household, both as eunuchs and as trusted servants. It appears that aristocratic households followed this pattern, if on a smaller scale.[15] The gender construct that society had developed for eunuchs required that they be separated from their homes and families of origin.

Although the childhood of eunuchs was rarely discussed, a few glimpses are available. We know some details of the childhood of Constantine, a powerful eunuch of the late ninth and early tenth centuries who appears elsewhere in this book. Constantine came from a community in Paphlagonia that regularly castrated children and then sent them off to Constantinople to make their fortunes. Constantine himself was castrated, named, weaned, and then taught "the holy word" before being sent to serve the empress Zoe Karbonopsina, the fourth wife of Leo VI ("the Wise"; 886–912). This, at least, is what Constantine wanted posterity to believe when he rewrote his past after he became wealthy and powerful. We know, in fact, from other sources that Constantine started his career at the palace as a young eunuch serving under the powerful eunuch *praepositus sacri cubiculi,* Samonas. Samonas then passed him on to the emperor's son, Constantine VII, as a gift.[16]

The author of the vita of the eunuch St. Niketas Patrikios (d. 836) outlines a career path for his hero that is superficially similar to that of Constantine.[17] Niketas is depicted as having been born in Paphlagonia late in the eighth century. His parents claimed to be distant relations of the empress Theodora, wife of the emperor Theophilus (r. 829–842) and regent for Michael III (r. 842–867). Niketas was castrated by his parents, educated, and at age seventeen, was sent to the capital where the empress Irene took him into her household.

One of the most coherent discussions of the acculturation of eunuchs is found in the vita of the eunuch Nikephoros, bishop of Miletos.[18] The vita describes the parents of Nikephoros as being of independent means, "neither overly wealthy and arrogant because of their surfeit, nor, wanting of necessary things, constrained through want, suffering in their life choices."[19] As a child Nikephoros proved to have a talent for mathematics. For this reason, when he was eight years old, he was sent to Constantinople.

> No childish things kept him from achieving greater maturity and growth. For it [i.e., such] is characteristic when a youth is separated from natural affection. But when a youth chances upon no lesser care he is more carefully modeled in the direction of good conduct. He is not hindered by tender love from training his natural will, or by the tendency of the parents to push him toward the greatest of deeds, while the child is greatly vexed. For fear resulting from torment encourages laziness and disdainfulness. This is why the saying rightly says, "the blow is greater and more painful when it is not fitting."
>
> So, after he was castrated by his parents, he was sent to the imperial city during the time when Romanos [Romanos I, 920–944] held the scepter because of the weakness and youth of the heirs of the throne. He [Nikephoros] was received providently and kindly by the *magistros* Mosele and was trained in the Holy Scriptures alone, since his protectors did not dare to disgrace the genuine and fertile nature of the child's soul with unsound teachings.[20]

This vita clearly suggests the importance of formal training and acculturation in the preparation of a eunuch for his proper role. In this case, of course, acculturation is focused on service and on rejection of the family, sexuality, and related earthly ties. Nikephoros was castrated by his parents, removed from their care, and turned over to the *magistros* Mosele in Constantinople for training.

There is also evidence describing the formal training of eunuchs as singers for Hagia Sophia and other churches. Leo VI founded the monastery of St. Lazaros for eunuch-monks some time after his accession in 886. It was located near Hagia Sophia and other important churches, and it is reasonable to assume that the monastery was involved in the training of young castrati singers for one or more of those churches.[21]

From a number of different sources, we can piece together several details about the upbringing of one of the best-known eunuchs in Byzantine history, John the Orphanotrophos.[22] Skylitzes tells us that John, like Constantine the son of St. Metrios and Niketas Patrikios, was born in Paphlagonia. John was castrated and reared to be a eunuch either at court or in a noble household. His parents were certainly not noble—it has been suggested that they were moneychangers, since Skylitzes[23] tells us that John's brothers Michael and Niketas were trained as moneychangers and understood the adulteration of money. John began his career as a eunuch in the household of the emperor Basil II (r. 976–1025), and was greatly favored by that emperor. He continued at court through the reign of Constantine VIII (r, 1025–1028) and then served under Romanos III (r. 1028–1034). He was responsible for the introduction of his brother, Michael, into the palace and for the later elevation of both his brother, as Michael IV (r. 1034–1041), and his nephew, Michael V (r. 1041–1042), to the imperial throne. John was subsequently exiled by an ungrateful Michael V.

Michael Psellos admired John the Orphanotrophos and had served with him at court. He indicates that John's nature was changeable (ποικίλος ἦν τὴν ψυχὴν), a characteristic assumption about eunuchs that we have already seen in chapter 2. Psellos notes that John's facial expression rarely changed and that when he looked at you, he raised his eyebrows high on his forehead. While we would regard such an expression as quizzical, in Byzantine culture, as in Late Antiquity, it was read as a sign of pride, haughtiness, superciliousness, and effeminacy.[24]

The final goal of this process of selection and acculturation of young eunuchs was to produce perfect servants, a goal hinted at in another source. Theodore the Protospatharios (first sword-bearer, d. 845) was one of the forty-two martyrs captured at Amorion in 838 and later martyred. He is generally regarded to have been a eunuch, and this is the way he is usually depicted in art. According to his ninth-century vita, he was offered clemency by the leader of the Arabs: "You are wellborn and have been honored by your emperor with the most exceptional signs of office." This sentence implies that Theodore was selected by the emperor and served him in an important administrative capacity.[25]

The fact that this acculturation process resulted in a distinctive personal affect is suggested by a certain amount of evidence that eunuchs reared at court or in large aristocratic homes acquired distinctive mannerisms, speech patterns, body language and gait, and facial expressions that were considered appropriate to their gender. The sources regularly make reference to the "chattering" of women and eunuchs, which is characterized by both the pitch of their voices and their patterns of vocalization. We have hints that the speech pattern of eunuchs may have been more rapid than the speech of people gendered as normal males and that it had a deliberately different rhythmic quality. Like women, eunuchs were assumed to be unable to control their emotions, which resulted in their voices being "weepy."

The gait of eunuchs was criticized as similar to that of women. Compared with the controlled stiffness of a proper adult male, a eunuch's walk was considered to be rather slack and loose-limbed. Eunuchs are described (or accused) of holding their hands away from the body with palms lifted, in an "unmasculine" manner.

There was also much to criticize in the facial expressions of eunuchs. They never looked one in the eye. As they carried out their business, they looked down their noses with eyebrows lifted, betraying both arrogance and an effeminate countenance. In their general mannerisms, both eunuchs and women were assumed to be incapable of physical, psychological or emotional self-control.[26] Both eunuchs and women were assumed to abuse food and drink, with the result that eunuchs were often accused of being fat and drunk.[27] Both were believed to talk too much, and eunuchs were accused of speaking out or laughing inappropriately (see the example of the court eunuch John Angourios, below). Both eunuchs and women were thought to be acquisitive rather than generous, to cry easily, and to let their emotions get the better of them.[28] These traits carried negative overtones because they were associated with women and represented the antithesis of the personal bodily control and self-presentation important to the dominant male gender construct.

One example of this common acculturation and distinctive personal affect among eunuchs is seen in the account of a eunuch discussed in chapter 2 in the Vita of St. Andrew the Fool. Recall that the saint's companion, Epiphanios, was a childhood friend of

> a young eunuch who was the chamberlain of one of the nobles. His face was like a rose, the skin of his body white as snow, he was well shaped, fair-haired, possessing an unusual softness, and smelling of musk from afar.[29]

This passage is one of our better descriptions of the worldly eunuch since it conveys in a few words the physical appearance, softness, good grooming, elegance, and careful training of the eunuch servant of a wealthy man.

As the preceding passage suggests, many of the traits exhibited by these eunuchs could easily be presented in a pejorative light. This is a recurring theme in our sources and reflects both the centuries-long accumulation of negative tropes as well as the underlying ambiguity of their gender construct. Thus it was easy to label the actions of eunuchs as examples of inappropriate affect and unsuitable behavior.

Throughout the Byzantine period eunuchs were accused of being morally weak and liable to corruption. In the ninth century the great patriarch Photios wrote a letter to a court eunuch, John Angourios, the *sakellarios* (head of the imperial department of finances) who, Photios believed had fallen prey to the exploitation of the Devil. In this letter Photios accuses John of laughing aloud during a church service and of allowing his voice to become the tool of the Devil:

> To John the patrician descended from the Angourioi. Those who are wise among the Greeks liken you to Attis, calling you one of the *galli.*[30] Our wise men confine you in the women's quarters and consider and call you androgynous. Whence

> [from the women's quarters] you have overstepped the rules on either side and intruded yourself upon the mysteries of God's church, turning everything upside down and through your corrupt nature, making the most fertile and prolific church of Christ fruitless and useless.

Clearly even a small case of inappropriate behavior allowed a critic of eunuchs to call into rhetorical play the whole range of anti-eunuch invective. John is compared with Attis, the self-castrated god, and with the *galli,* the castrated priests of the cult of Attis. His sterility destroys the fruitfulness of the church, rendering it barren and useless. He is accused of being effeminate because he was raised by women and therefore shares their nature.

> But know well [that] you have inscribed your deeds upon Hades and its gates in a more shameless manner by what you are doing. Even if you are weaker [than we are], we, and with us the populous and holy choir of Christ, will cross-examine you, even if we distress you. Whether [or "In spite of"] that architect of the worst evils [the Devil] with his gateways, one of which you happen to have since you have given [them] up to him in their entirety—your mouth and tongue and voice . . . but his entire battle array, through truth, has been shown ineffective and powerless against the church of Christ.[31] How long will you ceaselessly and in a shameful manner release the arrows of madness toward the heavens without thinking? Through these actions you move your companion demons to laughter, and cause distress regarding your loss [of your soul] to the saints, and you show your kind to be even more hated than before and famous throughout for evil.[32]

Because of his physical and moral weakness, this eunuch, through his inappropriate behavior, has fallen prey to the Devil and has become his gateway.

Certainly the opportunity for the acculturation of eunuchs existed at court. Young castrated servants were traditionally raised in the women's quarters under the supervision of older eunuchs. By the tenth century we have significant evidence that free young men were inducted into a system of education and acculturation designed to produce court servants, a system supervised by established eunuchs. These young eunuchs were educated either at court or in special schools designed to prepare them for career paths open only to eunuchs.

Yet another indication that young eunuchs were trained together in a segregated context is embedded in the common derogatory phrase that says that eunuchs were "reared in the shade."[33] In other words, they were nourished, like women, within the confines of the palace or aristocratic residences. We will see later on that this was not always the case, but the imagery remains a central part of the cluster of traits assigned to eunuchs by this culture.

We also find assumed traits and appearances that were more positive. Within the canons of the age, eunuchs were considered beautiful. Our sources regularly indicate that young eunuchs were valued for their beauty and grace. Their physical appearance contributed to the texture of a courtly setting.[34] Eunuchs played a prominent role in court ceremonial, standing like beautiful angels around the imperial throne, an image that is, perhaps, echoed in traditions in Byzantine painting. Young eunuchs, beautifully dressed and coifed, with good bearing and impeccable manners, were an asset to the court. The wealthy aristocratic woman Danelis was obviously aware of this when she made a gift of one hundred eunuchs to the court (see fig. 1). "For the wealthy old woman knew, as it seems, that there always was space in the palace for these eunuchs, for they descended upon the imperial palace in greater numbers than flies upon a sheepfold at springtime."[35]

Exactly what eunuchs represented as objects of aesthetic display is difficult to grasp from this cultural distance. Byzantine society clearly admired prepubescent boys for their asexuality, ethereal beauty, and innocence. Youths castrated before puberty retained many of the outward signs of youthful beauty and purity.[36] As indicated above, the physiological consequences of childhood castration meant that their bodily appearance and carriage was notably distinct from that of whole men.

The Late Antique and Byzantine world regularly debated whether eunuchs could participate in sexual activities and experience love. We find hints about this, as well as about cultural assumptions contrasting the sexuality of women and eunuchs, in the ninth-century Vita of St. Anna the Younger, a woman depicted as living in a monastery and pretending to be a eunuch.

> A particular trial befell the saint caused by a certain man who had the appearance of a monk but [who] in deeds and conduct was more like those who are attached to the evil-loving demon. His deed was no other than to pour out harsh and shameful verbal assaults against the saint, like those spoken against a eunuch, and openly to accuse her. She [the saint] took no account of these but, rather, considered the things said against her [to be] benefits. [Mean]while a certain God-loving woman maintained strongly, after having heard the shameful and reprehensible words of the one who was blasphemous and shortly thereafter to be a murderer, said: "Take care brother, in the event [s]he [the saint] is not a eunuch as you suspect, nor filled with passions, but a woman and without passions, and you have as your reward the fiery Gehenna for having been disparaging toward the passionless one, and for having polluted those who have listened to you. For, some years ago, a certain woman, after distributing all her belongings, disappeared. In the event that she may be the one you call eunuch, you lead your soul

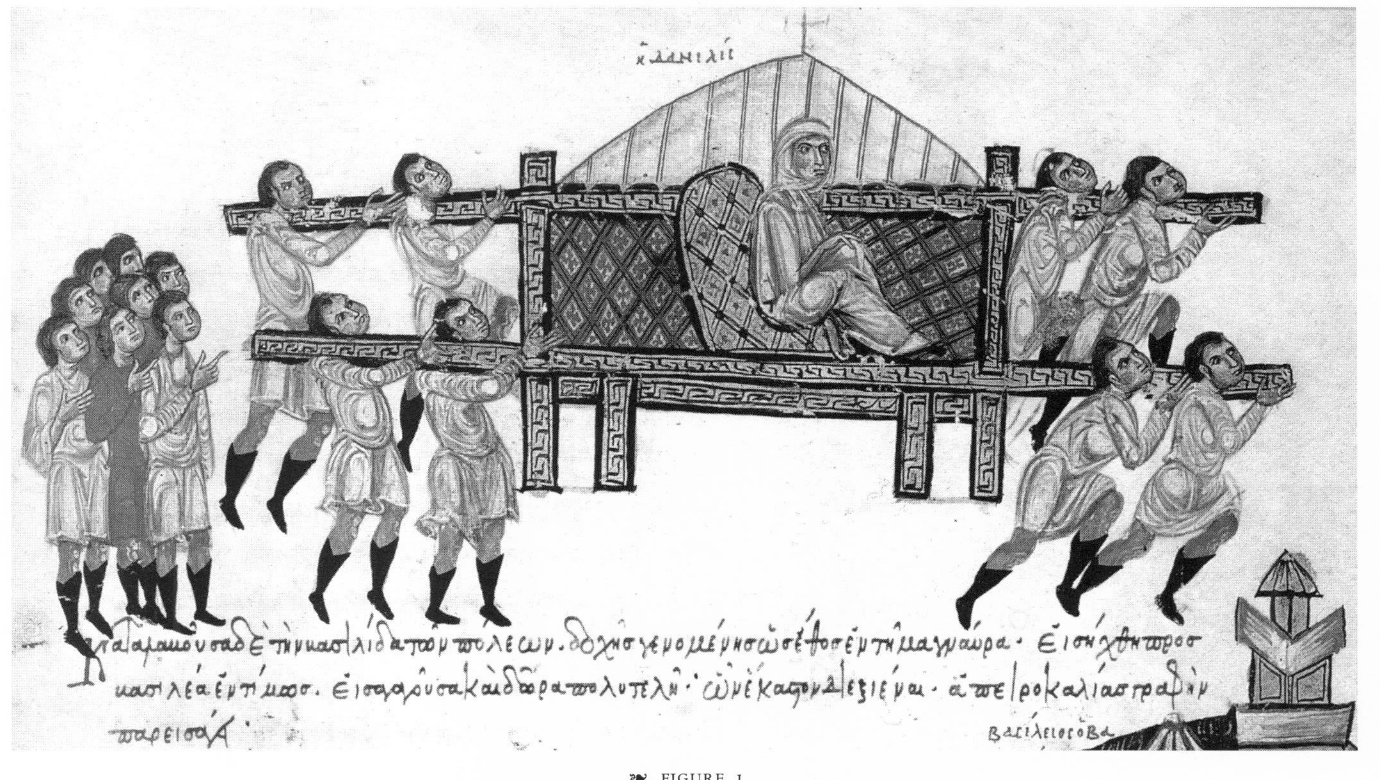

❧ FIGURE 1

The widow Danelis, her litter carried by eunuchs, brings gifts of eunuchs to the Byzantine court. Miniature on parchment, Madrid, BN, Skylitzes Chronicle, Ms vitr. 26-2, fol. 102 r., detail. In Anthony Cutler and Jean-Michel Spieser, *Byzance médiéval, 700–1204* (Paris: Gallimard, 1991), p. 81, fig. 53.

> down to destruction." That loathsome and treacherous one [attacking the saint] added this to his own evil, and spoke out these words to many, disseminating abuse. He quickly sought a way to push the holy woman down a precipitous place so that if her clothing was thrown up about her he would see her bared and would know with confidence [whether she was a eunuch]. Not long afterwards he did this but saw nothing, for he became paralyzed by divine force. And getting up from there he went to his own residence.[37]

While the passage is about the saint, what is interesting here is the use of hostile stereotypes against an assumed eunuch and the assumption that a eunuch could be expected to experience sexual desire, while a woman would not. One should not assume from this that eunuchs necessarily desired men. In fact, our sources rarely specify sexual object choice as an element in the gender construction of eunuchs. This does not, however, mean that eunuchs always escaped sexual predators, and the passage suggests that whole men sometimes expected eunuchs to be sexually licentious.

In addition to the physiological characteristics that made prepubertal castrates identifiable and the self-presentation that characterized some eunuchs, it appears that at least in some settings eunuchs routinely wore distinctive clothing that distinguished them as eunuchs. It is easiest to document this within a courtly setting. There, eunuchs often wore special costumes and were honored with the privilege of wearing distinctive jewelry that was denied to whole men outside the imperial family.[38] Tradition and legend tell us that eunuchs often wore white robes. Between the imagined parallels of divine and imperial courts and the use of white robes, it is not hard to see why eunuchs were regularly mistaken for angels. In the Vita of St. Symeon the Stylite the Younger, for example, Symeon has a vision that includes "a corps of angel-like men who were eunuchs, whose clothing was white as snow."[39]

Whether eunuchs always wore white robes or not, they seem to have worn distinctive clothing on many occasions. A miracle in the Vita of St. Tarasios, patriarch of Constantinople, tells us of a group of women with an uncontrollable issue of blood who came to the saint's tomb hoping for a cure. Since they were women, they were not allowed to enter the tomb area. They then disguised themselves as eunuchs, making it possible for them to enter and be healed.[40] In the Vita of St. Matrona, which features a woman who transforms herself by disguising herself as a monk and her subsequent ascent up the spiritual ladder, we find a woman who can accomplish her goals by presenting herself as a eunuch. Thus, when St. Matrona wishes to escape her abusive husband and enter a monastery, she cuts her hair and disguises herself as a eunuch. At one point the text says specifically that she put on the garments of a eunuch, although it never tells us just what made these garments distinctive.[41] The confusion that arose because of the characteristic garments worn by eunuchs is illustrated in one of the foundation legends associated with Hagia Sophia. In the course of this legend, St. Michael the archangel appears at the building site. Because he appears to be a eunuch, has a beautiful face, and is wearing a dazzling garment, a young boy at the building site assumes that he is a eunuch from the royal palace.[42]

The most detailed descriptions of the costumes worn by court eunuchs appear in the *De ceremoniis* of Constantine Porphyrogennetos and in the *Kletorologion* of Philotheos. These texts make it quite clear that the eunuchs at court wore special attire that whole men were not permitted to use. This attire set them apart as a distinctive and honored group. The gold *paragaudium* (or outer robe) worn by the eunuch-*koubikoularios* is an example discussed at length in the *De ceremoniis.*[43] Aside from the custom of wearing robes with specific decorations in courtly ceremonial settings, it is clear that eunuchs wore some sort of distinctive attire outside of the palace, but it is not clear what made that clothing characteristic of eunuchs.

Thus dress, mannerisms, speech, body language, and sexual status were linked in a way that identified eunuchs as a separate gender. Society had well-defined expectations about eunuchs and had institutionalized the process of selection and acculturation that fulfilled these expectations.

Socially Assigned Gender-Specific Roles

Gender and acculturation also involves the assignment of specific and often exclusive roles in society. Although Western society tends to establish gender categories based on choice of sexual object, many other societies, including that of Byzantium, emphasize occupation and appearance in the construction of gender status while rarely mentioning sexual object choice.[44] Eunuchs were assumed to be the normal or even exclusive practitioners of several roles and functions assigned to them in Byzantine society. Many of these roles were perceived as unmasculine or else involved tasks that were traditionally performed by women. Many of these roles involved mediational activities. Both at court and in the church, eunuchs were acculturated to become perfect servants. These are topics explored in the conclusion. As chapter 8 shows, their roles at court were very specifically gendered; many important court offices could only be held by eunuchs and reflected traditions dating from at least the third century.

Since the bulk of our information about the roles assigned to eunuchs comes from texts that describe court ceremonial, it is difficult to create a coherent picture of the roles assigned to eunuchs within the church or the lay community. At court, eunuchs acted as personal servants to the emperor and empress. In the palace context, eunuchs are mentioned briefly in several specific roles, and they controlled access to sacred space within the palace. They tended to be managers and supervisors engaged in tasks that would probably have been the province of wellborn women in a large noble household. These include such tasks as supervision of the cooking, serving meals, care of the wardrobe, management of the bedchamber, and preparation of the dead for burial. Beneath these eunuch–palace managers there probably were lesser eunuchs who served them, but they rarely rise to view in our sources. Other eunuchs filled positions that would traditionally be filled by the major-domo in a large noble household.[45] They regulated the access to the palace itself, controlled the palace doors, protected private portions of the palace, and supervised ceremonies. The chief eunuch of the palace often acted as an intermediary between the emperor and his staff of attendant nobles, even speaking on his behalf on ceremonial occasions.

Court eunuchs were also responsible for several other tasks that aristocratic males traditionally avoided. These included bookkeeping, managing money, and management or speculation in real estate. Other court eunuchs were assigned to serve as go-betweens in transactions involving women and children or individuals outside of the court, activities inappropriate for a proper male. They also served as tutors and their responsibilities for education royal children apparently strengthened their ties with imperial women at court.[46] Eunuchs played a key role in the orientation of empresses from outside court circles to court life and ceremonial.[47]

There are numerous specific examples of eunuchs carrying out tasks appropriate only to them. From the time of the persecutions of Late Antiquity we find Protas and Hyacinthus, eunuch servants of St. Eugenia,[48] a noble woman, and Inda, the companion of the lady Domna.[49] Both Origen (d. 254) and Leontios, bishop of Antioch, had themselves castrated so that they could live with or work with women. Pulcheria (ca. 400) put anonymous court eunuchs in charge of Athenais/Eudokia,[50] and the eunuch Mardonios was *paedagogos* to the emperor Julian.[51] The infamous fourth-century eunuch, Eutropios, arranged marriages,[52] and Lausos welcomed Melania the Younger (d. 439) to court at Constantinople.[53] Honoria's faithful servant, Hyacinthus, sought Attila's assistance on her behalf.[54] The eunuch Arsacius escorted Honorius's wife to her mother,[55] while John acted as godfather to Peter the Iberian,[56] and Stephen tutored Maurice's sons.[57] It was an anonymous court eunuch who took Constantina and her daughters to sanctuary,[58] and the eunuch Theophylaktos (latest date 705) was sent to fetch Justinian II's wife and child when he was restored to power.[59] Elissaios the scribe (latest date 844) was left in France to teach Rotrude, the daughter of Charlemagne,[60] and Theoktistos served as the tutor of Michael III.[61] It was an anonymous eunuch[62] who was sent to fetch the emperor's mother,[63] the eunuch Baanes carried Basil I's child to his baptism,[64] and Nicholas, the eunuch servant of St. Euphrosyna the Younger, arranged for her lodgings, away from visitors and noise.[65] The eunuch Samonas (latest date 908) sponsored Constantine Porphyrogennetos at his baptism,[66] and the eunuch Theodore was his tutor,[67] while Theophanes escorted Maria, the granddaughter of Niketas Magistros, to her marriage to Tsar Peter of Bulgaria.[68] We hear of Leontakis the Paedagogos[69] and of the eunuch servants and tutors of Anna Komnene.[70] Eunuchs are identified as barbers, bloodletters, and physicians, all activities that involve intimate personal service. Eunuch singers were found both in the court and in cathedral churches, a tradition that is almost certainly the ancestor of the castrato tradition in the West.[71] Finally, both eunuch-priests and eunuch-doctors were preferred by the regulations governing monasteries for women.[72]

As suggested earlier, most of the eunuchs who appear in our sources were connected with the world of the court, but this reflects the unevenness of our sources. We also have references to a number of eunuchs in the ecclesiastical world. Their acculturation may have been somewhat different, but the sources allow only tentative inferences on this point. By the ninth century, however, we find ecclesiastical eunuchs as property managers, priests, deacons, bishops, and in several cases, as patriarchs.[73]

Conclusion

Byzantine culture and society constructed a collective identity for its eunuchs. The result was something that modern gender analysis recognizes as perhaps the ultimate case of socially constructed gender. This is particularly the case if we accept that in the Byzantine context the primary indicators of gender were not sexual object choice but rather physical appearance, societal function, relationship to reproduction, and capacity for relating to what we would consider the spiritual world. Eunuchs represented a very special "other." They exhibited traits of both men and women. They were "unnatural" (in the sense that they were artificially, culturally created); they existed outside of what was perceived to be the natural order of the biological world. As we will see in the following chapters, eunuchs, because of their special gender status, were associated with preternatural realms. This made them fascinating, dangerous, and desirable in ways that are hard for the modern reader to grasp.

This chapter has shown aspects of the acculturation process that defined these people both in their own eyes and in the eyes of the society around them. The process involved many things familiar to modern gender awareness: systematic preparation and education based on implicit assumptions; the appropriateness of specific forms of dress; and inculcation of distinctive speech patterns, facial expressions, and body language. The process normalized eunuchs as the appropriate agents for carrying out a variety of roles in society, particularly mediating between distinctive groups, defining the sacred space around the emperor, and connecting that space to the regular world. The roles of eunuchs also tended to include supervision, management, and protection of imperial and household finances and domestic affairs and guardianship and care-giving functions. All of these roles were centered on personal service. Finally, the ambiguity of eunuchs, in a profoundly religious society, resulted in their being credited with preternatural powers not available to ordinary males or females, powers that associated eunuchs with both demonic forces and with holy men, saints, and angels.

It is tempting to ask how this came about, but that implies a fruitless search for first causes. Perhaps it is more constructive to inquire as to what made this multigendered society work in such a way that eunuchs persisted as a distinct group for a thousand years in this context. One possible answer is found in the work of the late Byzantine historian, Alexander Kazhdan. Kazhdan has characterized Byzantine society as both politically centralized and marked by rigid separation between men and women in terms of location, activities, and living space. He also has pointed out that "there was no stable layer between the bureaucratic elite of the capital and the working population."[74] As we have seen, many of the roles assigned to eunuchs developed out of household and domestic tasks and obligations that in many cultures, and in the lower reaches of Byzantine society, fell within the gender construction of women. But in an elite society in which women were severely segregated, women were unavailable to supervise or carry out many of these tasks. Such tasks still had to be performed, however, either by males whose gender construct would have required revision or by some other class of people. It should not surprise us, therefore, that the range of activities defined as normal for eunuchs overlapped considerably with areas otherwise allotted to the domain of women. This inevitably brought with it the insertion of elements of what our culture would call effeminacy into the gender construct of eunuchs. At the same time, however, their liminal, mediational, and administrative functions at court and in large households carried a growing element of power and prestige.[75] In an important way, eunuchs were "necessary" as go-betweens in a society where elite men and women were separated from each other and the elite as a whole was rigidly separated from the rest of society.

Thus, for all of the ambiguity and negative rhetoric associated with them, eunuchs constituted a permanent third gender in the Byzantine world. This produced the contradiction that Byzantium officially and legally abhorred the practice of castration even as eunuchs perennially occupied important societal niches. By their existence they both made possible the rigid social structures around them, while at the same time solving problems inherent in such a society. The consequence was a fascinating tolerance for alternative gender categories, a tolerance that grew from Late Antiquity until the middle of the twelfth century.

We have seen how the configuration of the eunuch gender had changed by the tenth century, and this change is further demonstrated in subsequent chapters. This normalization of eunuchs within the mental universe of tenth-century Byzantium is also seen in the changing content of acculturation. By the tenth century many Byzantine eunuchs came from the educated, propertied, freeborn classes within the empire and had been castrated within its boundaries. Unlike their predecessors, these later eunuchs often retained ties to their families and used their positions at court or in the church to promote the status of their relatives. Eunuchs had for centuries been assigned social roles as teachers, doctors, guardians of women and children, personal servants, entertainers, and singers. Now we find that these roles have been expanded. By the 900s several important court offices were reserved for eunuchs,[76] and an important part of their gender construct was centered on their perceived loyalty, trustworthiness, intellectual abilities, unique spiritual capacities, and their ability to transcend social and spiritual boundaries.

Judith Herrin suggests that eunuchs were central to the maintenance of the symbolic tradition of imperial power. They oversaw court dress and ritual. Much of the lore about imperial ritual was not systematically recorded but was instead transmitted as oral tradition reserved to court eunuchs. Consequently the imperial corps of eunuchs was crucial to the perpetuation of the ceremonial that helped stage imperial authority.[77]

It is possible to see a difference in the constructs assigned to court eunuchs and the eunuchs who served in church offices, differences that might support two distinct gender categories for these two groups. The gender construct for earlier court eunuchs carried with it a number of negative attributes, many of them part of a long tradition. Castrated servants were often assumed to achieve status as passive partners in sexual relationships with powerful men, and many commentators considered this part of their gender construct. Some court eunuchs were accused of accumulating fortunes at the expense of other individuals who sought influence at court. This left them open to charges of greed and worldliness while simultaneously their distinctive dress and manner contributed to the sense that they were a cultural "other."

By the tenth century eunuchs were acquiring a more positive image, partly associated with supposed spiritual powers and new ways of achieving sanctity. We can begin to document their role as guardians of sacred spaces, and as chapter 5 shows, eunuchs associated with the church were being assigned a gender construct that was more positive than that of the court eunuch. Honored for their celibacy and asceticism, eunuchs assigned to this gender construct exhibited the antithesis of the negative attributes traditionally assigned to court eunuchs. This aspect of their gender category is evident in Theophylaktos's essay when he says that, despite negative opinion about "eunuchism" (a direct translation of his term), it is a valued and holy condition.[78] In this context, castration was an asset because it helped eunuchs in the church to remain celibate. Thus chroniclers and hagiographers celebrated high churchmen who had been eunuchs, including the eighth-century patriarch Germanos,[79] the ninth-century patriarch Ignatios[80] and possibly the patriarch Methodios. The following century saw such prominent eunuchs as the patriarchs Stephen II[81] and Polyeuktos.[82] Hostile commentators, however, reminded people that the infamous iconoclastic patriarch Niketas of the eighth century was also a eunuch and one open to much hostile rhetoric.[83] The hagiographers also celebrated lesser eunuchs in the church and at court. St. Nikephoros and St. Niketas Patrikios are of interest here because they signify the normalization of eunuchs in tenth-century society. St. Nikephoros, bishop of Miletos, exemplifies the normality of castration, since he was castrated by his parents and brought to Constantinople to become a courtier. He later left the court to enter the church.[84] Niketas was also castrated by his parents, was trained, and then entered the household of the empress Irene. Only after a career as a civil servant and military commander did he become a monk and specialize in healing men tormented by sexual desires.[85] Scholars have suggested that Symeon the New Theologian might have been a eunuch,[86] and we have the early twelfth century Symeon the Sanctified, an important eunuch at court, who left the palace to become a monk.[87]

Clearly at least some court eunuchs were engaging in activities that conveyed an aura of sanctity. Powerful court eunuchs founded monasteries and sponsored hagiographical writings that celebrated their faith and worthy deeds. Thus the court eunuch Constantine probably sponsored the writing of the *narratio* of his father, St. Metrios. This text celebrates Metrios's faith and honorable behavior, for which he was rewarded by God with a son and given divine permission to castrate him and send him to serve at court.[88]

In general, by the tenth century the gendered status of eunuchs had improved and been normalized in society. The image of the court eunuch as what we would call a gendered construct had not only become more positive but had come to overlap partially with the distinct image of the virtuous ecclesiastical eunuch.

What is intriguing here are the ways in which the elaboration of the eunuchate and the increasing status of eunuchs in middle-period Byzantium were reflected in how authors invented or reinvented important historical and pseudohistorical eunuchs as important figures of Byzantine culture and history.

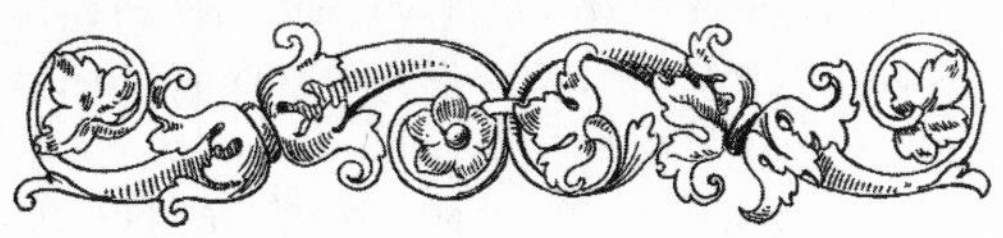

CHAPTER 4

Making Sense of Tradition: Regendering Legendary Narratives

In the late eleventh century, Theophylaktos of Ohrid, in compiling a list of famous eunuchs, posed the question, "What is Daniel to you?"[1] In so doing he asserted that one of Byzantium's biblical heroes was a eunuch. This is striking confirmation that the eunuch, as a distinctively gendered individual, had become a normal part of Byzantine society.

This chapter shows how deeply this assumption was established by illustrating how Byzantine culture rewrote the legends and stories about some of its most important figures—the prophet Daniel and the emperors Justinian and Constantine. Daniel was regarded as one of the precursors of Christ himself and was one of the most important figures in Greek Orthodoxy. Constantine and Justinian were the great leaders who founded, organized, and sustained the Byzantine empire and whose achievements were legendary.

Well, what *about* the prophet Daniel? As we shall see, as early as the tenth century the Byzantines assumed that Daniel was a court eunuch, and this was clearly Theophylaktos's assumption. In countless subtle ways Daniel fulfilled roles assigned, in the Byzantine mind, to the court eunuch. His rearing and his relationship to the king of Babylon clearly fit a pattern characteristic of the Byzantine court eunuch. The Byzantines came to assume that he was a eunuch, and by the twelfth century they were quite comfortable casting a favorite Old Testament figure in this role.

Confronted with earlier attitudes about eunuchs, Theophylaktos's matter-of-fact presentation of Daniel as a court eunuch also tells us that the status of the court eunuch was very different from what it had been in Late Antiquity. This is substantiated by the fact that by the twelfth century, eunuchs were accepted as holy men and could hold the highest offices in the church, including that of patriarch of Constantinople. Indeed, the status that Theophylaktos attributes to eunuchs in the twelfth century was already two hundred years old and had emerged in the tenth century. We will see that authors of the tenth and eleventh centuries also recast the lives of cultural heroes and invented earlier "historical" eunuchs who were given important roles in the lives of emperors. The tenth-century depiction of Daniel and his castrated companions, the boys in the fiery furnace, as well as the language used in connection with these figures, illustrates important issues about the ways in which gender categories were constructed and reconstructed in the Byzantine Empire.

Theophylaktos's Vision of Daniel

The normalized gender and status of eunuchs in the tenth century clarifies the meaning of Theophylaktos's rhetorical question, "What is Daniel to you?" The prophet Daniel presented Byzantine commentators with a major Biblical figure who, in their minds, was associated simultaneously with the status of courtier and that of prophet. As a prophet, his story endowed him with all the attributes of a Byzantine religious ascetic. Yet to a Byzantine audience the context of his story identified him unequivocally as a court eunuch, a category often associated with negative stereotypes.[2] Thus the figure of Daniel provides an important example of the way in which the court eunuch was assimilating attributes of the ascetic holy man, uniting these two very different images in one single individual. The ways in which authors from two different periods treated the tension between these aspects of Daniel's story offer insight into the dynamics of gender in Byzantine society.

The traditional story of Daniel comes from the Book of Daniel in the Old Testament. It recounts how Jerusalem was conquered by Nebuchadnezzar and how Daniel and his three companions were among the children of noble birth carried off to Babylon.[3] King Nebuchadnezzar instructed his chief eunuch to select the best and brightest from among the captives for his own household. Those selected had beautiful bodies and showed potential for training and education. Their names were changed, and the king commanded that they be fed from his own table. The Septuagint never directly states that Daniel was a eunuch, yet the assumption lurks in the background, if only because Daniel and the three boys were turned over to the chief court eunuch for training.[4] In some commentaries on the Book of Daniel (the fourth-century commentary of Theodoret of Cyrrus,[5] for example), and in some Byzantine historians who deal with historical events recorded in the Old Testament, we routinely find the Daniel story accompanied, without comment, by the quotation from Isaiah 39: "And some of the sons who will be born to you, sons of your own begetting, shall be taken and shall be made eunuchs in the palace of the king of Babylon."[6]

It is not surprising that Byzantine society of the tenth century, a culture that was accustomed to having eunuchs at court, should assume that Daniel was a eunuch. After all, he was a prisoner in a foreign land, his name was changed, he was reared in the king's *oikos,* destined to be a courtier, and the king was concerned about his physical and intellectual formation. Daniel was eternally youthful and lived outside the structure of the traditional aristocratic family—that is, he had no offspring. He was disassociated from any aristocratic or religious party and functioned as a moral control over the absolutism of the king. He was physically attractive and reared to present himself in ways that would bring honor to the court. He acted as an intermediary between his God and the king, between men and women (as in the story of Susanna)[7] and between the weak and the powerful. In this capacity he acted as a guardian of the weak, especially of women and children, a role that is especially clear in his relationship to the three boys and to Susanna. He functioned as a guardian and purifier of sacred space (as in the story of Bel and the story of the Dragon).[8] He had "magical" properties, especially as an interpreter of visions and dreams.[9] Finally, and perhaps most important, he was the trusted servant of the king, loyal to him first of all after his God.

This was the context within which Daniel's story was read in the tenth century. Our perception of that context and of the dynamics of gender construction are brought into clear relief by the way in which the traditional story of Daniel was reconfigured to conform to tenth-century Byzantine conceptions of the court eunuch. At the same time, the figure of Daniel also retained the qualities of a holy man.

Daniel and St. John Chrysostom in the Fourth Century

In the fourth century these two conceptions of Daniel, court eunuch and holy man, would have been so distinct that they would have been almost impossible to combine in a single individual. Court eunuchs were distasteful, worldly figures of ambiguous sexual status. Holy men were intact men favored by God. By the tenth century, however, it was possible to resolve this dichotomy, resulting in a new portrayal of Daniel that presents him as prophet, holy man, eunuch, and courtier.

While the following pages are based on a close reading of the Septuagint and several commentaries on the book of Daniel, the two sources that offer the best opportunity for comparison are St. John Chrysostom's fourth-century commentary on the book of Daniel[10] and Symeon Metaphrastes' tenth-century work on Daniel.[11] Both authors were certainly familiar with religious ascetics and with court eunuchs.

St. John Chrysostom, patriarch of Constantinople from A.D. 398 to 404, is a familiar fourth-century figure. He was born in Antioch at some time between 340 and 350 and died in 407. He was well-educated and famous for his oratorical skills. During the time he was patriarch, John Chrysostom carried out an extended political battle with the powerful court eunuch, Eutropios. Chrysostom's *Homilia in Eutropium eunuchum patricium,* which tradition says was delivered over Eutropios as he cowered beneath the altar in Hagia Sophia seeking sanctuary, is familiar to most scholars of Late Antiquity and Byzantium.[12] Although Chrysostom himself never tells us that Eutropios is a eunuch (the title is a later addition), it would have been quite apparent to his audience. In his oration Chrysostom uses a wealth of words and verbal imagery conventionally associated with eunuchs.

Chrysostom was a prolific writer, whose works are primarily exegetical homilies on the New and Old Testaments. His *Commentary on the Book of Daniel* is one of the latter. His works were widely read and held in high regard by his contemporaries. Writing in the fourth century, Chrysostom faithfully recounts at least some of the story of the prophet Daniel as it appears in the Septuagint. Tension between Daniel's image as a holy man and Old Testament prophet and his position as a court official with functions associated with court eunuchs in Byzantium runs through the document. Chrysostom tells us how Daniel and the three boys were brought to Babylon but never suggests that they may have been eunuchs. The line that says that the boys were selected because they were beautiful in appearance, however, elicits a long and rather tortured gloss. "Everyone knows," he says, "that beauty is an impediment to chastity and the acquisition of wisdom, so why should the king require boys who had well-formed limbs and surpassed others in beauty?" Chrysostom was certainly aware of the sexual role played by the young eunuchs at court, and he needed to recast this Biblical line.[13] "Beauty, in and of itself and as long as it is not connected with sexual sin, is not bad," he says, "and if the king, a barbarian, demanded beauty, then surely God, the lover of beautiful souls, also deserved beauty in his servants. Why," he asks, "would the king seek beauty when what he really ought to be looking for is wisdom and mental perception? He does so because he is a barbarian and as such is committed to the material world, a world in which the physical beauty of his servants brings him honor."[14] Next, Chrysostom discusses with approval Daniel's acculturation into the king's household. Daniel's studies will help him to do God's work and will make him effective in learned debate. Throughout this section Chrysostom regularly compares Daniel to Moses and Joseph, both of whom were boys from the royal house who were carried off to foreign countries and reared as part of a foreign king's household, becoming prophets who served kings.

Chrysostom then discusses the fact that Daniel and the three boys would not eat the food or drink the wine from the king's table. Discussions of food are interesting because, as we have seen, food is often gender-linked in the Late Antique and Byzantine world. You were what you ate, and the foods that were considered healthy for aristocratic women, children, and eunuchs were different from the foods appropriate for aristocratic adult men, just as the resultant flesh of adult men was different from the flesh of eunuchs, children and women.[15] Chrysostom's readers thus assumed that the proper feeding of young eunuchs contributed to the physical changes in development brought about by castration.

Chrysostom hedges in his explanation of why Daniel and the others refused the king's generosity. He says that Daniel rejected the wine because it might have been sacrificial wine but that he had no such concern about the food. Rather, he was following the law. "But," says Chrysostom, "what law? Laws governing ascetic dietary practice," he observes, "did not yet exist in Daniel's day."[16] Yet Chrysostom never suggests the obvious, that Daniel was following Jewish dietary laws.

Chrysostom tells us that Daniel and the three boys nourished themselves with a diet of raw grains and water. This conforms to the norms for the diet of a Byzantine religious ascetic, a diet that Chrysostom here projects backward onto an Old Testament prophet. Then he describes how God miraculously made Daniel and the three boys plump and beautiful on this diet so that they would please the king. Here God is facilitating the physical changes in them that are required if they are to serve the king. This miracle, Chrysostom says, is beyond nature.

> Behold the Maker of the World who finally shows His effectiveness. For He, most of all, seems an image-maker who not only is able to forge and form bronze, but also He, no less, is able to correct the shape of a statue that has already been made. Likewise also in Daniel and these boys He shall have recognized the same sort of thing. For that bodies, after such nourishment exhibit fat was no less an indication of the faculty of the creator than to have formed man from earth."[17]

By emphasizing this miracle, Chrysostom resolves the tension between Daniel's conflicting identities, holy man, prophet, and eunuch, and evades the possibility that Daniel was a eunuch.

Daniel and Symeon Metaphrastes: Making Sense of the Story in the Tenth Century

Six hundred years later, Symeon Metaphrastes tells the story in a way that highlights Daniel's dual identity far more openly than does Chrysostom. Our knowledge of Symeon Metaphrastes is meager considering his rich legacy of religious and hagiographical writings. He is believed to have died about the year 1000 and may have been a high official at court.[18] He would almost certainly have known of the castrated illegitimate son of the emperor Romanos Lekapenos, Basil the Parakoimomenos,[19] also called Basil Lekapenos or Basil the Nothos (the bastard), who served as chief eunuch under the emperors Nikephoros Phokas, John Tzimiskes, and Basil II, and was exiled in 985 when the emperor Basil II broke away from his tutelage. Basil the Parakoimomenos may well have been a model for Metaphrastes in his presentation of Daniel. Symeon Metaphrastes is best known for his collections of older saints' lives, which he reworked to suit linguistic and thematic traditions of his day. He compiled a *menologion* or collection of saints' lives arranged in accordance with the ecclesiastical calendar. It filled ten volumes and became the standard *menologion* for the Byzantine ecclesiastical world. Although we know little about Symeon Metaphrastes, it is clear that contemporary intellectuals admired and commented on his work.

In Metaphrastes' version of the story of Daniel, he is openly portrayed as a court eunuch and holy man rather than as an Old Testament prophet. Initially, as Metaphrastes recounts the story, he follows the Septuagint faithfully, explaining that it was necessary for Daniel and the three boys to be beautiful in body and soul so as to demonstrate their good breeding and descent from the royal line. Symeon Metaphrastes then goes on to say,

> When the king had made them eunuchs [and here he uses terminology, τούτους οὖν ἐκτομίας ποιήσας, or "cut men," the characteristic way of referring to surgically altered eunuchs in the tenth century] and arranged that they be fed from his own table, he turned them over to teachers so that they might learn foreign wisdom and the highest lore of the Chaldeans. . . . Their names were changed. . . . The king loved them and looked very favorably on them, praising their shrewdness, for not only were they well disposed toward mathematics,[20] but also each was very distinguished because of his judgment and decorous behavior. Thus did the king behave toward the youths.[21]

This is interesting for two reasons. First, Metaphrastes' acceptance of Daniel as a eunuch is unequivocal. Second and more significant, the roles of king and chief eunuch are altered to parallel the realities of the Byzantine court. The chief eunuch assumes a secondary role and the real operant relationship, from the time Daniel and the three boys arrive at court, is between the king and the children. Thus it is the king who takes direct responsibility for their castration and training.

Symeon Metaphrastes handles the issue of the boys' diet more straightforwardly than does Chrysostom. Daniel and the others will not partake of anything that had life. That is, they will not eat animal flesh. This, they say, is the way they were brought up. Daniel then asks the chief eunuch to provide them with seeds, herbs, beans, and dates. A review of the diets of holy men and women in Symeon Metaphrastes' other writings shows that he considered this to be standard fare for ascetic men and women.[22] Again, the chief eunuch expresses concern that the children will become thin and unattractive, but, miraculously, this diet makes them look as though they live in great abundance and luxury. The tensions between the two images, eunuch and holy man, may ultimately be resolved by a miracle, but it does not require the circumlocutions of Chrysostom's discussion.[23]

According to the Septuagint tradition, Daniel's first encounter with King Nebuchadnezzar is as a result of the king's dream. The king has a dream and remembers that it is important, but he cannot remember its details. When his wise men are unable to reconstruct it for him, he orders them put to death. Daniel prays to God and is granted insight into the nature of the dream, then retells it to the king and interprets its meaning. When he is finished he is rewarded by the king.

Chrysostom, in the fourth century, had explained Daniel's skill in interpreting the king's dream by saying that God made this happen in order for Daniel to appear wise.[24] His credentials had to be established before the Chaldeans in order to offset the fact that he was young, a captive, and a member of a foreign religion. Chrysostom then reminded us of Joseph's interpretation of Pharaoh's dream, again tying Daniel into the Old Testament tradition. For Chrysostom Daniel continued to be an Old Testament prophet. King Nebuchadnezzar was so astounded and grateful that he fell down at Daniel's feet and worshiped him, ordering that incense and offerings of bread be placed before him.[25]

Symeon Metaphrastes, in the tenth century, handles this story in a significantly different way. When Daniel discovers the nature of the dream he comes before the king. "Entering, at first he excused himself, not wishing to seem wiser than the other Chaldeans, and said that since none of them had been able to find the dream he would tell them." He could do this, not because of his own experience, not because of his intellect, but rather, he says, "because God was merciful to those in danger of death, and after I prayed for my own soul and the souls of those who are of my people, He disclosed the meaning of the dream and its message. I did this caring no less for my own distress or for your glory, oh king, who ordered such good and honest men to be unjustly put to death, from whom you asked nothing [that was] derived from human wisdom, but rather an explanation of something that was the work of God alone."[26]

This is a very different scene from the parallel one in Chrysostom. Here Daniel is deferential to the king, although his criticism of the king's autocratic behavior is clear. After Daniel has revealed the meaning of the dream, the king "was astounded by Daniel's wisdom, and straightway setting aside all small things and the empire itself and the dignity of his rule, he got up off his throne and honored Daniel with equal honors to those given to gods, and he made Daniel guardian of all his kingdom."[27] In Metaphrastes' world, the chief court eunuch, for all his power, would have treated the emperor and his other advisors deferentially. The emperor certainly would never have bowed down to his chief eunuch or worshipped him. Here again the relationship between the king and Daniel, his chief eunuch, has been altered to reflect the world of the tenth-century Byzantine court, a world that Metaphrastes almost certainly knew well.

Additional differences emerge when we examine the tale of the three boys in the fiery furnace. The three boys, Shadrach, Meshach, and Abednego, were accused of failing to properly honor the god of the Babylonians. They were thrown into a fiery furnace from which they emerged unharmed. Chrysostom asked why Daniel was not present and also cast into the furnace. He speculated that it was because the chief eunuch had given him the name of Balthazar, the name of the god of the Babylonians, and therefore the Babylonians were afraid of being charged with having burned up their own god. Or else, Chrysostom wrote, perhaps the king had become too fond of Daniel and shielded him.[28] Chrysostom then recounted the traditional tale of the three boys cast into the fiery furnace, describing how, "they sang and their singing was beyond nature. God honored them beyond nature. Behold a musical chorus singing hymns praising God as if from one mouth. Those who looked into the mouth of the furnace saw a theater of piety."[29] Can he be inadvertently referring to the eunuch singers and actors so regularly maligned by churchmen in the Late Antique world? Or, more likely, to the chorus of eunuch singers who provided music both at court and in the church? The evasiveness of Chrysostom's approach to Daniel's status as eunuch seems to emerge once again.

Symeon Metaphrastes introduces his version of the tale of the three boys in the fiery furnace with an addition to the Septuagint and to Chrysostom's story. In this passage Metaphrastes says that "a little while later it happened that, through the envy [of others], these [the three boys] fell into danger because they offended the king in this way." Again, notice the concern for maintaining a proper relationship with the king. Metaphrastes continues by telling us that the king was "proud and puffed up" and, as a result, decided that he could "not only make gods in one day but also sought to prove that the works of his own hands were [those of] gods."[30] Metaphrastes then returns to the traditional text of the Septuagint to recount the refusal of the three boys to worship the image. The author says that the boys refused both because they would not disobey the sacred law that says that one cannot bow down to a statue and because part of God's plan was that they should show how unjust the king was. Metaphrastes' text continues, "Those who accused the boys went forth and said, 'Oh king, those to whom you gave the royal imperium (a royal appointment), that is, Sidrach, Misael, and Abdenago, did not adore the image or obey your orders.'"[31] Notice that Metaphrastes does not specifically identify the boys as Jews, although the Septuagint and Chrysostom do.

When the king hears that the boys will not bow down to the image, he cannot believe that it is true. Their refusal "so angered the tyrant that he ordered strong men to throw Azarias (Hebrew name for Abdenago) and the others, bound as they were, wearing leggings, into the furnace."[32] The king is here again being presented as an individual who is capable of abusing his power. Here, too, the author has modernized the text, for in the Septuagint the boys wear Persian dress and their garments are named. In Metaphrastes, except for the leggings, which are retained, the boys wear specifically Byzantine dress. Again, Metaphrastes is casting the story into a contemporary context.

The story of Balthasar's feast and the writing on the wall is treated by both Metaphrastes and Chrysostom. King Balthasar, a descendent of King Nebuchadnezzar, held a great state banquet and used as table service holy vessels that had been seized from the Temple in Jerusalem. Immediately the fingers of a human hand appeared and began to write a cryptic message on the palace wall. Frightened, Balthasar called upon Daniel to interpret the writing. Daniel told Balthasar that God had found him wanting and that his kingdom would soon fall. That night Balthasar was killed and his kingdom seized by Darius the Great.

Chrysostom's version of the story of Balthasar's feast puts no emphasis on the service aspect of Daniel's life. For Chrysostom the explanation of the writing on the wall merely offers another opportunity for God to demonstrate to the king his power and that of his servant. In Chrysostom's version of the story the king keeps his promise to reward Daniel.[33]

Symeon Metaphrastes' version of the story of Balthasar's feast presents interesting changes from the account in either the Septuagint or Chrysostom. Here we again see Daniel reconfigured by Symeon Metaphrastes. When Balthasar's aunt suggests that he consult Daniel, she describes him as

> one of those who had been led here from Judea as a captive (whose name was Daniel), a man who had the power to find out those hidden things known only to God, who told King Nebuchadnezzar, when no one else was able to explain [tell him] the things he wanted to know, he [Daniel] knew all things well. If you send for him you will quickly find out what you want to know.[34]

Before Daniel explains the meaning of the writing on the wall, the king offers him great rewards, but Daniel "asked that the king keep his rewards for himself, since a wise and divine man is not motivated [literally, "captured"] by gifts. He gets his reward from helping those who are in difficulty."[35] Later, when the king does not like the explanation for the writings, he refuses to give Daniel the promised reward, an interesting change from the Septuagint text.[36] Here Metaphrastes is underscoring Daniel's role as a divine intermediary as well as a loyal servant, and suggesting that, in his experience, kings and emperors don't always keep their promises.

Chrysostom has little to say about Daniel's two sojourns in the lions' den or the story in which Daniel slays the dragon. Chapter 9 of Chrysostom's text begins with the arrival of the Archangel Gabriel. Here the theme is clearly salvation and the return of the Jewish people to their homeland. The commentary concludes with a few brief comments about Daniel's destruction of Bal, the killing of the dragon, and Daniel's second visit to the lions' den. Chrysostom makes it clear that God intervened to bring Habatuch and his food bowl from the Holy Land so that Daniel, whom God now treats like a prophet (and there is a certain implication here that he was not so treated at the beginning of the story), will not have to endure famine in the lions' den because unpolluted food is not available. God wanted to avoid the problem with food that existed at the beginning of the story.

Symeon Metaphrastes offers a much more elaborate version of the destruction of Bal, the killing of the dragon, and Daniel's second stay in the lions' den, and then inserts a new chapter that is not in any other source. This chapter 17 seems to be an effort on Metaphrastes' part to bring Daniel into the lives of his readers in a concrete way. He tells us that "since Daniel was powerful and splendid he built a tower, beautiful and well made, in Ecbatana of Media,[37] which is preserved even until this day. Those who see it think it is newly built, admire its beauty, and marvel at its age. The kings of the Medes and Persians are buried there, and a Jewish priest is in charge." Perhaps Metaphrastes is here thinking of the great building projects of the powerful eunuchs of his day[38] and their role in arranging for royal burials.[39]

Metaphrastes then goes on to elaborate upon the story of the cleansing of the temple of Bal, during which Daniel cleverly proves to the king that the priests of Bal are tricking him,[40] followed by the story of the slaying of the great serpent worshipped by the Babylonians. Daniel tells the king that he can prove that the serpent is not a god and that he will slay it without sword or staff. He then proceeds to kill it with a clever ruse, using a disguised pike and relying on the creature's gluttony. The fact that he will not use a sword or staff is Metaphrastes' addition to the story.[41]

This version is a clear echo of the Byzantine assumption that eunuchs, when they engage in active combat, almost always rely on cleverness rather than on skill with military weapons. Daniel's act brings the wrath of the cult priests down on his head, and they demand that he be thrown into the lions' den for a second time. God again aids Daniel. He seals up the mouths of the lions with a divine hand and makes them act like friendly (εὖνοι)[42] bodyguards (δορυφόροι), good and faithful (πιστότατοι).[43] The language of Metaphrastes' description of the lions' behavior is typical of the language routinely used to describe the eunuchs of the Byzantine court.[44] Again Metaphrastes is subtly connecting Daniel to court traditions, language, and imagery of his own day. Metaphrastes continues with a discussion of Daniel's fasts in preparation for his visions about the future, and he uses language that is characteristic of his other vitae. Finally, he concludes with a chapter that is an addition to the text of the Septuagint:

> Not just from these events [visions] but also from others, Daniel was shown to be great in visions and marvelous in wisdom. Where we might omit other things, we cannot bypass the judgment of Susanna, which is superior to many others and which he accomplished when he was still a youth. What more remains that can surpass that? She had been faithful to her husband but was condemned to death because of unjust false charges by those who looked upon her with unchaste eyes and was in danger of suffering a fate similar to Joseph's. Daniel's wise judgement after cross-examining the evil actions of the elders, showed them more worthy of death and brought about their end. This was the greatness of his wisdom (σύνεσις) and grace (χάριτος), and of the extent of his visions (μεγέθους θεωριῶν), since he understood even the hidden secrets of God, and the mysteries of the double presence of the Word [i.e., Christ] he saw with his spirit. [He understood] other things that are most worthy, and those that will take place before the end of time, and the grief that will take place, and the resurrection of men from the earth, and the glory of the saints and the never-ending shaming of the impious, and the depths of God, while he [Daniel] was still in the flesh, [these things] he knew by examining these things with his spirit. After he was released from the bonds [of his earthly existence], he joyously delivered earth to earth and went on to God, whom he desired, he a man filled with yearning. He is always with his three friends, the children, and with the prophets, but he has not, in any

> way, withdrawn from caring for and aiding us, to the glory of the Father, Son, and Holy Spirit, the marvelous Holy Trinity, which deserves honor and veneration into the ages to come. Amen.[45]

Here Metaphrastes is summing up his perception of Daniel's strengths, both as a holy man and as a eunuch. He is an intermediary between men and women, the weak and the powerful, the material and the spiritual worlds. He and the three boys can occupy this position because they are freed from the desires of the flesh. In Metaphrastes' mind they are gendered as eunuchs.

The Reconfiguration of Daniel

Both Chrysostom and Metaphrastes were confronted by the fact that while Daniel was an Old Testament prophet, in the context of Byzantine assumptions about gender the traditional narrative had the potential for placing Daniel simultaneously in two different categories, court eunuch and holy man. The tension that this created shaped both versions of the Daniel story in different ways. In general, Chrysostom treats Daniel as an Old Testament prophet, and his interpretation emphasizes Daniel's development as a prophet, the favor God shows him, and the way God's will is fulfilled through Daniel. As far as Chrysostom is concerned, the various kings of Babylon are fools, and very little time is expended on their relationship with Daniel. Chrysostom is reluctant to present Daniel as a court eunuch, a category that was negatively perceived in his day.

Chrysostom is aware of the developing image of Daniel as a holy man, and for him this is the more comfortable of the two available Byzantine categories. In one of the most beautiful passages in his account Chrysostom describes Daniel's mortification of the flesh, his fasting, his tears, and his wearing of sackcloth. Chrysostom says that Daniel does this in order that his body should remain pure, and that the ashes remind him of his own mortality. The sackcloth presses him down with its roughness. The fasting reminds him of the way things are in paradise. These are the customs of the holy man. Then he puts these words into Daniel's mouth, "I am not worthy of the earth," he said, "nor of clothing, nor of things, which exist *in accordance with nature,* but am oppressed by a *heavier punishment,* I who *am dressed in Persian garments and wear a Persian headdress*" (see fig. 2).[46] Chrysostom is certainly aware that traditionally Daniel is depicted artistically as youthful and beardless wearing Persian clothing and a Persian style headdress.

The message here is that Daniel has rejected the material world yet must bear a heavier punishment. He must wear the costume of a Persian courtier. It is quite possible that wearing this kind of an Eastern costume may also have been associ-

❧ FIGURE 2

This ninth-century depiction of Daniel shows him beardless, reclining on a couch and wearing Persian court dress. To Byzantine eyes the iconography would clearly identify him as a court eunuch. Khludov Psalter, Historical Museum, Moscow, Ms 129 d, f. 64r. In Anthony Cutler and Jean-Michel Spieser, *Byzance médiéval, 700–1204* (Paris: Gallimard, 1996), p. 61, fig. 37.

ated with eunuchs in Chrysostom's mind. In any case, Chrysostom evades the probability that Daniel was a court eunuch, although he is aware that Daniel might well be viewed as a eunuch even in the fourth century. This is confirmed both by his treatment of Daniel's beauty and by the inadvertent use of images that were applied to eunuchs in his day. Given the negative attributes ascribed to eunuchs in Late Antiquity, Chrysostom prefers to present Daniel as an Old Testament prophet and holy man.

For Symeon Metaphrastes both images are well developed, and he rather baldly presents Daniel as both a court eunuch and a holy man. Metaphrastes eases the tension between the two by downplaying the older image of Daniel as prophet and by reframing the context so that it resembles the Byzantine court. Daniel's dominant image becomes that of court eunuch, and his function is to provide moral guidance to an emperor before whom he is always deferential. The complications inherent in eating the wrong gender-specific food are still solved by a miracle, but the contextualization and reliance on familiar Byzantine categories allow Metaphrastes to merge the two images.

We can draw larger generalizations from this exploration of these two accounts of the vita of Daniel. The fact that for Metaphrastes these contradictory images could both be taken for granted and successfully merged indicates that gender categories in tenth-century Byzantium were more complex than we are inclined to assume. The strength of the image of Daniel as an ascetic at the expense of the image of him as a Hebrew prophet certainly supports what we know to be the increasing importance of ascetic holy men and monks in Byzantium.[47] The development of the image of Daniel as a eunuch in Metaphrastes' account suggests a clarification or cultural codification of the status of eunuch, especially at court. Indeed, it seems likely that, in the prophet Daniel, Metaphrastes was offering a model for the "good eunuch." Such positive stereotypes of court eunuchs are relatively scarce, but this model certainly matches the rather specific one offered by Theophylaktos of Ohrid in the twelfth century.

An Invented Eunuch for the Emperor Justinian

If it is striking that tenth-century writers found it helpful to recast the gender context of Daniel, one of the central figures in the Byzantine religious tradition, it is almost as noteworthy that they did something similar to stories about people at the courts of emperors Constantine (r. 324–337) and Justinian (r. 527–565). Constantine was both the founder of the city of Constantinople and the ruler who legalized Christianity as a religion in the Roman state. Justinian was equally important for his reconstruction of the Roman/Byzantine Empire and played a key role in Byzantine self-identity. Like Daniel, Constantine and Justinian and their courts were made more intelligible to the Byzantine audience of the tenth century by rewriting legends associated with them and imposing tenth-century gender assumptions on them.

In the case of Justinian, which is the less dramatic of the two recontextualizations, the rewriting took the form of Justinian's association with an "invented" eunuch who came, as did the updated version of Daniel, from the pen of Symeon Metaphrastes.[48] This vita is set in the reign of Justinian the Great, and the events involved are not themselves of great historical import. On the contrary, they affected the emperor in a highly personal way and thus involved people who were part of his innermost retinue. For our purposes, therefore, the real significance of the story lies in the way in which the scenario is constructed and the relationship between the individuals involved.

In the part of the vita that concerns us, the emperor has fallen ill with a painful medical condition that afflicted his genitalia, and none of his doctors can agree about a possible cure. In great pain and discomfort, and after watching his doctors argue futilely about treatment, the emperor decides that they are all useless and appeals to God for help. After much prayer, the emperor has a dream in which he sees a multitude of doctors, standing in order, dressed in splendid garments. He also sees a certain eunuch approach, clad in a garment woven of gold thread and dressed like a *praepositus sacri cubiculi* (chief eunuch).[49] The eunuch points out a certain individual from among the doctors. This individual has a humble manner, fittingly gray hair, and neat, trim clothing. To make certain the emperor knows the significance of this doctor, the eunuch says, "This doctor alone, and none of the others, is able to give you release from your illness."

When he awakens, Justinian is convinced that only the doctor that he has seen in his dream can cure his illness. He summons all the doctors and looks them over carefully, seeking the doctor in his dream. Finally one of his doctors brings St. Sampson to him and the emperor recognizes the saint as the man pointed out by the eunuch in his dream. He rejoices and kisses him. The saint cures the emperor's illness and reminds him that he has been afflicted in order to prove to him that although he is an emperor he is also a mortal man.

The entire story is a moral tale in which God teaches the emperor an important lesson about his own power. What concerns us is the way in which the crucial divine message is conveyed. In Symeon Metaphrastes' world, an emperor *had* to have a chief eunuch as his channel of communication with the world, and the costume of that official was a golden robe. Whether the court setting described was real or appeared to the emperor in a dream, it represents the way in which the tenth century perceived the court. The person who orchestrated the elements of the dream and acted as intermediary between God and emperor was a eunuch, *praepositus sacri cubiculi.* In any context of symbolic or ritual importance, the principal way that the emperors of the ninth through eleventh centuries interacted with their world was through eunuchs as mediators. By inserting a eunuch as intermediary into this moral tale, Symeon Metaphrastes makes it intelligible to his audience.

Eunuch for the Emperor Constantine

If Justinian was important to Byzantine history and self-perception, Constantine the Great was foundational, and the updating of his court life was much more dramatic. He was the founder of Constantinople, which by 1000 was the greatest city in Christendom. Constantine's achievements gave rise to many legends and traditions and he, too, was endowed with an invented eunuch by later commentators. In this case, however, the focus is not a personal crisis and a moral tale but instead the heroic actions associated with converting the empire and building Constantinople.

Here the story involves the figure of the eunuch Euphratas.[50] Euphratas is almost certainly an invention of the ninth century since he does not appear in any earlier sources, and there are references to him scattered throughout a number of ninth- and tenth-century sources. He is presented as a eunuch (although this is not always explicitly stated) and as the right-hand man to the emperor Constantine the Great. This story involves two simultaneous reconfigurations. In the most obvious sense, it creates a court eunuch whose status and aura are both extremely high and very positive. At the same time, it reshapes the way in which the emperor himself exercises agency as ruler.[51]

The centrality granted Euphratas is striking. According to both the *Writers on the Origins of Constantinople*[52] and an unedited text that is part of *Sabaiticus* 366 of the Greek Patriarchate of Jerusalem,[53] Euphratas is credited with converting the emperor Constantine I to Christianity. Supposedly, on the night before the battle of Milvian Bridge, Constantine is deeply concerned about the numbers of Maxentius's forces and the extent of their preparations. At that moment the eunuch Euphratas comes to Constantine and advises him that he can tell him how to win the battle without loss of men. When Constantine eagerly asks how this might be possible, Euphratas urges him to give up his pagan gods and worship Christ. He observes that large numbers of people already have become Christians and that those who have not, like the Jews, have either died or been scattered and forced into slavery. Those who have persecuted the Christians, like Maximian and Diocletian, have come to bad ends. He urges Constantine to pray to Christ for help in winning a victory. Constantine not only agrees but also decides to carry the Cross before his forces.[54] With the help of Christ, the newly converted emperor wins the battle the next day.

Another text, taken from the Patmos legend, credits Euphratas with a whole list of accomplishments.[55] Although this source never directly says that Euphratas is a eunuch, several elements in the text point in that direction. Euphratas is credited with the founding of the city of Constantinople. As the text says,

> And a certain one of those who were faithful servants to him [Constantine], whose name was Euphratas, spoke thus. "My lord, at that spot it is loving to God to build a city in honor of His mother the holy Theotokos." When he had heard these words the emperor immediately, on the spot, went and examined the place, which happened to be a high hill [or mountain], and put Euphratas in charge of the work of building a city that would be pleasing to the Theotokos. This happened in the twelfth year of his reign.[56]

In chapter 10 of the same text the author continues with a description of the way in which Euphratas carries out his task. He begins by planning the city, laying out its boundaries and the arrangement of its districts. He then builds underground canals and cisterns and digs wells designed to provide drainage and fresh water for the city.[57] Both of these tasks, as well as the way in which Euphratas supposedly approaches them, fit the gender configuration of an intelligent, educated, skilled eunuch official cum administrator.

Part of the trope about eunuchs is that while people might marvel at the accomplishments of a eunuch they also envied them. Thus,

> [s]ome, wanting to slander him [Euphratas], went to the emperor and said, "Those funds given by the emperor to Euphratas are wickedly being squandered by him for he has not undertaken the work because he holds you in scorn. Also, if he so much as perceives you coming he will probably flee."[58]

Here we see the courtiers, jealous because the eunuch Euphratas has the emperor's ear, exploit traditional charges about the avarice of eunuchs who make a profit at the emperor's expense. The author of the text clearly understands this, for he says, "But jealousy prowls everywhere in the city, and the envious eye could not stand to see the good [works]."[59]

The emperor is also assumed by the author to be aware of this dynamic, since the text continues:

> When the emperor heard these things, he acted as if he had not heard anyone speaking and . . . he [Euphratas] remained in the emperor's good favor. And see

> the emperor's gentle goodwill. For when Euphratas was near at hand, he [Constantine] did not say anything hurtful to him, but rather with a joyful countenance he said, "How goes the city?" Euphratas replied, "Well, my lord, with your patronage."[60]

Euphratas takes the emperor on a tour of the city, a tour led by a great throng carrying torches. They examine all the cisterns, canals, and courtyards and then proceed up to the square where the great statue of the emperor stands, a statue that Constantine's mother, St. Helen, had brought from Rome. There they examine the great drainage works designed to remove contaminated water and other wastes from the city.

> "When the emperor looked at these [works] he wondered what they might be. Euphratas said, "In these things, master, the people of the city will find a use, for if the rains become heavy, they will run off and the citizens will be safe. It will be easy to build fortification walls." The emperor marveled at the man's wisdom (φρόνησιν) regarding these things. He also greatly thanked God that such things could be inspired under Him through Euphratas, and he praised the man [Euphratas] exceedingly. After granting him high honors, he said, 'Since your works are so worthy of approval, I believe that you will take care to populate it, with God's help, not only with Romans, but you will bring peoples from all nations." Euphratas replied, "So I will do with God's help. But I beg your support, Your Majesty, so that when I send them [the seal rings] to your court [at Rome], each of the seal rings of the highest members of the Senate is approved with a sealed letter." And the emperor agreed. And so in time it came about and was accomplished. This happened in the fourteenth year of Constantine's reign.[61]

Even Constantine marvels at Euphratas's wisdom and accomplishments. He also thanks God for the work that Euphratas has accomplished, which suggests that this could not have happened without Euphratas's role as intermediary between earthly imperial power and God's power. In his turn, Euphratas says that he cannot complete his work on the city unless he has the seals of each of Constantine's foremost courtiers and stamped letters of authorization from the emperor. Here Euphratas is insisting on his right to act as an intermediary between the emperor and his nobility.

The story then tells us that Euphratas sends to Rome the seal rings of the noble families. He summons men from Rome who are skilled in the construction of princely houses. He arranges with them that a house should be built in the new city for each noble family, each of them exactly identical to the family's house at Rome. The appearance of the house and its location has to be copied exactly.[62] Next he sends the seal rings to the wives of the nobility, with written guarantees, making it appear that all of the senators are asking [or commanding] their wives to join them and ordering them to move their households to the new city.

> And they, not knowing the act [Euphratas's deception] but rather filled with joy as they would be going to their own husbands, boarded ships with their entire households and their most valuable goods, and they all came to Byzantium [Constantinople] and in the city of the Mother of God they recognized their houses, identical to their homes in Rome, and each entered her own filled with no small amazement.[63]

The arrival of the aristocratic families is part of a remarkable, if somewhat duplicitous, arrangement, one that is orchestrated by an extraordinarily clever man. Again we see distinctive attributes ascribed to eunuchs in Euphratas's use of a combination of skill, cleverness, and duplicity to fulfill the emperor's plans.

Meanwhile, the emperor has recaptured the city of Chalcedon, defeated the Persian army, and taken its treasury. The text tells us that "the most faithful Euphratas went out to meet him, requesting the following . . ." that the emperor should bring his nobles to the new imperial palaces by ship on a dark night.[64] Each noble's hand would then be placed in the hand of Euphratas so that he could lead the noble to his home [in the dark of the night]. There each noble would find his house, exactly like his house in Rome, with his wife, children, attendants, and even his animals. As a result,

> [a]t dawn all the nobles came with one accord to the emperor and marveled at what he had done . . . "The Virgin has called you," the emperor said, "and I believe through her begotten Son, Christ, our true God, we will not lack in any of the necessities, but will be filled in His goodness and that beyond our desires."[65]

Once again Euphratas has orchestrated an almost miraculous event, one that is supposed to illustrate the favor that the Virgin has showered upon Constantine. Euphratas has acted as an earthly intermediary between the emperor and the power of Heaven. The narrative goes on in the same vein in later chapters as the author credits Euphratas with the planning of the Church of the Holy Apostles and the construction of a church and poorhouse in honor of the Virgin.

While at one level Euphratas is a figure intended to explain the name of one of the city's districts (the Euphratas district), overall he bears all the stereotypes of eunuchs of the ninth through eleventh centuries. He is a trusted agent and servant, intelligent, well trained, and loyal. He is also disliked by the nobility, who accuse him of avarice. He is capable of acting both as an intermediary for the emperor and as his representative. He also is not above tricking a gullible audience in order to maintain a mystical aura both for himself and for the emperor.[66]

Conclusion

The reconfiguration of Daniel and the invention of eunuch servants and agents for Justinian and Constantine tell us a great deal about both the court and about gender assumptions in middle-period Byzantium. The invented court eunuch who is the intimate servant and advisor of the emperor is indicative of the growing distance between the emperor, with his semimagical or spiritual power, and the empire over which he rules. The eunuch himself is highly placed, constructive, and an essential mediator between the emperor and the ordinary world that the emperor wishes to reshape. At a more general level, the eunuch is the idealized "perfect servant." As we will see in chapter 8, this is an elaborate and detailed symbolic construct that was important in the legitimation of imperial authority.

Is the analysis put forth in this chapter, however, anything more than smoke and mirrors? Did aristocrats outside the highly refined world of the church even dream of associating court eunuchs with the Prophet Daniel? In the tenth century, they certainly saw on a regular basis the interaction between emperor, his eunuch servants, and the actual exercise of imperial authority. I think they did perceive the connection, and I offer this vignette from the chronicle of Skylitzes, an eleventh-century chronicler who worked from earlier sources, to illustrate my point.

Skylitzes tells us that when one of Basil II's court eunuchs was disloyal and tried to poison him, Basil threw him into a den of lions.[67] It is unlikely that Basil actually did this, and the real point is that authors of the Byzantine chronicle tradition had the imagery of the emperor and the lion's den at hand as an image that they assumed would resonate with their audience. It seemed an appropriate way to depict an emperor disciplining a court eunuch.

Byzantium was a Christian, post-Roman society that was also rooted in the long-standing cultural traditions of the eastern Mediterranean. Inevitably it had to reconcile or ignore the contradictory assumptions about gender construction embedded in those traditions. The preceding examination of the ways in which the story of Daniel was reworked between the fourth and eleventh centuries amply illustrates the complexity and multiplicity of gender categories in Byzantine culture. It was constantly necessary to reconcile the tensions between the bipolar and multiple gender constructs that coexisted in this eastern Mediterranean world. At the same time, the story of Euphratas documents the degree to which the intermediate gender category of the eunuch had become normal at the center of power. It was so normal that even Constantine, who legalized Christianity as a religion within the Roman Empire and who was the legendary founder of Constantinople, was more intelligible when shown working within the tenth-century gender framework familiar to the audience of that era.

PART II

Becoming Protagonists

Rather than looking at generalized patterns, part 2 looks at behavior and careers attributed to eunuchs or to groups of eunuchs. Some of these people are identifiable as historical persons; others are characters invented for various rhetorical and narrative reasons by Byzantine authors. This examination reinforces our findings about the distinctive gendering of eunuchs. It also documents two important ways in which their gender construct was enhanced during the ninth through twelfth centuries. First, by the tenth century, important and positive changes had taken place in the way in which eunuchs were regarded by some of their contemporaries. Second, and more concretely, eunuchs were seen in a variety of roles that were once closed to them. These roles sometimes seem "inappropriate" because later historians have relied on sources that emphasize negative rhetorical traditions about eunuchs, traditions held over from Late Antiquity. This change in status and gender attributes is evident in the world of religion and the church, in the world of politics, administration, and military leadership, and in the world of mediation between the areas of social and spiritual activity that constituted the map of elite Byzantine society.

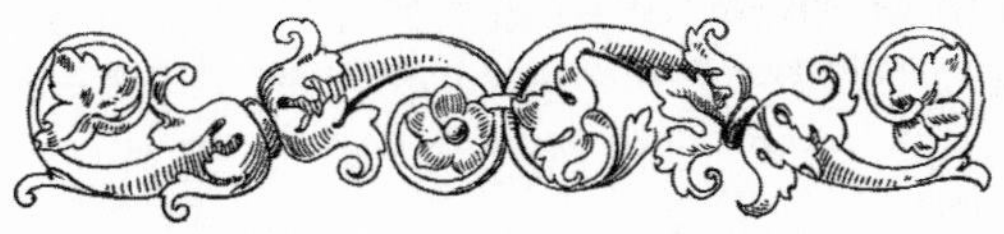

CHAPTER 5

Passing the Test of Sanctity: Eunuchs and the Ecclesiastical World of Byzantium

This chapter explores the relationship between individuals gendered as eunuchs and the ecclesiastical world of Byzantium. This is an extremely important part of the evolving position of eunuchs in Byzantine society, and a complex one. Some eunuchs in early Byzantium managed, despite significant disdain and scorn from the rest of society, to gain prominence, but rarely as religious figures. The church routinely condemned castration and, in the earlier centuries of the empire, associated eunuchs with licentiousness and immorality. Monastic foundation documents (*typika*), for example, occasionally use language that excluded eunuchs from monasteries.[1] At the same time, however, regulations for monasteries for women recommended the use of eunuch priests, stewards, spiritual directors, and doctors when the nuns required such services.[2]

More specifically, the church was uncertain and suspicious about the degree to which eunuchs could achieve the ascetic sanctity that came to mark the pinnacle of true spirituality in this society. The problem in part was that, while all eunuchs were incapable of reproduction, and many of them were celibate of necessity because they were unable to engage in sexual activity, critics thought that eunuchs' celibacy came too easily because it was the result of involuntary or self-inflicted castration. If eunuchs had never had to struggle against the temptations of their own flesh, how could their sanctity be genuine?

By the tenth and eleventh centuries, however, eunuchs were established in important positions throughout the church, up to and including the patriarchate.

We find them in many monasteries, and we find them portrayed as saints. What this chapter shows, therefore, is a dual process: the concept of sanctity itself was redefined in ways that made it accessible to eunuchs, while eunuchs came to be numbered among the important personalities and historical actors of the Byzantine church.

The church was deeply concerned about the relationship between castrated eunuchs and the spiritual life, a concern that projects great skepticism and many negative assumptions. St. Basil of Caesarea wrote in the fourth century that the eunuch was "damned by the knife."[3] Yet in the tenth century, as we saw in the preceding chapter, Symeon Metaphrastes reconfigured the life of the Old Testament prophet Daniel to fit his audience, in the process offhandedly identifying Daniel as a eunuch and discussing his castration.[4] Equally interesting is the language used in the tenth-century *typikon* of the emperor John Tzimiskes for the Monastery of Prôtaton on Mt. Athos. While a prohibition of "boys, beardless youths, and eunuchs" is clearly stated, the *typikon* also says that if admission of a boy, beardless youth, or eunuch cannot be avoided, admission is possible if the *protos* and superiors of the Mountain give their consent.[5] The generally enhanced status of eunuchs in the ecclesiastical world points to striking intellectual and cultural transformations. What kinds of stereotypical language and imagery came into play in this process, and what can the process tell us about the society of middle-period Byzantium?

Celibacy and Sanctity

The negative images of the eunuch found in the sources for Late Antiquity help explain the fact that in that era eunuchs were presented as unable to achieve sanctity. During the ninth through twelfth centuries, however, while eunuchs still could not achieve sanctity through the denial of the flesh—a process that had signified sanctity in earlier centuries—they could achieve sanctity through other forms of denial and selflessness. This shift was one of the various ways in which the gender construct of eunuchs was changing.

Although the real goal of the celibate life was probably to avoid the complications of earthly ties, literary topoi emphasized the role of the Devil, who used sexual desire to entrap men pursuing the celibate life. If eunuchs were sexually active and represented a source of sexual temptation to men striving for celibacy and if eunuchs thus assisted the Devil in his evil work, how could they possibly achieve holiness themselves? What role could a eunuch play in the emerging structure of Christian sanctity?

Two leitmotifs regarding male holiness emerged with early Christianity that affected the status and perception of eunuchs. One focused on the man who achieved holiness through the renunciation of the world and family duties, the most important of which was procreation. The Devil, using the beauty of women, eunuchs, and boys as bait, preyed upon the ungovernable nature of men's genitalia in his attempt to bind mankind to the world. This concern for control of sexuality, and stereotypes about eunuchs as a source of sexual temptation, explain the almost ritualistic prohibition of boys, beardless young men, eunuchs, and female animals from monastic establishments. These prohibitions are found in many monastic foundation documents.

Moreover, when a holy man overcame his sexual drives, he defeated the Devil's snares and won another battle for the heavenly kingdom. The signs of victory for the holy man were the inactivity of his sexual organs and the absence of nocturnal emissions. For obvious reasons, eunuchs were perceived to be unable to participate in this drama. Because of their physical condition they were immune to the temptations of the Devil and therefore incapable of participating in or claiming victory over him.

The other motif that complicated any association between eunuchs and sanctity focused on the moral duties of the Christian holy man and teacher working within the world. A holy man who wished to serve women and children in the church had to be above sexual reproach or suspicion. The Devil would whisper accusations of sexual sin against the holy man in order to entrap him and frustrate his efforts, and the only effective defense was perfect, demonstrable celibacy. This helps to explain some Late Antique religious figures who had themselves castrated in order to serve God more effectively. This approach was controversial from the beginning, and Eusebios calls these individuals "foolish and youthful to think that they can thus achieve salvation and continued youth and be able to minister to women as well as men."[6]

Motifs involving castration and celibacy spawned a hagiographical topos in Late Antique and Byzantine sources in which a woman posing as a man[7] is accused of fathering a child and is ultimately revealed as a woman and therefore incapable of the deed.[8] The companion story to this, which is discussed in detail later, is one told about the Patriarch Methodios. In this story, Methodios is accused of fathering a child outside of wedlock. Methodios publicly displays his mutilated genitalia, proving that he is a eunuch and thus incapable of the deed.[9]

Faced with the implications of these two emerging motifs—achieving sanctity through victory over one's sexuality and castration for the sake of holy service—the church fathers of Late Antiquity confronted several serious theological problems regarding eunuchs. This chapter attempts to answer only one, namely, could a castrated man achieve true holiness, since the measure of holiness was determined by each man's ability to control his sexual desires? In other words, did eunuchs "cheat" because they were not required to "struggle" to achieve the celibacy that was central to sanctity?[10]

Faced with this question, the church fathers appealed to the Old and New Testament for guidance. They looked at Isaiah 56, which says:

> Do not let the foreigner joined to the Lord say, "The Lord will surely separate me from his people"; and let not the eunuch say, "I am just a dry tree." For thus says the Lord: "To the eunuchs who keep my Sabbaths, who choose the things that please me and hold fast my covenant, I will give, in my house and within my walls, a monument and a name better than sons and daughters; I will give them an everlasting name that shall not be cut off."[11]

As we will see, the eunuch as a dry tree or twig metaphor comes up frequently and was subjected to interesting modifications in Byzantium by the twelfth century.

The church fathers also asked why the eunuch of Queen Candace[12] could achieve the honor of being baptized by one of the Apostles, given that he was a eunuch. They wrote numerous glosses on Matthew 19:12, "For there are eunuchs who have been so from birth, and there are eunuchs who have been made eunuchs by others, and there are eunuchs who have made themselves eunuchs for the sake of the kingdom of heaven."[13] This passage led them to ask questions about what a eunuch was, what was the relationship between castrated men and those who forced themselves to be celibate, and who among the above could enter the kingdom of heaven and achieve true sanctity.

Creating Categories of Eunuchs

These Late Antique commentaries on Biblical texts regarding eunuchs again illustrate the fact that the term *eunuch* did not carry a very specific meaning. Chapter 2 noted that in the fourth century *eunuch* was an omnibus term applied to a variety of nonreproductive individuals that included not only castrated men but men and women who were voluntarily celibate.

Most Late Antique and early Byzantine commentators assumed that Matthew 19:12 should be interpreted literally. In their interpretation, the passage was assumed to apply to three categories of men, those who were born without sexual desire, a particularly blessed state, those who had been castrated by others, and those who chose to remain celibate. Epiphanios, in the *Panarion,* sets up his categories in a slightly different way. He says that the passage refers to three groups of people, those castrated involuntarily by others, those who have castrated themselves, which he sees as a wicked act contrary to the power of Christ, and celibate men who "imitate the angels."[14] In the same vein, Clement of Alexandria offers an elaborate classification system for eunuchs: those men born without desire for women; those born without fully functioning sexual organs or those who are made eunuchs "of necessity" by others; and those who conquer their own bodies through the practice of celibacy.[15] One is also reminded of Eusebios's comment that Origen took Matthew 19:12 too literally when he castrated himself to attain celibacy.[16]

Athanasios glosses the passage by dividing eunuchs into two groups. One includes people castrated by other men "for the sake of the kingdom of women, to guard them and be conspicuous over others," a worldly goal of which Athanasios disapproves. Here Athanasios is almost certainly thinking of servants of wealthy households and the imperial court. He also reiterates two standard charges against castrated eunuchs, that they live in the soft and effeminate world of women rather than in the open and public world of men and that they attempt to overcome their sexual deficiencies by behaving arrogantly. Athanasios's second group is made up of men who castrated themselves.[17] But he uses this phrase in a metaphorical sense, saying that such individuals have elected to ignore their sexual natures and to live the celibate life for the sake of the kingdom of heaven. For Athanasios, this is the highest goal to which a man could aspire.

Epiphanios echoes Athanasios's negative opinion about castrated eunuchs by saying that "these [eunuchs castrated by men] cannot be foremost in faith." They can achieve salvation but get no points for their celibacy. He goes on to say that those who "castrate themselves for the sake of the kingdom of heaven" are men who, though remaining whole in body, practice celibacy as the Apostles did. These will enter the kingdom of heaven.[18]

St. John Chrysostom also divides eunuchs into two groups, those castrated by other men and those who castrate themselves, again metaphorically, and live the celibate life.[19] Those in the former group, he says, deserve no reward for their virtue since their enforced celibacy comes from having their nature imposed on them rather than from their own efforts. The latter group will be crowned in heaven because its members have practiced celibacy through their own efforts. Chrysostom goes on to suggest that castration is the Devil's work since it injures God's creation and allows men to fall into sin. Here Chrysostom almost certainly means worldly and sexual sin.

Epiphanios agrees with Chrysostom when he says rather explicitly that

> [I]t does not matter whether castration is done by one's self or by another. It still does not count toward sanctity. It still is not done "for the sake of the kingdom

> of heaven." He [the castrated eunuch] has failed to win the prize or win the game, since he has not achieved grace by shedding his own power, but rather has destroyed his sexual desire through the removal of those parts that lie under his penis. He who mutilates his own limb is like one who cuts down another's vineyard, for he does not do this in accordance with law but in accordance with a plan that is counter to the holy power of Christ.[20]

Gregory of Nazianzos adds another hostile twist in his gloss of this passage. He identifies as eunuchs the first group, those born without sexual desire. The second group, those who are "castrated by others," refers to men who have been taught celibacy by others. The third group, those who choose celibacy on their own, have the spiritual power to teach it to themselves. Castrated eunuchs have no place at all in Gregory of Nazianzos's gloss.[21]

Thus we find that by the late fourth century, as celibacy is becoming an important measure of sanctity, the physically castrated eunuch is being denied participation in the holy life. This is because the eunuch was perceived to be an individual who did not have to confront the sort of personal, spiritual effort that was required of a whole man striving for true celibacy. Furthermore, since eunuchs were perceived to belong to a class of individual that was associated with sexual sin and worldliness, their mutilation was perceived to be "against nature," contrary to God's plan, and perhaps even a part of a trap set by the Devil himself.

The evils attributed to eunuchs in Late Antiquity are summed up in the vituperative letter from St. Basil of Caesarea to Simplicia, a letter quoted in chapter 1. The tone of the letter is angry and negative, but St. Basil's rhetoric about eunuchs was standard for Late Antiquity and was aimed at a group that he clearly dismissed as less than human. St. Basil says that the eunuch is damned by the knife and that although he is chaste, his chastity will go unrewarded. He claims that eunuchs cannot make moral judgments because "their feet are twisted."[22] Backward feet were a sign of being in league with the forces of evil, particularly the Devil. Finally, St. Basil claims that eunuchs did experience sexual passion and that they raved with intemperate passion in general, but this passion could not achieve fruition. St. Basil's writings were widely cited by later commentators as the definitive "word" on eunuchs, and they became a standard part of the repertoire used by authors critical of eunuchs.[23]

A More Positive View

Recently other Late Antique and early Byzantine sources, which were kinder to eunuchs, have come to light. In 1992, Pascal Boulhol and Isabelle Cochelin published an important article that surveyed the hagiographical commentary on eunuchs in Late Antiquity. They found numerous references to eunuchs, including eighteen eunuchs in a sample of 541 masculine saints. They found that eunuchs were generally well regarded in Late Antique hagiography. These texts present eunuchs as sexually continent and scholarly and offer an antidote to the Late Antique portrait of the evil eunuch. In these texts we find eunuchs who have noble character, are kind to colleagues and servants, are good-tempered, and exhibit personal integrity. They are characterized as sincere, brotherly, pious, without malice, careful of what they say, abstemious of food and drink, unwilling to take bribes or play favorites, and generous in their philanthropy. In many cases these eunuch saints are fictional characters, but the characterizations remain useful.[24]

This pattern of positive references to eunuchs persists long after the period touched on by Boulhol and Cochelin.[25] The Byzantine hagiographical corpus includes remarkably few examples of negative rhetoric about eunuchs. Those that do appear usually portray the eunuch in question as the servant or agent of a superior authority while persecuting a victim. This is yet another example of the mediator function that was part of their gender construct. Thus we have cases in which a eunuch servant of either the emperor or a high civic official questions, torments, or punishes the saint.[26] The Vita of Saint Basil the Younger tells us of Samonas, a historical eunuch of the late ninth and early tenth centuries, about whom we know a great deal, who interrogates the saint in a particularly offensive way.[27] A similar example can be found in the Vita of St. Niketas of the Medikion (d. 824), who is persecuted by Anthimios the eunuch, head of the monastery in which the saint is confined for punishment.[28] Similarly the eunuch Gregory, who works for the city *eparch* (the head of the civil administration of a city), punishes and torments Pope Martin when he is brought to Constantinople to stand trial.[29] In general, however, it is difficult to find examples of bad eunuchs in the hagiographical literature. This presents a strong contrast with the better known, more secular historical sources.

The Evolution of the Sanctity of Eunuchs

The low esteem in which eunuchs were held in Late Antiquity and early Byzantium is reflected in the near absence of eunuchs from church offices in the early centuries of the Byzantine Empire. The sources of the fifth, sixth, and seventh centuries rarely mention eunuchs who were also churchmen or holy men. The few that we know include the eunuchs Calipodios and Tigris. Calipodios served as fiscal officer and property manager (οἰκονόμος) of Hagia Sophia in the early sixth century,[30] while Tigris, who was a priest, was a supporter of St. John

Chrysostom (398–404). The text implies that he was part of the church hierarchy at Hagia Sophia.[31]

This attitude appears to change in the eighth century, when eunuchs begin to appear in prominent religious positions. This trend, as well as a variety of hagiographical sources, documents the growing acceptance of eunuchs in ecclesiastical positions. This reflects a corresponding expansion of the attributes that conveyed spirituality and sanctity. Some of these figures are important court eunuchs appointed to high ecclesiastical posts, but most achieved their status within the church itself.

Two of the first really prominent ecclesiastical eunuchs were the patriarch Germanos (715–730) and the iconoclastic patriarch Niketas (766–780). Germanos had been castrated when he was already an adult, as a political act. He held office as patriarch under Anastasios II, Theodosios II, and Leo III.[32] Niketas was the target of much political slander because of his iconoclastic policies but not because he was a eunuch.[33] He was followed by Methodios, who was probably a eunuch and served as patriarch of Constantinople from 843 to 847, in the reign of Michael III,[34] and then by Ignatios the patriarch, who served from 847 to 858 and from 867 to 878. Our sources are careful to point out that Ignatios was not just any eunuch. He was the son of the emperor Michael I Rangabe (r. 811–813) and was castrated to end his imperial ambitions when his father was deposed (see fig. 3). He was made a monk and was patriarch in the reigns of Michael III and Basil I.[35] Nikephoros was trained for a career as a court eunuch but instead became a priest and one of the royal clerics before becoming bishop of Miletos.[36] The eunuch Sergios, a cleric and subdeacon at Hagia Sophia, appears in the Vita of Luke the Stylite.[37] Stephen, bishop of Amasia, was a eunuch who was patriarch in 925–928 after the death of Nicholas in 925.[38]

Polyeuktos the patriarch was a much admired eunuch whom we have already encountered.[39] Anthony the Fat (ὁ παχύς) was a eunuch who was a relative of Michael IV. He was named bishop of Nikomedeia "openly considering that the episcopal office was without dignity."[40] He later supported the eunuch John the Orphanotrophos's attempt to become patriarch of Constantinople. There is no evidence that either Anthony or John had any formal training in the church.[41] The eunuch Nikephoros the Priest was made head of the military forces of the east by Constantine IX Monomachos (r. 1042–1055). Nikephoros had once been a priest and had served Monomachos before he became emperor.[42] John, bishop of Sidon, was a eunuch who served in the administration of Michael VII Doukas (r. 1071–1078).[43] The eunuch Solomon served as bishop of Laodikeia in Phrygia in the reign of Manuel Komnenos (r. 1143–1180),[44] and it was the eunuch Niketas, bishop of Chonai and godfather of Niketas Choniates, who foretold that Manuel I would defeat his brother Isaac and rule the empire.[45] By the beginning

❧ FIGURE 3

St. Ignatios the Younger. He was patriarch of Constantinople (847–858, 867–877) and son of the emperor Michael Rangabe (r. 811–813). When his father was deposed, Ignatios was castrated so that he would have no claim to the Byzantine throne. He was later elevated to the office of patriarch, and his image joined the mosaics of other church fathers decorating the area just below the dome of Hagia Sophia. Ignatios was one of several eunuch patriarchs and, unlike most patriarchs, is shown as a beardless man. From Cyril Mango and Ernest J. W. Harkins, "The Mosaics of St. Sophia at Istanbul. The Church Fathers in the North Tympanum," *DOP* 26 (1972): 1–47, fig. 12.

of the twelfth century, therefore, the issues surrounding the role of eunuchs in the church outlined by Theophylaktos of Ohrid reflect a much-changed situation compared with that of Late Antiquity and the early Byzantine Empire.[46]

While there was a clear distinction between the world of the court eunuchs and that of the ecclesiastical figures who were eunuchs, there is scattered evidence that eunuchs sometimes moved between the two domains. The scattered evidence of such career crossovers may reflect the fact that the chronicles say little about the inner workings of the church hierarchy. While they sometimes identify a churchman as a eunuch, they rarely detail his professional background. Ecclesiastical sources treat court eunuchs in the same way.

The most common crossover involved the situation in which a powerful court eunuch became a monk and lived out the remainder of his life in a monastery. This kind of "retirement" to a monastery replicates a pattern followed by wealthy and powerful men and women, and it is not surprising that it should appear once eunuchs were normalized as a gendered component of elite society. While such retreats to monasteries were often voluntary, they also could be a form of exile or incarceration imposed by the emperor upon a court eunuch who had fallen from favor.[47]

Aside from those who "retired" to monasteries late in life, we have few examples of eunuchs crossing over from the court into the church, of which the eunuch John the Orphanotrophos's aspiration to the patriarchate is a prominent example.[48] This reinforces the inference that eunuchs in the imperial service were acculturated into gender patterns that were different from those instilled in young eunuchs destined for church office. Examples of ecclesiastical eunuchs moving into the court are also uncommon, but that crossover seems to have happened on occasion. As mentioned above, the eunuch Nikephoros was put in charge of the army in the reign of Monomachos, abandoning the priesthood "in favor of worldly pride and glory."[49] John, a eunuch who was bishop of Sidon, made a similar move into government service.[50]

The number of eunuchs who held important church offices from the ninth century onward clearly suggests a change in assumptions about the relationship of eunuchs to sanctity. We continue to find that their positions were ambiguous, at least in the eyes of lay authors, and the need to deflect this skepticism created interesting and revealing explanatory narratives. One of the best is the attempt to create a legend that would explain the castration of the great patriarch Methodios. In this narrative, Methodios was accused of rape. At a hearing on the charge, he removed his patriarchal robes and revealed that he was a eunuch. Then he told his story. As a young man he had been greatly troubled by sexual desire and, on a visit to Rome, prayed for help from St. Peter. St. Peter visited him that night in a vision and, after a painful night, Methodios awoke to find his testicles shriveled and useless. If this kind of rehabilitation was useful, it suggests that society, as well as the church, was still somewhat ambivalent about the whole issue of eunuchs, sexuality, and celibacy.[51]

Despite persistent concerns about the issue, by the time of Theophylaktos of Ohrid in the eleventh century, such hesitations were counterbalanced by a well-articulated, alternative interpretation of the problem. As noted earlier, the word *eunuch* had been accepted as an omnibus term referring to nonreproductive men of all sorts. Within this large group, castrated men were identified using specific terminology, such as "crushed" or "cut," terms that described their mutilation. Thus, when Theophylaktos writes his gloss on Matthew 19, he does so in terms that are similar to those of Gregory of Nazianzos. Eunuchs "born as eunuchs" are those that are born lacking sexual desire or functioning genitalia. Those who are made eunuchs by men are those who have learned celibacy from others. Those who are "eunuchs for the kingdom of heaven" are those who have been able to teach themselves celibacy.[52]

Theophylaktos's silence on the category of castrated men suggests an important shift in the rhetorical approach to eunuchs in general and to castrated men in particular. For Theophylaktos, the Biblical passage references men, castrated or not. His rhetorical strategy in this gloss and in his *Defense of Eunuchs* is to present eunuchs as individuals whose souls are untouched by the physical nature of their bodies. For Theophylaktos there are good and bad eunuchs just as there are good and bad men, and the physical fact of castration is not relevant to the quality of an individual's soul.

He reminds his readers that the term *eunuch* covers a wide variety of individuals, some castrated, some not. Some of these people were honorable, celibate men, while some were not. Theophylaktos then applauds the virtues of castrated bishops, saints, and patriarchs, while acknowledging the faults of the eunuchs of the palace and the theater. His central message is simple. One should examine eunuchs on a case-by-case basis. While admitting that eunuchs are aided in their chastity by their castration, he argues that celibacy is still a matter of personal choice between good and evil.[53]

This attitude is also reflected in some monastic foundation documents. Michael Attaleiates's rule for the Monastery of Christ Panoiktirmon in Constantinople specified that it could admit only eunuchs as monks, ostensibly because the temptations of city life were too distracting for monks who were whole men. The rule for the Monastery of the Mother of God Kosmosoteira near Bera nominally forbade eunuchs but specified exceptions for eunuchs of high standing and suitable wealth.[54] Clearly Theophylaktos was not alone in his willingness to be tolerant of eunuchs.

Theophylaktos's open-mindedness regarding the act of castration is, however, startling in view of modern and Late Antique attitudes toward the topic. He maintains that there are two sorts of castration, with very different motivations. The first is castration that is done to an adult of his own volition. This, he says, is wrong. He defines it as a sin equal to murder and an act that is against nature.[55] I suspect that Theophylaktos's real objection to this kind of castration is that it represents a voluntary change in a man's gender assignment after he has passed puberty. Given prevailing ideas about acculturation and gender hierarchies, Theophylaktos probably found this culturally unacceptable.

Theophylaktos views the second kind of castration, however, very differently. This is the castration arranged for a young child by a concerned parent who is helping that child to fulfill God's plan for his life.[56] This kind of castration is praiseworthy. Theophylaktos's logic and language here are subtle but important. Evoking a distinction pointed out in chapter 2, he claims such castration is not an "unnatural" act that violates nature because the resultant eunuchs are not "unnatural" but rather, like monks and holy men, they live "beyond nature."[57]

One of the things that helps Theophylaktos to perceive this second type of castration as constructive is the prevailing model for individual maturation and gendering discussed in chapter 3. This model lets him perceive prepubescent children not as "unripened" men and women but as unformed, malleable beings, destined to be molded by forces outside their own control. As we have seen, the idea that society molds a male child into a model of perfect masculinity is very well established in Greek society.[58] It is a short step to Theophylaktos's suggestion that it is appropriate for concerned parents and teachers to "mold" a prepubescent boy into a perfect servant either of God or of powerful men through castration and special training. Not only were such "servants" freed from the distractions and taints of active sexuality, but they had access to careers that could enhance family status while acquiring a new and semiangelic persona.

Theophylaktos reinforces this logic by reminding his Byzantine audience that these are difficult times and that the Devil's many temptations make it difficult to remain chaste.[59] Under these circumstances, early castration is helpful because it ensures a child's chastity. He concludes by cataloguing the positive contributions that eunuchs have made to Byzantine society. They are excellent and devoted servants of society, the church, and God. They guard and provide for women and orphans and engage in generous philanthropy. As far as their potential for achieving holiness through celibacy and chastity, Theophylaktos considers that eunuchs are no better or worse than other men. Some are celibate and some are not, although for obvious reasons castration aids them in their struggle for chastity.[60]

Is Theophylaktos's essay an anomaly or had eunuchism achieved the level of acceptance within the religious community that he portrays? Other evidence suggests that, in contrast to the Late Antique situation, eunuchs had achieved a high level of acceptance in religious circles despite the negative rhetoric still found in many sources of the tenth through twelfth centuries. Theophylaktos himself stands at that interesting intersection between the period when eunuchs exercised a great deal of political power at the Byzantine court (the tenth and eleventh centuries) and their subsequent political marginalization (in the later twelfth century under the Komnenoi). Theophylaktos is looking back over a period in which the status of eunuchs both at court and in the church had developed in significant ways, and his *Defense of Eunuchs* reflects these changes.

Sanctity, Eunuchs, and Hagiographical Sources

Theophylaktos of Ohrid notwithstanding, sources from the ninth through the eleventh centuries exhibit contradictory attitudes about eunuchs. On the one hand, Byzantine historians recounting political developments and court life frequently replay the hostile rhetoric and attitudes of Late Antiquity. On the other hand, the rich hagiographical sources of this period tell a different story. While they contain some of the standard negative tropes about eunuchs, we also have many positive narratives involving eunuchs. These sources show that the positive attitudes articulated by Theophylaktos were widespread well before he set them down in systematic form.

It is easy to find hagiographical vignettes that reflect positive assumptions about the sanctity accessible to eunuchs. This is illustrated by stories about eunuchs in the vitae of St. Niphon of Constantiana and St. Basil the Younger. The first example, a more dramatic version of Theophylaktos's *Defense,* places the saint in a situation in which angels and demons are fighting for possession of a eunuch's soul. Their debate evolves into a discussion about whether, given his sins, this eunuch can achieve salvation. Using well-known negative stereotypes, the demons claim that he cannot be saved. To make matters worse, they claim that he has been a passive partner in sexual activity with a man. The angels, however, argue that because the eunuch is remorseful, even his sexual activity can be forgiven and the eunuch proceeds, "limping," into heaven. Meanwhile, another eunuch in the same vita is damned because he has been greedy, and no forgiveness is possible.[61] The two cases in this vita clearly suggest a more open attitude about whether a eunuch could attain salvation and broader standards for holiness than that of perfect celibacy. While one eunuch's failure to achieve celibacy could be forgiven, another eunuch's lack of charity could not. The fact that the individuals were eunuchs is specifically ruled out as a factor in their salvation.

A similar contrast appears in the Vita of St. Basil the Younger.[62] There we find a detailed portrait of the eunuch Samonas, a historical figure of the ninth century who was *praepositus sacri cubiculi* under the emperor Leo VI. He is accused of all the traditional eunuch faults: arrogance, undisciplined temper, and sodomy. Yet in the same vita we find the hagiographer celebrating the eunuch Epiphanios, a very holy and ascetic monk, and the Gongyles brothers, Constantine and Anastasios.[63] The latter were both retired court eunuchs whose philanthropy included generous support of their Constantinopolitan community. Once again we see new criteria for sanctity supplementing asceticism and celibacy, in this case, both general holiness and philanthropic generosity.

Several other vitae of the period center on the holiness and sanctity of individuals who clearly have been castrated. Among them we find the Vita of St. Niketas Patrikios (d. 856), who ended his career as a monk who specialized in healing men who were tormented by sexual desires.[64] The same pattern appears in the Vita of St. Nikephoros, bishop of Miletos,[65] who began his career as a court eunuch, and in the Vita of St. Kosmas, who was *koitonites* (personal attendant) to the emperor Alexander in the early tenth century.[66] The attribution of sanctity is applied indirectly in the *narratio* of St. Metrios.[67] In this case an angel rewarded St. Metrios's good deeds with a son, to be called Constantine, and Metrios is told that he could "do as he wished" with the boy. Metrios had the boy castrated. Constantine became a court eunuch in the reign of Leo VI and eventually the favorite of the Empress Zoe. We have similar attributions in the vitae of the eunuch patriarchs Germanos,[68] Ignatios,[69] and (probably) the patriarch Methodios.[70]

The recognition of a considerable number of eunuchs not only as churchmen but as figures of recognized sanctity takes us back to the theme of chapter 4. There we focused on Symeon Metaphrastes's rewriting of the vita of the Biblical prophet Daniel. As we saw, Symeon had no hesitation in attributing sanctity to Daniel while at the same time matter-of-factly describing Daniel's castration and training as a court eunuch.[71] As a dramatic case involving a particularly important figure in Greek Orthodoxy, one could argue that the story is anomalous. But in the context of a variety of hagiographical writings, which offer several avenues to sanctity and recognize numerous eunuch saints, it seems safe to conclude that by the ninth through twelfth centuries Byzantine culture had redefined sanctity. By expanding the signs of sanctity, it became possible for eunuchs, once associated with very negative spiritual forces, to achieve the highest levels of reverence in the world of the Byzantine church.

A similar argument can be made with regard to Theophylaktos of Ohrid's logic about whether it was appropriate for parents to castrate their sons. Since his position is embedded in a rhetorically constructed dialogue meant to reinforce the legitimacy of eunuchism, his position must be regarded with skepticism.

This skepticism is especially valid given the continued existence of legal strictures forbidding just such castration.

Theophylaktos's argument must be seen in a larger context, including a number of well-known vitae. The vitae of the *patrikios* Niketas and of Nikephoros, bishop of Miletos tell us that they were castrated by loving parents who wanted to preserve their sons' chastity. In the case of St. Metrios, castration of his son was clearly authorized by God and followed the example of Metrios's neighbors.[72] As in the story of Patriarch Methodios, God, through St. Peter, seems to have approved the crucial act![73] This would seem fairly convincing support for Theophylaktos's assertion that the ancient laws against castration were indeed irrelevant in the context of the Byzantium of his era. Clearly the eunuchs of his time, gendered as imperial servants or people of the church, had moved out of the shadows of earlier negative rhetoric and become protagonists in the historical processes of the time.

By the tenth century we find that not only do eunuchs appear in popular stories but that they are described using language and imagery previously reserved for celestial beings. Eunuchs and angels are increasingly being confused with one another, perhaps because they are portrayed as doing similar tasks. Chapter 8 will discuss this wider topic of the spiritual potential attributed to eunuchs, but the trend reinforces the conclusion that gendered eunuchs had become appropriate representatives of sanctity, religiosity, and the dignity of high church office.

St. Symeon the Sanctified

St. Symeon the Sanctified is the most visible historical example of this trend toward eunuchs celebrated for their sanctity. Symeon was a court eunuch who served as *droungarios* of the watch until the reign of Nikephoros III Botaneiates (r. 1078–1081). There is considerable evidence that after Nikephoros came to power he continued to use Symeon as an emissary. Later, Symeon seems to have become a close confidant of the emperor Alexios I Komnenos (r. 1081–1118), serving as an ambassador and, perhaps, as his spiritual father.[74] Shortly before 1078, with the emperor's permission, Symeon retired from court life. He became a monk and took over the restoration of the Monastery of Xenophon on Mt. Athos. As the Acts (formal documents) of Paul, *protos* (director) of the Athonite monasteries put it in 1089,

> [w]hile the emperor still lived and ruled, the great *droungarios* [that is, Symeon] took over the monastery. He was from the great city [that is, Constantinople], a

> good man whose life was ornamented by holy virtue, bursting with much wealth and honored no less by the emperor [Nikephoros III Botaneiates] than any other lord. He sought the emperor's permission to leave the world and become a monk.[75]

Little is said about the fact that Symeon was a eunuch, even though an old and powerful tradition forbade the residence of eunuchs on Mt. Athos. Blithely evading the issue, the text simply says, "In as much as upon the earth he had been deprived of his genitals and was a eunuch, in that place [Mt. Athos] he would lead the angelic life."[76] With the emperor's help, Symeon took over the Monastery of Xenophon. With a large sum of money, he set about restoring its buildings, beautifying its church, and improving its agricultural holdings. In the process he was tonsured and changed his name from Stephen to Symeon.

The story rapidly gets complicated and suggests that the monks at Athos were not entirely happy about the situation. Unfortunately, Symeon brought with him three beardless boys from his household, Eusebios, Candidos, and Hilarion, and sponsored their entry into the monastic life.[77] The restoration of the monastery went well and it soon attracted new monks. Nevertheless, dissent arose for reasons that are not totally clear. The text seems to suggest that the older monks considered Symeon's three followers to be excessively arrogant. Consequently, when the monks of Athos met for their general meeting, they expelled Symeon and the three boys. The charge against Symeon was the introduction of beardless boys into Mt. Athos in violation of a regulation (found in the *typikon* of John I Tzimiskes of 972), which prohibited such introductions.[78] Symeon and his followers left the mountain, perhaps journeying to Thessalonica, where they may have established a monastery for eunuchs.[79]

But that is not the end of the story. When Alexios I Komnenos became emperor in 1081, Symeon approached him to plead his case against his expulsion from Mt. Athos. Symeon asked for and got a royal decree signed by the emperor that forced the monks there to reinstate him and his three followers. The emperor even sent his own personal representative to see that the decree was carried out.[80] Despite Symeon's apparent victory, however, it was agreed that this would be a singular exception to the traditions of Mt. Athos and that no other beardless boys would be admitted. Once again, nothing specific was said about eunuchs. Even so, the act of 1089, within which this imperial decree is embedded, concludes by reiterating the traditional exclusion of eunuchs, beardless boys, and women.

This historical vignette, set in the most rigorously ascetic community in the Byzantine world, reflects both old and new attitudes about eunuchs. Eunuchs, like beardless boys, could still be feared as objects of sexual ambiguity and desire and as individuals who blurred the boundaries between sanctity, maleness, and femaleness. Court eunuchs entering the religious world also brought with them the burden of years of participation in the secular life. This worldliness made them the object of suspicion within a strict monastic community. At the same time, eunuchs were often perceived as men of great spiritual power, men who had the resources to enrich a monastery. A court eunuch like Symeon used his political connections to acquire and hold onto his monastery, to enrich and endow his monastic house. The fact that he managed to establish himself on Mt. Athos, even as an exceptional case, reflects significant changes in the status of the eunuch.

Moreover, it is not clear just how exceptional his case really was. The new *typikon* that Constantine IX Monomachos gave to those monasteries on Mt. Athos subject to imperial authority includes language that clearly indicates the presence of at least some eunuchs among the monks of Mt. Athos in the eleventh century.[81] Symeon was controversial mainly because he was powerful and because he brought young male protégés with him. The fact that he was a eunuch provided rhetorical tools that could be used against him, but his gender was not so exceptional in itself. Clearly eunuchs still confronted limits and constraints at the extreme limits of formal sanctity, but it is striking that the rear-guard battle of conservative defenders of traditional sanctity took place in the confines of Mt. Athos itself.

These historical and hagiographical sources, like Theophylaktos's essay, support the hypothesis that by the twelfth century the gender construct and social placement of castrated eunuchs was very different from their situation in the fourth century. Castrated eunuchs of the twelfth century often were the offspring of well-established families. They were highly educated and dedicated to a life of perfect, loyal service within the aristocratic family, at court, or in the church. This chapter has shown how the eunuchs of Byzantium, reviled and existing at the margins of true sanctity in Late Antiquity, became protagonists who regularly acted at the center of the stage of Byzantine religious life.

CHAPTER 6
Transgressing Gender Boundaries: Eunuchs in Authority

Much as the authors of many religious sources regarded eunuchs with distaste, most of the sources of the political and narrative history of Late Antiquity and early Byzantium also treat them with hostility and suspicion. By the ninth through the twelfth centuries, as attitudes toward eunuchs changed, their gender construct had become more elaborate, and eunuchs were visible in many prominent roles. This chapter looks at some of the evidence for that shift, especially where eunuchs appear as protagonists in the military and political arenas.

First, however, we need to elaborate on what we mean by the term *protagonist.* It is a word that can be used in various ways, and at first glance some of those uses are out of character with the gender construction built up around eunuchs. Traditional historical narratives present protagonists as central figures whose actions shape the world and historical trends around them. They present such individuals as autonomous agents—a much more specific form of protagonism than the generic visibility and acceptance discussed in the preceding chapter.

Such protagonism, implying independent agency, is at odds with the central aspect of the prevailing gender construct for eunuchs. That construct cast eunuchs both as mediators between a variety of distinctive realms and social groups and as perfect servants. The eunuch as a perfect servant implies a contradiction with the concept of the independent historical actor. It presents eunuchs as extensions of their masters rather than as actors in their own right.

In practice, the distinction between eunuch as agent and eunuch as extension of his master or superior is not clear-cut. Our sources repeatedly present eunuchs in crucially important roles and situations where they are simultaneously cast as major personalities and as servants or mediators, usually for the emperor or empress. That is the somewhat ambiguous form of protagonism explored in the following pages. As imperial functionaries and generals, eunuchs are often shown simultaneously as imperial servants and as military leaders in their own right. Success in the latter role, however, implies behavior and personality traits that are out of character for eunuchs and transgress the norms of their gender.

A modest number of well-known Byzantine eunuchs have traditionally figured as historical protagonists. Because they played secular political roles, the evaluations of these individuals have at best been mixed. In the fourth and fifth centuries we have the infamous Eutropios, who was influential during the reigns of Theodosios I (r. 379–395) and Arkadios (r. 395–408), and also Chrysaphios, a powerful eunuch in the reign of Theodosios II (r. 408–450). The sixth century features one of the most prominent eunuch protagonists, Narses, who was the great general and *koubikoularios* of Justinian I (r. 527–565). In the ninth century we encounter Theoktistos, who served both Leo V (r. 813–820) and Michael III (r. 842–867),[1] and Samonas and Constantine, both of whom served Leo VI (r. 886–912). The tenth and eleventh centuries include Theophanes in the reign of Romanos I Lekapenos (r. 920–944) and Basil Lekapenos, the latter's illegitimate son. Basil first served his own father, then Constantine VII Porphyrogennetos (r. 913–959), Nikephoros II Phokas (r. 963–969), John Tzimiskes (r. 969–976), and Basil II (r. 976–1025). This period also included the prominent eunuch John the Orphanotrophos, who was active in the reign of Basil II (r. 976–1025), Constantine VIII (r. 1025–1028), Romanos III Argyros (r. 1028–1034) and Michael IV (r. 1034–1041).

Historians focus on these individuals when generalizing about eunuchs, even though their powerful roles in government were the exception rather than the rule within the "tribe" of eunuchs. Such individuals were not, in fact, typical of their gender. They represented the type of protagonist who used his office to accumulate power. They operated simultaneously as servants exercising power as imperial surrogates *and* as individuals who were respected and feared because of their apparent ability to act as independent agents. Such individuals are presented as prominent figures because they exercised political and military power in a world where those forms of power seemed important to writers of that age and to subsequent historians.

The biography of Basil Lekapenos, also called Basil the Nothos or Basil the Bastard, serves as an illustration.[2] One of the most prominent eunuchs in Byzantine history, Basil was the bastard son of Romanos I Lekapenos (r. 920–944) and an unidentified woman. There are suggestions that his mother was of Scythian origin, but this may just be a pejorative topos. He apparently was castrated as a child[3] and served his father at court, though we do not know in what capacity. When Romanos was deposed, Basil seems to have stayed in favor at court, rising to the rank of *protovestiarios* (πρωτοβεστιάριος or first dresser) in the reign of Constantine VII and later to the rank of *parakoimomenos* (or first eunuch), the highest office reserved for eunuchs. He was very influential in the government of Constantine VII, who sent him out to lead military expeditions. When Romanos II took over the throne in 959, Basil seems to have gone into semiretirement, and his role at court was assumed by Joseph Bringas, a rival eunuch. With the accession of Nikephoros Phokas, however, Basil returned to favor. He had actively supported Nikephoros Phokas's bid for power and was rewarded with his former position as *parakoimomenos* and with a new title, president of the senate (πρόεδρος).[4] After John Tzimiskes murdered Nikephoros Phokas and took his place on the throne, Basil became one of John's supporters and remained in the office of *parakoimomenos.* He assisted John in the removal of Nikephoros Phokas's supporters and relatives and helped him banish the former empress Theophano. Basil also advised John Tzimiskes to marry Theodora, the daughter of Constantine VII, and when John became emperor, served him in his military campaigns. The chronicles suggest that Basil bribed John's cupbearer to poison him. They claim that John had discovered that Basil was in possession of rich farmlands only recently conquered by the empire and that Basil's eagerness to accumulate wealth and property angered the emperor.

One should approach these stories with care. Contemporaries believed that eunuchs, like women, rarely fought men honorably and instead resorted to poison and to other underhanded tricks. It was also asserted that eunuchs, like women, were pathologically greedy and assiduously sought property and wealth. What we can be sure of is that the emperor John Tzimiskes became ill on campaign, returned to Constantinople, and died there.

John was the last of the long series of "guardians" of the "born in the purple" princes, Basil II and Constantine VIII. With John's death, Basil Lekapenos became a kind of regent for the young princes. Thus, even though he was a eunuch, Basil Lekapenos effectively ruled the empire until around 985. At that point the young emperor Basil II, restive and eager to assume control of the state, sent Basil Lekapenos into exile, where he died.

Basil Lekapenos was an unusual eunuch if only because he was the son of an emperor. He singlehandedly ran the empire for several years. He successfully shifted his allegiance from one emperor to another without being brought down. These are all activities that contradict the usual gender stereotype of the Byzantine eunuch. Consequently, although he was well thought of, he was also criticized, and the criticism leveled against him was couched in terms of traditional negative stereotypes about eunuchs.

The roles of eunuchs like Basil Lekapenos are well known and, along with examples of less prominent eunuchs, color our perceptions about the eunuchs in Byzantium. These powerful court eunuchs filled important roles as confidants and surrogate bearers of imperial power. They constantly had to weigh the necessities of their positions against the possibility of overstepping the bounds or giving the appearance that they wielded more authority than the emperor, thus challenging his position (to say nothing of his masculinity). However, we should remember that these powerful eunuchs were noticed, in part, because their activities were out of place in their culture.

The sources reveal a number of trusted court eunuchs who held important positions as generals and admirals. They led major campaigns, acting as protagonists. Some were brilliant successes and others were dismal failures, but there is little to suggest that the ratio of success to failure was any different among generals who were whole men. Moreover, eunuchs continued to be given military and naval commands throughout the period that is the focus of this book.

Of course, most Byzantine generals were not eunuchs. What is interesting here is, first, that a surprising number of eunuchs did hold military commands and, second, the way in which such eunuchs are presented in the sources. Byzantine authors wrestled with the question of how a eunuch could be an effective military leader. If he proved to be a successful general he was applauded for his intelligence, logistical skills, and loyalty to the emperor. The inevitable comment was, "He was skilled, for a eunuch." If he was unsuccessful he was said to be cowardly, untrained in war, devious, and effeminate and, therefore, unable to lead men successfully.

There are two logical explanations for the presence of Byzantine eunuchs in the role of military leaders. First, when an emperor was unwilling or unable to lead his army himself or when a woman or minor sat on the throne, military commands were entrusted to eunuchs. Under such circumstances it was especially important that the military command be held by individuals acculturated to the idea of acting as reliable surrogates providing perfect service, in this case to the nominal ruler.[5] History had shown the emperors of Byzantium that if the ruling emperor was not a strong individual, generals connected to rival aristocratic families used the army to seize the throne. Second, in a practical sense, when an emperor or empress was willing to follow an aggressive military policy, we find more eunuch commanders, if only because there were more military campaigns.

Eunuch commanders appear early in Byzantium. Eutropios, the powerful eunuch who served Theodosios I and Arkadios, led an army against the Huns and became head of the Roman forces in the east before his fall in 399.[6] Beginning with Justinian I's reign (r. 527–565), eunuchs were increasingly common in prominent military roles.

The most famous eunuch commander, of course, is Narses. Narses was sent to assist Justinian's great general Belisarios in his conquest of Italy.[7] Prokopios, one of our major historical sources regarding Narses, says, "At that time it was reported to Belisarios that Narses had come with a great army from Byzantium and was in Picenum. Narses was a eunuch (an Armenian from Persia) and the guardian of the royal treasuries, but for the rest keen and more energetic than would be expected of a eunuch."[8] Ultimately Justinian recalled Belisarios and made Narses sole commander of the forces in Italy. Prokopios says that Justinian did this either because he knew that the army would follow Narses or because Narses' appointment fulfilled an odd Tuscan prophecy that said that when a steer mounted the bull that represented Rome the city would fall.[9]

Prokopios believed that the removal of the testicles destroyed the seat of a man's natural powers. Nevertheless, he was lavish in his praise of Narses.[10] He marveled that a eunuch raised in the women's quarters and accustomed to a soft life could overcome his inherent traits and command so successfully. In effect, Prokopios depicts Narses as an anomalous example of his gender.

The historian Agathias is also generous in his assessment of Narses. He observes that the Goths underestimated him, judging him, sexually, to be a caricature of a man, overly accustomed to a life of pleasure in the shadows of the women's quarter, lacking manliness and virility. They (the Goths) acted as if there was no reason why they had to fear "a manikin who lived effeminately in the bedchamber and was effeminate, having set aside his masculine side."[11] The Goths were thus unprepared for Narses' military prowess.[12] He disproved the Goths' assumptions and roundly defeated them. Agathias ascribes Narses' success to his shrewdness, to the measured nature of his war making, and to the fact that he was neither insolent nor indecent. He didn't engage in pleasure after battle. In fact he discouraged such action on the part of his men, saying that it drained their masculinity. He was known to be generous, fair with his men, and magnanimous toward his enemies. He was prudent, industrious, flexible, and good at explaining things to others, attributes that were ascribed to him because he was the emperor's loyal eunuch.[13]

The explanations of Prokopios and Agathias for Narses' success are typical of sympathetic chroniclers and are examples of the way that gender assumptions color explanations. Both authors stress Narses' planning and execution of large operations. They depict him as intelligent and good at organizing things, both traits that were expected of eunuchs. Narses was loyal to the emperor and good to his men, who received regular rations and were paid on time. He was not a courageous warrior of the sort that the Goths favored, yet, given the military technology of his day, he had other qualities that were much more important. Thus neither Prokopios nor Agathias attributes Narses' success to traditional, courageous manliness. His success is attributed instead to the "cleverness" and "deviousness" that they perceived as attributes of eunuchs. Here we see that Narses is prominent in our sources because he was a major protagonist and also because he transgressed the boundaries assumed to surround his gender construct.

Narses was not Justinian's only eunuch general. The eunuch Solomon, who came from the region of Daras on the eastern frontier, served on Belisarios's staff. Prokopios makes a point of telling us that Solomon had not been castrated "through the treacheries of men." Rather, while still an infant in swaddling clothes, his genitals had been accidentally damaged."[14] In a passage that parallels his explanation for why Narses was sent to conquer Italy, he tells us that Solomon was sent to lead the Roman forces against the Moors in North Africa. Supposedly this was because of a legend among the Moors that the power of the Vandals (allies of the Moors in North Africa) would fall when a beardless Roman general brought a force to North Africa. When the Moors saw Solomon, "a beardless Roman general," they broke off their alliance with the Vandals and made peace with the Romans.[15] Prokopios says that Solomon was a brave fighter but tells us little more about him, although he does criticize him for promoting members of his own family (see chapter 9). While Prokopios chooses his words carefully in the *History of the Wars,* he is freer with his criticism of Solomon in his *Secret History.*[16]

Leo the Deacon notes that in the reign of Nikephoros Phokas (r. 963–969) when the Russians were confronted by an army led by the eunuch Peter Phokas, they ridiculed him as a "little woman reared in the shade." Leo then tells us how Peter surpassed all expectations by killing a Russian general in single-handed combat.[17] Despite that example of manliness, however, eunuchs were normally assumed to be successful commanders because they were clever and therefore good at organizing campaigns and at devising tactics and strategy. In general, eunuchs of lower rank who went on military campaigns were put in charge of the organizational aspects of the campaigns such as supplies, equipment purchases, and logistics. Their gender construct directed them to the usual forms of "eunuch work," even in a military context.[18]

The inventory of other eunuch military leaders is substantial. Theophanes tells us that the eunuch Leontios was the leading general of Emperor Phokas (r. 602–610). When Leontios was defeated by Khosroes II, king of Persia, Phokas had him led back to Byzantium in chains.[19] The eunuch Andrew, *koubikoularios* to Constans II (r. 641–668), was sent out to put down the Armenian rebel, Saborios.[20] Soon afterward, Andrew commanded a military force that destroyed the Arab garrison at Amorion.[21] Constans II also sent his *koubikoularios* Kakorizas to fight Muāwiya in Cyprus.[22]

As suggested above, when the empire was ruled by women or minor children, eunuchs were often sent out to lead military forces. John the Sakellarios (a high-level administrator who often had financial responsibilities) was a trusted eunuch of the empress Irene (r. 797–802).[23] In 781, John was sent out with the thematic armies to guard the passes against the Arabs.[24] Aetios and Staurakios, the two most powerful eunuchs of Irene's reign, both led forces in the field. Aetios led the armies of the Anatolic and Opsikion themes[25] and made his brother chief general of Thrace and Macedonia. Staurakios led a force against the Slavs with such success that he was allowed to celebrate a triumph in the Hippodrome[26] and won the loyalty of the troops in Thrace.[27]

Staurakios inspired the twelfth-century historian Kedrenos to give us what is certainly our most cited (and hostile) quotation about eunuchs.

> But a throng of eunuchs, among them especially Staurakios and Leo called Klokas,[28] took over the empire for themselves and put Nikephoros on the throne. So greatly did the counsels of these worst of people dominate the state that Chrysaborios, an elderly and important man, said, "If you have a eunuch, kill him, if not, buy one and kill him."[29]

A few eunuch generals were celebrated, if grudgingly, for their personal fighting skills. One example is the *protospatharios* Theodore, discussed in chapter 3, who was one of the forty-two martyrs of the battle of Amorion in 838.[30] After his capture, Theodore is interrogated, threatened, and coerced. The interrogator says,

> "You are wellborn and have been honored by your emperor with the most exceptional signs of office. Therefore I shall spare your gray hairs and set two propositions before you. If I can be persuaded that you will curse the one born of the Virgin Mary and support us in secret, you will be rewarded with much wealth. If not, you will be slain." The unholy barbarian was hoping that he could get somewhere with such proposals and that because he [Theodore] was a eunuch and grown old, he could be frightened and it would be easy to also drag the others to the same point of transgression. But his soul was strong and his judgment firm, and his name means God's gifts, and he was a champion.[31]

This raises the possibility that Theodore Krateros may have been freeborn; it is clear that he is valued by the emperor. The interrogators are being presented as individuals who would assume that a eunuch could be easily frightened and would be willing to serve them as a double agent. The hagiographer reminds us, however, that Theodore is a man of God and that his soul is strong, despite the condition of his body.

Another story about Theodore Krateros appears in Theophanes Continuatus, an anonymous continuation of the writings of the chronicler Theophanes. It is a later source and one that one would expect to be hostile to the iconoclastic emperor, Theophilos.[32] The events are set during a victory celebration held by Theophilos in the Hippodrome at Constantinople. One of the Arab captives was famous for his skill in handling spears and chariots. When the emperor saw him, knowing his reputation, he ordered him to circle the Hippodrome demonstrating his skill.

> And when he [the Arab] had done that and pleased those who had not seen such a display before, Theodore, called Krateros, who in a short time became leader of the cohort of the forty-two holy martyrs, approaching the emperor, sneered at the Arab, saying that the display was neither manly nor amazing. To this the emperor, angered, said, "With the strength that you have, effeminate and unmasculine creature, what have you accomplished similar to this feat?" He [Theodore] replied at once: "Emperor, I am not trained, nor can I handle two spears, for in battle there is no value in such frivolities. Using one spear and having absolute faith in God I will bring him down and throw him from his horse." The emperor, not liking his [Theodore's] frank speech, swore an oath against him [Theodore] that he would execute the holy man [Theodore] if he didn't truly turn his words into action. Theodore got on his horse and, taking his lance in his hand, quicker than a word, in a few circuits, he threw the Arab down off his horse, with the result that no one was impressed in any way with the Arab's performance. The emperor was shamed when he saw the Arab totally defeated by a man who was a eunuch and not of noble birth. Having always been cunning [shrewd?], the emperor, respecting the virtue of the man [Theodore], spoke to him with kind words and, honoring his pious way of life, gave him gifts of robes and cloaks.

Here we see that traditional assumptions about eunuchs' lack of military ability persisted, yet these assumptions could be overcome in exceptional cases.

The eunuch Theoktistos is best known for his role in the restoration of Orthodoxy in 843. He served the emperors Michael II (r. 820–829)[33] and Theophilos (r. 829–842) and assisted the empress Theodora as regent for Michael III (r. 842–867).[34] He is presented as a courtier and administrator, not as a military leader. Yet in 843 he led a successful naval expedition against the Arabs in Crete, and in 844 he led a force against the Arabs in Cappadocia. He died in 855 at the hands of his enemy, Bardas Skleros.[35] Both of Theoktistos's important campaigns took place while he was assisting the empress Theodora as regent.

Basil I (r. 867–886) apparently disliked eunuchs and did not send them out to lead his armies. His son, Leo VI (r. 886–912), however, regularly sent trusted eunuchs out to lead the imperial forces. These included the *droungarios* Damian of the *excubitors* (head of the palace guard),[36] who led a force against the island of Strobilos (an important island off the southwestern coast of Asia Minor) and Theodosios, *protovestiarios* (an honorific title at one time associated with the imperial wardrobe) to the emperor, who was sent out with a force to fight Symeon of Bulgaria. In the latter case the entire army was lost, and Leo grieved immeasurably for Theodosios.[37]

Eunuchs played prominent roles at court and in military service throughout the tenth and eleventh centuries. Many of the eunuch commanders of this period were both courtiers and long-term members of the *oikos* of the emperor or empress. Though nothing is known about the origin or early history of the eunuch Theophanes, *protovestiarios* of the emperor Romanos I Lekapenos (r. 920–944), it is clear that by 925 he was the most powerful person in the state after the emperor. He was very loyal to Romanos and a trusted advisor. In 941, as leader of the fleet, he successfully turned back and burned a Russian fleet that attacked the city.[38]

Such military campaigns of eunuchs were not always so successful. In 949 the command of an expedition to Crete was turned over to Constantine Gongyles, one of three trusted eunuchs who had advised the empress Zoe while she was still regent for Constantine Porphyrogennetos. Leo the Deacon comments that

> because of the unmanliness [cowardice] and inexperience of the general, who served as a eunuch of the bedchamber, who was a manikin raised in the shade and who came from the land of the Paphlagonians (his name was Constantine, his surname Gongylas), even though he was honored by the distinguished title of *patrikios*, the entire aforementioned army, except for a few men, was cut down by the barbarians and was entirely lost.[39]

When Constantine Porphyrogennetos was finally able to claim the throne for himself, he was assisted by the eunuch Basil Lekapenos. Basil participated in a major military campaign in 951 led by the future emperor John Tzimiskes against the Hamdanid emir, Sayf al-Dawla.[40] For his participation, Basil was rewarded with a triumph. In 971, when John Tzimiskes made his great campaign against Sviatoslav in Bulgaria, Basil Lekapenos was put in charge of the back-up forces, the baggage train, and supporting materials.[41] Again we see that organization of support services seems to be a military role customarily assigned to eunuchs.[42]

The emperor Nikephoros Phokas (r. 963–969) named the eunuch Niketas commander of a great fleet sent to invade Sicily. When Niketas was captured, the emperor went to a great deal of trouble to secure his release.[43] Peter Phokas (the Patrikios), the eunuch general mentioned earlier, became one of Nikephoros Phokas's most important generals. Kedrenos[44] tells us that Peter Phokas was born a slave, that he was one of Nikephoros Phokas's personal eunuchs, and that, though a eunuch, he was an energetic man. One may speculate that he was purchased as a youth by the Phokas family, then trained in military matters and used by Nikephoros as a member of his personal guard. As part of the *oikos,* he took the Phokas name. All of our sources recognize him as an outstanding fighter and effective general. At some point midway through his reign Nikephoros Phokas appointed Peter *domestikos ton scholon* (head of the imperial guard, a military unit quartered around Constantinople). Peter also took part in Nikephoros's invasion of Syria, acting as commander and leader of the reinforcements at the successful siege of Antioch.[45] Peter seems to have survived the murder of Nikephoros Phokas and appears in the reign of John Tzimiskes (r. 969–976), during which he was sent to fight the Russians. When John Tzimiskes died in 976, one of his most powerful supporters, Bardas Skleros, expected to inherit the throne. In fact, with the aid of the eunuch Basil Lekapenos, Basil II, the legitimate heir to the Macedonian dynasty, took control of the state. During the ensuing civil war, Peter Phokas fought against Bardas and was killed.

Clearly the chronicler Leo the Deacon admired Peter yet shared a general skepticism about what could be expected of a eunuch in battle. "Peter abounded in bodily strength and spirit beyond peoples' hidden suspicions about him." The Russian emissary, realizing that his army was to do battle with Romans (Byzantines) led by Peter Phokas, supposedly said:

> I see no reason for the Roman Emperor to come out to meet us. Therefore let him not trouble himself in coming into this land. For soon we will pitch our tents at the gates of Byzantium [Constantinople] and will surround it with a fortified camp. And if he [the emperor] leaves the city, if he persists in such actions as to fight against such a force, we will receive him bravely and teach him that we are not lowborn fellows living by the labor of our hands but rather men of noble bloodlines, prevailing against the enemy with our arms. This we will do if he, in ignorance—just like weak women reared in the shade—tests the strength of the Russians in battle and tries to threaten us with these threats as if we were like children at the breast threatened by some sort of she-monsters.
>
> The emperor, when this reply reached his ears, knew that he could not postpone the conflict and prepared for war in anticipation of the Russian invasion, setting up fortifications against the attack on the city. Immediately he summoned a company of brave young men, whom he called the "immortals," and ordered them to stand at his side. Then he summoned the *magistros,* Bardas Skleros, the

> brother of Maria, the late wife of the emperor, an energetic man of strength and singular courage. He also summoned Peter the Patrikios [Peter Phokas, the eunuch], recently named commander (στρατοπεδάρχης) by the emperor Nikephoros because of his innate virtue and brave deeds during wars. It is said that once, when the Scythians [Russians] had invaded Thrace, Peter, although a eunuch, and his legion were arranged for battle. The leader of the Scythians, a man of enormous size, securely armed, with a spear like a log, rode out in the space between the two forces, inviting anyone who dared to fight with him in single battle. Peter, strong and spirited, overturned everyone's expectations. Quickly spurring his horse and strongly brandishing his lance in both hands, he threw it at the Scythian [Russian]. So powerful was the blow that he split his body from front to back, the breastplate didn't make any difference, and the great enemy fell to the ground without a word. The Scythians [Russians] were so surprised they ran away.[46]

Here we see all of the traditional tropes about eunuchs as military commanders. Outsiders, here the Russians, fail to understand the relationship between the emperor and his trusted eunuch general. To the outsider, the use of a eunuch general implies that the emperor is weak and effeminate. Yet the eunuch more than fulfills the emperor's trust, successfully leading the troops and overcoming the Russians' champion in single-handed combat. Here the author, Leo the Deacon, clearly recognizes that the eunuchate, as an institution, is unique and beyond the understanding of outsiders.

Just as Peter Phokas was a long-time member of Nikephoros Phokas's *oikos,* so also the emperor John Tzimiskes (r. 969–976) relied on a long-time servant of the imperial household, the eunuch Nicholas the Patrikios, as an army commander. Nicholas was an experienced military leader and was commander of the forces on the eastern frontier who successfully fought the Arabs.[47]

In 976, under the influence of the eunuch Basil Lekapenos, the new emperor Basil II (r. 976–1025) sent his *protovestiarios,* the eunuch Leo, as commander of the imperial forces confronting the revolt of Bardas Skleros. Leo was promptly captured in 977.[48] At the end of his reign, Basil II sent "one of his most faithful eunuchs," Orestes, to lead an army from the western themes on an expedition into Sicily. Orestes did not fight well and had to be replaced by another general and by the eunuch John, head of the fleet.[49] These two cases are exceptions for Basil II, who seldom sent eunuchs to command his forces.[50]

Throughout much of the complicated period after the death of the childless Basil II in 1025, the imperial household was served by the eunuch Nicholas. He began his career under Constantine VIII (r. 1025–1028), the brother and heir of Basil II, serving him as a high-level army commander[51] and finished his career as *parakoimomenos* for the emperor Constantine IX Monomachos (r. 1042–1045).[52] He is identified as a long-term retainer, loyal to the Macedonian house. Under Constantine IX Monomachos, Nicholas led an army into Armenia. He was not successful and was replaced as head of the army by a Saracen eunuch, Constantine, another long-term personal servant of the emperor.[53]

During the period when the eunuch John the Orphanotrophos was in power (about 1030–1041), he often sent his brother, the eunuch Constantine (whom he eventually named duke of Antioch), out to lead the imperial forces. As leader of a military force, Constantine saved the city of Edessa. He then was sent out as head of the eastern army to aid in the Abchasian civil war.[54]

Also in the reign of Constantine IX Monomachos, the eunuch Nikephoros the Priest was given the command of the forces of the eastern frontier. Kedrenos says that he was "not made head of the army of the East because he was strong, warlike or industrious, but because he was faithful to the emperor."[55] Nikephoros had served Constantine IX Monomachos long before Constantine took over the throne in 1042. Nikephoros had been a priest but had left the priesthood to serve Constantine in a secular capacity, for which he was much criticized by the church.

When Constantinople was besieged by the Russians in 1047, the eunuch John the Patrikios, also called John the Philosopher, organized the city defenses. He had been one of the *koubikoularioi* since 1042 and was loyal to the empress Zoe. He was selected because he was trustworthy, and "he easily accomplished his task."[56]

Demonstrating that eunuch generals could also be incompetent, in 1042 the emperor sent the eunuch George Probatos out with an army to fight Stephen, prince of Zeta (a Slavic principality). George was defeated and lost his entire army because he didn't consider the difficulties of the terrain on which he would have to fight.[57]

During her brief reign in 1055–1056, the empress Theodora named the eunuch Theodore as *domestikos* (commander) of the eastern army and sent him out against the Turks. The sources are very specific that he was one of her personal eunuchs, and, therefore, trustworthy. A few years later, in the reign of Michael VI (r. 1056–1057), Theodore led an army against the rebellious Komnenoi.[58]

In the reign of Nikephoros III Botaneiates (r. 1078–1081) the eunuch and courtier John the Protovestiarios was sent out to take over the army of the east then under the command of Alexios I Komnenos. An interesting series of events is reported by Nikephoros Bryennios, who, like most of his family in this period, was a military leader. Nikephoros Bryennios later married Anna, the daughter of Alexios I Komnenos, making him a supporter of the Komnenoi and of Alexios, who seized the imperial throne in 1081. It was in Nikephoros Bryennios's interest to show Nikephoros III Botaneiates as a weak ruler who depended on incompetent eunuchs to lead the forces of the Byzantine state.

Nikephoros Bryennios reports that in 1080 the nobleman Nikephoros Melissenos rebelled against the emperor Nikephoros. The emperor ordered Alexios Komnenos, who was in command of a substantial army, to attack him. Alexios, whose family had close ties with the Melissenoi, refused. The emperor then ordered him to turn his army over to the eunuch John the Protovestiarios. Nikephoros Bryennios tells us that John had long been a servant of the emperor, that he loved honor, but was of unstable temperament.[59] Before turning over his army, Alexios Komnenos first rode out to review his troops and dazzled them with an equestrian display. The eunuch John attempted to duplicate Alexios's feat and fell off his horse, at which the soldiers all shouted "Klu, klu," a derogatory phrase "which is customarily said to eunuchs."[60]

Once he had a force behind him, the eunuch John undertook a campaign in Bithynia. He immediately began to have problems with his subordinate military officers. He tried to lay siege to and recover the city of Nicaea but was ultimately forced to retreat. Soon the retreat turned into a rout, and John was only saved through the kind help of George Palaiologos.[61] When they returned to the city, however, John spoke to the porter and the doors of the palace were closed to George Palaiologos, and John continued to plot against him.[62]

As we approach the period during which the Komnenoi and Angeloi ruled the empire, we find that eunuchs are far less likely to be entrusted with high military commands. In the reign of Alexios I Komnenos (r. 1081–1118) the eunuch Eustathios, who had served as *kanikleios* (keeper of the imperial inkstand, an important position because its holder controlled the preparation of imperial legislation at the highest level), was sent out as *droungarios* (commander) of the fleet to secure the harbor at Kuriakon when it was attacked by Bohemond of Antioch.[63] An unnamed eunuch gathered a force and defeated Andronikos Angelos when he rebelled against imperial authority.[64] Nikephoros the *parakoimomenos* of Andronikos I Komnenos (r. 1183–1185) commanded one-quarter of the imperial army against the Latins.[65] In the reign of Alexios III Angelos (r. 1195–1203), John Ionopolites, the *parakoimomenos,* was sent to deal with the problem of the false Alexios.[66]

The conclusion here is not particularly surprising. Eunuchs could and did command armies, especially in situations requiring sophisticated tactics and organizational skills. Some eunuchs even had the necessary charisma to lead fighting men. Many monarchs, especially those who were not too secure on their thrones, were more comfortable turning military forces over to individuals who, because of their physical disability, could not rise up and attempt to use these forces to seize the imperial throne. These emperors were far more likely to entrust military power to a eunuch who was a perfect servant, a loyal long-term family retainer.

Although it is clear that some eunuchs were highly skilled military leaders, rhetoric that questions their military abilities runs through the literature. The phrase, "He was skilled, for a eunuch" is seen again and again. By the eleventh century, as the power of the great noble families grew and as aristocratic male values that applauded individual courage and military skill increasingly colored historical accounts, we find eunuch commanders subject to open ridicule. These critiques highlighted their gender difference and the author's perception of the incongruity of having a eunuch command troops. This is especially evident in Nikephoros Bryennios's comments about the eunuch John, cast in a role that Nikephoros Bryennios considered unsuitable for a eunuch's gender construct.

The fact that eunuchs were often successful in positions of authority created a rhetorical dilemma for Byzantine commentators. On the one hand, eunuchs were clearly not supposed to be individuals of great political or military power. On the other hand, they were supposed to act as surrogates or perfect servants for their masters, and such service might easily include exercising political or military leadership. The way in which an author depicted these eunuchs reflected his own reaction to what he considered a transgression of the eunuchs' gender limitations. The more successful eunuchs were as generals (in the style of whole, aristocratic male generals), the more difficult it was for some observers to explain their successes. Consequently, those successes were treated as the result of administrative and organizational skill rather than as feats of military valor. Where the valor was undeniable, commentators fell back on exceptionalism as an explanation for success by a eunuch. The fact that they were repeatedly treated as individuals who transgressed their designated gender construct is evidence for just how deep-seated such gender categories were within Byzantine culture. Underlying the tension in these accounts is the fact that Byzantine society accommodated more than two gender constructs and that, in this regard, it differed from its neighbors—a difference recognized by authors like Leo the Deacon.

CHAPTER 7

TRANSCENDING THE MATERIAL WORLD: EUNUCHS AND ANGELS

In the last two chapters we have seen how Byzantine society normalized eunuchs as a socially constructed gender and accommodated them both as important religious figures and as powerful military and political leaders. This chapter looks at a very different aspect of the roles assigned to eunuchs by Byzantine culture. Rather than a problem of transgression, this is a case of transcendence. Our sources repeatedly attribute to eunuchs an ability that was important in most premodern cultures, the capacity to transcend boundaries that constrained ordinary men and women. Eunuchs were considered able to gain access to spiritual realms, both divine and demonic, that men and women could not reach. This mediation with the spiritual involved activities for which eunuchs were perceived to be uniquely endowed, and it represents an important form of protagonism and an intriguing aspect of gender role assignment by the society.

Byzantine culture did not draw sharp distinctions between man and God, between Constantinople and heaven, between the "real" and the "spiritual." In place of clearly demarcated realms we find a spectrum of overlapping domains, some primarily material in nature, others associated with heavenly or satanic power. The latter realms, while they could not be contacted directly, were believed to exist. While most ordinary people were unable to access those realms, it was believed that, to varying degrees, certain distinctive individuals could attain them. Among the latter were angels, holy persons, prepubescent boys, magicians, and it would appear, eunuchs. Since interaction between the material and the spiritual involved access to realities that ordinary men and women believed in but could not contact directly, it also rendered individuals such as eunuchs important protagonists in many settings.

This is one of the many aspects of the gender construct of eunuchs that rendered them so ambiguous to their own society. It is not surprising, therefore, that we find eunuchs associated with a variety of roles and professions that linked the real with the divine, the imagined, and the spiritual. In many cases these are activities that took place well outside the court and palace, forcing us to step away from stereotypes based on traditional chronicles and historical narratives. Moving beyond the eunuch generals, courtiers, and church personalities we have already mentioned, we also find eunuchs in occupations and situations that many cultures associate with liminality and marginality.

Eunuchs and Angels: Parallels and Mistaken Identities

Of all of the situations wherein eunuchs were perceived as having readier access to spiritual matters than ordinary men, the most striking involve the perennial confusion between eunuchs and angels. André Grabar has suggested that the portraiture of the heavenly court is based on the portraiture of the imperial family.[1] I would like to suggest that, in a reciprocal way, patterns of visualizing heaven became the model for the Byzantine imperial court, and that each image reinforced the other (see fig. 4). This may give us at least part of an explanation for the associations between eunuchs and angels that we find throughout Byzantine sources. A glance at descriptions of the angelic hosts written by the Syriac fathers[2] or Theodore the Studite[3] reveals what could easily be a description of the eunuch servants at the imperial court of the tenth or eleventh centuries. Angels sing hymns and control access to God. They stand beside the throne of God as guardians, act as doorkeepers and ushers, and guard the relics and temples of God. They also bring God's gifts to men and bring God's mysteries to earth. As we will see presently, these are all roles assigned to eunuchs both in the imperial court and in the aristocratic household. Cyril Mango has convincingly suggested that, at least for the popular mind, the Byzantine court was a mirror of the court of heaven and vice versa.[4] He also suggests that this angelic imperial iconography originated outside the church in a non-Christian milieu before the fifth century.[5] In this representation St. Michael the Archangel is the *praepositus sacri cubiculi* and presides over a heavenly court in which angels play the roles that eunuchs play in an earthly court.

❧ FIGURE 4

The Archangel Gabriel in court dress, reflecting the assumed parallel between angels in the heavenly court and eunuchs at the imperial court. Wall painting, apse of monastery of Mavriotissa, Kastoria. In Stylianos Pelekanidis and Manolis Chatzidakis, *Kastoria* (Athens: Melissa, 1985), p. 71, fig. 71.

Eunuchs, like angels, were thought to have special powers beyond those of other men (see fig. 5). Eunuchs were an integral part of the material world of mankind but, because of their distinctive gender, they could also penetrate farther along the material-spiritual spectrum than ordinary men. This perception lies behind the ambivalent but ultimately positive attitude of the church toward eunuchs as holy men and church officials.

The ease with which eunuchs could cross over into spiritual realms is illustrated in literary themes that regularly play upon the frequent confusion between eunuchs and angels. There is no question that the two categories were closely associated in men's minds. This association is reflected in descriptive language and in the very structure of the language used to describe these categories.[6]

It was thought that angels were organized in a hierarchical manner and that the heavenly hierarchy was echoed in the hierarchical structures of both the church and the imperial court. For example, the eleventh-century theologian Niketas Stethatos outlines hierarchies that suggest parallels between the heavenly kingdom and the world of the church. In Niketas Stethatos's structure, the first tier of angels—the thrones, cherubim, and seraphim—are equated with earthly patriarchs, archbishops, and heads of monastic communities. This first group of angels stands closest to God in a circle and without intermediaries and exalts Him with songs and praises. The second circle includes dominions, virtues, and powers whose earthly counterparts are the heads of lesser monasteries, priests, and deacons. In this tier, the dominions are perfect servants; they have abandoned all worldly things and want only to serve God. The third circle of angels includes principals, archangels, and angels, all of whom serve God and transmit His wishes to earth. On the earthly plane these angels are paired with subdeacons, readers, and monks.[7] This interesting construction of hierarchies of proximity and service to a ruler, celestial or earthly, also appears as an aspect of the eunuchs' role in court ceremonial, which is analyzed in chapter 8.

The angelic tasks mentioned above are also characteristic of the imperial corps of eunuchs. There are endless references to eunuchs carrying messages, an area where their liminal function is always on display. They facilitate interactions between men and women, old and young, rich and poor, emperor and peasant. They act as supervisors and organizers of the imperial sacred space. This is obvious in the case of the imperial court where, by the tenth century, the *koubikoularios* had become one of the most powerful officials at court. By the twelfth century there is also clear evidence that the concept of sacred space guarded by eunuchs has been expanded to include places like the imperial hunting preserve, with its trees "planted by God."[8]

In another parallel with the corps of court eunuchs, the corps of angels, with the exception of a few specific individuals like St. Michael, is a homogeneous

FIGURE 5

A tenth-century court eunuch, the *patrikios, praepositos,* and *sakellarios* Leo. In this donor portrait Leo offers a beautifully illuminated manuscript, now known as the Leo Bible, to the Virgin. It will be a treasured possession of a monastery ruled by Leo's brother. This is an exemplary portrait of a historical eunuch. Unlike most mortals, he dares to look the Virgin squarely in the eye—perhaps a hint of the eunuch's presumed access to spiritual realms unavailable to ordinary men. From *Die Bibel des Patricius Leo: Codex Reginensis Graecus 1 B,* ed. Suzy Dufrenne and Paul Canart (Zurich, 1988), fol. 2v.

group. All angels look alike and present themselves in the same way. At each hierarchical level they function as a group, not as specific individuals. By the tenth century this was also true of the corps of eunuchs at the imperial court. We have seen how they were often reared at court and how they were acculturated with a specific body language, a certain kind of bearing, specific facial expressions, distinctive voice patterns, characteristic dress, and distinctive body ornaments. All of these engendered elements set them aside and marked them out as a group, separate from other men.

One of the texts I will use to illustrate the overlap between angels and eunuchs is a well-known selection from the *Patria* of Constantinople, a literary genre devoted to local topography, monuments, history, and legends.[9] One legend in the *Patria* is set during the reign of Justinian the Great and centers on the building of the church of Hagia Sophia. Although the *Patria* is difficult to date, there seems to be an emerging agreement that it was written between the eighth and the tenth centuries. Here we are dealing with a single narrative, but this legend apparently enjoyed enormous popularity, with several variants in general circulation. Versions of the basic story can be found in a number of texts, and it even appears in a Russian variant in the thirteenth and fourteenth centuries.[10]

The story includes three main characters and a case of mistaken identity. The cast includes the emperor Justinian; St. Michael the Archangel, who comes to earth as a messenger (see fig. 6); and a prepubescent boy, the son of the foreman of the building project. The confusion of identities involves the St. Michael and a nonexistent eunuch.

The choice of St. Michael for the story is intriguing and may not be accidental, since he is associated with a number of early cults featuring gender ambiguity. There is excellent evidence that St. Michael entered both Judaism and Christianity from Babylonian religious beliefs. By the fourth century A.D., cults to St. Michael were appearing in Egypt and later appeared in Nubia and in Anatolia at Chona in Phrygia and in Pythia. At its fall, Constantinople had thirty-five sanctuaries dedicated to St. Michael, although many had probably fallen into disuse. Seven of them had come into existence before the eighth century. The eastern provinces of the Byzantine Empire saw many new sanctuaries dedicated to St. Michael. In Egypt, a pagan cult to Saturn was converted into a cult dedicated to St. Michael, as were pagan cults in other regions.[11] Mango suggests that cults dedicated to St. Michael took over those of the Anatolian mother goddess Cybele through the Syria Dea.[12] These cults were connected with the *galli,* the castrated priests of the mother goddess.

The basic structure of the foundation narrative presents St. Michael, God's administrator for heavenly affairs, interacting with God's administrator for earthly affairs regarding the building of an earthly structure that will be dedicated to

❧ FIGURE 6

The Archangel Michael in court dress. The Byzantine esthetic associated the same sort of beauty with angels, eunuchs, and prepubescent boys. Wall painting, late eleventh century, Hagioi Anargyroi, south aisle. In Stylianos Pelekanidis and Manolis Chatzidakis, *Kastoria* (Athens: Melissa, 1985), p. 47, fig. 26.

spiritual matters. The intermediary between the two key individuals is a prepubescent boy who acts as a liminal figure and facilitates their interaction.

Work has been going well on the great new church, and Strategios orders a break for a celebratory lunch. All the workers are invited. The foreman leaves his young son to guard his tools while everyone else goes off to lunch. We are specifically told that the boy is fourteen years old, placing him on the verge of sexual maturity. As he is sitting there alone, the boy is approached by someone he assumes to be a eunuch wearing a shining garment (εὐνοῦχος λαμπρὰν ἐσθῆτα ἠμφιεσμένος). The stranger is beautiful and youthful, and the text says that he looks like someone sent from the palace. He approaches and asks the boy by whose authority the workmen have left for lunch. The boy politely explains that they will return presently. The visitor reminds him that the completion of the church, to be called Hagia Sophia, is very important and orders him to go and get the workmen. When the boy protests that he cannot leave the tools unguarded, the visitor replies: "Leave quickly and tell them to return right away, and I promise you, child, that by the holy wisdom, which is the word of God . . . I will not leave this place, for I have been appointed to work here and guard it by the command of God until you return."

The boy rushes off to his father, who takes him to the emperor. The boy explains the orders and says they were delivered by a palace eunuch. The emperor summons all his court eunuchs and parades them in front of the boy. "The eunuch I saw is none of these," the boy says. The boy then specifically describes the visitor as wearing a white robe, with cheeks that shot forth flames and an appearance that was strange (ἐνηλλαγμένη). Here the Greek word, which comes from ἐναλλάσσω, has the sense of being changed from one form or appearance to another.[13]

At this point the emperor realizes that the boy's visitor is not a eunuch at all. He is an angel, a messenger of God sent to inform the emperor about God's desires regarding the name of the church. What is important for the narrative is that the angel has promised to guard the church until the boy returns. The emperor consults with his advisors and high churchmen, and they all agree that the boy must never enter the church again. With his father's permission, the boy is given money and sent into "honorable exile" in the Cyclades islands. Thus the eunuch/angel ambiguity has helped the emperor to "trap" St. Michael into becoming the guardian angel for Hagia Sophia forever.[14]

What is significant for our purposes is that this text brings together three important elements: angels, eunuchs, and young boys. The idea that eunuchs and angels might be connected is not new; it appears too often in hagiographical texts, for example, to be accidental. Among the more prominent examples is the tale told in chapter 4, in which Justinian I suffers from a seemingly incurable disease. The solution comes to the emperor through a vision in which a eunuch appears as a *praepositus sacri cubiculi* and points out the modest man who can provide the needed treatment.[15] Thus it is a eunuch, acting as angels often do, who directs the emperor to a miraculous cure.

Certain details of appearance were common to both angels and eunuchs. It is imagery that echoes well-known passages in the Bible, such as Moses' appearance after he has seen God and Christ's appearance at the transfiguration.[16] In chapter 3 we saw how Symeon the Stylite the Younger had a vision that included "a corps of angels like men who were eunuchs whose clothing was white as snow."[17] The same distinct appearance of eunuchs is demonstrated in the story of women, suffering from an uncontrollable issue of blood, who were not allowed to enter the tomb of St. Tarasios because they were women. They "covered their female genitals with manly garb and disguised their faces as eunuchs and secretly took refuge at the wageless coffin of the very dexterous steersman, entering the shrine, where they were healed."[18] In the vita of Anthimios, when evil Maxentius's henchmen are beating up the saint, he is saved by three men with fair faces, wearing white robes, men who were frightening to look at.[19] In the Vita of Aberchios, God sends a youth as a messenger to the saint as he sleeps. The youth is fair and beautiful and holds a staff, which he gives to Aberchios.[20] Similarly, the pillar-dwelling Saint Daniel the Stylite has a vision in which he visits St. Symeon the Stylite's column and sees St. Symeon, accompanied by two youths, standing on his column. Their clothing is bright and radiant.[21] The Vita of St. Andrew the Fool includes a description of the angel who comes to cook a pot of soup for Epiphanios. "He saw a beautiful young man of wonderful stature dressed in a divine robe, his face shining brighter than the sun . . . sometimes it was like snow, sometimes, like dazzling fire . . . [He had] blond hair on his head, like gold in appearance.[22] In another vita, St. Michael appears with a large retinue clad in the garments of a *praepositos*.[23] Such clothing appears over and over. In the Vita of Paul the Younger of Latros we find an angel in the form of a human, specifically, a boy of no more than twelve, wearing a linen tunic white as snow, who proves to be an angel.[24]

Considering further similarities between eunuchs and angels can give us a more detailed glimpse of the heavenly court. The Vita of St. Basil the Younger talks of a heavenly palace with angels: "Couches and tables were supplied for their [the holy men's] use, watched over by holy angels set in order under Christ."[25] The Vita of St. Philaret the Merciful offers a vision of paradise run by a "man with such a radiant appearance that he seemed to be made of fire and was holding a golden staff."[26] This angel is cast in the role of a Byzantine courtier. The vision of St. Kosmas offers a description of heaven in which there is a heavenly palace run by eunuchs "resplendent as lightning."[27] Even more explicit is a coincidence of angels and eunuchs in the vita of St. Lazaros on Mount Galesion. This vita includes a vision of Christ with a eunuch on each side. The one on his right appears to have a ruddy complexion; the one on his left has darker hair and a face the color of ripe wheat. The *hegoumenos* (director) of the saint's monastery interprets the dream to mean that the eunuchs are angels. In another part of the vita we find a vision in which a mounted eunuch rides into the courtyard of the monastery and, when asked where he has come from and why he has come, says that he has come from the emperor and, had he not come on time, St. Lazaros would be dead.[28] Similar overlaps between angels and eunuchs are found in the Vita of St. Niphon of Constantiana.[29]

The most dramatic example of the angel/eunuch parallel comes from the Vita of St. Andrew the Fool. In that passage, four eunuchs minister to a fifteen-year-old martyr named Theodore:

> After he had spent a few days in prison together with all the others who had been confined on this occasion, that apostate and lawless emperor was killed in the war and the revered boy was released together with all the other prisoners. When he came home, his friends, comrades, and relatives together with his parents, kissing his wounds, questioned him and said, "What did you feel, Sir Theodore, when you hung on the stake and your holy flesh was torn by the claws?" He refused to tell, but at last yielded to their entreaties, giving them the following account: "At first when I was hung on the stake and they began to touch me I had to force myself, and to encourage myself. I said, 'Poor Theodore, be courageous and endure this bitter suffering, for if you fail, you will be thrown into the eternal fire!' As I said this I looked up, and behold, there were four eunuchs with beautiful faces, like roses, and one of them held a basin, as it were, which was white and very bright, through its appearance blinding the vision of a human being and throwing him into ecstasy, while another held a golden flask filled with divine oil which was like rose water, the other two held linen cloths, white as snow and folded into four, on their outstretched hands. When they were beside me, one of them said to the one holding the shining basin, 'Bring it here!' And when he had brought it, he said to the one holding the golden flask, 'Pour here!' As he poured, the oil came out and struck my eyes like a flash of lightning, spreading through my entrails to all my limbs, so that the sweet smell of the oil conquered and overcame the terrible pains inflicted on me by the torture. One of the two holding cloths came forward, soaked his cloth in the basin and put it over my face, holding it there for a long while, so that, as I said, from this most sweet pleasure I was made to forget my pain. When he removed it the other stood ready to put his cloth over my face, and so they continued until my tormentors stopped and took me down from the stake. The moment this happened they departed from me at once. De-

> prived of this most sweet pleasure I felt very sad. I wanted my torments to continue, for God assures us that this matter is such that the human mind cannot imagine anything similar. It is only the beginning of the sufferings and the sight that contain the testing; the full force of the tortures applied is not felt thanks to the power of the grace of God."[30]

Not only do the eunuchs in this story perform in a manner reminiscent of angels, but the way in which they minister to the tortured Theodore reflects the caregiving role that was part of their gender construct.[31]

Angelic Parallels and Perceptions of Identity and Gender

In the minds of those who told these tales and of those who wrote them down, eunuchs and angels shared a number of attributes. Both are depicted doing similar jobs in the heavenly and earthly courts. Each of these courts is run by an absolute ruler who is assisted by a specialized corps organized in an elaborate hierarchy.[32] Both eunuchs and angels serve the personal, private needs of the rulers of their respective courts. Eunuchs serve as guardians of their masters; and angels, as guardians of the souls of men. Both are especially called to service during the dangerous hours of the night.[33]

Modern society tends to devalue the role of the personal body servant. Thus it is important to emphasize that as both the emperor and God, his celestial analogue, became increasingly distant from ordinary men and as the emperor's person enjoyed increased sanctity, the nature of the individuals who dealt with him in a private, personal way became more important. They took part in the private, closely guarded community that was the center of imperial power, both earthly and heavenly. As the emperor's servants they became extensions or surrogates of the imperial person, gaining in the process some of the emperor's worldly might. They shared the emperor's sacred space as well and were thus extensions of his spiritual power.[34] They had access to the imperial person, his feeding and bodily needs, and the sacred regalia. As eunuchs were increasingly associated with the court as a separate, private world, they gained power, and their liminal functions became increasingly important.

The imagery that associates eunuchs with angels extends to their angelic function as intermediaries between heaven and earth and to such angelic functionaries as majordomos, doorkeepers, and singers in the court of heaven. Angels report events on earth to God and carry messages back and forth. They guard tombs, holy sites, and other special places.[35] Angels appear before men and women, acting as God's messengers to earth.

Our sources often present angels as guardians of tombs. While I have found no evidence of eunuchs acting formally as tomb guards in Byzantium, this is a function that they acquire in Islamic societies.[36] There is, however, ample evidence that Byzantine eunuchs were regularly involved in the ceremonials surrounding death, preparation of bodies, and burials.[37] Finally, there is scattered, though convincing, evidence that eunuchs, like angels, served as singers both in the church and in the court.[38]

Conceptual Similarities between Angels and Eunuchs

The complex conceptual parallels that Byzantine culture came to perceive between angels and eunuchs were reinforced by some of its other assumptions about identity, gender, and personality. In this context it is important to remember some of the patterns outlined earlier in this study. Byzantine culture, like classical Greek culture, equated certain physical attributes with sexual maturity. Both the physical appearance of sexually mature men and the definition of maturation included an elaborate constellation of things that went well beyond the development of sexual organs and secondary sexual characteristics. Sexually mature men were assumed to exhibit particular patterns of behavior, speech, and carriage that were specific and culturally defined.[39]

Thus, eunuchs and angels not only shared gender characteristics, but both were clearly different from the sexually mature or whole man of the time. When angels appear in Byzantine art and literary sources, they are presented as young or prepubescent boys. They are beardless, with fair complexions and rosy cheeks. They are beautiful in the way that boys were perceived to be beautiful in Greek society before their features and complexions were altered by puberty. In Byzantine culture, these traditions set the stage for eunuchs as earthly representatives of angels.

While confusion between angels and eunuchs was almost a commonplace in Byzantine sources, and especially in hagiographical sources, the vita of St. Niphon of Constantiana provides an especially rich example.[40] Although Niphon was bishop of Constantiana in Egypt, the vita is set in Constantinople.

> As we were returning from prayer we arrived at a residence where prostitutes lived. There St. Niphon saw a certain man who seemed to be a eunuch standing outside of the residence. The supposed eunuch appeared to be very dejected, he held his face in his hands and wept uncontrollably, gazed up into heaven, and groaned. Then he extended his hands to heaven and groaned again, grabbed his jaw and stood there desperately and began to groan again with downcast eyes.

> The just man [St. Niphon], beholding how the supposed eunuch mourned and how he could not set his grief aside, went to him and said, "Tell me, what event has caused you such bitter tears? What habit makes you cry out so bitterly and stand with downcast eyes, not withdrawing from this inn? Tell me, I appeal to you. I wish to know why you mourn so." In answer to St. Niphon the eunuch said, "Honored Niphon, I am an angel of God. All the Christians from the time of their baptism are assigned an angel to guard their lives. I have been sent, like the rest, to guard a certain man. It is his lawlessness that distresses me, and now he is in that inn you see, lawlessly lying with a certain prostitute. Seeing this sin, how can I not lament the image of God that has fallen to such darkness?" The blessed saint said, "Why didn't you instruct him to escape the darkness of such a sin? The angel replied, "I have no place to approach him, for since he began committing this sin, he is a servant of the demons, and I have no authority over him."

The dialogue continues as the saint asks the angel why he doesn't have the power to save this man. The angel replies that God created man to have free will and allowed him freedom to choose the road of his liking. The angel disappears back into heaven.[41] One of the interesting angel/eunuch overlaps is coded into the inability of the angel to enter a place [the brothel] controlled by demons. This exemplifies the kind of space wherein eunuchs sometimes replace angels.

In another section of the same vita the saint, while traveling, meets a man who is sitting down and eating bread with his wife and children. Then the saint sees certain people, equal in number to the family members, people whom he takes to be eunuchs, with handsome faces and brilliant clothing, standing around among those who are eating bread. God then shows him that these are angels who "are present at the dinner table and flee if slander or evil speech takes place."[42]

St. Niphon also tells his disciples a story about the blessed Sozomenos who did a good deed for a poor man. Later Sozomenos had a vision in which a eunuch came to him and led him to the gates of heaven, where Christ rewarded him. Yet neither Sozomenos nor the eunuch, because they were living mortals, could actually enter heaven.[43] Angels and eunuchs were readily interchangeable in many contexts, but eunuchs faced some limitations that were not imposed upon angels.

Angels thus possessed certain qualities that set them apart as a special category distinct from human beings. They brought messages from God, had distinctive appearances that emanated supernatural power, wore distinctive clothing, and guarded humans against their own weaknesses. As the gender construct for eunuchs evolved, it picked up many of these same qualities.

As noted earlier, by the tenth century, probably because of the increasing prestige of the celibate life, the perception of eunuchs as a third gender distinct from men and women had begun to change. Eunuchs were more likely to be referred to as male, but males of a different, separate gender. As we have seen, they were acculturated into gendered patterns of behavior quite distinct from those of sexually active, aristocratic men, yet they were still considered to be a type of man. At the same time, they were considered to resemble angels, something that was possible because eunuchs were not contaminated by sexuality, nor were they tied to the world by attachments involving family life and its complex expectations. Thus they were closer to the "angelic life," the life of asexual purity that was granted to angels, aspired to by monastics, and promised to all who achieve admission to heaven. They shared the "perfect service" of the imagined angelic host.

Finally, eunuchs, like angels, were perceived to exist outside of space and time. This perception is not as clearly documented as some of the other characteristics attributed to eunuchs and involves an implicit rather than an articulated assumption. One modern historian raises this suggestion in connection with some of the writings of the eleventh-century courtier and historian, Michael Psellos. At one point Psellos discusses why angels are so frequently pictured as carrying spheres:

> [T]he sphere shows quickness. It can arrive, independent of time and in less than an instant wherever it wishes. It is ἀχρόνως, outside of time. In contrast, our bodies are governed by time and move slowly and heavily, groaning with the weight of the earthly tents we live in and inclined downward.[44]

Mango questions Psellos's interpretation of the globe and also that of Symeon of Thessalonica, who claimed that it represented the sanctification of the Holy Spirit and that it was a symbol of the knowledge of God, knowledge that had no beginning or end. Mango argues quite convincingly that the globe represents imperial authority as early as the sixth century.[45] For our purposes the actual meaning of the globe is not as important as what Michael Psellos and Symeon of Thessalonica thought it meant: the angel's life outside of earthly time, the knowledge of God that existed beyond earthly time. Some of the same characteristics seemed to adhere to eunuchs, since they did not age in the normal way and were not caught up in a normal family-based life cycle. And as Marmon has shown, the same logic applied to eunuchs in late medieval Islam.[46]

Eunuchs and the Darker Side of the Spiritual World

In a culture that, despite the efforts of the church, acknowledged in various ways the existence of the demonic powers and magical traditions of the pre-Christian

Mediterranean, the spiritual aura associated with eunuchs extended to more than just an angelic strain. The distinctiveness of eunuchs was also expressed in terms derived in part from the transitory gendered ambiguity of prepubescent boys, which contrasted with the nature of the sexuality attributed to women. Thus it is not surprising that some of our sources hint that one rationale for castrating young boys was to assure that they would retain the physical and spiritual qualities of prepubescence. This is difficult to prove, since the reasons for castration are rarely addressed directly in our sources. As we have seen, however, the medical literature of the era makes it clear that castration preserved, or at least altered, a eunuch's physiological makeup in ways that were seen as characteristic of prepubescence.

The association between eunuchs and prepubescent boys probably relates to a long tradition that predates Christianity, one in which angels and prepubescent boys share magical properties. This is best seen in the Greek magical papyri in which, to cite but one example, a prepubescent boy acts as an intermediary for a magician who has cast a spell in order to summon an angel to act on his behalf.[47] The boy guarding the tools in the story about the building of Hagia Sophia referred to above clearly is playing a similar role, since he acts as an intermediary between St. Michael and the emperor. His presence in the narrative allows the emperor to outwit St. Michael and trap the angel into becoming the permanent guardian for Hagia Sophia. Since eunuchs were perceived to share so many attributes with both angels and boys, it is hard to avoid the inference that eunuchs were also assumed to have access to magical properties.[48]

Is this what Theophylaktos of Ohrid is hinting at when he says that "foolish men say that eunuchs, like monks, are ill-omened?" Authors of Late Antiquity, like Lucian, who was much read and admired in the Byzantine world, suggest that eunuchs are spiritually polluting and should be kept away from holy places. "It is an ill-omened sight," he says, "to meet a eunuch in the morning."[49] This same kind of imagery spews from the pen of St. Basil of Caesarea when he says that eunuchs are unclean creatures, like lizards and toads, accursed, with twisted feet.[50]

Pejorative language, which attributes negative preternatural power to eunuchs, crystallizes around the much-reviled eunuch Eutropius who died in 399. Claudian says that Eutropius frightened people because he was ill-omened. Claudian compares him with a corpse or an unholy ghost.[51] Eunapios of Sardis compares Eutropius with the Gorgon's head. It looks at you just once, and you are finished.[52] Eunapios also develops an elaborate snake image that he applies to Eutropius: he hisses and leaves a snake's trail behind him; he winds and coils and destroys men in his coils. In the Late Antique Mediterranean this kind of image of the snake is regularly associated with women, sexuality, changeability, and autochthonous cults associated with fertility. In the earlier classical tradition one immediately thinks of Tiresias who, upon striking copulating snakes, was changed from a man into a woman. In Byzantine hagiographical literature, snakes often represent demonic forces, especially sexual ones.

Another cluster of negative images about eunuchs and the preternatural world cluster around the idea that eunuchs are poisoners. In the fourth century Ammianus Marcellinus carries this a step further and tells us that there is a poisonous vent at Hierapolis that produces fumes that kill every living thing, except eunuchs. He also tells us that in A.D. 364 a chariot driver was convicted of apprenticing his son, who was just entering puberty, to a mixer of poisons so that he could be instructed in secret practices forbidden by law.[53] Can we assume from this that the special qualities of prepubescent boys and eunuchs, those same qualities that gave them access to the preternatural world of angels, also facilitated their entry into this mysterious world of secret chemical mixtures and perhaps even of other kinds of magical practices?

While rhetorical flourishes and imagery that paint eunuchs as participating in the evil arts can be found in our Late Antique sources, they almost completely disappear after the fifth century. In the eleventh century the author of the continuation of Skylitzes attacks the eunuch Nikephoritzes by saying that he is "on the left" (ἐπεὶ σκαιὸς). In this context it means that he is associated with the ill-omened side of things. He goes on to say that Nikephoritzes drew the emperor into his magic working.[54] But references like these are few and far between by the later Byzantine period, bringing us full circle back to Theophylaktos's remark about foolish men who say that eunuchs and monks are ill-omened.

None of our authors offer an explanation for this association between eunuchs and the preternatural world of negative spiritual forces. Psellos and Theophylaktos scoff at the idea and call it foolishness. Yet, in the Vita of St. Andrew the Fool, we find a eunuch who is the instrument of the Devil and who competes with a eunuch/angel for the soul of a wicked monk.[55] Perhaps the answer lies in the Pseudo-Psellos *De daemonibus,* which says that the most characteristic thing about demons is their changeable nature. They can make appearances as men, women, or animals even though they are really none of the above. If the changeable nature, both physical and psychological, of eunuchs reminded men of angels, then perhaps it also reminded them of demons.[56]

Eunuchs and the Limitations of Angels

While eunuchs and angels performed many of the same tasks, their domains did not overlap completely. As we have seen, the eunuch, while serving as a spiritual guide on the path to heaven, could not actually enter heaven. At the same time, eunuchs carried out tasks, sometimes at God's behest, that were outside the assumed jurisdiction of angels. This is illustrated in another text from the *Patria*. Again, the narrative involves the miraculous appearance of a figure who is unambiguously a eunuch, a figure who facilitates a miraculous event important to God.[57]

In the legend, the emperor Justinian has continued work on his great church, but he is running out of money. One morning as he is inspecting the work site, a eunuch appears and tells the emperor that if on the next day he will send out a group of his noblemen, he (the eunuch) will bring out as much gold as the emperor needs. The next morning all is ready. The group leaves the city through the Golden Gate, entering a suburban neighborhood. There they stop at a magnificent palace. It is "marvelously made" (παλάτια κτιστὰ θαυμαστά), a phrase that, in this context, conveys the sense of not having been made by human hands. The eunuch and his crew climb a magnificent staircase, and the eunuch opens a door with a golden key. Inside is a room, its floor covered with golden coins. The eunuch shovels them up with a winnowing shovel, the men load the gold on the pack animals, and they all return to the emperor.

The next day the emperor speculates about returning to the house for another load, but the eunuch cannot be found. The crew, sent to what they believe to be the same location, finds only an empty plot of ground. Here we clearly have a eunuch acting in a "magical" or miraculous capacity, in a setting in which we would expect to find an angel. Perhaps he was an angel, yet our text consistently identifies him as a eunuch. Our anonymous author has no trouble with a disappearing eunuch and a disappearing mansion that was not made by human hands. This eunuch, while not an angel, has moved a significant distance into that liminal world that lies between the worldly and spiritual courts.

A similar story can be found in Skylitzes.[58] The context is Michael the Paphlagonian's controversial marriage to Zoe. A certain cleric on the bishop's staff had a dream in which he saw a eunuch with a fiery countenance (ἐξαστράπτοντα τὴν μορφήν) wearing a white robe (εὐνοῦχόν τινα λευχείμονα). The eunuch set three sacks down in front of the cleric and ordered them to be opened and emptied. From the first rushed a serpent, a viper, and a scorpion; from the second, toads, adders, lizards, bees, and other venomous creatures. From the third came beetles, gnats, wasps, and other stinging animals. When the cleric had been struck dumb by this sight, the splendid man, the eunuch (ὁ δὲ φαιδρὸς ἐκεῖνος), approached him and said, "These things will happen to you because you violated God's law and facilitated the infamous deed against Romanos and his wife."[59] While this is obviously a polemical critique of clerical support for the empress Zoe's dynastic marriages, it is of interest here because of the nature of the messenger.

Why a eunuch instead of an angel? In the two preceding examples we see that eunuchs are magical, operating on behalf of spiritual objectives, but in areas that involve profane, earthly mysteries that, at some level, were considered inappropriate for direct angelic intervention. In these two cases, after all, eunuchs act in miracles that involve money and sexual transgression. This is clearly the case in the incident with the lizards and snakes. Kazhdan suggests that in the similar appearance of lizards and snakes in the Vita of St. Andrew the Fool the creatures are connected with sexual sin. This motif is seen often in hagiographical sources, and it is almost certainly connected with sexual transgression.[60] Nor is the role of the miraculous eunuch surprising in the story of finding the money for Hagia Sophia, since eunuchs frequently handled financial matters at the court. They served as accountants and bookkeepers and regularly informed the emperor about the availability of funds. Perhaps a "magical" infusion of money orchestrated by a disappearing eunuch was an appropriate way for the emperor to explain away his financial embarrassment. An angel would not have been nearly as appropriate.

Other kinds of sexual misconduct and sexually related medical problems were similarly better left to eunuchs. The curing of the emperor Justinian's genital abscesses (see chapter 4), while it involved a miracle of sorts, was arranged by a eunuch rather than by an angel.[61] Once again we see a eunuch conveying divinely inspired vital information and presented as an angel-like being. Like the eunuch with the three sacks of vermin, he clearly has been sent to bring a message to the powerful of the material world. Eunuch messengers, in this context, are simply fulfilling some of their many roles, those of organizing sexual liaisons and marriages and of arranging for the material well-being of the emperor. The story also provides an instructive contrast to that of the guardian angel who could not enter a brothel because of its identification with demonic forces and sexuality.

Thus eunuchs could be miraculous messengers who were analogous to angels but were more appropriate when the message dealt with worldly topics. They, too, could mediate the flow of information between heaven and earth but were chosen when the information was too inherently polluting for divine beings to handle. Eunuchs regularly performed functions that were located on the worldly side of the boundary between the mundane and the spiritual—preparing the dead, guarding sacred space, seeing the future, serving as physicians and other kinds of healers,[62] and living in proximity to persons with "special" powers.

Another illustration, drawn from the Vita of St. Euphrosyna the Younger,[63] makes this point. The emperor Leo VI (r. 886–911) and the empress Zoe have visited Euphrosyna, begging her to pray that they might have a male heir. She

FIGURE 7

The Archangel Gabriel as the angel of the Annunciation. Angels and eunuchs both carry messages. They were also believed to share physical attributes. Mosaic, ca. 1100, Daphni. In Anthony Cutler and Jean-Michel Spieser, *Byzance médiéval, 700–1204* (Paris: Gallimard, 1996), p. 152, fig. 203.

does so with great diligence. After a few days of continuous prayer she finally dozes off and has a dream. In her dream an angel "with a radiant appearance" (ἀστράπτων μεν τὴν μορφήν), "wearing a distinguished robe that shone as if radiant and transparent," visits her and tells her that her prayers will be answered. The empress will bear a male child (see fig. 7).

Euphrosyna then arises and summons Nicholas the monk, a eunuch who tends to her personal needs. She writes a note to the emperor and entrusts its delivery to Nicholas. He, with a "radiant face" (φαιδρῷ τῷ προσώπῳ), delivers it to the emperor. Here the eunuch/monk fulfills the liminal function served by the prepubescent boy in the first story, conveying miraculous information between the saint and the emperor.

Conclusion

The similarity in descriptive language associated with these angels and eunuchs forcefully underscores the connections and overlap between the two in the minds of our Byzantine authors. In the first of the stories discussed in this chapter St. Michael the Archangel, who is mistaken for a eunuch, has a brilliant garment, a shining face, and a strange appearance. The depiction exactly follows Biblical angelic convention. The eunuch who appears and miraculously provides Justinian with the gold he needs for Hagia Sophia wears a white robe, a common Biblical convention for angels. The eunuch with the three sacks in the passage from Skylitzes wears a white robe and his face shines. The angel in the passage from the Vita of St. Euphrosyna has a shining form and a splendid robe, while the eunuch's face shines with joy.

In chapter 1, we examined the ways in which the language used in our sources dealt with and adapted to eunuchs as a distinct gender category. That language, as well as narrative structure, suggests that eunuchs, like angels, were considered capable of operating in the supernatural realm that lies between heaven and earth. Both eunuchs and angels were perceived as "changeable," and eunuchs were characterized as ambiguous beings whose sexual indeterminacy led to psychological instability. Thus it was easy for Byzantine authors to portray them in very diverse roles. The terminology used was similar to that applied to magicians and demons, who changed their demeanor as did angels. Angels, after all, had great ability to change their physical appearance, presenting themselves on earth as soldiers, horsemen, animals, and beautiful youths.[64] Even when they appeared in the guise of human beings, angels transcended conventional human appearance. This quality is captured in the description of St. Michael.[65]

Thus both angels and eunuchs shared a strong quality of "otherness" for which the Greek language lacked descriptive adjectives that applied directly. Both also shared a kind of third-gender quality that allowed them to transcend the differences between the worlds of earthly materialism and heavenly spirituality.

This linguistic indirection was also characteristic of attempts to describe God and Christ. It comes as no surprise that the same linguistic solution would be applied to angels, but the fact that it was also used for eunuchs reinforces the proposal that eunuchs were believed to be (or suspected of being) capable of operating in similar divine ways. "Eunuch" was a constructed category that was nevertheless defined clearly enough to achieve accommodation from a language that lacked a vocabulary to express its nature directly.

Finally, both eunuchs and angels were, in a sense, created beings. Our sources go to great lengths to assure us that angels were created by God to serve Him.[66] They were not preexisting spirit beings. Likewise, one can suggest that eunuchs, through castration and acculturation, are "created" beings, creatures "beyond nature," created by society to serve the imperial and ecclesiastical courts and provide access to the dangerous and unknown realms between earth and heaven.[67]

CHAPTER 8

Eunuchs at the Palace: Gendered Space and Confirmation of the Imperial Numen

Without any doubt the most prominent way in which eunuchs appear as historical protagonists is through their role in the organization and functioning of the imperial palace. This is the role of eunuchs that has been most prominent in the histories, chronicles, and political narratives that have long dominated the presentation of Byzantine history. Byzantine historians have long puzzled over the powerful position of the eunuchate in ninth- through eleventh-century Byzantium.

By the ninth century eunuchs controlled the most important functions in the imperial court and household, the reference point for most social and political life in Byzantium. This chapter explores a tentative model that may help to explain both the powerful role that eunuchs played at the Byzantine court and some of the limitations that were placed on their role in society. We will explore these questions through a discussion of the ceremonial roles set out for eunuchs in the *De ceremoniis* of Constantine Porphyrogennetos[1] and in the *Kletorologion* of Philotheos.[2]

It is important to recognize that the *De ceremoniis* is a composite document, brought together by an emperor with marked antiquarian tendencies. It contains information on ceremonies that may well span the fifth through the tenth centuries, and thus some of the ceremonies described were probably anachronistic even in Constantine Porphyrogennitos's day (r. 913–959). The examples presented here, however, are securely datable to the ninth and tenth centuries.

In *Eunuchs and Sacred Boundaries in Islamic Society,* Shaun Marmon explores the traits attributed to the eunuchs who served as guardians for Muhammad's tomb. She suggests that eunuchs existed outside of time and space as we conceive these concepts and that, because eunuchs were castrated, they could operate in realms that were denied to whole men.[3] In constructing her model, Marmon suggests that Muhammad's tomb was thought to exist outside of worldly, mundane space. It was a house in which Muhammad continued to "live," though in another time frame.[4] Eunuchs were therefore appropriate guards for Muhammad's tomb because they, too, lived outside of time.[5] I would suggest that Marmon's model is valid for cultures that predate Islam and that a parallel tradition was operating in the Byzantine world up until the time of the Komnenoi. In fact, if we could reach more clearly into the shadows of the Sassanian Persian world, I suspect that we would find the origin for these beliefs there.

In Byzantium this eastern Mediterranean conjunction of space, time, and gender intersected in the gendering of space. Michel Foucault, in his studies of the classical Greek cultural tradition, suggests that the Greek tradition included a spatial distinction between the enclosed, feminine world of women and household functions and the open, masculine world of the forum and palaestra.[6]

Christianity then added another element to the mix. While presbyters in the Eastern Church were not required to be celibate, early Christianity developed as a set of institutions within which asceticism and denial of sexuality were crucial components of true sanctity. At the same time, the church as an institution aspired to mediate between ordinary mortals and the spiritual realms that housed God and the heavenly court.

During the early Byzantine period, a powerful imperial tradition emerged at Constantinople in which the emperor and his court were also a focal point for power and spiritual forces in society.[7] In a Christian culture the emperor was not divine, but he nevertheless possessed a numen or special form of divinity that placed him in a realm separate from that of ordinary humans. This quality, as well as needs of practical politics, defined the imperial household as a distinctive space that could not be entered without appropriate ritual and mediation.

Out of this emerged a capital city, Constantinople, that was spatially divided into three realms: the world of the church, centered on the great church of Hagia Sophia and controlled by the patriarch of Constantinople and his staff, the world of the imperial palace controlled by the emperor and his staff of eunuchs, and the world of the city, controlled by the city *eparch*.[8]

By the Byzantine period, the "box" that was the Greek household controlled by women had become, in the case of the imperial family, the imperial palace under the control of eunuchs. As we have seen, the eunuchs, and especially those employed in the palace, were men gendered into a distinct, perhaps new, gender configuration that combined some of the attributes of both men and women. Eunuchs were also thought to have preternatural properties appropriate to individuals who had, because of their castration, concentrated their powers within their own bodies rather than dissipating them through sexuality.

Within the palace complex the presence of the empress gave rise to a women's area or household parallel, if subordinate, to that of the emperor.[9] By the middle period of the empire, the empress maintained a separate formal life and presided over a ceremonial hierarchy of the wives of important men at court. The most prominent of these women held the position of *zoste patrikia,* the one female title that appears in the description of the official hierarchy around the emperor.[10] The empress was also the head of the "women's quarters." This is a somewhat misleading phrase meant to evoke the normally secluded women's portion of the Greek household. Whether the empress shared the emperor's own quarters or resided in the women's area, she headed that portion of the imperial household.

Details are scarce, but it seems clear that the empress ran this domain with a combination of eunuchs and female servants and that the empress's eunuchs were organized in a hierarchy similar to that of the emperor's *cubiculum* (see fig. 8). The one subtle distinction that has been suggested is that the gender barriers between male and female in Greek culture encouraged close personal bonds between the empress and her staff of eunuchs. Those gender differences made it difficult for an empress to exercise effective authority in the male dominated world of political and military affairs. Consequently, when empresses were in a position to exercise actual power (e.g., Irene, Zoe, Euphrosyne, Theodora), they relied heavily on eunuch confidants from within the empress's entourage. One can interpret this as relying on ineffectual, effeminate agents who represented decadent orientalizing influences or as relying on a corps of dedicated, educated, and experienced administrators. Obviously both characterizations are couched in extreme terms, but the situation demonstrates that the gender traits of eunuchs facilitated the exercise of power by certain empresses. The role of eunuchs as perfect servants, their specialized training, and the capacity to transcend conventional social boundaries all contributed to the complexity of female rule.

While this helps to explain the interaction between emperor, empress, and power, it was an internal component of the larger structure of symbols and ceremonial through which the emperor and imperial authority were organized and presented to the world outside the palace. Not all servants who worked in the imperial palace were necessarily eunuchs, but those who controlled access both to the imperial palaces and to ancillary spaces used temporarily by the emperor

❧ FIGURE 8
The empress Theodora and her court. This mosaic, from the mid-sixth century, includes Theodora's chief eunuch, who is seen holding back the curtain over the door. He is beardless and wearing a distinctive robe that marks his office. The liminal function of eunuchs is often on display in this manner. Mosaic, sixth century, San Vitale, Ravenna. In André Grabar, *L'Age d'or de Justinien: De la mort de Théodose à l'Islam* (Paris: Gallimard, 1966), pp. 161–62, fig. 172.

were required to be castrated men and held particular offices reserved for them alone. In contrast, the city *eparch,* who controlled the open spaces of the city, its markets, commerce, and judiciary, was required to be a "bearded man." He was, after all, the "father" of the city. Only two other imperial offices, that of *domestikos,* or head of the guard, and that of *quaestor,* a kind of judge, were reserved for bearded men.[11] It is clear that in the Byzantine world at least some offices and the spaces in which they functioned were "gendered."

The Imperial Offices Reserved for Eunuchs

When we turn to the imperial palace, or, more properly, to the spaces charged with imperial numen, we discover that it is impossible to talk about the emperor, his household, or his administration without talking about eunuchs. This is a constant theme as we study the boundaries and crossovers in the *De ceremoniis.* Eunuchs were not simply court functionaries but gendered beings integral to the coherence of imperial authority. This section explores specific contexts and roles assigned to eunuchs in tenth-century court ceremonial as revealed by a close reading of this text. To provide a necessary perspective on this theme, I also suggest a tentative interpretation of the role of the city eparch and the ways in which he and the urban space associated with him constituted part of a larger context for our depiction of the palace and its eunuchs.

Much of our information about the roles of eunuchs in the imperial administration comes from *taktika* (s. *taktikon*), written lists of precedence. Nicholas Oikonomidès has edited and translated five of these *taktika* from the ninth and tenth centuries. His work outlines clearly the historical difficulty in dealing with Byzantine titles and offices and the distinction between them.[12]

Titles generally were honorary and were often purchased. Their holders may or may not have directly fulfilled the court function nominally associated with the title. Offices, however, were appointive and generally reflected actual duties performed by their holders. Some titles and offices were reserved only for eunuchs, while a few were reserved exclusively for bearded men. Since the precise list of offices reserved to eunuchs changed from time to time, any detailed description will probably seem inconsistent with one *taktikon* or another. Furthermore, many titles were open to both eunuchs and bearded men. The lists of both titles and offices changed over time. Thus they vary between the *taktika* discussed by Oikonomidès.[13]

The following is a summary of the titles reserved to eunuchs according to the *Kletorologion* of Philotheos, a *taktikon* written in 899. They are arranged in ascending order of prestige. The lowest class of eunuch titles were held by the holders of the washing bowl, the *nipsistiarioi.* These eunuchs held the bowl when the emperor ceremonially washed his hands, and, at banquets, they ceremonially purified the emperor's food with drops of water. Next came the *koubikoularioi,* who served the emperor in his private quarters and attended him on ceremonial occasions. When the emperor was on campaign they preceded him carrying the Cross. After about the eighth century many eunuchs bought the title of *koubikoularios* but did not actually fulfill the duties of the office. The third title was that of *spatharokoubikoularioi* (*koubikoularioi* armed with swords). Their insignia was a sword that was awarded from the emperor's own hand. These eunuchs escorted the emperor on horseback on ceremonial occasions and had the right to be armed in the emperor's presence. The next title was that of *ostiarios,* a term that originally meant doorkeeper. The *ostiarios* ritually introduced individuals to the emperor as a part of the imperial ceremonial. The badge of office of the *ostiarios* was a jeweled staff given from the emperor's own hand. Next came the *primikerios,* literally the first eunuch within a given category of eunuch servants. Above him in rank was the *protospatharios* or commander of the eunuch *spatharioi* or spear-carriers. His insignia was a gold collar trimmed with pearls and was given by the emperor's own hand.

The most important eunuchs were the *praepositoi.*[14] The *praepositos* was the chief of the corps of eunuch household servants. He was responsible for financial, administrative, and ceremonial matters. The importance of this office is suggested by the fact that the *praepositos* carried the same insignia (ivory tablets, but not inscribed) as a *patrikios* (patrician) and received them directly from the emperor's hand. We will see that in the *De ceremoniis* the *praepositos* often acted as the eyes and voice of the emperor and provided liaison between the emperor and the *epi tes katastaseos* (master of ceremonies), who played a role in coordinating court ceremonial.[15] Finally, both eunuchs and bearded men could hold the title of *patrikios* (patrician). The insignia for this high office was inscribed ivory tablets received from the emperor's own hand. The eunuch patricians took precedence over bearded patricians.

There were also clearly functional offices reserved to eunuchs. Unlike titles, which might simply be honorary, officeholders fulfilled appointed duties connected with their offices. These included, in ascending order, the *papiai* of the lesser palaces and the *deuteroi* of the Daphne and Magnaura Palaces.[16] The *papias* and his assistants functioned as guardians of the doorway and thus were eunuchs who controlled access to imperial space. This meant that they controlled the division between the emperor's sacred space and the city outside the palace doors. The *papias* was in charge of the ceremonial for opening and closing the palace and he censed the emperor and carried the Cross in certain religious festivals. The *papias* supervised a corps of servants who worked in various parts of the palace, including bath attendants, lamplighters, fire tenders, clock tenders, and those who hit the great gong. The *deuteros* was responsible for the imperial furniture and clothing and supervised those who cared for the ceremonial clothing, the dressers, the guardians of the imperial insignia, and those who prepared the apparel for new dignitaries. He kept the key to the oratory of St. Theodore, where the most important imperial regalia and insignia were stored.[17]

The next in importance was the cupbearer (ὁ πιγκέρνης). The emperor and the empress each had a eunuch who was responsible for provisioning and serving beverages. The cupbearer accompanied the emperor when he left the palace and was responsible for the emperor's own special cup.

Above the cupbearers in this hierarchy we find the *deuteros* and *papias* of the Great Palace, then the masters of the empress's and emperor's tables (ἐπὶ τῆς τραπέζης). The master of the table organized imperial banquets and assisted the *atriklines* (a bearded official who was a kind of protocol officer) in drawing up invitations and arranging the seating at banquets. The master of the emperor's table greeted guests, invited them to take off their outer garments, seated them at the table, orchestrated the entertainment, and generally kept order. On campaign he marched at the emperor's side and saw to the provisioning of the imperial table and to the emperor's comfort.

Next in importance is the first dresser, the *protovestiarios.* He was in charge of the imperial wardrobe, which included the emperor's apparel and also his table service, lamps, clocks, shoes, swords, the uniforms for his servants, pharmaceutical products, and a large amount of silver. The *protovestiarios* supervised the emperor's dressers, slept in the imperial chamber, carried the holy icons of Christ in religious processions, signaled the emperor's presence at ceremonies, gave the signal for the opening of the curtain that hid the emperor from view, and received the imperial vestments that the emperor was to wear. He was the only person allowed to touch the imperial vestments without permission. His sign of office was a golden baton.

The most important eunuch official became the *parakoimomenos* (παρακοιμώμενος), "one who sleeps beside the bed." The lesser bedchamber attendants under his supervision were called the *koitonitai* (κοιτωνίται). In the eighth century these terms of office seem to have replaced the terms *koubikoularios* and *praepositus sacri cubiculi,* yet the latter terms seem to have been retained and used for titles reserved to eunuchs. The duties of the *praepositos* became more ceremonial, while the duties of the *parakoimomenos* centered on actually guarding and personally serving the emperor.[18]

It is clear that the eunuchs protected the physical space that surrounded the emperor (see fig. 9). Although I am reluctant to label this surrounding area "sacred space,"[19] it bears a strong resemblance to the "sacred space" that Marmon perceives as surrounding the tomb of Muhammad. As we will see, it is certainly true that the emperor's numen was protected from physical intrusion, that a kind of invisible wall was placed around his person on ceremonial occasions, and that eunuchs maintained this ritual barrier.

Some of this specially charged personal space was permanent and immovable. This is certainly the case with regard to the space within the *cubiculum,* the emperor's personal quarters in the imperial palace. It was also the case for the spaces within the smaller *cubiculi,* which were scattered about Constantinople and which served as the emperor's temporary personal quarters when he visited churches and other large buildings.[20] Whichever *cubiculum* was in use on a given occasion, it was controlled by eunuchs in their capacity as ritual personal servants. It also was the place where the emperor's crown was routinely put on and removed from his head. As we will see, this was one of the rituals surrounding the emperor that was definitely gendered.

❧ FIGURE 9

The emperor Nikephoros III Botaneiates and his courtiers. The two beardless officials to the left of the emperor are eunuch officials of the court. According to Henry Maguire, they hold high posts because they are in the favored position at the ruler's right hand. Nearest the throne stands a beardless eunuch in a splendid white silk robe decorated with medallions containing lions woven in red and gold. He is designated *protoproedros* and *protovestiarios*. Next to him, in the red and gold cloak over a blue tunic, is another beardless eunuch. He is identified as *proedros* and *epi tou kanikleiou*, indicating that he is the emperor's private secretary. The inscription reads, "You hold the throne, which shines like the morning star, wreathed above with all virtue. Beside you stands the pinnacle of those who are most loyal to you, chosen men, moreover noble in their soul." Miniature on parchment, Paris, BN, Ms Coislin 79, fol. 2r Inscription translated by Harry Macquire. In Helen C. Evans and William D. Wixom, eds., *The Glory of Byzantium: Art and Culture of the Middle Byzantine Era, A.D. 843–1262* (New York: Metropolitan Museum/Harry Abrams, 1997), p. 208, fig. 143.

The personal space around the emperor was also "portable" and could be established in temporary locations when the emperor was in transit. Such was the case when the emperor left the palace in a formal procession. On these occasions, the enclosed world of the palace was extended out into the open world of the city like a river flowing out of the palace into the desert. The individuals who rode closest to the emperor, both defining and guarding his ritually charged space, were either eunuch servants or eunuch guards. Thus the emperor was always escorted by the *praepositus sacri cubiculi,* the eunuch *koubikoularioi,* and the *protospatharioi,*[21] all of whom were eunuchs. On occasion, he was also accompanied by members of the *cubiculum* who were not eunuchs, such as the dressers (some of whom were bearded)[22] and the bearded *protospatharioi.* Nevertheless, any bearded men who were part of the procession usually walked or rode outside the screen of eunuch escorts.[23]

One can cite several examples that illustrate this arrangement. The emperor only took communion in the presence of the members of the *cubiculum.*[24] When he ceremonially proceeded to the hippodrome the *spatharokandidatoi, spatharioi,* and *patrikioi*[25] formed a line on one side of him; and the most important members of the *cubiculum,* on the other.[26] When the patriarch visited the palace with high church officials in attendance, only the emperor and members of the *cubiculum* were present.[27] When the emperor processed to the Church of St. Mokios, he was initially accompanied by a variety of palace officials, but when he reached the church he was ringed by his *koubikoularioi.*[28] Even when the emperor processed formally within the palace he was escorted by members of the *cubiculum,* while other high officials bowed down to the group as it passed.[29] We have a detailed description of the arrangement of persons around the imperial throne that probably dates from the time of Constantine VII. The eunuch *spatharioi* stood in a semicircle immediately behind the imperial throne, with the bearded *spatharioi* immediately behind them. The eunuch *spatharioi* directly associated with the *cubiculum* and the *koubikoularioi* stood to the immediate right and left of the throne.[30]

Chapter 12 of book 2 of the *De ceremoniis* details the arrangements when the emperor went to the baths at Blachernai. He was accompanied by a large retinue of eunuchs and bearded men who stayed with him during elaborate devotions at the Church of the Virgin of Blachernai. Yet, when it was time to enter the inner parts of the church and the baths, the *koubikoularioi* closed the doors to the baths, saying, "Bearded men cannot enter here, only *koubikoularioi.*"[31]

Thus on ritual occasions, the emperor was usually "surrounded" by members of his *cubiculum.* While some of his personal servants were bearded men, the bearded *protospatharioi,* and in some periods, some of his dressers, were bearded men, it is clear, as in the case of the announcement at the bath, that members of the *cubiculum* were assumed to be eunuchs.[32]

By way of caveat, I should say that these ceremonial rituals do not necessarily offer a literal description of the emperor's world. We have more than one example of the emperor moving unprotected among ordinary people, and we ought not to assume that the emperor was always escorted and protected in this way. For example, Arethas, in an oration dated 902, describes Emperor Leo VI's reception of the relics of Lazaros when they were brought from Cyprus: "The emperor came down, weeping abundant tears, like Moses bringing the tables of the law down from the mountain, or rather like Jesus, for he mingled freely with the people, and laying imperial pomp aside, went about without escort."[33] Such cases aside, it is important to emphasize that these rituals defined the formal, official ordering of society and power and symbolized how the Byzantine elite thought things ought to be.

While the emperor was not considered divine, the office conveyed a transcendent quality upon its occupant, a quality, which I refer to as the imperial numen. This special quality, which had to be shielded from the polluting effect of inappropriate contact, contact with ordinary men, occurred only under special circumstances. While the emperor's feet and knees were kissed by bearded men in a ritual way as an act of obeisance, the remainder of his body was rarely touched by bearded men in any way. Aside from eunuchs, only the patriarch was allowed regular personal contact with the emperor in this symbolic context. Even gesturing at the emperor with a bare hand was not permissible for bearded men, as is illustrated in the ceremony that celebrated the feast and procession of the Virgin. We are told that in this ceremony the emperor is announced and his way is cleared of obstacles by the *epi tes katastaseos,* a bearded man. The *epi tes katastaseos* is instructed to wrap his own hand in his tunic before gesturing toward the emperor in order to clear his path.[34]

We also see evidence for the need to control the transfer of numen from the emperor to other persons in the way in which objects were transferred from the imperial hand to the hand of another. The importance of direct contact is reflected in the fact that only the highest dignitaries received their badges of office from the emperor's own hand. This was a very special honor. The *De ceremoniis* is always specific about whether objects passed directly from the emperor's hand to the recipient or were transferred to the recipient via the hand of another. Such intermediaries were always eunuchs. Thus the emperor gave insignia with his own hand only to bearded men with the rank of *kouropalates*[35] and above.[36] Similarly, he gave such insignia only to eunuchs of the rank of *spatharokoubikoularios* and above.[37] As an exceptional honor on Palm Sunday, the emperor placed flowers and palms directly into the hands of the senators and gave silver crosses to the *magistroi*[38] and chief eunuchs.[39] Thus it is a mark of respect that objects given by the emperor to the patriarch or to God always came directly from the emperor's own hand.[40] A purse of gold or silver coins was given directly to the patriarch or placed on the altar. These same items, when given to lesser officials, were passed by the emperor to the chief eunuch, who then handed them to the recipient.

In the same vein, almost all objects passed to the emperor came from the hands of his chief eunuch. The rare exceptions included important religious objects, such as the crosses brought from Hagia Sophia,[41] the symbols of fidelity brought to him by the *orphanotrophos*,[42] or the *libellum* given him by the domestic of the schools.[43] In rare ceremonial situations, as when the emperor accepted a candle, an incense pot, consecrated bread, or oil directly from the hand of the patriarch, he took it into his own hand.

The most common ceremonial form is illustrated by the almost daily ceremony that involved the lighting of ecclesiastical candles. The chief eunuch took a candle from a supply carried by one of the eunuchs of the *cubiculum*, lit it, and then handed it to the emperor. When the emperor completed the part of the ceremony requiring candles, he handed the candle back to the chief eunuch, who passed it to a lesser eunuch, who then placed it in a ceremonial candleholder.[44]

Finally, the chief eunuch, especially in a ceremonial setting, acted as a voice for the emperor. We rarely see references to the emperor saying anything in the course of a formal ceremony in the palace. He nodded and signaled his chief eunuch, but outsiders never heard his voice. The chief eunuch interpreted his signals and relayed them by voice to the *epi tes katastaseos*.[45]

Hierarchies of Imperial Proximity

When we look carefully at the *De ceremoniis*, therefore, we find that in ceremonial settings the emperor moved about his palace and his city surrounded by carefully defined space that was marked and guarded by eunuchs. He could not touch or be touched except under exceptional circumstances. The objects that passed through his hands were controlled and mediated by transferring them via the hands of his chief eunuch. His spoken words were also mediated.

All of these nuances identify a hierarchy of ceremonial proximity to and contact with the emperor. Ordinary men, women, and eunuchs other than those at court seldom approached or touched the emperor. Indeed, entrance to the palace itself was controlled by the *papias* and his assistants, all of whom were eunuchs. Bearded men of social importance had some rights of ceremonial proximity or access, but these were carefully controlled and the degree of access depended on the individual's place in the official hierarchy. Nevertheless, the eunuchs of the *cubiculum*, especially the *praepositos* or chief eunuch, ranked higher than any of the bearded aristocracy, at least in terms of proximity to the imperial numen. Not surprisingly, the highest degree of ceremonial access to the emperor was given to the patriarch.

A similar hierarchical structure governed those who were allowed to view the emperor, even from a distance, when he was on his throne. This was true both when the throne was in its usual location in the apse of the *khrysotriklinos* in the palace[46] and when it had been moved to a location outside of the palace. The second book of the *De ceremoniis* gives us the general observances on this point for occasions when the emperor visited a ceremonial location outside of the palace, in this case, the Church of the Holy Apostles.[47] The imperial throne was moved to the required location by a crew of young men drawn from the highest levels of the aristocracy. When the emperor was seated, however, he was encircled "by the most secret order of the servants of the bedchamber so that he might not be seen easily by the multitude." Once again, this time at a visual level, eunuchs were mediating contact with the emperor's numen. In this case, he is shielded from sight while his attendants change his shoes. The imperial purple shoes were one of the most important symbolic elements of the imperial regalia.

Even inside the royal palace the emperor was shielded from improper viewing with a curtain. This curtain was moveable and was carried about by the same eunuchs of the *cubiculum* who were responsible for designating the emperor's personal space.[48] The curtain was transported and hung by eunuchs. While it was usually opened and closed by bearded men, they did so at the direction of the chief eunuch. One exception to this was the festival on the Saturday before Easter Day.[49] On this occasion, as the assembled choirs sang "Christ Is Risen," the eunuch *koubikoularioi* themselves opened the outside curtain. They left in place the inner golden curtain, which seems to have been transparent. This allowed the spectators outside the entrance to the *khrysotriklinos* the unusual opportunity of seeing the emperor, seated on his throne, through a golden haze.

The parallelism of Byzantine conceptions of the heavenly and imperial courts is echoed here in a passage from the Vita of St. Andrew the Fool. After being led past singers with fiery eyes and through various firmaments, Andrew is brought to a fine curtain. The curtain is drawn aside by an immense dove to reveal Christ on his throne. Andrew then makes obeisance, after which Christ speaks directly to him three times.[50]

Some of the most intriguing regulations regarding seeing and touching the emperor surrounded the ceremonial putting on and taking off of the imperial crown. The emperor wore a variety of headgear, including crowns as we think of them, floral garlands, hats, and wreaths. These were often changed during a long and complex ceremony, and the time and place for such changes, as well as the nature of the headgear worn for each occasion, are carefully outlined in the *De ceremoniis.*[51]

Whatever the time, place, or type of headgear, it is clear that no bearded man was allowed to see the emperor's crown actually being put on or taken off except at the imperial coronation.[52] For example, in the directions for the observances on the feast and procession of the Ascension we are told that the emperor could reach his destination, the shrine to the Virgin of Pege outside the Theodosian Walls, either on horseback or by boat. If he went by sea, when he disembarked he instructed the chief eunuch to tell the nobles that they could come into his sight. As they did so, the eunuchs of the *cubiculum,* wearing [bearing?] purple cloaks,[53] stood in a circle. The emperor entered the center of the circle and was crowned by the chief eunuch. The text tells us specifically that this was "because the emperor cannot be crowned before the faces of bearded men."[54] The emperor was then robed and escorted to the baptistery of the church of the Virgin of Pege. He then passed through the church to the adjacent palace, where the chief eunuch removed the emperor's crown, again in a private *cubiculum.* The crown remained off, and later his nobles saw him without it.

Bearded men could see the emperor with or without his crown; what they were not permitted to see was the transitional moment when the crown was actually taken off or placed on his head. This could only be witnessed by the eunuchs or the patriarch. Thus, when the emperor was dressed—and his clothes might be changed several times during a single ceremony—dressers who were not eunuchs had to be dismissed before the chief eunuch or the patriarch placed the crown on the emperor's head.

The *De ceremoniis* does describe one exception to this rule about who can observe the changing or removal of crowns. The case involves the elevation of an individual to the position of head of the senate.[55] In this instance, the individual, in addition to receiving the insignia and regalia of office, was honored with the right to walk next to the chief eunuch (and therefore in close proximity to the emperor) in the procession. More significantly, he was also allowed to be present when the emperor's crown was put on or taken off. Traditionally, both of these prerogatives were denied to bearded men. This suggests that the particular ceremony being described was in fact that of the elevation of the great court eunuch Basil Lekapenos to the position of head of the Senate. This particular section of the *De ceremoniis,* dating to the period between 963 and 969,[56] certifies the relevance of the surrounding symbolic acts to the context of the tenth century. There is really no other way to explain these rather singular additions to the rights and prerogatives normally granted to the head of the Senate.

Thus the rituals and regulations that surrounded the crown and its handling replicate the same hierarchies of space and contact that we saw in other aspects of court ceremonial. Commoners and bearded, male aristocrats could have nothing to do with the crown, which was closely linked to the imperial numen. This was a spiritually charged domain reserved to the court eunuchs and, at the highest level, to the patriarch.

The rituals involved with this phenomenon extended beyond managing the spaces immediately around the emperor, and while the details are a bit tedious, they reinforce the proposition that eunuchs had special capabilities and were divinely designated for their tasks. In addition to placing the crown on the emperor's head, the chief eunuch of the *cubiculum* and his staff were responsible for the protection and storage of the imperial crown and the other imperial regalia. The objects were stored in boxes that were kept in the Oratorium of St. Theodore, which was located in the palace. The boxes in question were brought out in a ceremonial procession so that the crown could be properly stowed away and protected when it was not actually being worn. This happened, for example, during religious services when the emperor's role required him to set aside the imperial regalia.

This shrine was ritually important in three ways. It was closely associated with imperial ceremony, its regalia, and the ritual changing of imperial clothing and crowns. It was thought to have been a possible storage place for one of the relics of the True Cross. Finally, it was intimately associated with the court eunuchs themselves, since the *oratorium* played a major role in the ceremonies associated with investing eunuchs with the office of *koubikoularios,* a promotion that made them part of the emperor's inner entourage.

Hierarchies of Ceremonial

The hierarchies and spatial patterns around the emperor suggested above can also be seen in the ceremonial accoutrements worn at court and in the arrangements whereby formal visitors were escorted to imperial audiences. One passage in the *De ceremoniis* touches on both of these points. It describes the ceremonies appropriate to the reception of foreign ambassadors and includes a reference to a particular ceremonial reception for a group of Saracen envoys. The emperor was eager to put his best foot forward and therefore had the envoys escorted into his presence by the *katepanos* of the *basilikoi* and the *komes tou staulou.*[57] Both of these officials were bearded men. On this occasion these escorts and several other bearded officials were granted the privilege of wearing ceremonial robes much more beautiful and valuable than they usually wore at court, along with torques embellished with precious stones and large pearls. The texts tells us that such torques, gems, and large pearls were not customarily worn by bearded men, but that the emperor Constantine VII had ordered that the bearded officials be allowed to wear them on this particular occasion.[58] While it is easy to assume that court dress was elaborate and that it varied as a marker of hierarchical status, it is more difficult to find concrete documentation of this phenomenon. This passage shows clearly that eunuchs normally wore the most prestigious markers of status while occupying the spaces near the emperor.

One intriguing aspect of this system of symbolic display involves the wearing of pearls—not small pearls that encrust a garment as a decoration, but large single pearls. Such pearls were regularly worn by members of the imperial family, and they decorated even the imperial war-horse on ceremonial occasions. Of all the officials of the court, however, only the eunuch *protospatharioi* wore pearls as part of their official regalia. Moreover, their regalia differed from that of their bearded counterparts only in that they *were* allowed to wear pearls and their bearded counterparts were not. This symbolic use of pearls was most prominent in connection with the women of the imperial household, although pearls were also worn by the emperor. Pearls also appear in angelic iconography, sometimes in association with St. Michael. All of this leads one to suspect that pearls had a spiritual and gender significance, which led to their being reserved for the imperial family and their eunuchs.

The definition and gendering of space around the emperor and the hierarchy of persons allowed access to his person are also evident in the role of eunuchs as escorts in imperial ceremonials. Many readers are familiar with the famous passage from Liutprand of Cremona in which he describes his imperial audience before Nikephoros Phokas. He says that he was brought before the emperor leaning on the shoulders of two eunuchs. There is a good deal of evidence to suggest that Liutprand's experience was exceptional. The *De ceremoniis*, compiled just ten years before the events described by Liutprand, describes this kind of formal "escort on the shoulders of two eunuchs" as being reserved for the emperor, the empress, the patriarch, and a few high officials. Most ambassadors were escorted up to the throne by bearded men of a lower rank.

The hagiographical sources that echo this ceremony reserve the honor claimed by Liutprand for Christ, the Virgin, and the saints (see fig. 10). Thus, Liutprand may have been accorded a signal honor of which he was not aware. Alternatively, he may have been elaborating his account to make himself appear more important in Constantinople than he really was.[59] The ambiguity here may also be another warning that we must be careful of the often anachronistic nature of the *De ceremoniis.* It also reminds us that the *De ceremoniis* is often a reflection of how some people thought that things *ought* to have been, not necessarily the way that things actually were.

The numerous examples of ceremonial escorts suggest two points—the escorts are usually of comparable rank to those being escorted, and the most important personages are always escorted by eunuchs of appropriately high rank. Thus the *komes*[60] who is to be promoted,[61] as is appropriate to his high rank, is

FIGURE 10

This miniature shows two angels assisting Christ during the Ascension. Angels are frequently depicted as supporting heavenly figures and eunuchs routinely performed similar functions for important persons at the imperial court. New York, Pierpont Morgan Library, cod. M639, fol. 391. From Gary Vikan, ed., *Illuminated Greek Manuscripts from American Collections* (Princeton: Princeton University Press, 1973), p. 120, fig. 50.

escorted by the *domestikos* of the schools and count of the ceremonies (both bearded men of high status). The first (and presumably less important) group of individuals received by the emperor in an audience is escorted by the captain of the imperial guard and the *logothetes* (supervisor) of the public roads (both bearded men of lesser status).[62] The patriarch merits an escort of two eunuch *koubikoularioi*,[63] while a person about to be named caesar or *nobilissimus* (honors usually reserved for the imperial family) is escorted both by the *praepositos* (highest-ranking eunuch) and the *magistros* (who was a bearded man).[64] The *praepositos* also escorts the *zoste patrikia*, the highest-ranking woman courtier, when she is promoted.[65] When the *praepositos* himself is promoted he is escorted by the senior eunuchs of the *cubiculum* at the ceremony.[66]

Similar descriptions of escorts at imperial audiences appear in various other sources, and it is not at all clear that the hierarchies were as consistent as the *De ceremoniis* would lead us to believe.[67] In two such tales, however, there is no question about the importance of the persons being escorted or about the special nature of the eunuchs who served as escorts. One of the vitae of Athanasios of Athos includes a vision of the Virgin escorted by eunuchs. The Virgin is richly dressed and the eunuchs wear white robes. One eunuch leads her carrying a torch, the other follows as she distributes gifts to the monks.[68] Finally, we have the example from the Vita of St. Lazaros of Mt. Galesion, which was discussed in chapter 7 above. In a dream a monk saw two eunuchs escorting a third person out of a church. This dream was interpreted to represent Christ guarded by two angels.[69] While these two cases are obviously not examples of court protocol, they document the unconscious cultural conviction that eunuchs were the proper escorts for the most important individuals in the Byzantine mental universe.

The Elevation of a New *Koubikoularios*

The question still remains as to what afforded eunuchs this special position in court ceremonial. This has been the focus of previous chapters, but through the ceremonial that surrounds the appointment of a eunuch as a *koubikoularios* we can approach the topic from a different angle. This office moved a eunuch from the general palace staff to the emperor's personal entourage or else honored a eunuch with a high imperial title.[70]

The *De ceremoniis* gives an account of this ritual:

> At the beginning of the daily procession, when the emperor is seated in the *khrysotriklinos*, if he wishes to announce the elevation of an individual to the rank of *koubikoularios*, he informs the chief eunuchs.[71] These chief eunuchs take, as is customary, two *koubikoularioi* and two *spatharokoubikoularioi*, an *ostiarios*, and the *primikerios*, one of these being the *primikerios* of the *koubikoularioi*, and they enter the *khrysotriklinos*. The chief eunuchs, entering through the western curtain of the *khrysotriklinos*, make obeisance to the emperor, while the remaining members of the *cubiculum* do not make obeisance. The *deuteros* [assistant doorkeeper, a eunuch] opens the *oratorium* of the holy and great martyr Theodore.[72] All enter and hang the golden *paragaudium* (ceremonial robe of a *koubikoularios*)[73] from the gate of the chancel *bema* or from the sacred door. Then the chief eunuch leaves and brings in, either from the Pantheon or through the Horologion, the eunuch who is to be

> made a *koubikoularios.* The *koubikoularioi* dress the one who is to be honored at the chief eunuchs' order, either outside the *oratorium* or inside the curtain of the *oratorium* of Holy Theodore, in a tunic and uncover his head. Then, in this fashion, they bring him into the *oratorium* and place him in front of the sacred doors.

At this point the chief eunuch makes a customary exhortation, instructing the candidate that he should not lay a violent hand on any bearded man except at the emperor's orders. He should not be a drunkard and a braggart, should not concern himself with affairs that are not his business, and should not associate or be friendly with men of bad reputation or those who are "innovative." Here "innovative" refers to those who stir up political trouble or rebellion against the emperor. He should not reveal any of the emperor's secrets to such men. It is important to note that these instructions are all negative; they all define what the *koubikoularios* may *not* do.

The candidate is then told that he should honor all those of the first rank in office, those who are his equal in office, all members of the council, and most of all, the chief eunuch. After this exhortation has been delivered to the new *koubikoularios,* the chief eunuch says:

> Observe whence comes this dignity which now you have received. It is completely clear that it comes from these holy doors. Recognize that you have received your dignity from the hand of the Lord. Guard yourself diligently that so long as you live you maintain these precepts and keep them close to your heart. Displaying and ornamenting yourself with the greatest virtues, you will achieve the highest levels of honors by dispensing our wealth and [from] the holy emperor, and you will be glorified among the members of the holy *cubiculum.*

Having said this, the chief eunuch orders the candidate to lie prone on the ground facing east and venerate and give thanks to God. Then the chief eunuch takes the golden *paragaudium* from the sacred door and places it on the candidate. The other chief eunuch then embraces and kisses him and so do the others. Then they lead him outside the curtain of the *oratorium* of St. Theodore, where he falls on the ground and gives reverence to the emperor. The new *koubikoularios* is then led by the *praepositoi* and *koubikoularioi* into the *lausiakos* (a meeting hall located near the *khrysotriklinos*), where he is embraced by the senators and by all the members of the *cubiculum.* This done, he again covers his head, takes his seat among those of his own order, and, the ceremony over (established in high rank), returns to his own house.

What do we learn from this? The candidate for office receives his regalia from the chief eunuch, who acts in the ceremony as an agent of God. The text is very specific about telling us that the charge of the new *koubikoularios* comes from God, not from the emperor. Only the eunuch courtiers received their offices from God rather than from the emperor. The analogous ceremonies for bearded men were not religious in nature, and it is clear that their power is given them by the emperor.

The regalia given to the new *koubikoularios* are blessed in the Oratorium of St. Theodore, where the saint acts as the intermediary between God and the regalia. The saint controls this regalia just as he maintains the holiness of the imperial regalia stored there.

The temporal instructions to the new *koubikoularios* come from the chief eunuch, and the new recruit is addressed specifically as a eunuch, not as a bearded man. We see this in the things that he is instructed not to do. He should not harm a bearded man unless the emperor orders him to do so. This reflects the longstanding rhetorical perception that eunuchs, like women, cannot control their emotions and are likely to commit violent acts. He should not be a drunkard or a braggart. Again, like women, eunuchs are believed to be unable to control their desires for food and drink and are assumed to be arrogant and talk too much. He should mind his own business. Being overly inquisitive is a charge regularly leveled at women and eunuchs. The new *koubikoularios* is told that he should not become friendly with men who have a bad reputation or might make trouble for the emperor.

The final instruction is for the new official to take his place in the hierarchical structure of the palace and honor those who are his equals or stand above him. In return, he is promised honor and the right to dispense the wealth of the emperor. Notice that we have here a pact made with God but one that involves only worldly rewards. As part of the imperial entourage, the eunuch is not automatically entitled to spiritual rewards or happiness in the afterlife. It is true that the eunuchs guarded the emperor's numen and vicariously shared it. They were associated with the ceremonial parts of the imperial construct that came to be expressed in terms of divine powers, and therefore their office was presented as one that comes directly from God. Despite the religious appearance of the ceremony surrounding their induction into the ranks of the *koubikoularioi,* however, their duties and rewards were worldly.

Imperial Space and Gender

While these court eunuchs were assumed to have a greater capacity to function in spiritual realms than ordinary men, and those capacities were often presented as resembling those of angels, there was no question about eunuchs being mortal beings. If gender is socially constructed, they were the ultimate socially constructed category. The emperor was not personally responsible for their castration, but indirectly he was their creator. His household (in the largest sense of the term) was the context for their acculturation. The palace provided a societal niche for them, a niche that encouraged parents to send children into this kind of imperial service and one perceived as crucial to the functional integration of the imperial court.

These eunuchs were thus the essence of perfect servants. This is not simply a matter of performing the menial tasks of a household. They were perfect servants because they were uniquely qualified extensions of the imperial person—they partook of and guarded his numen and they carried with them the divine legitimation and special powers of the emperor wherever they went in his service. Indirectly, they made it possible for some empresses, either as regents or as rulers in their own right, to transcend gender boundaries and exercise real authority. As keepers of ancient ceremonial lore, they were crucial to the continuity of imperial ceremonial and tradition and thus of the emperor's numen.[74] They managed the emperor's wealth. They were separated from the sexual activity that implied family and patrimonial connections and thus lived in a world separate from that of aristocratic families. Like Shaun Marmon's eunuch tomb guards, they lived outside of conventional space and time. They could achieve honor and power, but only in so far as they served the imperial household.

The emperor was by definition a whole man, but was also one with special powers. The spaces around him were not only distinct from female space, but they were also kept free of normally gendered males, at least on the ritual level. In effect, the space constituted by the palace and the surroundings of the emperor was eunuch space, gendered in a distinctive way that defies any more apt designation.

While the whole pattern of spatial regulation and the divine charge given to eunuchs makes this gendering of space in the palace quite clear, it is made more manifest with a brief, if speculative, suggestion about the gendering of other ceremonial spaces in Constantinople. If the imperial palace was a realm of eunuch space, somehow apart from ordinary time and space and reserved only to the imperial family, then one can suggest that the city, under its *eparch*, was space that belonged to bearded men. That space was the site of trade and traditional justice where everyday work flourished. It was the realm of the noble families. The *Kletorologion* of Philotheos offers evidence that, at least in a ceremonial sense, the court recognized that the palace eunuchs and the *eparch* with his staff belonged in two very different realms.

This separation of elite society into two domains is suggested by a passage in Philotheos that discusses a series of dinner parties given by the emperor as a part of the Christmas festivities.[75] Occurring during a twelve-day span, the feast days honored specific groups, marked by an invitation to dine with the emperor. The guests included the patriarch and his staff, the heads of monasteries and their senior monks, representatives of the city factions, and foreign dignitaries. On the seventh day the honored guests included the city *eparch* and his staff, the *drounga-*

rios of the fleet and his staff, and judges, while on the eighth day the honored guests were the staff of the *cubiculum.*

The *De ceremoniis* provides other hints that the social landscape of the palace and the city administration were differently gendered and that their interaction had to be carefully mediated. The city *eparch,* though an important and powerful official, is rarely mentioned in the *De ceremoniis,* despite the many occasions when the text describes elaborate processions into the city. On such occasions the city *eparch* was involved only in that he was instructed to clean the streets, assure their safety, and decorate the parade route with flowers and greenery.

The only time the *eparch* was invited to enter the palace was for the Christmas dinner and at the time of his investiture. Even this investiture is an unimpressive ceremonial at best,[76] given that the *eparch* was probably the most important official in civic government. The ceremony is best characterized as "external" to the imperial space. The emperor first informed the *praepositos* of the name of the individual he was appointing as *eparch.* The entire ritual was handled by the *praepositos,* who acted as the emperor's surrogate and performed the actual ceremony. As a part of the ceremony he refers to the *eparch* as the "father of the city." The symbolic relationship is obvious: if the *eparch* is to be "father of the city" then he must be a bearded man.[77] If the city is a family, its space/time environment is distinct from that of the eunuch space of the palace.

The role of the *eparch* thus appears to be analogous to that of the *praepositus sacri cubiculi.* The city *eparch* rules the city and its public space, which in the classical Greek tradition is considered to be masculine space. The public space of the city is the place where bearded men engage in the necessary, mundane activities of the world. Indeed, the stipulated duties of the *eparch* reflect this. He is chief judge of the city and supervises trade and manufacturing. The *praepositus sacri cubiculi,* in contrast, presides over a differently gendered world, one that exists on a far more spiritual plane, one that is enclosed, secret, and defined by different rituals.

This distinction between city and palace does not imply a dual structure. As I suggested at the start, the church was another focal point for these complex patterns. As discussed in chapters 5 and 7, the spiritual or magical powers assigned to eunuchs posed a problem for the church but also facilitated access by eunuchs to church office. Moreover, because we know little about the inner workings of the women's quarters, little can be said about spaces assigned to women and gendered as female. Based on classical and Hellenistic patterns of household organization, however, we have to assume that large areas of domestic life in the city were so defined. The gendered elements in the eunuchs' roles in the palace and its ceremonial are very evident. The degree to which gender regulates the larger physical structure of the city is less clear.

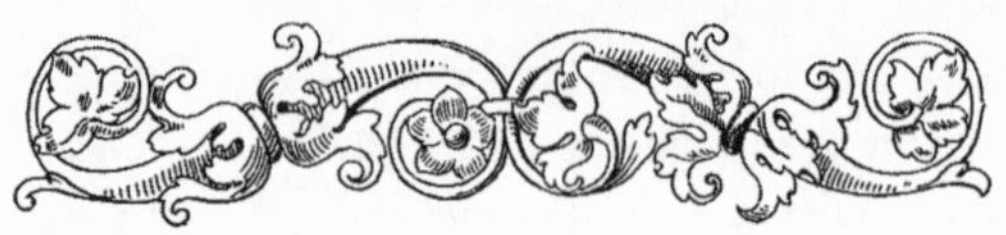

CHAPTER 9

Social Reproduction and Integration

Analysis of language, medical lore, acculturation, and perceptions of eunuchs as active participants in historical narratives have shown that eunuchs were socially constructed as a distinctive gender and were deeply embedded in Byzantine society for many centuries. They were neither exotic nor marginal, even though elements of their gender construct included the notion that as individuals they had "outside" or servile origins.

In fact, eunuchs constituted a distinctively gendered group and were integral to Byzantine society for a thousand years. Although incapable of normal biological reproduction, this group of individuals reproduced itself, trained itself, and became the repository for courtly traditions. This apparent contradiction suggests that we need to look more systematically at the origins of eunuchs, how they were recruited into their distinctive gender category, and how they integrated into society. Conventional assumptions about their origins and evidence about actual recruitment tell us a great deal about how Byzantine eunuchs were integrated into their society.

Eunuchs Gendered as "Outsiders"

In the Late Antique construct discussed in chapter 3, one of the basic characteristics of the gendering of eunuchs was that they were distanced from their own extended and biological families. Traditionally this was accomplished through enslavement, which usually moved an individual into another physical and social environment and cut him off from parents and relatives. At the same time, the act of castration, since it precluded marriage, biological children, and new marital kin, further distanced eunuchs from their families. This dissociation from the past and lack of family was characteristic of most eunuchs of the Late Antique and early Byzantine periods.

This isolation from social origins, exclusion from normal family and dynastic affairs, and separation from standard domestic life cycles divorced eunuchs from "normal" time. It shaped their relationship to the family dynasticism that characterized the society and politics of Byzantium. Ironically, the strength of some of the invective used against eunuchs suggests transgression of the gender norm requiring social isolation.

The counterpart to this process of separation from society was a pattern whereby eunuchs were acquired by aristocratic families and became part of their *oikoi.* The same was also true of the eunuchs in the emperor or empress's domains within the larger context of the imperial palace.[1] Such eunuchs were assumed to reserve all of their personal loyalty for their adoptive families, receiving in turn a fictive family relationship similar to that of slaves in many parts of African society.[2] This image of social "disconnectedness" was an important factor in making a eunuch a perfect servant. It was a quality that eunuchs shared with strictly cloistered monks and with holy men who rejected their families and who concentrated their "familial" loyalty on their comrades in the monastery, all of whom attempted to be perfect servants of God. Regarding this parallel with holy men, Rosemary Morris notes that holy men sometimes refused to reveal their origins and that this was a device used by their hagiographers to emphasize their separateness from familial and worldly ties. She also suggests that this quality made it possible for them to act justly in both spiritual and social terms.[3] Here we see one of the important ingredients in a gender construction based on the ideal of the perfect servant, an ingredient that remained central even after normalization of recruitment of eunuchs from within Byzantine society. The image of the eunuch as outsider, separated from his place of birth and family, was enshrined in rhetorical tradition and recurs as a theme as long as eunuchs existed in Byzantine society.

By the tenth century our sources clearly document the social mechanisms that allowed eunuchs to reproduce themselves. As eunuchs were increasingly recruited from within Byzantine society it became inevitable that they should become intimately involved in the interplay of family and clan politics that was the backdrop for official policies and institutions. The range of powerful positions they occupied clearly suggests that eunuchism, as an institution, fell within the dynamics of society. Eunuchs were not modeled as either descendants or progenitors of biological families, but neither were they entirely outsiders to society.

Social Reproduction: From "Outsider" to "Insider"

One indicator of the changing status of eunuchs in Byzantium is violation of that aspect of their gender construct that assumed absence of a biological family. Whatever the prevailing rhetoric of our sources, from the sixth century on we find examples of powerful eunuchs who maintained extensive connections with their own families. Phrased differently, established families sought to place sons in important offices open only to eunuchs. Families castrated some of their sons as part of an age-old strategy for familial advancement. Many Byzantine authors observed that eunuchs were using their offices to promote their natal families. This violation of traditional norms for the behavior of eunuchs was perceived to be an "inappropriate" transgression of gender boundaries and became a source of criticism aimed at eunuchs. Despite such negative rhetoric, however, by the tenth century the assumption that eunuchs had to abandon their biological families was becoming a less salient part of their gender construct.

A few examples of eunuchs who used their office to promote the interests of their natal families can be found as early as the sixth century. The career of the prominent eunuch general Solomon is outlined by the historian Prokopios of Caesarea (see chapter 6). Prokopios tells us that a careless nurse had swaddled Solomon incorrectly and had destroyed his testicles. Given what we know about the techniques for infant castration, this looks suspiciously like a rhetorical device used to explain Solomon's deviation from the traditional gendered norms for eunuchs.[4] By suggesting that Solomon had not become a eunuch in the conventional way—which implied being castrated and sold into slavery from outside of Byzantine society—the author legitimizes Solomon's future status as a general and governor, along with membership in his extended biological family.

Solomon was *domestikos* for Belisarios, Justinian's great general, when he was sent to North Africa to fight the Moors, first as head of the army, then as governor of the province. When Prokopios discusses this North African war in volume 4 of his *History of the Wars,* we find that Solomon brought into the army four of his nephews, Bacchus, Cyrus, Sergios, and Solomon the Younger, to serve under his command. This appears as a routine example of family patronage.

Prokopios, however, is quite hostile toward these young men. When Solomon died, he was succeeded by one of his nephews, whom Prokopios presents as incompetent.[5] As any aristocratic man of the period would have done, Solomon had facilitated the advancement of his biological family. The explanation for

Prokopios's attitude derives in part from his judgement that Solomon, a eunuch, had transgressed gender boundaries. While Solomon's own condition as a eunuch commander was resolved with a literary device, his behavior in promoting his family remained suspect.

We get another glimpse of a eunuch deeply embedded in the affairs of his own family from Prokopios's references to the eunuch Euphratas in the reign of Justinian I (r. 527–565).[6] Euphratas is best known from Prokopios's account of how, as an Abchasian eunuch, he was sent to the kingdom of the Abchasians in hopes of ending the practice of castration in that region. Prokopios mentions Euphratas in both his standard historical works and in the *Secret History* (also called the *Anecdota*).[7] One passage involves Euphratas's attempt to bequeath his estate to his nephew. The emperor Justinian, however, confiscated the estate, possibly in deference to long-standing legislation that discouraged eunuchs from adopting children and passing their estates on to their extended families.[8] In the relevant passage, Prokopios appears to side with the eunuch Euphratas. Citing it as an example of Justinian's greed, Prokopios presents Justinian's action in the hostile light that permeates the *Secret History.*

For the sake of a rhetorical jab at Justinian, therefore, Prokopios had no trouble overlooking the apparent gender transgression involved. In principle, having an extended family to which an estate could be left was contrary to the expected gender structure established for eunuchs, and it is therefore not surprising that Justinian was opposed to the practice.

We get glimpses of two more powerful eunuchs, Staurakios and Aetios, enmeshed in dynastic and family politics during the reign of the empress Irene (r. 797–802). Theophanes, in his *Chronographia,* suggests that the two had a falling out because each was plotting to seize the imperial throne for his own family. In this struggle, Staurakios acquired a large following but died before he could successfully promote his own family. Aetios was more successful, making his brother Leo commanding general of the armies of Thrace and Macedonia. He was also thought to have had plans to elevate this Leo to the imperial throne.[9] Both of these figures were not only deeply involved in dynastic politics but also were working to further the interests of members of their natal families.[10]

Another prominent eunuch with a somewhat anomalous career was Samonas, an important figure during the reign of Leo VI (r. 886–912). Samonas was, in a certain sense, an outsider, since he came from Syria and is assumed to have been from a Muslim family.[11] Unlike most eunuchs in earlier stereotypes, however, Samonas is presented as coming from an elite background. He maintained relations with his biological family and even entertained his father in Constantinople while the latter was there as an envoy to arrange an exchange of prisoners. If we can trust the chronicle, Samonas's father was a very important person in his own right and was received by the emperor at the Magnaura Palace. He was even allowed to see the sacred church vessels at Hagia Sophia, a remarkable concession to a visitor who probably was not even a Christian.[12] During his visit, Samonas's father was so impressed with Constantinople that he suggested to his son that he might settle there. Samonas was not receptive to this suggestion, and the sources give no indication that Samonas attempted to place members of his biological family in the Byzantine military or administration.

Nevertheless, Samonas actively extended his "familial" influence in other ways. As a wealthy and powerful individual who was also a eunuch, Samonas was active at court from 900 until he disappears from the historical record in 908. He developed his personal *oikos,* which included the poet Constantine of Rhodes and the eunuch Constantine, a trusted servant, who is described as "his [Samonas's] own man" (ἄνθρωπον αὐτου). The former began his career as Samonas's secretary and later was *asekretis* to Constantine VII.[13] The latter, Constantine the eunuch, moved up through the palace hierarchy under Samonas's sponsorship and served the empress Zoe as *patrikios* and *parakoimomenos.* In an additional trace of Samonas's evolving *oikos,* the vita of St. Basil the Younger indicates that the two Gongyles brothers, both important court eunuchs, were relatives of Constantine, Samonas's protégé.[14]

This example demonstrates one of the ways in which a powerful eunuch, although distanced from his own family, could extend his influence within the court by promoting other eunuchs as a part of his own *oikos.* In this case, Samonas's plan failed. The increasing power of Constantine ultimately helped to topple Samonas from his place at court. This example retains the image of the court eunuch as separated from his origins (in this case, located in Muslim Syria)[15] but retaining contact with his elite family there. He exploits the fictive kinship of the *oikos* to build a network clearly modeled after the habits of family promotion.

The letters of Leo, metropolitan of Synada, also offer a fleeting glimpse of the process whereby eunuchs at court constructed *oikoi.*[16] Within this correspondence we find evidence that John the Ostiarios, a eunuch at court, was almost certainly the nephew of Leo the Protovestiarios, a eunuch who commanded the imperial forces during the revolt of Bardas Skleros in 976. It is probable that Leo sponsored John's career at court in the same pattern described regarding Samonas.

The changing assumptions about the putative relationship between eunuchs and Byzantine society are even more evident in the *narratio* of St. Metrios, father of Constantine, the eunuch patronized by Samonas.[17] This case shows how recruitment of eunuchs from within Byzantine society became an accepted convention. It also illustrates how eunuchs built their own family networks in spite of the older assumption that eunuchs were individuals separated from their biological families. Thanks to his faith and honesty, God enabled St. Metrios to have a son. Moreover, God authorized the son's castration as part of rearing him for an important career at court. As we saw in chapter 3, the son, who was the eunuch Constantine, became a protégé of the empress and attained the title of *patrikios* and office of *parakoimomenos.*

St. Metrios is presented as an independent peasant farmer from Paphlagonia. Life was difficult for his family, and Metrios envied his neighbors who had sons whom they could castrate and send off to Constantinople, where they were expected to become rich and powerful and send money home to help their families. Metrios had not been able to follow this course even though he had prayed for a son. His prayers were finally granted after he proved his saintliness by returning a large, mislaid purse full of gold to an itinerant merchant. Not only did Metrios return the gold after hiding it until the merchant returned, but he refused the financial reward offered by the merchant.

At this point St. Metrios was rewarded with a vision of an angel who promised that a male son would be born to him. The angel instructed him to name this son Constantine; Metrios was told that he "could do with him [the son] as he wished." The angel also informed Metrios that this son, "after he is weaned and brought into the queen of cities, will be held in honor on the earth and will fulfill all sorts of good things for you and for your family." As soon as Constantine was named and weaned and had been taught the holy word, his mistress, the empress, brought him to the emperor, Leo VI (son of Basil I; r. 886–912). Subsequently the empress arranged for Constantine to be honored as *patrikios* and *parakoimomenos.* She had "a thousand good things" done for his parents and family. Given Constantine's role in the fall of Samonas, it is hardly surprising that Constantine's previous relationship with Samonas has been dropped from the story.

St. Metrios also appears in a second story based on the same plot—lost gold faithfully returned to its rightful owner—but this time the miracle takes place at the end of Metrios's life. It appears in the Pseudo Symeon Magistros, a tenth-century chronicle.

> Constantine had an elderly father, a man who was very religious and full of fear of God. Near that same place of Nosiai [or Nosia, where Leo VI built a monastery in Constantine's honor] Constantine's father had a very small farm by the sea. On the farm there was a spring that poured water into a cistern and refreshed travelers who passed by. It happened once that a soldier came to the spring and, after refreshing himself, he took out money that he had received for his just labors in order to count it. There were three pounds of gold. Then, aris-

> ing and mounting his horse, he set off on his journey, leaving the gold in that place. And so the old man, as had been his custom, went to the cistern and found the gold and was concerned about the man who had lost it. Keeping it with him he prayed to God day and night that its owner would return for it. When the soldier had gotten to Pylai, he remembered the money, but since [he] thought it hopeless to try to recover it he continued, sadly, on his journey.
>
> Three years later he [the soldier] came to Nosiai [or Nosia] again and got off his horse to water him, and he also drank and sat thinking. With a sigh he said, "In this very place I lost my whole livelihood." The old man heard and asked him, "What happened, sir?" He replied, "I lost my money here." Immediately he showed him the place and described his purse and the amount [of gold]. At once the man of God [Metrios] extracted the purse from a fold of his garment and said, "Do you recognize this?" He was struck dumbfounded but managed to say, "Yes, that is what I lost." And Constantine's father said, "Take it, with the assurance that I did not open it, nor did I see what was inside." Taking the purse, he begged the old man take as much as he wanted of the total. He refused to take anything. Therefore the soldier, happy, went on his way giving thanks to God.
>
> That night in a dream the old man saw Christ coming to him and saying, "Because you treated the soldier in this way, tomorrow you will hear that your son has become *parakoimomenos,* and this estate of yours will become a great monastery to my glory. And you yourself will be rewarded for these things." The next morning the announcement was made. Soon after, the emperor Leo agreed to take over all the expenses for the monastery's construction and dedication.[18]

In the first tale Metrios is rewarded for his holiness by the birth of a son who, as the story specifies, will bring wealth and power to his family. In the second tale, the son's success brings status (and wealth) to his father's community in the form of an imperial subsidy for a large monastery.

This reinforces our case that eunuchs increasingly retained contact with and sponsored their own families. Sent into service at the court as a eunuch, Constantine clearly knows who his father is, does not hesitate to celebrate him, and provides favors to his biological family.

This inference is supported by other aspects of Constantine's career. He brought his sister to Constantinople, arranged for her marriage, and introduced her into the highest levels of the aristocracy. His success in this is suggested by the fact that she was married to Leo Phokas, uncle of the emperor Nikephoros II Phokas (r. 963–969). Among the letters of the patriarch Nicholas Mystikos there is a warm letter of condolence written to Constantine at the time of his sister's death.[19]

Thus, we not only have the accounts of eunuch generals and officials from powerful families as seen in chapter 6, but we also find eunuchs constructing their own *oikoi.* These eunuchs were active participants in deciding the imperial succession and remained closely supportive of the biological families that castrated them and sent them into service at court. Eunuchs' subsequent attempts to promote members of their biological families at court run counter to older traditions and gender assumptions about eunuchs but were increasingly common after the eighth century.

The mechanism for the social reproduction of eunuchs as a gender is clearly sketched in the story of St. Metrios. Indeed, there is an odd twist to the story of St. Metrios since, despite the persistence of formal legislation banning castration, God authorizes him to castrate the son whom God has miraculously bestowed upon him. Castration and life as a eunuch, which at one time had implied total separation from familial and societal background, has been legitimated by God. It had become yet another strategy for family promotion, a strategy that is a crucial part of the explanation of how the institution of eunuchism maintained itself in Byzantium over several centuries.

The most striking example of family advancement by a eunuch is John the Orphanotrophos. John, like the eunuch Constantine discussed above, was from Paphlagonia, a region that was the source of many eunuchs during this period. His family was not noble, and in fact our sources suggest that it engaged in some kind of distinctly ignoble business, possibly moneychanging. John was probably the eldest of five brothers. Two of the other four, Constantine and George, were also eunuchs, while the other two, Niketas and Michael, grew up as whole men. John is first seen at court in the reign of Basil II (r. 976–1025) where he served as *protonotarios* (head notary) and in other minor administrative positions. We are told that Basil held him in high regard. When Basil died and the imperium passed to Basil's brother Constantine VIII, John seems to have continued in office. We know that he served the emperor Romanos III Argyrus (r. 1028–34), who was the husband of Constantine VIII's eldest daughter, Zoe.[20] Toward the end of the reign of Romanos III, John brought his youngest brother, Michael, to court and introduced him to the emperor and empress. Michael was young and extremely handsome, and the empress was very taken with him. According to the historian and courtier, Michael Psellos, an inveterate gossip, they had an open love affair.[21] Soon after this, Romanos III died, and it is inevitable that our sources suggest that John was guilty of having him poisoned. After Romanos died, John encouraged the widowed Zoe to marry Michael and make him emperor. Zoe agreed, and John's brother became the emperor Michael IV (r. 1034–1041).

This spectacular example of family promotion is only part of the story. Our sources, especially Michael Psellos, all comment on John's devotion to his family and the way he actively promoted his relatives. Skylitzes notes that "with John's help all of his brothers became members of the emperor's *oikos*."[22] In addition to Michael, he brought his other three brothers to court, as well as his sister Maria, for whom he negotiated a fine marriage. He arranged for his brother Niketas to be named duke of Antioch. Skylitzes tells us that Niketas was greatly hated in Antioch, at least by the aristocracy, who probably resented his modest social origins. Niketas died young and was replaced in Antioch by his brother Constantine.[23] Constantine was more popular in Antioch than his brother. This is the same Constantine who saved Edessa from an Arab attack.[24] He seems to have had some talent for military leadership, for he later served as head of the scholian guard and was sent out to command the army of the eastern frontier.

John also promoted his relatives within the palace. Early in his rise to power Symeon, the imperial *protovestiarios*, resigned his office in protest against John's actions and retired to Mt. Olympus. John promptly took the opportunity to name one of his eunuch brothers, George, as *protovestiarios*.

The marriage that John arranged for his sister Maria was to the *patrikios* Stephen, the admiral who botched the Byzantine expedition into Sicily and Southern Italy.[25] Meanwhile, Stephen and Maria had a son, Michael, whom John introduced into the imperial court as a potential replacement for the ailing Michael IV. The younger Michael, John's nephew, was adopted by the empress and, after the death of John's brother Michael IV, ruled as Michael V from 1041 to 1042.

Despite his uncle's role in placing him on the throne, Michael V did not treat John, the patron and nominal patriarch of his family, in the way that John thought that he should be treated. As a result, John began looking for a replacement for Michael, and his eye fell on another nephew, yet another Constantine. We do not know whether this Constantine was a son of Maria and Stephen, of Niketas, or of some other unnamed member of the clan. Psellos claims that John hoped that Constantine would unseat Michael V. To facilitate this John managed to gain legal power to be the sole judge of those who challenged the emperor's authority.[26] This was too much for the emperor Michael V. He exiled John to the Monastery of Monobatae in 1041. A year later John was blinded at the order of the patriarch, Michael Keroularios, then executed at the order of the emperor. Michael V himself was overthrown in 1042, while John's brother Constantine, the *nobelissimos*, stood by him to the end. They even had their eyes put out side-by-side. We do not know what finally happened to Constantine, nor can we be certain what happened to John's brother George.[27]

Whatever the fate of John's brothers, we have evidence that John's efforts at family promotion extended beyond his immediate relatives. There is a brief reference to Anthony the Fat, a eunuch related to the family, who was named bishop of Nikomedeia, much to the disgust of our sources.[28] We are also told that Constantine Phagitzes, a eunuch from Paphlagonia and long-time friend of Michael IV, was sent on a special diplomatic mission.[29] Skylitzes claims that when Romanos III died, the empress Zoe had hoped to bring to court eunuchs who had long served her father and thus were a part of her *oikos.* John blocked this plan, bringing in women servants from his own family whom he assigned to serve Zoe.[30] Psellos tells us that when Michael V deposed John the Orphanotrophos he also castrated "all his male relatives, most of whom were adults and held high office."[31] No other eunuch was as successful at advancing his family as John the Orphanotrophos. He was hated by the aristocracy for engaging successfully in behavior considered normal for an aristocratic family, and it is not clear whether their antipathy was because of his gender or because of his success in promoting the status of a family that was not part of the older elite.

Some sources, especially the chroniclers, characterize John's actions as "unnatural." This is couched in terms far more dramatic than mere disapproval of a politically successful strategy. Skylitzes intersperses his discussion of the rise of John the Orphanotrophos and his family with heaven-sent famines, floods, heavenly portents, hailstorms that strip the fruit off the trees, and locust plagues. He uses language drawn from the centuries-old rhetorical tradition about "bad eunuchs," employing terms that present a fruitful earth made fruitless under the reign of fruitless men.[32]

One of the things that this book shows is that this vigorous language against an overly powerful eunuch who had apparently transgressed traditional gender boundaries did not reflect the general realities of the time. The real indignation was directed at certain individuals who were perceived to have too much influence at court. The fact that they were eunuchs opened the door to a particular set of rhetorical weapons. The negative language about gender was, by the eleventh century, a rhetorical device built on a social anachronism that ignored the evolving process of acculturation and training of eunuchs that made them distinctive but normal within the Byzantine society of the eighth through the eleventh centuries.

Regardless of the negative language in some of our sources, established families had become accustomed to the idea of castrating sons for careers that would support the family trajectory in the imperial city. They had also come to accept the socially constructed gender assigned to eunuchs. This, in turn, meant that they believed not only in the limitations imposed on eunuchs by society but also in the special talents and spiritual potential that eunuchs were perceived to possess.

CONCLUSION

Past and Present Perceptions of Gender

A medievalist grounded in the structure of Western European feudalism would suggest that the eunuchs of the Byzantine court were castrated so that they could not have sons who would try to inherit their fathers' offices. Alternatively, they were castrated so that they would be less motivated to use their positions of power to promote the dynastic interests of their own families. Leaving aside a few examples of men who were castrated for dynastic reasons, like Basil Lekapenos,[1] this explanation is too simple and reductionist for the Byzantine context.

If today's medieval historians are willing to accept that gender is a socially constructed phenomenon consisting of a variety of ascribed traits and characteristics, some assigned by society as a whole and some internalized and reinforced by members of the gender group itself, then we may be able to come closer to an explanation for eunuchism as a cultural phenomenon. In this final chapter I would like to suggest that the model around which the gender of eunuchs was organized is that of the "perfect servant," a model of great antiquity in the eastern Mediterranean. We have seen elements of this model throughout this book. Before addressing it, however, I want to return to a striking eleventh-century Byzantine source that deals with eunuchs in a remarkably coherent, sympathetic way. This is an essay, in the form of a mock dialogue, written by Theophylaktos, bishop of Ohrid, under the title *Defense of Eunuchs.* Citations to portions of Theophylaktos's essay have appeared in previous chapters, but so far it has not been presented in its entirety.

Theophylaktos of Ohrid Reflects on Eunuchs

Theophylaktos of Ohrid was a respected writer and churchman of his era, and both he and his family were well established in the church. He wrote extensively on eunuchs, sometimes in ways that have been perceived as highly critical. The twelfth-century depiction of eunuchs that emerges from his work sits quite comfortably alongside a representation structured around modern gender concepts.

Theophylaktos himself recognized that there were conflicting opinions about the institution of eunuchism and about eunuchs themselves in his own time. In his *Defense of Eunuchs* he makes it clear that he believes that those who judge eunuchs simply on the basis of appearance, assuming that the outward appearance of the body reflects the quality of the soul, are wrong; each person must be examined based on his own personal merits.[2] This contradicts directly some of the medical lore about eunuchs discussed in chapter 3. Theophylaktos sets up his discussion as a dialogue between two persons, one (a monk) who is hostile to eunuchs and one (a eunuch) who is favorably disposed.[3] The dialogue takes places over the head of the recently castrated nephew of the eunuch and is overheard from a secret place by the author. This is, of course, a rhetorical device, as is Theophylaktos's claim to impartiality, since Theophylaktos's own goal is to support eunuchism as an institution.

The dialogue starts out with the opponent of eunuchism stating his case.[4] The opponent criticizes the recent castration of the eunuch protagonist's nephew, saying that such an act is opposed by the Creator. Furthermore, castration is contrary to the laws of gods and men; the law of Moses refused to allow eunuchs to be part of the religious community. The canons of the Apostles and church fathers, and the civil legislation of Justinian all forbade the removal of testicles; indeed, the legal tradition dating back to the earliest emperors had forbidden castration within the Roman Empire. In addition castration changes the character of the castrated child, making him morally weak, so that he easily yields to passions and greed and is prone to a long list of other weaknesses: miserliness, licentiousness, ambition, envy, a love of petty quarrelling, deceit, bad temper, irritation at small things. Eunuchs haunt the palace, and this increases their weaknesses. Since eunuchs live apart from men, in physical contact with women, they become prey to the passions of feminine sensibility. Eunuchs, with weak souls and strong passions, are controlled by women. Women, through their prudishness, two-facedness, slothfulness, and stupidity present models of effeminacy for eunuchs. Then there are the eunuchs who sing in the theater and warble lewd verses to traditional hymn songs and have brought pornographic songs into the church. The critic of eunuchs goes on to say that eunuchs behave like actors. They have an indecent appearance, they drink too much, they use filthy language, and most of them engage in random illicit sexual activity.[5] This is especially true of the eunuchs who serve as guardians of the women's quarters, which seems reasonable. Eunuchs hang out with theater people—like attracts like. They sing with libertines, and those who keep company with women arouse others with their passion. In any case, eunuchs are ill-omened and everybody insults them.

The defender of eunuchs, an articulate and educated man "and a living reproach to these charges," counters. He says that not all eunuchs are alike. He points out that there are many kinds of eunuchs, and the ones that are being criticized are surely eunuchs from Persia or the Arab lands. He then lists some of the honored churchmen who have been eunuchs and suggests that the critic of eunuchs, in order to make his point, has mentioned only evil ones, purposely looking for examples of eunuchs who have behaved badly. He suggests that the critic, who is a celibate man, is also, like a eunuch, subject to the accusation that he is at variance with God's intention. Marriage and procreation are part of God's plan, so how is the eunuch different from the celibate man, since both consider the genital organs to be superfluous? He points out that it makes sense to prune away unnecessary genitalia if a man does not intend to father children. If a child is born with a sixth finger and it is cut off, nobody calls this act "unnatural."

Is it any different or any more an attack on "nature" if unnecessary genitals are removed? The celibate man, since he desires virginity and hates the production of sperm, has modified the nature of the genital organs so that they do not produce sperm even though this is their natural function. Wouldn't it be just as reasonable to remove the genitals at an appropriate time? Such a decision would not be blameworthy. The defender of eunuchism goes on to criticize the celibate man for wasting away his body through asceticism and not eating or bathing. How is the destruction of the body different from the removal of the testicles? A Hellene might offer these criticisms since he puts nothing ahead of nature and his goal in life is to live according to nature and its laws. But those who have chosen to lead the ascetic life, a life beyond nature, have no right to criticize eunuchs.[6]

The defender of eunuchs then turns to a discussion of the laws against castration, arguing that they are outmoded, devised for a different time and a different kind of society. All written law is subject to interpretation, and one should look for the spirit rather than the letter of the law. The Old Testament honored eunuchs in Isaiah, and also, the prophet Daniel and the three children [Abednego, Shadrach, Meshach]. Such people should not be cut off from the Christian community, for they are neither barren nor fruitless in the sight of God, since they have descendants and family in Jerusalem. If one here means the earthly Jerusalem, then eunuchs do not have descendants, but they do if you are referring to the heavenly Jerusalem, which no one can enter unless he has the seeds of reason within him, seeds that encourage man to do good. Those of us who do not want to be expelled from the company of the faithful should respect eunuchism. The Hebrews condemn eunuchism because they (the Hebrews) "mark out the boundaries of goodness in terms of prolific childbearing."[7]

At this point the defender of eunuchism states that he cannot fully support the laws of the Apostles and the patriarchal canons as they apply to eunuchs. He agrees that those who come to manhood and then arrange for their own castration are murderers of the self. Men who are castrated by others, however, do not deserve the criticism directed at men who are responsible for their own castration. He cannot tolerate those who have themselves castrated so that they can be sexually active without impregnating women, calling them enemies of the creation of God. "They have not used their members for the reason [for which] they were created and have not considered that ejaculation is the object of coitus."[8] He supports legal sanctions against self-castration. On the other hand, he supports childhood castration saying,

> If anyone's testicles are cut off while still a child or an adolescent because he is worthy of every care by his relatives who desire to preserve his chastity and purity, and they assist him in his resolution to become a eunuch so that no danger can befall him [from sin], how can you still show the disapproving eye and express the bitterness that fills the canons?[9]

The defense goes on to comment that the Apostles forbade eunuchism because they related it to the heretical Symeon the Magician. Later the church fathers forbade it because it was practiced by the Marcionites and Manichaeans. These heretics taught that marriage and procreation were evil. Today men no longer believe this and practice ablation because of love of purity and piety. Celibate men avoid sexuality for the same reason, not because they consider marriage an institution created by the Devil.

The defender continues by suggesting that church law is not always perfect. Here he lists examples of laws passed by the church that he feels contradict Jesus' teachings.[10] He asks why men and women are not treated equally in church law regarding matters like divorce, and why divorce is allowed, even though forbidden by Jesus. Since such is the case in these examples, it is right to examine the law carefully and interpret it within the context in which it was written.

Moreover, he says, since there are so many high-ranking eunuchs in the state and in the church it is obvious that his interpretation of the law is correct.[11] The church fathers and the saints guarded their chastity and ignored their bodies. As the end of the ages approaches it has become increasingly difficult to face the front-line forces of the Devil, and so castration is now sometimes needed to preserve sanctity.[12] Doctors now administer treatments that are different from those recommended in past times, and if asked, these doctors say that these changes are because patients' resistance has changed. So, also, the church's method of healing has changed.

Here the implication is that castration is used as a way of avoiding sin. "If it were not so, how could it be that this very illegal act is overlooked by all the high churchmen and is accepted openly within the church? It is considered normal that the emperors should close their eyes to this practice, especially since it is in their interest to increase the number of this breed [eunuchs] since they are always well minded, as the true meaning [etymology] of their name implies."[13]

The defense continues by characterizing as laughable Justinian's legislation that abolished eunuchism. How could these laws have been enforced when Justinian himself had eunuchs at his court? This legislation was the work of Tribonian, Justinian's expert on Roman law, and was created because of the high mortality from castration at that time. If the laws were actually being enforced, where did all the court eunuchs come from? Or the general Narses? Emperors need eunuchs, so society should either abolish castration and neither employ eunuchs nor entrust them with the highest offices, or else it should legalize the practice of castration, recognizing its advantages. The defense says it cannot accept the justification that castration is a sin for others while emperors find eunuchs useful.

Likewise, claims that castrations are performed routinely because of sickness ought not to be condemned. Such a position is not really valid because those who oppose eunuchism haven't taken the time to explore the real reasons for castration.[14] If Justinian's law had teeth in it, why do we still have people who do castrations? Eunuchs today are not necessarily from barbarian countries, even though you claim that they are and that they were castrated by foreigners. You can't have barbarians doing important administrative jobs, nor can you turn these jobs over to slaves, who are stupid and coarse.[15] Justinian's legislation should be abandoned. The older laws against castration grew out of a need for soldiers, a need to keep up population levels. Constantine the Great abolished laws that penalized those who did not marry and introduced the practice of virginity into the city. Julian the Apostate hated eunuchs because they supported Christianity. If we accept Julian's rationale for disliking eunuchs, we would also have to accept his rationale for persecuting the martyrs.[16]

The defender of eunuchs then comments on the supposed vices of eunuchs, suggesting that to say, as the critics do, that eunuchs are reduced to a feminine state is not even worth commenting on. Such comments are more concerned with the small faults of eunuchs than with the big faults of whole men. Furthermore, how can society say that eunuchs are weak and at the same time complain that they are too powerful? It is said that they are greedy, yet they engage in philanthropy. Moreover there is no shortage of whole men who are guilty of all the same bad things attributed to eunuchs.

Theophylaktos's defender of eunuchs also comments on common perceptions of the eunuchs of the imperial palace. Again he argues that the criticisms aimed at palace eunuchs are group stereotypes, not reactions to real individuals. When the Greeks and the barbarians claim that eunuchs are objectionable, they are talking about them as a group. In fact, he points out, there are good ones and bad ones, and they model themselves on their masters and mistresses, and there are many very worthy palace eunuchs.

Similarly, one finds numerous eunuchs in churches and monasteries, and others who ornament the episcopate and priesthood, and they are very good persons. Theophylaktos's advocate for eunuchs agrees that there may be eunuchs who, in church, sing holy songs set to popular tunes, tunes that some might consider licentious. But, he argues, good tunes have long made holy songs attractive to the public and, in any case, it isn't fair to blame the eunuch who sets the words to the tune.[17]

The advocate then notes that critics point to a tradition of perceiving a eunuch as a bad omen. After all, he says, dull-witted men also say the same thing about monks. The church fathers may have said bad things about the eunuchs of their time, but they also said even worse things about the rulers of their time. But heretics in an older age were bad whole men and we don't criticize whole men today because there once were bad heretics who were whole men. The most winning image of eunuchs, modesty and dignity, should be the way of life that all strive to achieve.[18]

The defense goes on to point out that some commentators become enraged with eunuchs if they deviate from appropriate conduct, pointing out that spots are most conspicuous on luxurious clothing. When one is given much, much is also demanded. This is followed by an enumeration of good eunuchs, [and] there is at least one in every cohort of the Lord. The advocate starts with the eunuch of Queen Candace "who brought all Ethiopia to Christ" and is called the "hands for the Holy Spirit." He goes on to list many others, including eunuchs who have been martyrs, patriarchs, bishops, abbots, priests, deacons, and monks.

The defender of eunuchs then enters into a very interesting discussion of the eunuch and sexuality. Eunuchs can avoid nocturnal emissions and erections of the penis and thus avoid the "pricks of conscience" that afflict whole men. But eunuchs also are continent because they want to be, even though the condition of their bodies aids them in this choice. Indeed, some eunuchs do engage in lewd behavior, and therefore those who are chaste are chaste by choice. All men, he says, can escape nocturnal emissions if they desire purity and refrain from involuntary and natural pollution. Granted that castration allows eunuchs to avoid natural sexual desires more easily than whole men can, nevertheless eunuchs are chaste by choice, though aided by the condition of their bodies. In reply to those who say that many eunuchs behave unchastely, Theophylaktos says that there are also those who remain chaste by choice. In his experience it is difficult for whole men to remain chaste. This is even true of priests, despite their vows of celibacy. Finally he concludes that those who insult eunuchs do so without examination, because of lust or envy.[19]

Theophylaktos of Ohrid also wrote two poems dealing with eunuchs, one of which is often taken as hostile to eunuchs and as a contradiction of the message in the *Defense of Eunuchs.* Taken together, these poems show that he was comfortable with both praising and criticizing eunuchs. Placed in proper context, these poems are not contradictory. One of the themes that emerges is that he disliked eunuchs who were sexual predators and used castration as a way to facilitate sexual activity. The following is addressed to a eunuch who seems to fit that category:

> Many say that eunuchs are a marvel [monstrosity]
> because they have a changed nature.
> I would claim that you are a marvel among eunuchs
> for you are thoroughly corrupt when it comes to purity
> which is, of course, the natural privilege of eunuchs;
> as lustful, as profligate, as fond of
> fornication,
> as one who seduces virgins and despoils young women,
> more intemperate than a billy goat in your
> approach to illicit intercourse.
> Regarding intercourse you are a Priapus in your deeds
> or a Pan, child of many sorts of seeds, being, as the
> myth says enamored of Echo, a most outlawed
> love.
> I don't have time now to write more about what you do,
> for the tongue may happen upon a lie when it is
> being frank.[20]

At the same time, Theophylaktos could write the following, which is found in the preface to the work dedicated to his brother:

> My brother is the reason why I write this essay,
> because he is a eunuch, and a model for the well-ordered life.
> But, feeling disgusted regarding the things said about eunuchs,
> which some say unjustly,
> he seeks suitable consolation.
> As a way of offering it, I have written this treatise,
> the interest due a man who loves purity and is most wise,
> who can distinguish different facts justly
> without confusing their disparate nature,
> or censuring those most noble men
> when perchance one sees an evil eunuch.
> If we should allow this, then it would not be sufficient
> for one to hurl innumerable censures at testiculated men,
> even though they might have achieved the highest step of virtue.
> How many [whole men] are thoroughly evil among them?
> They are like the sand of the sea or dust of the earth.
> If anyone wishes to compare them with the eunuchs,
> those whom they thought to be most evil,
> one would find them to be lions compared with weasels and flies.
> And if any of the laws and canons forbid the
> excision of the testicles, think about the intention
> of the law and notice when it was written,
> and all the circumstances surrounding it, taking
> notice of the rules of rhetoric.
> When you have looked at them,
> you will find only one practice,
> one that was not adopted before
> for safety.
> I have not written this tract for a public audience,
> but for a father, a eunuch, great in knowledge.
> Although it is written as a private favor for my own brother
> I also, indeed, pour it out for all of you
> even though I have a special feeling regarding these
> things, I intend the goodwill to be for all.
> And to whomever these things are not agreeable,
> he may be fond of those, and I these.[21]

What emerges from this digest of Theophylaktos's work is in fact quite consonant with the findings in this book. The perceptions of eunuchs of his age were filled with a variety of stereotypes, many of them hostile. In many cases, as in the example of Theophylaktos's own poetry, negative stereotypes were used freely. It is important to recognize, however, that these stereotypes were often aimed at eunuchs who transgressed the norms for their gender and do not necessarily constitute a condemnation of the group as a whole.

The Perfect Servant and Mediation

In the broader perspective of this book, the gender construction for eunuchs was founded primarily on what I have characterized in various places as "perfect service." This element was, however, closely interlocked with a second trait, the perceived capacity to mediate across otherwise difficult boundaries in the service of masters, patrons, and others that needed assistance. This capacity has shown up at various points in the book but is complex enough to merit a brief direct discussion.

Because the eunuch could transcend boundaries he was usually portrayed as an extension of his master and as a go-between, transmitting crucial information across barriers that his master or mistress could not pass. This is seen most dramatically when eunuchs functioned as surrogates for imperial power.[22] Often acting in this capacity on behalf of a member of his *oikos,* eunuchs appear both as servants in the conventional sense and as altruistic helpers. This cultural mediation transcended the boundaries between the social and spiritual spaces of the mental universe of the people of Byzantium, a universe that regulated their beliefs and actions. Within this universe angels, holy persons, prepubescent boys, and eunuchs all functioned as messengers and servants moving across unseen, but very real, boundaries. These individuals provided mediation that had both a personal and a broader cross-cultural or anthropological content.

The eunuch's unique capacity for mediation made his role as a perfect servant possible. In chapter 4 we saw that commentators of the tenth century, as part of bringing the image of Constantine I (r. 324–337) up-to-date for an audience of a later era, invented the eunuch Euphratas and then cast him in the role of a perfect servant of the emperor. A servant like Euphratas extends the power of the emperor in numerous directions, including into the terrain of the miraculous. He carries out the emperor's wishes and counsels him on crucially important religious matters. He embodies the objectives of his master and enhances his personal authority. Euphratas acts as the emperor's surrogate. He is even allowed to use the imperial seal. He is bright, highly educated, unfailingly loyal, and unfairly attacked by the aristocracy because of his access to power. In creating Euphratas, the Byzantine world of the tenth century was not only providing the legend of the emperor Constantine I with an intelligible context but was also defining the eunuch as perfect servant.

Examples of eunuchs acting as mediators have appeared throughout this book. Certainly their oldest and most familiar mediational role is one in which they mediated between the separate worlds of men and women. In this social arena eunuchs frequently appear as guardians of women and children. In a culture where female chastity was honored and women, at least aristocratic ones, were secluded from contact with men, it is not surprising that castrated men served women as guards and as confidants. In some cases, they functioned as a "paternalistic" extension of the *oikos* to which they were attached; in others, they appear as the agents, servants, physicians, spiritual advisors, or protectors of the women and children. St. Euphrosyna the Younger had a eunuch servant who interacted with the world on her behalf and "attended to her needs." Recall that when the saint had an angelic vision that told her that her prayers endorsing the desire of Emperor Leo VI (r. 886–912) for a male offspring, it was this eunuch who took the good news to the emperor.[23] Similarly, when St. Irene of Chrysobalanton communicated with her sister, who was married to the Caesar Bardas, it was through the sister's eunuch.[24]

The tale of St. John the Almsgiver (see chapter 2 above), among others, illustrates both the paternal/tutorial aspects of eunuchs as servant-mediators and the degree of separation that social norms required between men and women of reproductive age, whatever their circumstances.[25] It is this kind of contextual material that clarifies the significance of Angeliki Laiou's observation that "after the eleventh century the confinement of women to the women's quarters was not a functional reality." 26

Just as eunuchs functioned as intermediaries in the transmission of messages, as bridges between worldly and spiritual settings, and as mediators between the court and the outside world, they also connected the world of the educated elite with that of the common people. A large gulf existed between the aristocratic and bureaucratic elite of the empire and the rest of society, and in such a compartmentalized society, mediation by eunuchs was crucial.[27] We particularly see this in Basil the Nothos's popularity with the common people,[28] John the Orphanotropos's charity to the eastern provinces after a famine,[29] and in the prevalent image of eunuchs as guardians of widows and orphans.[30] The hagiographical corpus also contains a familiar topos in which eunuchs served as "talent scouts" who drew individuals out of the lower orders into the elite. It is seen in the case of the eunuch tax collector in the Vita of St. Athanasios of Athos,[31] who is depicted as recognizing the virtue of a worthy young man of modest background, seeing to his education, and bringing him to court. There is an analogous story regarding the eunuch Theoktistos's early sponsorship of Sts. Cyril and Methodios, the famous apostles to the Slavs.[32] Eunuchs were also involved in the choice of imperial brides who, in some periods, were selected from modest backgrounds.

Eunuchs also acted across boundaries between the spiritual and material worlds. The assumption that they had special access to spiritual powers made them especially valuable as servants of powerful men and women and also enhanced the importance of those they served.

In the Byzantine mind the court at Constantinople was a place of power, prestige, and mystery. It was perceived to be an earthly replica of the court of heaven where the emperor functioned as Christ's representative on earth and was attended by an "angelic" corps of eunuchs who guarded him, regulated his contacts with the material world, and supervised and guarded ceremonial traditions and protocol.

That these parallels were clearly understood is seen in the imagery used by the author of the Vita of St. Kosmas the Monk.[33] Kosmas was *koitonites* (bedchamber attendant) to the emperor Alexander (r. 912–913), and after the emperor's death he became a monk. In 933, during a severe illness, he had a vision in which he was escorted to heaven and ushered to a seat at a great table in a magnificent hall staffed with eunuchs with shining faces. Their faces were like lightning and filled to overflowing with all kinds of joy. St. Kosmas was seated at the table, surrounded by other monks and servants of the emperor. They came from a "cosmic catalog." Yet he wasn't allowed to stay. After many hours a eunuch came and ordered that St. Kosmas be returned to his monastery, presumably to recover from his illness, and another monk be brought in his place. It seems that his disciples had so mourned and prayed for him that it was time for him to return from the dead. In this image of the heavenly palace the eunuchs act as intermediaries between the deceased and God, just as they act as intermediaries between the living and the emperor in the earthly palace.[34]

We have already seen many examples in which eunuchs and angels are interchanged and the earthly and heavenly courts are described with similar images. In the Vita of St. Athanasios of Athos, a monk named Matthew has a vision of the Virgin escorted by two eunuchs.[35] This parallels other descriptions of the Virgin being escorted to the throne of God, supported on the shoulders of angels and mirrors the way in which eunuchs escorted important persons to imperial audiences.[36] On a more exalted level, we can go back to our citation of St. Lazaros of Mt. Galesios, who had a vision in which Christ himself was accompanied by two eunuchs.[37] By the tenth century, therefore, it was a commonplace that the major dignitaries of both heaven and earth should be accompanied by individuals who guarded and escorted them. These escorts, whether angels or eunuchs, separated such dignitaries from lesser beings and acted on their behalf. The examples cited above show that eunuchs were considered appropriate, or even necessary, for that role.

Perhaps the most telling example of this that I have found is in the previously cited Vita of St. Niphon of Constantiana.[38] In this episode a eunuch guides the saint from the real world through the heavenly gardens right up to the gates of the heavenly mansion and then back to earth. Neither of them can pass through the gates of heaven because both are still mortal beings, but the eunuch guides the saint along the way, acting as his escort. The ability of this eunuch to move between worldly and spiritual realms is made quite explicit.

The preceding example embodies an unusual number of elements of mediation between the earthly and heavenly realms, and chapter 7 cites numerous similar cases of activity by eunuchs in regions where the material and spiritual worlds interacted. Angels, eunuchs, and young boys are presented with similar gender identity, beardlessness, shining faces, and clothing. They are described with similar language and bring messages, escort personages, occupy visions, and guide metaphysical travelers. These images are found in the *Patria,* in the chronicle of Skylitzes despite its frequent hostility to eunuchs, and in hagiographical topoi.[39]

Images that illustrate societal assumptions about eunuchs can readily be found outside of the courtly or hagiographical literary traditions. They appear in popular literature like the dream book of the patriarch Nikephoros. There it is considered good luck when someone dreams of a eunuch who looks like an angel.[40] They are also recognized by the author of the *Timarion,* an early twelfth-century satire.[41] The hero, Timarion, descends into Hell. There he sees the emperor Theophilos sitting among the judges of the lower world.[42] He observes that a eunuch is whispering in Theophilos's ear. "Oh no," replies his companion, Theodore, "that is his guardian angel." The image is amusing, but even more amusing is the author's choice of descriptive adjectives for the eunuch/angel: his face "shines like the sun." This language is a parody of the eunuch/angel confusion so common in the hagiographical corpus. It also illustrates the popular assumption that emperors needed eunuchs, special individuals who could function in both a material and a spiritual world, and that if such an individual was present at the emperor's side it must be a eunuch—unless, of course, it was a guardian angel.

This assumed capacity to mediate in such a variety of ways was crucial to the eunuch's function as "perfect servant," the cornerstone of the gender construct for eunuchs. As such, the eunuch functioned as both servant and agent for his master or patron and his role was well understood. This concept permeates the range of gender traits assigned to eunuchs; it is also a conception that changed subtly as eunuchs came to be recruited from within Byzantine society. In principle, the Byzantine world agreed with earlier traditions that said that the individual serves best who is not troubled by sexual desires or by family responsibilities. Writing in the third century, St. Hippolytus made this claim, even as he connected asexual servants with angels.[43] This asexual aspect of the eunuch as perfect servant was central to the gender construction of the eunuch.

I would suggest that their gender construct, including the core role as "perfect servant," is a variant on a much older and widespread model in the ancient and medieval eastern Mediterranean. It is a model that dates from well before the Christian era and it defined the role of the castrated man in eastern Mediterranean societies. Palace eunuchs in these societies were perfect servants of kings and emperors, and priestly eunuchs were perfect servants of their gods.

It is also likely that eunuchs who served in these ways before, outside of, or beyond the Byzantine construct dealt with in this book were similarly presumed to have no other allegiances. Not much has been written on this aspect of the topic, but the inference is supported by Shaun Marmon's work and by Biblical passages such as the story of the eunuch of Queen Candace. As in Byzantium, such eunuchs also seem to have had no ties to family, either natal or marital. They lived outside of conventional time. Frequently slaves, they commonly had no ties to a geographical place, with the result that they existed outside of conventional space. Thus, the loyalties of eunuch servants, whatever their society, were not easily divided even though they were not constrained by conventional boundaries.

Eunuchs appear as perfect servants in Biblical texts. The eunuch servant of Candace, queen of the Ethiopians, who appears in Acts 8:26–40, provides an excellent example (see fig. 11). The passage begins with the angel of the Lord directing Philip to go to the road from Jerusalem to Gaza. There he finds an Ethiopian eunuch, who remains unnamed but is described as head of the queen's treasury. The eunuch is returning from Jerusalem, where he had gone to worship, riding along in a cart reading the prophet Isaiah. As an Ethiopian and a eunuch, he is an outsider. Nevertheless, he is announced by a stereotypical angel and open to Philip's teachings. He is described as gentle and courteous, is quickly converted, and requests baptism.

It is not far from this story to the vita of the late third-century martyr, Eleutherios.[44] In this vita, which dates from the fourth century or later, the model of the eunuch as perfect servant is set out with remarkable coherence. Indeed, many aspects of this vita have affinities with the description of the invented eunuch Euphratas seen in chapter 4. We also find elements of the perfect servant model in many of the lives of eunuchs who were well regarded by Byzantine authors. The description of Eleutherios merits quotation at some length.

FIGURE 11

Depiction of the scene in Ps. 68:31 (Ps. 67:32 LXX). Phillip the Deacon encounters the eunuch, a high official of Queen Candace of Ethiopia. The eunuch is returning home from Jerusalem and reading the Old Testament. Phillip succeeds in converting the eunuch, showing that eunuchs are also part of God's kingdom. Historical Museum, Moscow, MS 129 D, fol. 65r. From M. Shchepkina, ed., *Miniatury Khludovskoi Psaltyri* (Moscow, 1977).

"Eleutherios, oh men, is a Christian name meaning "freely sharing." Throughout antiquity among ordinary people he was famous, though we don't know who his parents were and can only say that he was born either in Byzantium, now called Constantinople, a large city, or else in the East. The abundance of his virtue is celebrated. He is said to have been one of that order of men who hold the high office of head of the royal bed-servants, having great power with the emperor, even as the unwritten common tradition records. For he was dear to him and a friend and most faithful and held in an equal place with the emperor's sons, always living in the palace, joined with royal honors and piled with rewards. He was charming in all things, famous, outstanding, like a star from heaven shining through the night.[45] [He was] flourishing in the friendship of Maximian the emperor.[46]

He had not yet been baptized, although he was eager in his observances. For the holy Eleutherios was always doing good deeds, gentle, kindly, willing to do work appropriate to his high office and also that of his subordinates, a lover of peace, opposed to avarice, mild, not wrathful, he showed himself truly to be the spirit of the house, just and blameless, sincere and kind to his brother, reverent of God, and lacking in evil, never allowing his eye to wander, never allowing himself to be influenced by rewards, increasingly serious and modest, never indulging in false agreement (with others), liberal in his gifts to the poor and needy, always following those imprisoned and attempting to help them, he hastened to aid the cause of those unjustly oppressed.[47]

And finally he received the Holy Spirit that is able to dissolve mountains. He didn't take up the task of being a soldier, for he was not considered appropriate to engage in this work, but rather in the areas of wisdom and industry and teaching the Scripture. Since it was not the custom for him to be a combatant, he concentrated his attentions on learned study, instructing (others) in all things regarding the Holy Spirit. Since he could not easily persuade the emperor, who was then Maximian who has been mentioned above, who had been filled with hatred and burning enmity for the true Christians, he set out in greatest detail a plan of this sort, both best and most wise, a plan that claimed that he [Eleutherios] needed to go to a more salubrious place and breathe pure and healthy air. And so he departed, skillfully eluding the emperor and tyrant Maximian.

About this man and similar men of this sort God the all-powerful has said through Isaiah, "Let not the eunuch say, I am a dry branch and without fruit, for I tell you the eunuchs are chosen by me because I give to you in my house and within my walls a place that is better than sons and daughters and those things which follow.[48]

We get a less detailed version of the model of perfect service in connection with Justinian's eunuch general, Narses. Narses is portrayed as faithful to the emperor's requests despite the fact that his friends "tried to prevent him from marching with Belisarios, and they sought to show him how disgraceful it was for one who shared the secrets of the emperor not to be commander-in-chief of the army but to take orders from a mere general."[49]

Prokopios goes on to suggest that Narses' friends felt that if he wanted to take over the army the men would desert Belisarios. Apparently these "friends" assumed that the only reason one would leave the society of the emperor would be to seek fame as a war leader. Narses refused their suggestion that he usurp command and, elsewhere in Prokopios, is praised for his princely generosity and willingness to help others. As a result, he was "clothed with great power by the emperor."[50]

The tradition of the "perfect servant" permeated the culture of the eastern Mediterranean for centuries before the rise of Byzantium. It was associated with separation from one's own background, with asexuality and asceticism, and was linked to service in the household of both secular and religious masters—*oikoi*, rulers, and gods. It is also inseparably linked with eunuchs. Biology and a society constructed around complex family units rendered eunuchs well suited to this role, while social construction and conditioning accentuated the link. In Byzantium this developed into a complex, gradually evolving, and durable gender construct that became integral to society.

Conclusion

In the course of this book we have tried to understand the place of eunuchs in Byzantine society and culture. We looked at the language associated with eunuchs and saw that it had developed numerous ways of adapting to the ambiguities of a world that included more than male and female gender categories. At the same time, writers of Late Antiquity and Byzantium developed a repertoire of ideas about gender and physiology that incorporated many observations about the physical distinctiveness of eunuchs. Concurrently, we found plentiful evidence that many eunuchs were castrated young and both educated and acculturated into distinctive forms of speech, body language, and dress.

The resulting pattern clearly fits the modern conception of the social construction of gender. The prevalence and normalization of the construct within Byzantine culture is suggested by the fact that by the era of the ninth to the eleventh centuries Byzantine authors regendered the context of some of the most important figures in their religious and historical tradition. Thus the biblical narrative that framed the prophet Daniel, in which he was a courtier and moral counselor to the ruler, only made sense if Daniel was also a eunuch. Similarly, the activities of Byzantium's two greatest emperors, Justinian and Constantine, were only intelligible if implemented through the mediation of court eunuchs who also functioned as perfect servants.

When, in part 2, we examined the narratives and discussions around specific eunuchs, we found that these discussions are much easier to understand if we assume that the authors who wrote about eunuchs were responding to the sorts of explicit and implicit gender assumptions set out in part 1. By the ninth century it was increasingly easy to find eunuchs holding high church offices, despite earlier prejudices against them. This shift was accompanied by a broadening of the criteria that signified sanctity in ways that made it possible for eunuchs to assimilate to the religious culture of the era. This should be taken as an important indication of changes in the gender construct assigned to eunuchs by the society and of the growing normalization of that construct. Meanwhile, Byzantium witnessed a considerable number of eunuchs as generals and high officials—positions perceived as involving physical prowess and the assumption of autonomous agency. Since this violated assumptions about the incapacity of eunuchs in such roles, the apparent gender transgression was resolved in two ways that reflect the discourse about gender in many settings: such eunuchs had succeeded either by exploiting traits unique to their gender or by becoming exceptions to the perceived norm for their gender.

We then followed eunuchs into realms that were part of the Byzantine mental universe, realms that sometimes seem alien to the modern observer. We saw how eunuch servant/mediators were crucial to the ceremonial and symbolic structures that surrounded the emperor and the imperial palace. As they defined the charismatic space around the ruler, they reinforced the idea that the imperial office involved a special power or numen. At times they helped empresses to transcend their condition as women and occupy the space created for emperors. They ritually protected the ruler and his or her aura from contamination by ordinary mortals, in practice, creating a distinctively gendered space around the ruler. The spiritual and religious element of this function was established by the rituals that initiated eunuchs to the inner circle of the royal service. Unlike other positions associated with the emperor, which were granted by the ruler, these eunuchs received their charge directly from God in a distinctive ceremony. Because they had an effective monopoly on the lore that governed imperial ritual, they were crucial to the continuity of the imperial establishment.[51]

Moreover, we saw that in creating stories, narratives, visions, and dreams, it was routine for individuals to perceive a confusion or even interchangeability between eunuchs and angels. Eunuchs clearly were not angels, since they were undeniably mortal. Yet they functioned in ways that closely paralleled the supposed roles of angels, facilitating miracles, conveying messages between divine sources and mortal recipients, and escorting holy individuals. All of this illustrates how in the Byzantine mind, eunuchs, while not capable of some things that ordinary mortals could do, possessed a potential for holiness, asexuality, and access to spiritual realms that was not part of the makeup of ordinary mortals.

The preceding summary points to two parallel conclusions. Not only were eunuchs defined by their society as a distinct gender, but the nature of that gender construct changed substantially over time. One key aspect of this, reflecting the proposition that they were increasingly integral to society, was the changing process of social recruitment. As a result, while some of the rhetoric of "otherness" persisted with regard to the origins of eunuchs, in practice, they increasingly were recruited from within Byzantine society itself rather than from foreign populations. This meant that in certain ways their image of loyalty to their masters was compromised by loyalty to a biological clan but seems not to have affected the elements of their gender construct that involved mediation and perfect service.

Finally, if we assume that a gender is constructed around a few fundamental roles and traits, the crucial trait for eunuchs was service or "perfect service." Even though they often had loyalties or obligations to a personal *oikos,* eunuchs continued to be perceived as transcending normal physical, spiritual, and temporal constraints. Their nominal separation from the normal life cycle and from normal sexuality made them perpetually ambiguous but also perpetually dependent on the masters whom they served. At the same time, their unique combination of traits allowed them to transcend numerous boundaries within the Byzantine world, including boundaries between sexes, between palace and plebeian worlds, between holy sources of revelation and human recipients, between the emperor and his subjects. Thus, at one place on this spectrum eunuchs served and protected the poor and the orphaned, at another they carried divine news to mortal recipients, and at yet another they functioned as surrogates for emperors and empresses. As such they held important military commands, carried out diplomatic negotiations, and undertook major administrative tasks.

In so doing, however, they were not functioning as autonomous agents. Because of their gender-specific nature, they extended the ruler's persona into physical and spiritual spaces he (or she) could not reach directly. They not only provided the ruler with the physical reach required by military command and diplomacy but also were assumed to have access to spiritual spaces not easily reached by ordinary men and women. Seen this way, eunuchs were not just an oddity of Byzantine society or an example of suspect "oriental" influences. Rather, they were part of an ancient eastern Mediterranean tradition that in the Byzantine Empire became a well-defined third gender that was integral to the functioning of Byzantine society for a millennium.

APPENDIX

Spelling Equivalents, Traditional and Reformed

Traditional	*Reformed*
Aetius	Aetios
Anna Comnena	Anna Komnene
Anthimius	Anthimios
Belisarius	Belisarios
Cedrenus	Kedrenos
Cosmas	Kosmas
Ducas	Doukas
Epiphanius	Epiphanios
Eudocia	Eudokia
Eugenius	Eugenios
Eunapius	Eunapios
Eusebius	Eusebios
Glycas	Glykas
Lecapenus	Lekapenos
Leontius	Leontios
Nicholas I Mysticus	Nicholas I Mystikos
Nicephorus Bryennius	Nikephoros Bryennios
Nicetas Choniates	Niketas Choniates
Nicetas Pectoratus	Niketas Pectoratos
Nicetas Stethatus	Niketas Stethatos
Nicomedia	Nikomedeia

Ochrida	Ohrid
Paleologus	Palaiologos
Philaretus	Philaretos
Philostratus	Philostratos
Philotheus	Philotheos
Polyeuctes	Polyeuktos
Porphyrogenitus	Porphyrogennetos
Procopius	Prokopios
Psellus	Psellos
Socrates	Sokrates
Soranus	Soranos
Sozomenus	Sozomenos
Symeon Magister	Symeon Magistros
Theophylact Simocattes	Theophylaktos Simokattes
Theophylact	Theophylaktos
Theophilus	Theophilos
Zosimus	Zosimos

FREQUENTLY USED ABBREVIATIONS

AASS	*Acta Sanctorum*, 71 vols. (Paris, 1863–1940)
AB	*Analecta Bollandiana*
BHG	*Bibliotheca hagiographica graeca*, ed. F. Halkin, 3d ed., 3 vols. (Brussels, 1957)
ByzF	*Byzantinische Forschungen*
BZ	*Byzantinische Zeitschrift*
CIC	T. Mommsen, P. Kruger, R. Schoell, and G. Kroll, eds., *Corpus Iuris Civilis*, 3 vols. (1892; reprint, Dublin, 1967–1968)
De cer.	Constantine VII Porphyrogenitus, *Constantini Porphyrogeniti Imperatoris De ceremoniis aulae byzantinae libri duo*, ed. J. J. Reiske, 2 vols. (Bonn, 1829–1830)
De cer., ed. Vogt	Constantine VII Porphyrogenitus, *Le livre des cérémonies*, ed. A. Vogt (1935–1940; reprint, Paris, 1967)
Deltion	*Deltion tes Christianikes Archaiologikes Hetaireias*
DOP	*Dumbarton Oaks Papers*
FHG	*Fragmenta historicorum graecorum*, ed. K. Müller, 5 vols. (Paris, 1841–1883)
MGH	*SRG Monumenta Germaniae historica, Scriptores rerum germanicarum*, 2 vols. (Hanover, 1871–1965)
NOAB	*The New Oxford Annotated Bible with Apocrypha* (New York, 1994)
ODB	*Oxford Dictionary of Byzantium*, 3 vols. (New York and Oxford, 1991)

PBE	John Martindale, ed., *Prosopography of the Byzantine Empire, I (641–867)* (London, 2001; CD-ROM)
PG	J.-P. Migne, ed., *Patrologiae cursus completus, Series graeca,* 161 vols. in 166 pts. (Paris, 1857–1866)
PLRE	A. H. M. Jones, J. R. Martindale, and J. Morris, eds., *The Prosopography of the Later Roman Empire* (Cambridge, 1971–1980)
PL	J.-P. Migne, ed., *Patrologiae cursus completus, Series latina,* 221 vols. in 222 pts. (Paris, 1844–1880)

NOTES

INTRODUCTION

1. Here, in my English text, eunuchism is defined as the practice of making and employing eunuchs. The eleventh-century essayist Theophylaktos of Ohrid comes close to using an institutional definition for eunuchism when he uses the term ἐυνουχισμός. In general usage, this noun means castration, but Theophylaktos uses it in an almost institutional sense, as when he says ἐπιστομίζει δὲ τοὺς καθόλου τὸν εὐνουχισμὸν ὡς κακίας δημιουργὸν διαβάλλοντας [It completely silences those who in general slander eunuchism as the maker of evil]. *Defense of Eunuchs,* p. 291, l. 2 and l. 21, p. 293, l. 17.

2. John J. Winkler, "Unnatural Acts: Erotic Protocols in Artemiodoras' Dream Analysis," and "Laying Down the Law: The Oversight of Men's Sexual Behavior in Classical Athens," in John J. Winkler, ed., *The Constraints of Desire: The Anthropology of Sex and Gender in Ancient Greece* (New York and London, 1990); David M. Halperin, John J. Winkler, and Froma I. Zeitlin, *Before Sexuality: The Construction of Erotic Experience in the Ancient Greek World* (Princeton, 1990); David M. Halperin, *One Hundred Years of Homosexuality and Other Essays on Greek Love* (London, 1990).

3. In the introduction to a recent book, the editors comment: "Currently we labor under the constricting influence of two conceptual dichotomies: sex/gender, which too harshly compartmentalizes the phenomena of interest into the illusory categories of 'the biological' and 'the cultural' and into the supposed conflict between essentialism and constructionism, which is often played out as a duel between cultural and biological interpretations of human sexuality." Paul R. Abramson and Steven D. Pinkerton, eds., *Sexual Nature/Sexual Culture* (Chicago, 1995), p. xii. These authors argue that both biological and cultural influences are important and that one should study them as interacting phenomena. Byzantine

eunuchs illustrate this very well since, as will be seen, their society defined cultural and biological phenomena and their interactions in ways that differ greatly from the ways we define these same phenomena in modern culture.

4. Kazhdan's interest focuses on the later period of the empire. He traces the prominence and then abrupt decline of the political power of eunuchs at the end of the eleventh century. Alexander Kazhdan and Michael McCormick, "The Social World of the Byzantine Court," in Henry Maguire, ed., *Byzantine Court Culture from 829 to 1204* (Washington, D.C., 1997), pp. 178–180. Quotation from Alexander P. Kazhdan and Ann Wharton Epstein, *Change in Byzantine Culture in the Eleventh and Twelfth Centuries* (Berkeley, 1985), p. 67.

5. Julia M. Asher-Greve, "Mesopotamian Conceptions of the Gendered Body," in Maria Wyke, ed., *Gender and the Body in the Ancient Mediterranean* (Oxford, 1998), p. 14.

6. Gerald E. Kadish, "Eunuchs in Ancient Egypt?" in G. E. Kadish, ed., *Studies in Honor of J. A. Wilson* (Chicago, 1969), pp. 55–62.

7. G. Carter Stent, "Chinese Eunuchs," *Journal of the North-China Branch of the Royal Asiatic Society*, n.s., 9 (1877): 143–184. For a general survey on Chinese eunuchs, see Mary Anderson, *Hidden Power: The Palace Eunuchs of Imperial China* (Buffalo, N.Y., 1990).

8. Amélie Kuhrt, *The Ancient Near East, c. 3000–330* B.C.E., vol. 2 (London, 1995), pp. 529–530.

9. R. Ghirshman, *Iran from the Earliest Times to the Islamic Conquest* (Middlesex, 1954), pp. 150, 206.

10. A good selection of early Middle Eastern and Classical texts regarding eunuchs is found in Thomas Wiedemann, ed., *Greek and Roman Slavery* (Baltimore, 1981). An older source with extensive useful material is Charles Verlinden, *L'esclavage dans l'Europe médiévale*, 2 vols. (Bruges, 1977), vol. 2, pp. 118–131, 982–984.

11. Shaun E. Marmon, *Eunuchs and Sacred Boundaries in Islamic Society* (Oxford, 1995).

12. See, for example, Lynn E. Roller, "The Ideology of the Eunuch Priest," in Wyke, *Gender and the Body*, pp. 118–135.

13. Walter Burkert, *Structure and History in Greek Mythology and Ritual* (Berkeley, 1979), pp. 102–105; Mary Beard, "The Roman and the Foreign: The Cult of the 'Great Mother' in Imperial Rome," in Nicholas Thomas and Caroline Humphrey, eds., *Shamanism, History and the State* (Ann Arbor, Mich., 1994), pp. 164–190.

14. Laura Englestein, *Castration and the Heavenly Kingdom: A Russian Folktale* (Ithaca, N.Y., 1999).

15. Serena Nanda, *Neither Man Nor Woman: The Hijra of India* (Belmont, Calif., 1990).

16. *Wall Street Journal*, September 24, 1998, p. 1. For another article on *hirjas*, "Katni Journal. A Pox on Politicians: A Eunuch You Can Trust," *New York Times*, January 19, 2001.

17. Marmon, *Eunuchs and Sacred Boundaries*, p. 11.

18. Quoted in Will Roscoe, *The Zuni Man-Woman* (Albuquerque, 1991), which offers a modern example. Richard Trexler, *Sex and Conquest: Gendered Violence, Political Order, and the European Conquest of the Americas* (Ithaca, N.Y., 1995), pp. 64–117.

19. Mathew Kuefler, *The Manly Eunuch: Masculinity, Gender Ambiguity, and Christian Ideology in Late Antiquity* (Chicago, 2001), pp. 31, 61–69, 245–282.

20. This is the current *ODB* spelling for Abasgians.

21. Prokopios, *Wars* bk. 8, ch. 3, l. 12.

22. Scholars of the Roman and Byzantine period use the term *familia*. For the Greek-

speaking world, *oikos* also refers to the circle of dependents that surrounded an aristocrat. These included biological family, servants, and other dependents.

23. This has been carefully dealt with in an excellent doctoral dissertation. See Gary R. Brower, "Ambivalent Bodies: Making Christian Eunuchs" (Ph.D. diss., Duke University, 1996).

24. G. A. Rhalles and M. Potles, eds., *Syntagma ton theion kai hieron kanonon*, 6 vols. (1852–1859; reprint, Athens, 1966), vol. 2, pp. 29–30 (hereafter referred to as Rhalles-Potles, *Syntagma*).

25. There are references to legal action regarding this issue in both legal and literary sources of the late Roman Republic and the early Roman Empire. See Brower, "Ambivalent Bodies," pp. 16–22.

26. Modern scholars continue to debate whether this formal code of masculine behavior was actually imposed on Roman men.

27. For two excellent discussions of this problem, see Peter Brown, *The Body and Society: Men, Women and Sexual Renunciation in Early Christianity* (New York, 1988); and Maud W. Gleason, *Making Men: Sophists and Self-Presentation in Ancient Rome* (Princeton, 1995).

28. See especially the *CIC*, vol. 2, chapter 1, number 142, which repeats older legislation that forbids human castration within the Roman Empire and suggests that this older legislation was being flouted. The new legislation punished those who made eunuchs with confiscation and deportation to work in the mines. Both those who castrate and those who turn individuals over to the castrator are to be punished equally. Chapter 4, number 42 decrees that anyone who castrates within the Roman Empire is subject to capital punishment and anyone who tries to bring a castrated Roman into the empire to offer for sale or purchases one will be subject to the same penalty. Only barbarian eunuchs castrated outside the empire could legally be bought or sold in the empire.

29. Rhalles-Potles, *Syntagma*, vol. 1, p. 53.

30. This is discussed in detail in chapter 2.

31. In the eleventh century Theophylaktos of Ohrid observed that this legislation was outdated and unnecessary. His comments are discussed in the conclusion.

32. Within Christian monasticism of Late Antiquity, and also in Western monasticism, the terms εὐνοῦχος, εὐνουχίας, and ἐν εὐνουχίᾳ were sometimes used to refer to celibate men and women and their way of life. Women ascetics often cross-dressed and posed as eunuchs. See Sebastian P. Brock and Susan Ashbrook Harvey, *Holy Women of the Syrian Orient* (Berkeley, 1987), p. 59. This problem is particularly well handled in J. Anson, "The Female Transvestite in Early Monasticism. The Origin and Development of a Motif," *Viator* 5 (1974): 1–32.

33. According to Zachariä von Lingenthal, *Ecloga privata aucta*, a legal compilation that probably predates the tenth century, the term *eunuch* includes three kinds of individuals, the *spadones* (σπαδόνες), *kastratoi* (καστράτοι) and *thlibiai* (θλιβίαι). *Spadones* are those who, because of a mental disease or fault of spirit, cannot use their generative organs to produce children. *Thlibiai* are those who submitted to the crushing of the testicles by their nurse or mother. *Kastratoi* are those who have been excised "in accordance with their families' customs." *Kastratoi* and *thlibiai* may not adopt children since they cannot produce children themselves. The *spadones* may adopt children since for them there remains the hope of having children. Zepos and Zepos, *Jus*, vol. 6, bk. 4, p. 399. The term καστρᾶτος is not Classical Greek but is taken from the Latin. In plural it may be ξαστερτοι or καστρᾶτοι.

34. I am of the opinion that this type of castration, which involved removal of both testicles and penis, was rare in the Byzantine Empire, though it is very familiar to modern scholars because of an often-translated passage in Liutprand of Cremona. It is important to remember, however, that the three fully castrated young eunuchs that Liutprand mentions were purchased in the west where there was, indeed, a traffic in doubly castrated youths destined for a life as male prostitutes in Moslem courts. Liutprand brought these youths to the Byzantine emperor as a very special, and perhaps inappropriate, gift. Liudprand, bishop of Cremona, *Antapodosis,* in *Die Werke Liudprands von Cremona,* book 6, ch. 6, p. 209. See also chapter 3, note 55 below.

35. Pierre Chantraine, *Dictionnaire étymologique de la langue Grecque. Histoire des mots,* 4 vols. (Paris, 1968–1980), vol. 2, p. 385.

36. Galen, *Opera omnia,* bk. 1, ch. 15, p. 569; ch. 16, p. 585.

37. Clement of Alexandria, *Stromata,* pp. 3, 15, 97–99.

38. The theory of humors classified all human life as warm or cool, dry or moist. Bodies that were warm and dry were preferable to those that were cool and moist.

39. Brown, *The Body and Society,* pp. 10–12, points out the importance placed on the acculturation of young men and the need to develop them in accordance with socially determined ideals of masculine behavior to move them up the ladder of masculine perfection.

40. Thomas Laqueur, *Making Sex: Body and Gender from the Greeks to Freud* (Cambridge, Mass., 1990), p. 22.

41. Beard, "The Roman and the Foreign," pp. 164–190; Nanda, *Neither Man nor Woman.*

42. Michel Foucault, *The History of Sexuality,* vol. 1, *An Introduction* (New York, 1990), pp. 36–47, 103–114.

43. The term "eunuch by nature" is also used to categorize men who are simply born without functional sexual organs and without sexual desire.

44. Nikephoros, *The Life of Saint Andrew the Fool* [*BHG* 264b], vol. 1, p. 82, l. 1056; Nikephoros, Vita of Andrew Salos, p. 30. The *AASS* text says he is a eunuch by nature (τῇ φύσει).

45. Vilinskii, *Zhitie sv. Vasiliia Novago v russkoi literature,* pp. 285–290. To quote St. Basil: "Those who engage in the acts of sodomites in secret, even as you do—for Samonas was a eunuch by nature and handsome to look upon and the continuous recipient of the unholy acts—justly ought to be called unholy and accursed!" (p. 287, l. 25). The word for intimate relations involves a tantalizing double entendre.

46. Vita of Niphon of Constantiana [*BHG* 264b], p. 111, l. 9, p. 68, l. 1.

47. *De cer.,* bk. 2, ch. 25, p. 624. The context is the ceremony for elevation of a *koubikoularios.* One can also make an argument for the possibility that a "eunuch by nature" is a term used for a man born without fully developed sexual organs or born without sexual desire.

48. See the excellent discussion in Harriet Whitehead, "The Bow and the Burden Strap: A New Look at Institutionalized Homosexuality in Native North America," in *Sexual Meanings: The Cultural Construction of Gender and Sexuality,* ed. Sherry B. Ortner and Harriet Whitehead (Cambridge, 1981), p. 97.

49. Skyl., p. 406, l. 95, for example, uses the term unmanly (ἄνανδρος). This is regularly translated as "effeminate," which is a modern English meaning imposed on a term that really means unmanly. Liddell-Scott defines it as "want of manhood; unmanliness, cowardice."

50. St. John Chrysostom, *Homilia in Eutropium eunuchum patricium, PG* 52, cols. 392–414.

51. *Defense of Eunuchs,* p. 313, ll. 19–22.

52. Rodolphe Guilland, "Études sur l'histoire administrative de l'empire byzantine: Les titres auliques des eunuques. Le protospathaire," *Byzantion* 25–27 (1955–57): 649–95; "Les eunuques dans l'empire byzantine: Étude de titulature et de prosopographie byzantines," *Revue des études byzantines* 1 (1943): 197–238; "Études de titulature byzantine: Les titres auliques réservés aux eunuques," *Études byzantines* 12 (1954): 50–84, 14 (1956): 122–157; "Fonctions et dignités des eunuques," *Revue des études byzantines* 2 (1945): 185–225, 3 (1945): 179–214. These articles have been condensed and collected in Rodolphe Guilland, *Recherches sur les institutions byzantines,* 2 vols. (Amsterdam, 1967).

53. John Thomas and Angela Constantinides Hero, eds., *Byzantine Monastic Foundation Documents* (Washington, D.C., 2000), available on the World Wide Web at www.doaks.org; Roberto Romano, ed. and trans., *Timarione / Pseudo-Luciano, testo critico, introduzione, traduzione, commentario e lessico* (Naples, 1974).

54. We have a collection of military *taktika* and other manuscripts commissioned by the famous eunuch, Basil Lekapenos (also called Basil the Nothos), ca. 925–985. This collection includes the author's own work on naval battles. I have not yet seen this unpublished manuscript. *ODB,* 1: 270.

55. See chapter 3, n. 86.

56. Guilland, *Recherches.*

57. Keith Hopkins, *Conquerors and Slaves* (Cambridge, 1978).

58. Michael McCormick, *Eternal Victory: Triumphal Leadership in Late Antiquity, Byzantium, and the Early Medieval West* (Cambridge, 1986).

59. Brown, *The Body and Society,* pp. 10–11, 19, 169–171, 268–269. They are also treated in Kuefler, *The Manly Eunuch: Masculinity, Gender Ambiguity, and Christian Ideology in Late Antiquity.*

60. Peter Guyot, *Eunuchen als Sklaven und Freigelassene in der griechisch-römischen Antike* (Stuttgart, 1980).

61. Marmon, *Eunuchs and Sacred Boundaries.*

62. Piotr Scholz, *Eunuchs and Castrati: A Cultural History,* trans. John A. Broadwin and Shelley L. Frisch (Princeton, 2001).

CHAPTER 1

1. Averil Cameron, "Sacred and Profane Love: Thoughts on Byzantine Gender," in Liz James, ed., *Women, Men and Eunuchs: Gender in Byzantium* (London, 1997), pp. 1–23.

2. Very similar rhetoric was used against "bad" empresses. Liz James, *Empresses and Power* (London, 2001), pp. 16–17.

3. On early use of "third sex" terminology, see Claudian, *Against Eutropius,* 1, p. 172, l. 466: "You whom the male sex has discarded and the female will not adopt." Also Lucian, *The Eunuch,* p. 336, ch. 6, l. 12: "Observing that a eunuch was neither man nor woman, but something composite, hybrid, and monstrous, alien to human nature."

4. Kazhdan and McCormick, "The Social World," pp. 179–180.

5. On Symeon, see chapter 3, n. 86.

6. Gregory of Nazianzos, "Laudatio Athanasios," ch. 399, col. 1106; Aretaeus of Cappadocia, *De causis et signis acutorum morborum,* ed. C. Hude, book 4, sec. 5, pt. 4.

7. St. Basil, *The Letters,* no. 115. This comes from St. Basil's letter to Simplicia the Heretic and is one of the classic attacks on eunuchs. Because of St. Basil's eminence, it colored later commentaries. The letter, number 115, is found, with English translation in the Loeb Classical Library. I am here using Deferrari's translation, with changes reflecting the new edition by Yves Courtonne. The letter was probably written in 372. According to a letter of Gregory of Nazianzos (no. 38), a church in Cappadocia elected one of Simplicia's slaves as its bishop without her consent. She threatened St. Basil with retaliation by her slaves and eunuchs. Even after St. Basil had died she continued to agitate for the return of her slave. A codex containing the letter repeats the tradition that, when St. Basil was visiting a bath, Simplicia's eunuchs and maids took away his towels and brought the judgment of God down on their own heads! Simplicia tried to make amends, but St. Basil refused her overtures. Gregory of Nazianzos, *Discours.*

The actual letter begins with St. Basil saying that he will say little about the indignities that have been brought down upon him, knowing that God avenges all evil. He reminds Simplicia to remember that Judgment Day is coming and that he is far wiser than she. He continues with remarks about the eunuchs whom she has roused against him: "You have roused against us lizards and toads, beasts of spring forsooth, but nevertheless unclean. But there will come a bird from above to feed on these. For it matters to me, not how you think, but how God knows how to judge. And if there be need also of witnesses, slaves will not stand forth, nor any [of the] disreputable and utterly accursed race of eunuchs—yes, I mean just that—a race neither feminine nor masculine, mad for women, envious, of evil wage [I would translate "ill-fated"], quick to anger, effeminate, slaves to the belly, money-mad, coarse, grumbling about their dinner [or perhaps "weeping over their food"], fickle, stingy, ready to accept anything [I suggest "anyone" in a negative and perhaps sexual sense], disgusting, crazed, jealous [the last two items do not appear in the Courtonne text]—and yet why say more? At their very birth doomed to the knife! How then ["then" omitted in the Courtonne text] can these possess true judgment, whose very feet are twisted? They are chaste without reward—thanks to the knife; and they rave with passion without fruition—thanks to their own lewdness.

8. Skyl., p. 245, l. 40.

9. Leo Diac., p. 39, l. 11.

10. Leo Diac., p. 107, l. 4.

11. Vita of John Chrysostom, p. 1197.

12. Γαστρίδουλος (glutton), St. Basil, *The Letters,* no. 115; οἰνοφλυγία (drunkard), Galen, *Opera omnia,* bk. 18, pt. 1; οἰνόληκτος (drunken), Skyl., p. 370, l. 27.

13. St. Basil, *The Letters,* no. 15, l. 19.

14. Nikephoros, *The Life of Saint Andrew the Fool,* vol. 2, p. 80, l. 1035.

15. Nikephoros, *The Life of Saint Andrew the Fool,* vol. 2, p. 82, l. 1036.

16. Eunapios of Sardis, *FHG,* vol. 4, frag. 69, p. 44.

17. St. Basil, *The Letters,* no. 15, l. 21.

18. John of Antioch, *FHG,* vol. 4, frag. 198, l.2.

19. Eunapios of Sardis says that they are κατεμφορεύμενος. Eunapios of Sardis, *FHG,* vol. 4, frag. 67.

20. Ὀργῶσαν ὀργάω. Leo Diac., p. 42.

21. St. Basil, *The Letters,* no. 115. See note 7, this chapter.

22. Leo Diac., p. 42, l. 11.

23. St. Basil, *The Letters,* no. 115, l. 21.

24. Aretaeus of Cappadocia, *De causis et signis acutorum morborum,* bk., 4 sec. 5, pt. 5.

25. *Defense of Eunuchs,* p. 317, l. 13.

26. *Defense of Eunuchs,* p. 317, l. 12.

27. *Defense of Eunuchs,* p. 293, l. 9.

28. *Defense of Eunuchs,* p. 293, l. 8.

29. *Defense of Eunuchs,* p. 293, l. 12.

30. ἐπισυρμάμενον ἤδη πονηράς μαρτυρίας. The word ἐπίσυρμα means a snake's trail. See John of Damascus, "De eunichis," *PG* 95, no. 2, col. 1564. Here he quotes St. Nilus.

31. Ὁ βαρὺς καὶ μυριέλικτος ἐκεῖνος ὄφις. Eunapios of Sardis, *FHG,* vol. 4, frag. 68.

32. καθάπερ τις γενναῖος ὄφις, καθελίττων εἰς τὴν ἑαυτοῦ χρείαν. Eunapios of Sardis, *FHG,* vol. 4, frag. 69.

33. Eunapios of Sardis, *FHG,* vol. 4, frag. 68.

34. Leo Diac., p. 7, l. 5, p. 39, l. 11, p. 107, l. 4; Skyl., p. 245, l. 41.

35. Lucian of Samosata, *Lucian,* p. 340, pt. 8.

36. Lucian of Samosata, *Lucian,* p. 336, pt. 6.

37. Gregory of Nazianzos, "Laudatio Athanasios," *PG* 35, col. 1105, l. 20.

38. Leo Diac., p. 39, l. 5.

39. Photios I, *Epistulae,* vol. 1, p. 95, letter 50, l. 3; on John, *PBE,* Ioannes 447.

40. Psellos, *Chron.,* bk. 4, ch. 13, l. 2.

41. *Passio* of St. Eugenia, with Basilla, Protas and Hyacinthus, p. 179.

42. Leo Diac., p. 32, l. 19.

43. Agathias, ch. 15.

44. Skyl., p. 284, l. 9.

45. Skylitzes Continuatus, *He synecheia tes Chronographias,* p. 155, l. 10. This is a continuation of Skylitzes, perhaps an anonymous reworking of Attaleiates, *Historia.*

46. Theodore Studites, *Oration VI. On The Holy Angels, PG* 99, col. 729.

47. Choniates, *Historia,* p. 219.

48. Skylitzes Continuatus, *He synecheia tes Chronographias,* p. 155, l. 18. Women are also associated with "the left."

49. *Defense of Eunuchs,* 325, l. 9.

50. Aretaeus of Cappadocia, *De causis et signis acutorum morborum,* bk. 4, sec. 5, pt. 4.

51. Leo Diac., p. 40.

52. Photios I, *Epistulae,* vol. 1, letter 50, p. 95, l. 6.

53. Leo Diac., pp. 7, 39; St. Basil, *The Letters,* no. 115, l. 19; Gregory of Nazianzos, "Laudatio Athanasios," *PG* 35, col. 1105, l. 19.

54. Skyl., p. 245, l. 41.

55. Galen, *Opera omnia,* bk. 18, pt. 1, p. 43, l. 2.

56. Aretaeus of Cappadocia, *De causis et signis acutorum morborum,* bk. 4, sec. 5, pt. 4; Photios I, *Epistulae,* vol. 1, no. 50.

57. St. Basil, *The Letters,* no. 115, l. 20.

58. St. Basil, *The Letters,* no. 115, l. 20.

59. Theophanes, de Boor, p. 367, l. 17; Basil, *The Letters,* p. 229.

60. St. Basil, *The Letters,* no. 115, l. 19.

61. St. Basil, *The Letters,* no. 115, l. 18.

62. Photios I, *Epistulae,* vol. 1, letter 50, p. 95, l. 7.

63. *Defense of Eunuchs,* 295, l. 21.

64. *Defense of Eunuchs,* 295, l. 13.

65. *Defense of Eunuchs,* 295, l. 13.

66. *Defense of Eunuchs,* 293, l. 10.

67. *Defense of Eunuchs,* 309, l. 14. See also the conclusion.

68. Skyl., p. 351, l. 88, Bekker, *Symeon Magistros,* 754, l. 23; *Defense of Eunuchs,* 295, l. 24; Bekker, *Theophanes Continuatus,* 442, l. 22.

69. Agathias, ch. 15.

70. Leo Diac., p. 94, l. 7; Agathias, ch. 15.

71. Skyl., p. 472, l. 31.

72. To date I have found only one passage that directly confronts this issue. It comes from Hippolytus, an early third-century bishop at Rome who wrote on rites and ordinances of the church and also on theological issues. Hippolytus says, "The Logos accomplishes the fulfilling of the masculine and feminine. Those who are occupied with service to another or with public service have no need for active sexuality, either of a masculine or of a feminine sort." This citation, taken from Hippolytus's discussion of the role of the Logos in the material world, opens up a wealth of questions about the perceived role of sexuality within the material and spiritual worlds. It is clear that Hippolytus connects asexual servants on earth with angels, asexual servants of God. St. Hippolytus, *Refutatio omnium haeresium,* ed. P. Wendland (Hildesheim and New York, 1977), pp. 10, 33, 3–5.

73. Bekker, *Symeon Magistros,* 754, l. 20.

74. Skyl., p. 427, l. 31.

75. Prokopios, *Wars,* bk. 8, p. 26, l, 14.

76. Leo Diac., p. 94, l. 7.

77. Skyl., p. 464, l. 18.

78. *Defense of Eunuchs,* 313, ll. 13, 14.

79. Theodore Studites, Oration 6, chapter 12, cols. 745, l. 7; 740, l. 2; 745, l. 13; 740, l. 2; 740, l. 4; 745, l. 13; 740, l. 3; 745, l. 13; 745, l. 12; 740, l. 1; 745, l. 8. In this text angels are sometimes referred to as ἄγγελοι (masculine gender), sometimes as πνεύματα (neuter gender). As a result, the adjectives listed here appear in both the masculine and neuter gender.

80. Summaries of the nature of apophatic theology are found in John Meyendorff, *Byzantine Theology* (New York, 1979), p. 11; and Jaroslav Pelikan, *The Spirit of Eastern Christendom (600–1700)* (Chicago, 1978), p. 32.

81. Lucian of Samosata, *Lucian,* 336, section 6.

82. Lucian of Samosata, *Lucian,* 336, section 6.

83. Lucian of Samosata, *Lucian,* 336, section 6.

84. Leo Diac., p. 39, l. 6.

85. This is the *ODB* transliteration of the Arabic spelling. The name transliterates as Mauias from Greek. On Andrew, see *PBE,* Andrew; his latest date is 667.

86. This is my translation of the phrase βαβαί σοι Μαυΐα, which Mango translates as "Woe to you." I believe that the phrase "Bless me" or, though a bit modern, "Bless my soul," better captures the extravagance of the words used by the eunuch as imagined by the author.

87. Theophanes the Confessor, ed. Mango and Scott, pp. 488–489. The *ODB* now spells Sergios as in my text; it appears as Sergius in the Mango and Scott translation, which I am quoting directly.

88. A similar note of down-to-earth pragmatism is seen in a passage in Theophanes Continuatus that describes Theodore Krateros, eunuch general of the iconoclastic emperor Theophilos. Theodore eschews showy weapon handling in favor of a good spear and God's help. See chapter 6, p. 135 below; and Bekker, *Theophanes Continuatus*, p. 114, ll. 22 ff.

89. Nikephoros, *The Life of Saint Andrew the Fool*, vol. 1, pp. 27–37. Regarding the date, see pp. 41–56. See also chapter 3, note 29.

90. A *koubikoularios* was a member of a powerful individual's most private staff. The term, which comes from the Latin *cubiculum*, or sleeping room, is traditionally used to refer to those individuals who are the most intimate, and therefore powerful, servants of a great man or woman. In Byzantium, the most powerful eunuchs who served at the imperial court were usually *koubikoularioi*. In this context the eunuch of a powerful man might be described as his chamberlain.

91. This passage, with its lewd connotations, is explained by Rydén in n. 2, p. 315, where he has to emend the text. "Like Charles Du Cange, *Glossarium ad scriptores mediae et infimae Graecitatis* (1688, 1793; reprint, Graz, 1958), I write κωλοφωνίας rather than κολοφωνίας or κολοφονίς, understanding this otherwise unattested word as a combination of κῶλος (= πρωκτός) [my insert, meaning anus] and φωνία (meaning noise). Presumably the former half of the compound refers to the fact that the eunuch has earned his dates by satisfying the lusts of his master, while the latter is supposed to refer not only to wind-breaking but also to the φοίνικας [my insert, meaning date], with which the genitive form of φωνία, φωνίας, has a slight phonetic resemblance." Another possible interpretation is that the eunuch gave the saint dates because he had no figs. Figs are often associated with testicles.

92. Nikephoros, *The Life of Saint Andrew the Fool*, vol. 2, p. 81.

93. Symeon Metaphrastes, Vita of St. John the Almsgiver, *PG* 114, col. 936. Our earliest life of St. John the Almsgiver was written by his near contemporary, Leontios of Cyprus. See Leontios, *Vie de Syméon le Fou (et) Vie de Jean de Chypre*, ed. A. J. Festugière, which has a French translation. In the tenth century, Symeon Metaphrastes rewrote John's life based on a text drawn from that of Leontios and earlier texts by Sophronios and John Moschos, which are now lost. The Festugière version is closer to John's actual life and therefore usually cited, but the Metaphrastic life is a better reflection of the period we are dealing with.

94. The grammar here is problematic, but the sequence of events is unchanged by alternative readings. Vita of St. John the Almsgiver, *PG* 114, col. 936, ch. 45.

95. Symeon Metaphrastes is more detailed about the monk's mutilation than is Leontios. Symeon Metaphrastes, Vita of St. John the Almsgiver, *PG* 114, col. 936, ch. 47; Leontios, *Vie de Syméon le Fou (et) Vie de Jean de Chypre*, p. 374, l. 58.

96. Bellerophon was an unusually handsome and valiant man, a native of Ephyre. The wife of Proetus, king of the Argives, loved him and, when he did not return her affection, she told her husband he had tried to seduce her. Proetus sent Bellerophon to carry a sealed letter to the king of Lycia. The letter asked the king to arrange for Bellerophon's death. The king of Lycia sent Bellerophon off to fight the Chimaera, Solymi, and the Amazons, tasks

that Bellerophon accomplished successfully. There are many other legends attached to Bellerophon, including the capture of Pegasus, the winged horse. The author here seems to be alluding to a proverb about Bellerophon. The exact relevance of the proverb eludes me.

97. The Greek text says, "You hasten, like gourds, to gather up that which is worst." I have substituted the term "cupping glasses," a modern term. In Theophylaktos's time gourds were used to create a vacuum that would draw blood (and evil humors) out of the body.

98. *Defense of Eunuchs,* p. 297, l. 1 ff.

CHAPTER 2

1. For a general background on Byzantine medicine, see John Scarborough, ed., "Symposium on Byzantine Medicine," in *DOP* 38 (1984), especially his introduction, pp. ix–xvi.

2. The Methodists, among whom Soranos of Ephesus is best known, believed that illness was caused by an imbalance in the basic states of the body. They defined these states as relaxed, constricted, and mixed. Illnesses were classified according to the imbalance they brought to the body. Because the Methodists focused on the state of the body rather than its physiology, they tended not to differentiate between male and female bodes. Lesley Ann Dean-Jones, *Women's Bodies in Classical Greek Science* (Oxford, 1994), pp. 23–24.

3. G. Westerink, "Physiology and Medicine in Late Antiquity," *Janus* (1964), pp. 168–177; "Symposium on Byzantine Medicine," J. Scarborough, ed., in *DOP* 38 (Washington, D.C., 1984); *ODB,* s.v. "Medicine."

4. For an excellent summary of these issues, see Joan Cadden, *Meanings of Sex Difference in the Middle Ages: Medicine, Science, and Culture* (Cambridge, 1993).

5. Aristotle, *Generation of Animals,* 391, l. 27.

6. Brown, *The Body and Society,* p. 11.

7. Aretaeus of Cappadocia, *De causis et signis acutorum morborum,* bk. 4, pt. 5, p. 71.

8. Aristotle, *Generation of Animals,* p. 525, l. 8.

9. Galen, *Opera omnia,* bk. 13, p. 662.

10. Galen, *In Hippocratis,* p. 334.

11. Galen, *Opera omnia,* bk. 18, 41.

12. Alexander of Tralles, *Therapeutica,* p. 127, l. 13; Aetios of Amida, *Aetii Amideni Libri medicinales,* vol. 2, liber 6, p. 241, l. 10. Useful comments on the practical nature of Alexander's work are in John Duffy, "Byzantine Medicine in the Sixth and Seventh Centuries," *DOP* 38 (1984): 25–27.

13. Galen, *De alimentorum,* p. 334.

14. Galen, *De alimentorum,* p. 334.

15. *De alimentia,* pp. 268–269.

16. Simeo Sethus, *Simeonis Sethi Syntagma de alimentorum facultatibus,* ed. Bernhard Langkovel (Leipzig, 1868). For more general detail on food in Byzantium see J. Koder, *Der Lebensraum der Byzantiner: Historisch-geographischer Abriss ihres mittelalterlichen Staates in östlichen Mittelmeerraum* (Graz, 1984), *Gemüse en Byzanz: Die Versorgung Konstantinopels mit Frischgemüse im Lichte der Geoponika* (Vienna, 1993), and "Fresh Vegetables for the Capital," in *Constantinople and Its Hinterland: Papers from the Twenty-Seventh Spring Symposium of Byzantine Studies* (Oxford, 1993), pp. 49–56.

17. Alexander of Tralles, *Theraputica,* p. 497.

18. In a discussion of the treatment of quotidian fever, Leo the Physician, who proba-

bly wrote in the ninth century, says that this fever typically attacks women, children, castrated men, and inactive men. Leo the Physician, *Conspectus medicinae,* chap. 7, p. 95.

19. Galen, *Opera omnia,* bk. 13, p. 575.

20. Galen, *Opera omnia,* bk. 13, p. 569, l. 14.

21. Galen, *Opera omnia,* bk. 13, p. 575.

22. Translated in Gleason, *Making Men,* p. 47. The text of Polemo, *De physiognomia,* is in Foerster, *Scriptores physiognomonici,* vol. 1, pp. 162–164 ff. The passage in Adamanteus is in Foerster, *Scriptores,* vol. 1, p. 351.

23. Theophilos Protospatharios has been variously dated to the seventh, ninth, and thirteenth centuries.

24. Theophilos, *Peri tes tou anthropou kataskeues biblio E. De corporis humani fabrica libri V,* bk. 4, p. 178.

25. Theophilos, *Peri tes tou anthropou kataskeues biblio E* (bk. 5), p. 233.

26. This was a long discussion and is seen in Philostratos, *The Life of Apollonius of Tyana,* bk. 1, ch. 36.

27. This passage probably remained familiar to Byzantine authors because it dealt with the sexuality of eunuchs. The author of the vita of the tenth-century eunuch St. Nikephoros of Miletos refers specifically to this passage in discussing the saint's sexuality. Delehaye, V. Nikephoros Miletos, ch. 15.

28. Theophilos, *Peri tes tou anthropou kataskeues biblio E* (bk. 5), p. 255.

29. At puberty, the production of testosterone causes the growth plates in the long bones to close, completing growth. Without testosterone the growth process lasts longer than normal.

30. Paul of Aegina, *Surgery,* ch. 46, p. 86.

31. Paul of Aegina, *Surgery,* ch. 57, p. 97.

32. Paul of Aegina, *Surgery,* ch. 68, p. 111.

33. Unfortunately, Paul does not tell us who it is that these "powerful persons" wish to have castrated.

34. Soranos of Ephesus, *Gynaeciorum,* p. 83.

35. Psellos, *De legum,* p. 1027.

36. *CIC,* vol. 3, no. 142. See also the comment on Liutprand in chapter 1, note 34 above. One of the difficulties in this topic is that until the tenth century a eunuch was a eunuch and there was little discussion about his physical state. An often-cited passage of the sixth century says that only three out of ninety eunuchs survived castration. Given the status of boys who were castrated in the Byzantine Empire after 900 and the confidence with which Paul of Aegina approaches the surgery, I find this passage puzzling. It is possible that in the sixth century there were castrators who practiced total ablation, as was done in China. If they lacked the skill of the Chinese castrators, the high mortality rate is plausible. This may have been the kind of eunuch proffered by Liutprand. It is interesting to note, however, that a comment in Theodore Spandounis suggests that when the Turks conquered Constantinople in the fifteenth century, they were surprised that the harem was staffed by eunuchs who retained the penis and promptly introduced full ablation. See Theodore Spandounis in Sathas, *Documents inédits,* vol. 9, p. 205.

37. My collection of eunuch biographies includes references to at least 196 individuals,

about 150 of whom are specifically named. This includes 16 from the fourth century, of whom one is described as a castrated slave and another said to have castrated himself; 22 from the fifth century, of whom two are presented as castrated children living in their natal households; 38 from the sixth century, of whom two came as slaves from regions that traditionally castrated slave children and one was castrated as the result of an accident; 33 from the seventh century; 9 from the eighth century, of whom one was castrated for political reasons and two remained in contact with their natal families; 28 from the ninth century, of whom one was castrated as an adult (possibly by his own choice), one was castrated for political reasons, and two were castrated by parents to advance their careers; 30 from the tenth century, of whom one is identified as a castrated slave, one remained in contact with his relatives, one was born a eunuch, and three were castrated by parents; and 20 from the eleventh century, of whom five were castrated by their parents.

38. We have a number of scattered sources that discuss Eutropios, including Claudian, *Against Eutropius;* Eunapios of Sardis; Zosimos; John of Antioch; John Chrysostom, *Against Eutropius;* Sokrates; and Sozomenos.

39. Prokopios, *Wars,* v. 3, ch. 11, l. 5.

40. Cyril of Schythopolis, p. 240.

41. Niketas Paphlagonis, Vita of St. Ignatios, patriarch of Constantinople, p. 492; see also *PBE,* Ignatios 1.

42. Basil, who died sometime after 985, is also referred to as Basil the Nothos, a reference to his illegitimate birth.

43. Skyl., p. 328, ll. 67–68.

44. Psellos, *Chron.,* bk. 5, ch. 42, l. 8.

45. Psellos, *Chron.,* p. 147 (trans. Sewter).

46. Skyl., p. 244, l. 91.

47. Skyl., p. 390, l. 70. The sources never say specifically that John's parents castrated him, but given that two of his brothers were also castrated, and that the family, like that of Constantine, came from Paphlagonia, this seems a safe assumption.

48. *Narratio* of St. Metrios, ch. 4, p. 136.

49. Delehaye, "Vita sancti Nicephori episcopi Milesii," ch. 4, p. 136.

50. Papachryssanthou, "Un Confesseur de second Iconoclasme, la vie du Patrice Niketas (+836)," pp. 309–351.

51. Gautier, ed., introduction to *Theophylacte d'Achrida,* p. 16. Gautier accepts the possibility that Theophylaktos had a brother who was a eunuch. He does not suggest that this brother was castrated by his parents, that is my assumption. The possibility exists that this brother was born with incomplete genitalia or suffered a childhood accident.

52. Vitae of Eugenius et Maria eius filia, col. 348.

53. Symeon Metaphrastes, Vita of St. John the Almsgiver, col. 936.

54. A case of this kind is found in van den Gheyn, *Acta graeca SS. Davidis, Symeonis et Georgii Mitylenae ininsula Lesbo,* p. 240, l. 11. A friend of the holy man, whose name was Leo, brought his youngest son, George, to him. He was suffering from a hernia, and the plan was to turn him over to a castrator, but the saint healed the child. The Vita of St. Artemios (Crisafulli, *The Miracles of St. Artemios*) offers a number of healings and miracles involving male genitalia. In the twenty-fourth miracle (p. 145) a man named George is urged to see a doctor and have his testicles removed to heal a testicular disorder. The saint heals him. In the twenty-eighth

(p. 155) a child injures his testicles and is cured by the saint. When his mother realizes that he has been cured, she runs her hands along his thighs and assumes the cure involved removing his testicles. The forty-third miracle (p. 219) is similar. In the forty-fourth miracle (p. 219) a man with diseased testicles is considering having them removed but is healed by the saint. The saint appeared to him in the guise of a physician who did hernia surgeries. The saint bound up the man's testicle with a cord, an action that mimicked castration.

55. See chapter 1, n. 33 above.

56. I am grateful to several members of the Department of Endocrinology of the University of California, San Diego (UCSD) Medical School, for assisting me with these issues.

57. The above is speculative and based on unpublished data from colleagues at the UCSD Medical School and the Salk Institute.

58. Gleason, *Making Men,* pp. 61–67.

59. *Defense of Eunuchs,* p. 295, l. 10. See also chapter 3, note 3.

60. Symeon Metaphrastes, Vita of St. John the Almsgiver, ch. 46.

61. Skyl., p. 86, l. 51; Kedrenos, *Compendium historiarum,* vol. 2, p. 147.

62. For additional material on women who dress as eunuchs in order to undergo the more rigorous life in monasteries for men, see Brock and Harvey, *Holy Women of the Syrian Orient;* Anson, "The Female Transvestite"; Evelyne Patlagean, "L'histoire de la femme déguisée en moine et l'évolution de la sainteté féminine à Byzance," *Studi medievali,* ser. 3, 17 (1976): 597–623; and Constans, Vita of St. Mary/Marinos, introduction by Nicholas Constas. The last reference is in a volume that contains English translations of the lives of two famous women who entered monasteries disguised as eunuchs. See Featherstone and Mango, "Life of St. Matrona; and Constas, Life of St. Mary/Marinos. Other examples are found in the lives of Paul the Bishop and John the Priest (Papadopoulos-Kerameus, "Vita Paulus et Ioannes"), Pelagia of Antioch (Brock and Harvey, *Holy Women of the Syrian Orient*), Theodora the Alexandrine (Symeon Metaphrastes, Vita of Theodora Alexandrina), the martyrdom of Eugenia (*Passio* of St. Eugenia, with Basilla, Protas and Hyacinthus), the life of Indes and Domna (Symeon Metaphrastes, *Passio* of Saints Indes and Domna), and the life of Anna Euphemianos. A more complete list is found in Patlagean, "L'histoire de la femme déguisée en moine et l'évolution de la sainteté féminine à Byzance," *Studi medievali,* ser. 3, 17 (1976): 597–623.

CHAPTER 3

1. The exceptions to this are Justinian's sixth-century legislation against sodomites and castration as punishment for those who castrated others.

2. See chapter 9, which includes examples of how eunuchs formed their own lineages or attached themselves to the *oikos* or *familiae* of the powerful.

3. In *Defense of Eunuchs,* p. 321, l. 18, Theophylaktos objects to the cultural assumption that castration made all eunuchs alike, a "tribe" of physically, psychologically, and morally deformed persons. He asks that eunuchs, like men, be judged on a case-by-case basis. See also chapter 2, note 59 above.

4. *Defense of Eunuchs,* p. 319, l. 5.

5. Maud W. Gleason, "The Semiotics of Gender: Physiognomy and Self-Fashioning in the Second Century C.E.," in *Before Sexuality: The Construction of Erotic Experience in the Ancient Greek World,* ed. David M. Halperin, John J. Winkler, and Froma I. Zeitlin (Princeton, 1990), pp. 389–417; also *Making Men: Sophists and Self-Presentation in Ancient Rome* (Princeton, 1995), pp. 3–20.

6. Gleason, *Making Men*, pp. 46–47.

7. Gleason, *Making Men*, pp. 62–69.

8. Gleason, *Making Men*, p. 135.

9. Gleason, *Making Men*, p. 75.

10. Gleason, *Making Men*, p. 162.

11. Anna Marava-Chatazenikolaou, *Recherches sur la vie des esclaves dans le monde byzantin* (Athens, 1950), like many scholars, notes the contradiction that Byzantine emperors passed legislation condemning castration while having eunuchs at their own courts. Both civil and ecclesiastical law carefully separated the act of castration from the castrated individual. It is the act that must be punished, not the outcome. In this context, eunuchs were punished only if they arranged their own castration. Despite Judeo-Christian traditions favoring bodily integrity, eunuchs who were not responsible for their own castration could become priests, bishops, or clerics under canon law. Those who castrated others or arranged for their own castration were considered "homicides, hateful to God and unsuitable for church office." Rhalles-Potles, *Syntagma*, vol. 2, p. 676. The canons of the Council of Nicaea repeat these injunctions and point out that civil law traditionally punished those who castrate themselves with death, confiscation, exile, or fines. Although castration was illegal in the Roman Empire, the supply of eunuchs continued because barbarians could castrate other barbarians outside the empire and then import them. Rhalles-Potles, *Syntagma*, vol. 1, p. 53.

12. By the early tenth century the law code of the emperor Leo the Wise reflected the prevalence of castration and the need to adjust the law to current practice. Leo acknowledged that it was considered wrong to castrate and comments that castration created a creature "far different from what God intended," but objected to the severity of past punishments for the crime. His new law punished imperial servants who castrated with removal from court and large fines. Outside the court, punishments were reduced to fines, tonsuring, confiscation of goods, and exile. Victims, if slaves, were compensated with their freedom; if free, they received no compensation. *Law Code of Leo the Wise*, pp. 886–910.

13. Psellos, *Chron.*, bk. 2, ch. 3, l. 6 (trans. Sewter).

14. Psellos, *Chron.*, bk. 2, ch. 12, l. 10 (trans. Sewter). The shape and placement of the eyebrows were important markers in the physiognomic tradition.

15. Judith Herrin, *Women in Purple: Rulers of Medieval Byzantium* (London, 2001), p. 19.

16. On Constantine, see *Narratio of Metrios*. Kazdan suggests that this is a ninth-century source. For commentary on Constantine, see Bekker, *Symeon Magister*, p. 711; George the Monk, *Chronicon*, p. 868; Kedrenos, *Compendium historiarum*, vol. 2, p. 270. For background, see Romilly J. H. Jenkins, "The Flight of Samonas," in Romilly J. H. Jenkins, ed., *Studies on Byzantine History of the Ninth and Tenth Centuries* (London, 1970), first published in *Speculum* 23 (1948): 217–235; and L. Rydén, "The Portrait of the Arab Samonas in Byzantine Literature," *Graeco-Arabica* 3 (1984): 101–108.

17. Papachryssanthou, "Un Confesseur de second Iconoclasme, la vie du Patrice Niketas (+836)," pp. 309–351. See also *PBE*, Niketas 160.

18. Delehaye, "Vita sancti Nicephori episcopi Milesii," pp. 133–161.

19. Delehaye, "Vita sancti Nicephori episcopi Milesii," ch. 4, p. 136, l. 11.

20. Delehaye, "Vita sancti Nicephori episcopi Milesii," ch. 4. This may have been the *magristros* Romanos Mosele who obtained the title from Constantine VII. *ODB*, s.v. "Mosele."

21. Neil Moran, "Monasteries for Eunuchs, 890–1078," paper presented at the Conference on Byzantine Monasticism, Toronto, 2001.

22. The title *orphanotrophos* indicates that, among his other duties, he was director of the state orphanage. Under Michael IV, John the Orphanotrophos speculated about unseating the patriarch of Constantinople, Alexios Stoudites, and taking his place. The church objected, but its objections, as set out by Skyl., p. 401, did not refer to the possibility that John the Orphanotrophos was not qualified because he was a eunuch.

23. Skyl., p. 390, l.73.

24. Psellos, *Chron.*, bk. 4, ch. 13, l. 17: Ἐπελανθάνετο μὲν οὐδ' οὕτω τῶν περὶ τὴν βασιλείαν φροντίδων, κεχάλαστο δ' ὅμως τὸ βλοσυρὸν τῷ θηρὶ καὶ τὸ ἐπισκύνιον οὐδαμοῦ. Sewter translates this as "Even then [when he was drunk] he did not forget the cares of Empire, nor relax that fierce-beast look on his face or the sternness of his expression." Κεχάλαστο (from χαλάω), he did not relax, is often used with reference to letting down the eyebrows; ἐπισκύνιον refers to the skin around the eyebrows. I suspect that when the sources say that eunuchs look "haughty" that it is a reference to habits of presentation that were part of their acculturation.

25. ἀλλὰ γὰρ καὶ εὐγενὴς τυγχάνεις καὶ τῆς κατὰ πολὺ διαφερούσης ζώνης κατηξίωσαι παρὰ τοῦ βασιλέως ὑμῶν. This is Theodore Krateros, *patrikios* and *protospatharios* to the emperor Theophilos. He may have come from or taken the name of the noble Melissenoi family. Kazhdan was convinced that this was a ninth-century vita. Vasilievskii and Nikitin, "42 Martyrs of Amorion, Constantine, Theodore and Callistos" [*BHG* 1210], p. 31, l. 33. See also *PBE*, Theodoros 67.

26. The assumption that eunuchs, like women, were psychologically unstable and changeable is also discussed in chapter 2.

27. The supposed lack of self-control was assumed to produce an abuse of pleasurable activities. Our texts rarely elaborate on the appearance of eunuchs, and it is hard to know if the assumption was merited.

28. This is reflected especially well in St. Basil's angry letter (St. Basil, *The Letters*, no. 115) to Simplicia, in which he enumerates the traditional evils of eunuchs. He complains that they are insatiable, weep in their food, are quick to anger, are slaves of the belly, and are mad for gold. See also chapter 1, note 7.

29. Nikephoros, *The Life of Saint Andrew the Fool*, vol. 2, ch. 2, p. 28. This saint is probably fictitious. Nicephorus, V. Andrew Salos-Rydén, vol. 1, pp. 41–56; and L. Rydén, "The Date of the Life of Andreas Salos," *DOP* 32 (1978): 127–155, suggest that although the vita is set in the fifth century and the author claims that it is an eyewitness account, it was written in the tenth century and is a fabrication.

30. Attis was the castrated god associated with the mother goddess, and the *galli* were her castrated priests.

31. This sentence is very difficult and seems to be lacking a verb

32. Photios I, *Epistulae*, vol. 1, p. 95, letter 50. Also, *PBE*, Ioannes 447.

33. For examples, see Leo Diac., pp. 7, 39, 107; and Skyl., p. 245, l. 40.

34. Theophylaktos of Ohrid says that "Everyone aspires to introduce into his life the most attractive ornament of eunuchs, their *gravitas* . . ." *Defense of Eunuchs*, p. 325, l. 20.

35. Bekker, *Theophanes Continuatus*, p. 318, l. 7.

36. This ephebic beauty underscores much of the language used to talk about eunuchs.

Reflecting traditions in the classical world and Late Antiquity, Claudian says that a eunuch is a mixture of a child and an old man. He talks about the beauty of eunuchs that, like roses, fades and wrinkles. John Chrysostom uses similar language in his oration about Eutropios. It is filled with motifs about fading grass and flowers, clearly representing the fading beauty of the eunuch. Claudian, vol. 1, p. 144, l. 76; p. 146, ll. 110–113.

37. Vita of Anna Euphemianos, pp. 175–176, l. 39. See the introduction to this saint in the Dumbarton Oaks Hagiography Database. We also find this assumption about the sexuality of eunuchs in the life of St. Andrew the Fool. Court eunuchs were often charged with having sexual relations with emperors and empresses. It is impossible to evaluate these accusations.

38. On distinctive costume, see chapter 8 on the eunuchs in the imperial palace.

39. Van den Ven, *La vie ancienne de S. Syméon Stylite le Jeune,* p. 127, l. 31.

40. Efthymiadis, *The Life of the Patriarch Tarasios by Ignatios the Deacon,* p. 161, l. 15; Heikel edition, p. 421, l. 29.

41. Featherstone and Mango, "Life of St. Matrona," in *Holy Women of Byzantium: Ten Saints' Lives in English Translation,* ed. Alice-Mary Talbot, pp. 13–64 (Washington, D.C., 1996). The life exists in two forms. Kazhdan dates the older to the second quarter of the sixth century or the late seventh century. Mango and Featherstone suggest in their introduction that the older version was written after mid-sixth century, though the author may have worked from an account contemporaneous with the saint in the fifth century. The older life is in *AASS,* Nov., 790–823. In the tenth century the life was rewritten by Symeon Metaphrastes (*PG* 116, cols. 919–954), who changes the text to say that the saint put on the garments of *her own* eunuch.

42. This text is in *Scriptores originum Constantinopolitanorum,* published in the Bonn Corpus in connection with the pseudo-Kodinus. A better text is Preger, *Scriptores,* p. 86. See also Gilbert Dagron, *Constantinople imaginaire, études sur le recueil des "Patria"* (Paris, 1984), pp. 201 and 230, n. 84.

43. The spiritual importance of this garment is discussed in chapter 8. There is also reference to a *praepositus sacri cubiculi* in Symeon Metaphrastes, Vita of St. Sampson, p. 283. In this late tenth-century life, God sends Justinian I a dream in which he saw "a certain eunuch approach clad in a garment made of gold, dressed like a *praepositos.*"

44. Harriet Whitehead, "The Bow and the Burden Strap: A New Look at Institutionalized Homosexuality in Native North America," p. 97, in a discussion of American Indians, makes a statement that could apply to the Byzantine context: "[O]ccupational pursuits clearly occupy the spotlight, with dress/demeanor coming in a close second. Sexual object choice is part of the gender configuration, but its salience is low: so low that by itself it does not provoke the reclassification of the individual to a special status. In the Western system, the order of salience is virtually the reverse."

45. Many large noble houses were staffed by eunuchs in a pattern analogous to the staffing of the palace. The great eunuch administrator and general Narses, for example, had a staff of eunuchs who ran his household.

46. Herrin, *Women in Purple,* p. 17.

47. Herrin, *Women in Purple,* pp. 58–59.

48. See *Passio* of St. Eugenia.

49. Symeon Metaphrastes, *Passio* of Saints Indes and Domna, p. 1041.

50. Malalas, *Chronicle,* bk. 14, p. 354.

51. Sokrates Scholasticus, *Socratis Scholastici,* bk. 3, p. 369.

52. Zosimos, *Histoire nouvelle,* vol. 2, part 2, book 5, p. 9, l. 2.

53. *PLRE,* 2, Lausus 1.

54. *PLRE,* 2, Hyacinthus 2.

55. *PLRE,* 2, Arsacius 2.

56. *PLRE,* 2, Joannes 22.

57. *PLRE,* 3-B, Stephanus 53.

58. Theophanes the Confessor, *Theophanis chronographia,* p. 293, l. 8.

59. Theophanes the Confessor, *Theophanis chronographia,* p. 375, l. 26; *PBE,* Theophylaktos 1.

60. Theophanes the Confessor, *Theophanis chronographia,* p. 455, l. 23: *PBE,* Elissaios 1.

61. Skyl., p. 81, l. 7; *PBE,* Theoktistos 3.

62. In the text he is called σχολαστικός εὐνοῦχος. Mango and Scott, p. 422, n. 1, suggest that this eunuch's name is Σχολασικός, an opinion shared by the *PLRE,* iii, 1117, or that he might be the conspirator Romanus who is to be found in Dindorf, *Chron. Pasch.,* 696.8 and is called *scholastikus* (advocate).

63. Bekker, *Theophanes Continuatus,* p. 246, l. 15.

64. Leo Grammaticus, *Leonis grammatici chronographia,* 254, l. 9.

65. Vita of Euphrosyna, *AASS* text, ch. 28.

66. George the Monk, *Chronicon,* vol. 2, p. 863; Skyl., p. 185, l. 21.

67. Skyl., p. 206, l. 67.

68. Bekker, *Theophanes Continuatus,* p. 413; S. Runciman, *The Emperor Romanus Lecapenus and His Reign: A Study of Tenth-Century Byzantium* (1929; reprint, Cambridge, 1988), p. 97.

69. Nikephoros Bryennios, *Histoire,* bk. 2, ch. 14, l. 3 (p. 174).

70. J. Darrouzès, ed., *Georges et Dèmètrios Tornikès,* p. 263, l. 17; p. 231, l. 2. "She received her training in grammar from one of the eunuchs who was not low born" and "eunuchs served her in the palace."

71. The topic of castrati singers in Byzantium is explored by Neil Moran in "Byzantine Castrati," forthcoming in *Plainsong and Medieval Music* (2002). Typescript provided by author. The earliest eunuch singer I have found is Brison (*PLRE,* 2), fifth-century *koubikoularios* in the service of the empress Eudoxia. Sokrates Scholasticus, *Socratis Scholastici,* p. 690, l. 31, tells us that he was head of her household and of her singers. While leading a procession in opposition to the heretical Arians, he was struck and injured by a stone. He also appears in Sozomenos, 1564, l.2.

72. Alice-Mary Talbot, "Women's Space in Byzantine Monasteries," *DOP* 52 (1998): 120–121, 126. Thomas and Constantinides, *Byzantine Monastic Foundation Documents,* no. 27, "Kecharitomene: *Typikon* for the Convent of the Mother of God Kecharitomene in Constantinople," pp. 653–656, 678–679, 696.

73. This is explored in greater detail in chapter 5. The growing presence of eunuchs in ecclesiastical roles coincides with a change in conceptions of spiritual behavior, a change that was part of the enhanced place of eunuchs in Byzantine society.

74. Kazhdan and Epstein, *Change in Byzantine Culture,* p. 8.

75. These two roles were combined in cases of empresses who exercised real power. Their closeness to the eunuchs of the empress's household let empresses appoint those same

eunuchs to important offices and commands. James, *Empresses and Power in Early Byzantium,* pp. 6, 89; Herrin, *Women in Purple,* pp. 77–82, 241; Lynda Garland, *Byzantine Empresses: Women and Power in Byzantium, 527–1204* (London, 1999), pp. 77, 132.

76. Kathryn M. Ringrose, "Eunuchs as Cultural Mediators," *ByzF* 23 (1996): 75–93.

77. Herrin, *Women in Purple,* p. 18.

78. Theophylaktos of Ohrid presents "eunuchism" as an established institution that, through castration, protected a man's chastity during morally difficult times. *Defense of Eunuchs,* 305–309.

79. Lamza, *Patriarch Germanos I,* p. 202, l. 44.

80. Niketas Paphlagonis, Vita of St. Ignatios, Patriarch of Constantinople; Skyl., p. 106, l.18.

81. George the Monk, *Chronicon,* 902, l. 21; Bekker, *Theophanes Continuatus,* 410, l. 12. Also Skyl., p. 221, l. 80, though in this case the text does not specify that Stephen was a eunuch.

82. Skyl., p. 244, l. 90.

83. Theophanes the Confessor, *Theophanis chronographia,* pp. 440–453. These page reference numbers are also found in Theophanes the Confessor, *The Chronicle of Theophanes Confessor* (ed. Mango and Scott), pp. 606–625, which provides a translation of pp. 440–453 of the de Boor edition.

84. Delehaye, "Vita sancti Nicephori episcopi Milesii," pp. 129–166.

85. Papachryssanthou,"Un Confesseur de second Iconoclasme, la vie du Patrice Niketas (+836)," pp. 309–351.

86. In "The Political Saint of the Eleventh Century," in *The Byzantine Saint,* ed. Sergei Hackel (London, 1981), Rosemary Morris argued that Symeon the New Theologian, based on his background and office-holding career at Constantinople, may have been a eunuch. A. J. Van der Aalst, "The Palace and the Monastery in Byzantine Spiritual Life c. 1000," in *The Empress Theophano: Byzantium and the West at the Turn of the First Millennium,* ed. Adelbert Davids (Cambridge, 1995), pp. 326–327, agrees. Symeon's origin in Paphlagonia, a common source of eunuchs in this period, suggests that he might have been a eunuch, as does the fact that he was sponsored as a student by his uncle, a powerful eunuch in the service of Basil II and Constantine VIII. Symeon also served as a *spatharokoubikoularios* (ceremonial sword carrier in the emperor's personal service), an office often held by eunuchs. We are far from certain, however, that Symeon was a eunuch. In her more recent *Monks and Laymen, 843–1118,* Morris no longer makes this claim. Many provincials who came to the capital from Paphlagonia were not eunuchs, and powerful eunuchs at court sponsored young scholars who were not eunuchs, as in the case of the eunuch Theoktistos's sponsorship of Constantine and Cyril. The palace had both bearded and eunuch *spatharokoubikoularioi.* This question may only be settled by a close analysis of St. Symeon's writings.

87. Morris, *Monks and Laymen,* pp. 279–280.

88. *Narratio* of St. Metrios, esp. ch. 10. A similar story celebrating the holiness of the eunuch Constantine's father is in the continuator of Theophanes and in Bekker, *Theophanes Continuatus,* p. 713, and *Symeon Magister,* p. 713, l. 15.

CHAPTER 4

1. *Defense of Eunuchs,* p. 301, ll. 6–8, Isa. 56:3–5 OAB.

2. Saint John of Damascus reflects early eighth-century negative stereotypes about eu-

nuchs in his ecclesiastical commentaries on eunuchs. John of Damascus, *PG* 95, no. 2, col. 1563. John begins with Biblical commentary, then repeats the letter to Simplicia, with its vitriolic passages on eunuchs, attributed to St. Basil and quoted in chapter 1, note 7 above. John of Damascus continues with a quotation from St. Nilus, "Remove from your household the chattering of eunuchs. For even though the eunuch seems to be cut under his testicles, above he has two eyes in his face looking passionately and dragging out wicked lies." In quoting these two authors, John of Damascus summarizes the negative perceptions of eunuchs.

3. Greek authors had access to several versions of the Septuagint or would have relied on Origen's text of the Pentateuch. These would have included the sections on Susanna and Bel and the Dragon. Except in Roman Catholic editions of the Bible, these sections are now placed with the apocryphal books of the Old Testament. For a summary of the Greek textual tradition and its problems, see Hartman and Di Lella, *The Book of Daniel,* ch. 12. The edition of the Septuagint used is A. Rahlfs, *Septuaginta* (Stuttgart, 1952). The book of Daniel begins in vol. 2, p. 870.

4. Dan. 1:870–873, from Rahlfs, *Septuaginta.* Dan. 1:3–4 NOAB.

5. Theodoret, "Interpretatio in Danielem," pp. 1256–1546. See also the early sections of Georgios Kedrenos, which reflect Byzantine perceptions of events before the time of Christ. Georgios Kedrenos, *Compendium historiarum,* vol. 1, p. 199.

6. Mathew Kuefler, "Castration and Eunuchism in the Middle Ages," in Vern L. Bullough and James A. Brundage, eds., *Handbook of Medieval Sexuality* (New York, 1996), p. 295. Kuefler suggests that the assumption that Daniel was a eunuch has roots in Jewish tradition and was transmitted to the West by Jerome. He cites evidence for this in the Babylonian *Talmud* and Jerome's writings. I am indebted to Prof. David Goodblatt of UCSD for his help in dealing with the dating of the Babylonian Talmud and for other technical details. The Babylonian *Talmud* Sanhedrin 93b, cited by Kuefler, includes an early third-century Palestinian debate regarding whether Isaiah 39:7 uses "eunuchs" in a literal or metaphorical sense. In the context, a discussion constructed by the editorial layer of the Talmud and usually dated to the sixth or seventh century, the verse is applied to Daniel or to Daniel and the three young men. In Pirqe de Rabbi Eliezer 52, the verse from Isaiah is explicitly applied to the three young men and, at least in one witness to the text, to Daniel. The editing of this work is usually dated to the Islamic period, perhaps the eighth or ninth century, though it contains earlier material. Thus, as far as the Babylonian Talmud is concerned, we cannot assume a connection between Isaiah 39:7 and Daniel before the sixth century. Jerome, however, in the early fifth century, seems aware of Jewish traditions linking Isaiah 39:7 with Daniel and the three boys. In both passages cited by Kuefler (Jerome, *Adversus Jovinianum,* p. 255, and Jerome, *Commentarius in Danielem,* l, l, 3, pp. 778–779), Jerome suggests that Daniel and the three boys are eunuchs. As I have shown, early Byzantine authors made the same connection between Isaiah 39:7 and the story of Daniel and the three boys, though they are reluctant to openly call them eunuchs as does Jerome. Some ambiguity remains regarding what the Talmud and Jerome mean by "eunuch." In the context of Jerome's writings it clearly means "courtier," but it is not clear whether it refers to a castrated courtier or to a celibate one.

7. Rahlfs, *Septuaginta,* 864–870. The Susanna story is chapter 13 of the Greek version of the book of Daniel, Sus. 1–64 NOAB.

8. Rahlfs, *Septuaginta,* 936–941. Bel and the Dragon is chapter 14 of the Greek version of the book of Daniel, Bel and Dragon 1–69 NOAB.

9. Rahlfs, *Septuaginta,* 874–876.

10. St. John Chrysostom, "Interpretatio in Danielem prophetam," 194–245.

11. Symeon Metaphrastes, *Commentarius* on the Passion of the Prophet Daniel, pp. 372–404.

12. St. John Chrysostom, *Homilia in Eutropium eunuchum patricium*, p. 391. Chrysostom's themes point to the vanities of worldly pleasures and power and the changes and ambiguities that afflict the natural world. Eutropios is accused of abusing food and drink, despoiling widows and orphans, unlawfully seizing wealth and property, wearing silk robes, and displaying himself. This is standard fare in pejorative literature aimed at eunuchs. Images applied to Eutropios include the dry fruitless tree and the ephemeral drying rose, also familiar images applied to eunuchs. Chrysostom is familiar with the gender construct of the eunuchs of his day and dislikes it.

13. The idea that beautiful young eunuchs were passive sexual partners for powerful men runs through our sources. It is hard to verify since it is imbedded in pejorative stereotypes.

14. St. John Chrysostom, "Interpretatio in Danielem prophetam," 194.

15. See the discussion of this topic in chapter 2, p. 55.

16. St. John Chrysostom, "Interpretatio in Danielem prophetam," 197.

17. St. John Chrysostom, "Interpretatio in Danielem prophetam," 199.

18. *ODB*, s.v. "Symeon Metaphrastes." Symeon may have lived for most of the tenth century. Kazhdan eliminated one of the potential individuals who might have been Symeon, shortening the possible life span, and making the year 1000 as a death date a fair estimate for our purposes. Based on personal correspondence with Dr. Nancy Sevcenko.

19. The *parakoimomenos*, literally the one who sleeps beside the emperor, was chief of the eunuchs who served in the emperor's intimate quarters. The office may have appeared in the seventh century and was well established in the eighth as a replacement for the earlier office of *praepositus sacri cubiculi.* In the ninth and tenth centuries the office was politically important and was held by several powerful eunuchs. It declined, with the eunuchate, in the twelfth century. Guilland, *Recherches*, pp. 202–216.

20. From τὰ μαθήματα. E. A. Sophocles, *Greek Lexicon of the Roman and Byzantine Periods* (1914; reprint, Hildesheim, 1992) translates this as "mathematics," although it might also refer to general knowledge. Liddell and Scott specify that often, in the plural, as in this case, and in Aristophanes and Thucydides, the term refers to the mathematical sciences. Since my work indicates that eunuchs were considered adept at computation, I have chosen this translation.

21. Symeon Metaphrastes, Vita S. Prophetae Danielis, p. 372, ch. 1, l. 12.

22. A survey of the diet of holy men in Symeon Metaphrastes' other vitae in *PG* 114–116, indicates that St. Lucian (Symeon Metaphrastes, *Passio* of St. Lucian, p. 400) ate only bread and water; St. Theodosios the Coenobiarcha (Symeon Metaphrastes, Vita of St. Theodosios Coenobiarcha, p. 481) ate only dates, pods, cooked vegetables, and date pit meal; St. Euthymios (Symeon Metaphrastes, Vita of St. Euthymios, p. 672) ate bread, water, dates and wine once a week; St. Clement (Symeon Metaphrastes, Vita of St. Clement of Ancyra, p. 824) ate only vegetables and never touched meat. Symeon Metaphrastes specifically tells us that for St. Clement, "Vegetables were his only food. He didn't eat anything that moved, always remembering the three boys whose bodies, sharpened by abstinence, could not be defeated by the fire of debauchery or by the flames of the furnace." St. Kyriakos (Symeon Metaphrastes, Vita of St. Kyriakos the Anchorite, p. 929) ate only wild onions; St. Aberchios (Symeon Metaphrastes, Vita of St. Aberchios, 1236) ate only bread, wine, olives,

and oil. St. John the Abbot (Symeon Metaphrastes, Vita of St. John the Abbot, p. 44) ate only herbs; St. Melania (Symeon Metaphrastes, Vita of St. Melania, p. 769) ate only harsh food and hard bread, as did Saints Indes and Domna (Symeon Metaphrastes, *Passio* of Saints Indes and Domna, p. 1041).

23. Symeon Metaphrastes, Vita S. Prophetae Danielis, p. 373.

24. St. John Chrysostom, "Interpretatio in Danielem prophetam," p. 199.

25. St. John Chrysostom, "Interpretatio in Danielem prophetam," p. 209.

26. Symeon Metaphrastes, Vita S. Prophetae Danielis, p. 376, ch. 5, l. 5.

27. Symeon Metaphrastes, Vita S. Prophetae Danielis, p. 377, ch. 6, l. 3.

28. St. John Chrysostom, "Interpretatio in Danielem prophetam," p. 210.

29. This comment is a striking metaphor, given the way Chrysostom usually fulminated against the theater. St. John Chrysostom, "Interpretatio in Danielem prophetam," p. 211.

30. Symeon Metaphrastes, Vita S. Prophetae Danielis, p. 377, ch. 6, ll. 11, 15, and 17.

31. Symeon Metaphrastes, Vita S. Prophetae Danielis, p. 379, ch. 7, l. 8.

32. Symeon Metaphrastes, Vita S. Prophetae Danielis, p. 379, ch. 7, l. 23. By Symeon Metaphrastes' time, the image of the boys in the fiery furnace was used frequently as a metaphor for overcoming sexual desire. We see this in his other writings, as in the vita of St. Theophanes (Symeon Metaphrastes, Vita of St. Theophanes, p. 16), where he tells us that, just as the angel saved the boys from the flames of the furnace so, also, an angel saved St. Theophanes and his bride from the flames of sexual desire.

33. St. John Chrysostom, "Interpretatio in Danielem prophetam," p. 225.

34. Symeon Metaphrastes, Vita S. Prophetae Danielis, p. 385, ch. 12, l. 11.

35. Symeon Metaphrastes, Vita S. Prophetae Danielis, p. 385, ch. 13, l. 1

36. Symeon Metaphrastes, Vita S. Prophetae Danielis, p. 387.

37. The ruins of Ecbatana are in northern Media, on the Iranian plateau. Traditionally founded by Deioces as the capital of the Median Empire, it became the summer capital of the Achaemenid Empire and, like Susa and Babylon, a royal residence. Alexander captured Ecbatana in 330 B.C. and plundered a vast sum from the treasury. It remained a royal residence in Parthian times. *The Oxford Classical Dictionary,* ed. Simon Hornblower and Antony Spawforth, 3d ed. (New York, 1996), s.v. "Ecbatana."

38. One thinks of the large monastery built by Basil the Nothos. After the exile of this powerful eunuch, the emperor Basil II had the unfinished building pulled down, stone by stone. Zonaras, *Ioannes Zonaras: Epitome historiarum,* vol. 3, p. 554, l. 16. Since Daniel was honored as a prophet in Islam, it is possible that a building in Ecbatana was attributed to him.

39. Symeon Metaphrastes, Vita S. Prophetae Danielis, p. 389, ch. 17.

40. Symeon Metaphrastes, Vita S. Prophetae Danielis, p. 396, ch. 22.

41. Symeon Metaphrastes, Vita S. Prophetae Danielis, p. 396, ch. 23, l. 20.

42. From εὔνοος, kindly, friendly, well-disposed. This is a false etymology for eunuch.

43. Symeon Metaphrastes, Vita S. Prophetae Danielis, p. 400, ch. 23, ll. 6, 7.

44. Regarding the derivation of the word "eunuch," see chapter 1. The term δορυφόροι is specifically used for a king's personal bodyguard or sword-carrier. Both eunuchs and bearded men served this function, and the use of eunuchs in this role can be traced to the Assyrian Empire. The same word is also used for satellites revolving around planets. There is clearly an

association between eunuchs and personal servants and bodyguards as individuals who shared the ruler's personal space. See Symeon Metaphrastes, Vita S. Prophetae Danielis, p. 400.

45. Symeon Metaphrastes, Vita S. Prophetae Danielis, p. 401, chs. 26, l. 1 to end of ch. 27.

46. Italic added. St. John Chrysostom, "Interpretatio in Danielem prophetam," p. 238.

47. Morris, *Monks and Laymen*, p. 30.

48. Symeon Metaphrastes, Vita of St. Sampson, pp. 277–308.

49. This is an early title for the grand chamberlain, highest-ranking eunuch in the imperial service. By the fifth century this office had become very important and included duties beyond those of personal service in the palace. After the sixth century the office declined, and its important duties were taken over by the *parakoimomenos*. The title *praepositos* remained in use for eunuchs associated with court ceremonial. Guilland, *Recherches*, bk. 1, pp. 338–380.

50. Samuel N. C. Lieu and Dominic Montserrat, eds., *Constantine: History, Historiography and Legend* (London and New York, 1998). On p. 160, Lieu discusses the legend of Euphratas, summarizing the story and providing partial translations.

51. Halkin, "L'Empereur Constantin converti par Euphrates"; Opitz, "Die Vita Constantine des Codex Angelicus 22"; Kazhdan, "'Constantin imaginair': Byzantine Legends of the Ninth Century about Constantine the Great"; Halkin, "Les deux derniers chapitres de la Nouvelle Vie de Constantin." Euphratas also appears in the *Patria*. See Preger, *Scriptores originum Constantinopolitanarum*, fasc. 2, 147; and G. Dagron, *Constantinople imaginaire.*

52. Preger, *Scriptores originum Constantinopolitanarum*, fasc. 2, p. 147, ll. 12–13.

53. Halkin, "L'Empereur Constantin converti par Euphrates," pp. 7–8.

54. Halkin, "L'Empereur Constantin converti par Euphrates," p. 6.

55. François Halkin, ed., "Une Nouvelle vie de Constantin dans un légendier de Patmos," *AB* 77 (1959): 63–107, quotation from p. 70. Halkin considers that this vita could not have been written before the ninth century.

56. Halkin, "Une Nouvelle vie de Constantin dans un légendier de Patmos," p. 83, ch. 8, l. 19.

57. Halkin, "Une Nouvelle vie de Constantin dans un légendier de Patmos," p. 86, ch. 10, l. 1.

58. Halkin, "Une Nouvelle vie de Constantin dans un légendier de Patmos," p. 86, ch. 10.

59. Halkin, "Une Nouvelle vie de Constantin dans un légendier de Patmos," p. 86, ch. 10.

60. Halkin, "Une Nouvelle vie de Constantin dans un légendier de Patmos," p. 86, ch. 10, l. 12.

61. Halkin, "Une Nouvelle vie de Constantin dans un légendier de Patmos," p. 87, ch. 10, l. 37.

62. Halkin, "Une Nouvelle vie de Constantin dans un légendier de Patmos," p. 89, ch. 12, l. 1.

63. Halkin, "Une Nouvelle vie de Constantin dans un légendier de Patmos," p. 89, ch. 12, l. 9.

64. Halkin, "Une Nouvelle vie de Constantin dans un légendier de Patmos," p. 90, ch. 12, l. 22.

65. Halkin, "Une Nouvelle vie de Constantin dans un légendier de Patmos," p. 90, ch. 12, l. 38.

66. The idea that Euphratas was Constantine's architect and builder is also found in the historian Kedrenos, *Compendium historiarum,* vol. 2, p. 531.

67. Skyl., p. 367, l. 69.

CHAPTER 5

1. Thomas and Constantinides, *Byzantine Monastic Foundation Documents,* includes forty-six documents dated before 1300. Eleven refer to eunuchs. There are six references that are prohibitions on the entry of eunuchs, and three of them involve Mt. Athos. No. 13, "*Typikon* of Athanasios the Athonite for the Lavra Monastery, 973–975," pp. 248, 263, trenchantly rejects a eunuch or young boy, "even if he should be the son of the man who holds the imperial scepter."

2. Talbot, "Women's Space," pp. 120–121, 126; Thomas and Constantinides, *Byzantine Monastic Foundation Documents,* no. 27, "*Typikon* of Empress Irene Doukaina Komnene for the Convent of the Mother of God," dated 1110, pp. 654, 656, 678–679, 696.

3. Saint Basil, *The Letters,* p. 229.

4. Symeon Metaphrastes, *Commentarius* on the Passion of the Prophet Daniel, pp. 371–403.

5. Thomas and Constantinides, *Byzantine Monastic Foundation Documents,* no. 12, "*Typikon* of Emperor John Tzimiskes," pp. 232, 233, 238. See also Moran, "Monasteries for Eunuchs," pp. 4–5.

6. Eusebios of Caesarea, *Histoire ecclésiastique,* vol. 1, p. 8, l. 2.

7. Life in a male monastery was considered to be more rigorous than in a female monastery. In the hagiographical tradition women who sought spiritual perfection are often portrayed as pretending to be young men or eunuchs in order to enter male monasteries. See also Talbot, "Women's Space," p. 117.

8. See Nicholas Constas's excellent translation of the life of St. Mary/Marinos.

9. This tale appears in most historians who discuss his patriarchate: Bekker, *Theophanes Continuatus,* p. 158, l. 2; Skyl., p. 86, l. 52.

10. Other questions regarding eunuchs troubled the church. While castration was a solution to Late Antique questions about propriety between the sexes, it flew in the face of religious norms regarding the integrity of the body, especially that of the priestly body. Many saw castration as an unnatural act that violated the integrity of the body. Could religious duty justify this act, or was it, like murder, socially unacceptable? This takes us to the issue of cultural definitions of "nature" and the cultural relativism of the "natural" versus the "unnatural," which merits separate discussion.

11. Isa. 56:3–5 NOAB.

12. Acts 8:26–40 NOAB.

13. Mt 19:12 NOAB.

14. Saint Epiphanios, *Panarion,* in *Epiphanius,* vol. 2, p. 361.

15. Clement of Alexandria, *Clemens Alexandrinus. Stromata,* bk., 3, p. 1.

16. Eusebios of Caesarea, *Histoire ecclésiastique. The Ecclesiastical History,* vol. 2, ch. 2, par. 8 (p. 29).

17. Athanasios, *Homily on the Song of Songs, PG* 27, col. 1352.

18. Saint Epiphanios, *Panarion,* vol. 2, p. 360, l. 8.

19. St. John Chrysostom, *Homily XXXV on Chapter XIV of Genesis,* p. 599.

20. Saint Epiphanios, *Panarion,* vol. 2, p. 362, l. 7.

21. Gregory of Nazianzos, *Discours,* ch. 16, p. 305.

22. Saint Basil, *The Letters,* no. 115, l. 24.

23. John of Damascus, *PG* col. 1564. John provides several texts dealing with eunuchs.

24. Pascal Boulhol and Isabelle Cochelin, "La rehabilitation de l'eunuque dans l'hagiographie antique (IIe—VIe siècles)," in *Memoriam sanctorum venerantes: Miscellanea in onore de Monsignor Victor Saxer* (Vatican, 1992), esp. pp. 66–69. These sources contain references to many other eunuchs, often servants or courtiers.

25. A valuable new tool for analysis of this hagiography is being developed at Dumbarton Oaks in the form of the computerized Byzantine Hagiography Database, created by the late Alexander Kazhdan, Alice-Mary Talbot, and Lee Sherry.

26. Vilinskii, *Zhitie sv. Vasiliia Novago v russkoi literature,* pp. 285–290.

27. Vilinskii, *Zhitie sv. Vasiliia Novago v russkoi literature,* p. 285, l. 7.

28. V. Niketas of the Medikion, ch. 43. Gilbert Dagron, *Empereur et prêtre: Étude sur le "Césaropapisme" byzantin* (Paris, 1996), p. 197, considers that this vita was written before 840; see also *PBE,* Anthimios 6.

29. Robert Devreese, "Le Texte Grec de l'hypomnesticum de Théodore Spoudée," p. 73; *PBE,* Gregorios 149.

30. *PLRE,* Calipodius 2.

31. Sokrates Scholasticus, *Socratis Scholastici, Hermiae Sozomeni Historia ecclesiastica,* p. 711.

32. In Byzantine iconography the patriarchs Germanos, Niketas I, and Ignatios the Younger are shown beardless. See O. Meinardus, "The Beardless Patriarch: St. Germanos," *Macedonika* 13 (1973): 178–186; and *PBE,* Germanos 8.

33. Niketas's career is outlined in Theophanes the Confessor, *Theophanis chronographia,* pp. 440–453; also *The Chronicle of Theophanes Confessor,* pp. 606–625; and in *PBE,* Niketas 1. Theophanes reminds his readers that Niketas was a eunuch and a Slav, but his hatred of Niketas is not derived from the assumption that Niketas was ineligible to be patriarch because he was a eunuch. Theophanes emphasizes Niketas's policies regarding the icons and his irregular election. Indeed, Theophanes celebrates the heroism of the icon-supporting palace servants who, since they were *koubikoularioi,* were certainly eunuchs. *Theophanis chronographia,* p. 453. The twelfth-century chronicler Michael Glykas, however, does use the fact that Niketas was a eunuch to heap negative rhetoric upon him. Glykas, *Michaelis Glycae Annales,* 527.

34. Bekker, *Theophanes Continuatus,* bk. 4, p. 158, l. 4; and Skyl., pp. 86, l. 52, 87, l. 15. *PBE,* Methodios 1, does not identify Methodios as a eunuch, but other materials suggest that he may have been.

35. Niketas Paphlagonis, Vita of St. Ignatios, archbishop of Constantinople; Skyl., p. 106, ll. 18, 20; *PBE,* Ignatios 1.

36. Delehaye, "Vita sancti Nicephori episcopi Milesii," ch. 8, pp. 143–44.

37. Vita of Luke Stylite, p. 217, l. 26. Kazhdan dates this life to be of the tenth century.

38. George the Monk, *Chronicon,* p. 902; and Skyl., p. 221, l. 81, p. 223, l. 45, p. 225, l. 86.

39. Leo Diac., p. 32, l. 19; Skyl., p. 244, ll. 89–90, p. 245, ll. 21, 31, p. 247, ll. 73, 82, p. 248, ll. 2, 15, p. 249, l. 20, p. 259, ll. 60, 62, p. 260, l. 82, p. 261, ll. 89, 1, 6, p. 285, l. 24, p. 286, ll. 46,

67. The emperors were Constantine VII (r. 947–959), Romanos II (r. 959–963), Nikephoros (r. 963–969), and John Tzimiskes (r. 969–976). Leo Diac., p. 32, l. 20, says that Polyeuktos "was a man who had studied divine and human philosophy to the extreme. He had elected from childhood the monastic and unencumbered life and had attained communion with the divine beyond that of other men. It was not just his nature that made him this way, for he was a eunuch and had come to extreme old age, but also his poverty, lack of guilt, and simple way of life." Skyl., 244, l. 90, says, "On the third of April in the same indiction Polyeuktos the monk was appointed patriarch in his [Theophylaktos's] place. Polyeuktos was a man who had been raised and educated in Constantinople, had been castrated by his parents, and had become prominent in the monastic life. The emperor appointed him as patriarch because of his superior wisdom, the simplicity of his manner, and his love of poverty."

40. Skyl., p. 400, l. 30.

41. Skyl., p. 400, l. 29, p. 401, l. 8.

42. Skyl., p. 464, l. 14.

43. Attaleiates, *Michaelis Attaliotae historia,* p. 180.

44. Choniates, *Nicetae Choniatae Historia,* p. 124, l. 17.

45. Choniates, *Nicetae Choniatae Historia,* p. 219.

46. His discussion of Mat. 19 and *Defense of Eunuchs,* pp. 291–331, are particularly important.

47. For examples of this, see Skyl., p. 190, ll. 60, 89; p. 240, l. 68; p. 398, l. 85.

48. John the Orphanotrophos tried unsuccessfully to use his influence over the emperor to have himself named patriarch.

49. Skyl., p. 464, ll. 15–16.

50. Attaleiates, *Michaelis Attaliotae historia,* 180.

51. Kedrenos, *Compendium historiarum,* vol. 2, p. 147. The tale of Methodios's sterility is treated by historians who discuss his patriarchate. See Bekker, *Theophanes Continuatus,* bk. 4, p. 158; Skyl., p. 86, l. 52. The story is a version of a common "discovery" tale in which a holy person is accused of fathering a child and then found incapable of doing so, revealed either as a woman or a eunuch.

52. Theophylaktos of Ohrid, *Enarratio en evangelium Matthaei,* ch. 19, v. 12; *PG* 125, col. 352.

53. *Defense of Eunuchs,* p. 329, l. 9.

54. Thomas and Constantinides, *Byzantine Monastic Foundation Documents,* no. 19, "Rule of Michael Attaleiates for his Almshouse in Rhaidestos and for the Monastery of Christ Panoiktirmon in Constantinople," pp. 327, 348; and no. 29, "*Typikon* of the *Sebastokrator* Isaac Komnenos for the Monastery of the Mother of God Kosmosteira near Bera," pp. 787, 800, 824.

55. *Defense of Eunuchs,* p. 303, l. 10.

56. *Defense of Eunuchs,* p. 303, l. 22.

57. *Defense of Eunuchs,* p. 297, l. 13

58. Brown, *The Body and Society,* pp. 10–11.

59. *Defense of Eunuchs,* p. 307, l. 15 ff.

60. *Defense of Eunuchs,* p. 327, l. 3.

61. Vita of Niphon Constantiana, p. 111, l. 9, p. 67, l. 21.

62. Vilinskii, *Zhitie sv. Vasiliia Novago v russkoi literature,* pp. 285–290.

63. Vilinskii, *Zhitie sv. Vasiliia Novago v russkoi literature,* pp. 57, 305.

64. Papachryssanthou, "Un Confesseur de second Iconoclasme, la vie du Patrice Niketas (+836)"; *PBE,* Niketas 160.

65. Delehaye, "Vita sancti Nicephori episcopi Milesii."

66. *Vision* of St. Kosmas, pp. 73–99.

67. *Narratio* of St. Metrios, pp. 721–724.

68. Lamza, *Patriarch Germanos I,* p. 202, l. 44.

69. Niketas Paphlagonis, Vita of St. Ignatios, archbishop of Constantinople.

70. Kedrenos, *Compendium historiarum,* vol. 2, p. 147.

71. Symeon Metaphrastes, *Commentarius* on the Passion of the Prophet Daniel, pp. 371–404; and Kathryn M. Ringrose, "Reconfiguring the Prophet Daniel: Gender, Sanctity, and Castration in Byzantium," in *Difference and Genders in the Middle Ages,* ed. Sharon Farmer and Carol Pasternak (Minneapolis, 2002.)

72. Ringrose, "Eunuchs as Cultural Mediators," pp. 75–93.

73. Kedrenos, *Compendium historiarum,* vol. 2, p. 147.

74. Morris, *Monks and Laymen,* p. 86. I am grateful to Professor Morris for suggesting that I investigate the life of St. Symeon.

75. Papachryssanthou, *Actes de Xénophon,* p. 70, l. 19.

76. Papachryssanthou, *Actes de Xénophon,* p. 70, l. 23.

77. It is unclear whether the youths were eunuchs or prepubescent boys. In this period, eunuchs were not usually referred to as "beardless boys," especially in a text that talks about eunuchs and beardless boys as distinct categories. In his *Defense of Eunuchs,* Theophylaktos discusses Symeon and his monastic foundation(s). The passage can be interpreted to indicate that Symeon founded a monastery for eunuchs in Thessalonica or that he established a monastery for eunuchs on Mt. Athos, or both. Since the final settlement between Symeon and the officials on Athos involved an agreement in which Symeon would be the only eunuch on Athos, the assumption is that he restored the Monastery of Xenophon on Mt. Athos with the assistance of three beardless boys who were part of his *oikos,* after which he was forced to leave and founded a monastery for eunuchs in Thessalonica. *Defense of Eunuchs,* p. 329, l. 4. In the same volume (pp. 116–117), see Gautier's comments.

78. Papachryssanthou, *Actes du Prôtaton,* section 21, ll. 101–106. The *typikon* also forbids introduction of eunuchs onto the mountain, but this does not seem to have been the reason for Symeon's expulsion. Indeed, the *typikon* of John Tzimiskes (Thomas and Constantinides, *Byzantine Monastic Foundation Documents,* p. 232) includes a process whereby eunuchs could, in fact, be admitted to the monastery of Prôtaton.

79. Morris, *Monks and Laymen,* p. 279. See also Moran, "Monasteries for Eunuchs," pp. 4–5.

80. Papachryssanthou, *Actes de Xénophon,* l. 48–52.

81. *Byzantine Foundation Documents* no. 15, "*Typikon* of Constantine IX Monomachos," pp. 282–283, 285.

CHAPTER 6

1. *PBE,* Theoktistos 3.

2. See W. G. Brokkaar, "Basil Lacapenus," in *Studia Byzantina et Neohellenica Neerlandica,* ed. W. F. Bakker, A. F. Van Gemert, and W. J. Aerts, 199–235 (Leiden, 1972).

3. Brokkaar, "Basil Lacapenus," takes the position, which my research supports, that adult castration was considered dangerous and was rarely performed on important individuals. He discounts Kedrenos, Zonaras, and Joel, who say that Basil was castrated as an adult when Romanos was deposed. He and I favor Psellos's assumption that Basil was castrated young because he was a bastard. The problem is complicated by the fact that we do not know when Basil was born.

4. See chapter 8, which provides an account of the ceremony in which Basil was given this new title (*De cer.*, bk. 1, ch. 97). Events in the description of the ceremony make it clear that the official elevated on this occasion was a eunuch.

5. Herrin, *Women in Purple*, pp. 19, 77–82; James, *Empresses and Power*, p. 89; Garland, *Byzantine Empresses*, pp. 5, 77, 132.

6. In a campaign that his detractors neglect to mention, Eutropios led his troops successfully against the Huns in about 398. J. B. Bury, *History of the Later Roman Empire from the Death of Theodosius I to the Death of Justianian*, 2 vols. (New York, 1958), vol. 1, p. 126.

7. Malalas, *Chronicle*, pp. 486–492; Agathias, bk. 2, ch. 7; Prokopios, *Wars*, bks. 6–8.

8. Prokopios, *Wars* vol. 6, ch. 8, l. 4.

9. Prokopios, *Wars*, vol. 8, ch. 21, l. 7.

10. Prokopios, *Wars*, vol. 6, ch. 13, l. 1; ch. 116, l. 2.

11. Agathias, bk. 1, ch. 7.

12. Agathias, bk. 1, ch. 8.

13. Agathias, bk. 1, ch. 16.

14. Prokopios, *Wars*, vol. 3, ch. 11, l. 5.

15. Prokopios, *Wars*, vol. 4, ch. 8, ll. 12–17.

16. Prokopios, *Anecdota*, ch. 5, l. 15.

17. Leo Diac., p. 107.

18. This continues to be the case through the twelfth century, when the historian Niketas Choniates tells us that Alexios I Komnenos's men were unable to take the fortress at Prosakos because the eunuch in charge of tools failed to bring adequate equipment to dismantle the wall. Choniates, *Nicetae Choniatae Historia*, p. 505, l. 94.

19. Theophanes, *Theophanis chronographia*, p. 451.

20. Theophanes, *Theophanis chronographia*, p. 349, 351, l. 6; *PBE*, Andreas 1.

21. See J. F. Haldon, *Byzantine Praetorians: An Administrative, Institutional, and Social Survey of the Opsikion and Tagmata, c. 500–900* (Bonn, 1984), p. 188 and n. 415.

22. Theophanes, *Theophanis chronographia*, p. 344; *PBE*, Kakorhizos 1.

23. Irene was imperial consort to Leo IV. From 780 to 790 she ruled as regent for Constantine VI. Deposed in 790, in 797 she dethroned and blinded her son Constantine VI. She then ruled in her own right until deposed again in 802. *ODB*, s.v. "Irene, empress (797–802)."

24. Theophanes, *Theophanis chronographia*, p. 455, l. 4; *PBE*, Ioannes 14.

25. Theophanes, *Theophanis chronographia*, p. 475; *PBE*, Aetios 1.

26. Theophanes, *Theophanis chronographia*, p. 457.

27. Theophanes, *Theophanis chronographia*, p. 462; *PBE*, Staurakios 1.

28. *PBE*, Leo 14.

29. Kedrenos, *Compendium historiarum*, vol. 2, p. 29.

30. *PBE,* Theodoros 67.

31. The second vita, falsely attributed to Michael Synkellos, in Vasilievskii and Nikitin, "42 Martyrs of Amorion, Constantine, Theodore and Callistos," par. 31, l. 33.

32. Bekker, *Theophanes Continuatus,* p. 114, l. 22 ff.

33. According to Bekker, *Theophanes Continuatus,* p. 36, he helped Michael II the Amorian murder Leo V the Armenian. See also *ODB,* s.v. "Theokistos"; and *PBE,* Theoktistos 3.

34. Bekker, *Theophanes Continuatus,* bk. 4, p. 148; Kedrenos, *Compendium historiarum,* vol. 2, p. 139, l. 15; Herrin, *Women in Purple,* pp. 214–217.

35. F. Halkin, "Trois dates précisées grace au synaxaire," *Byzantion* 24 (1954): 11–14.

36. George the Monk, *Chronicon,* p. 878; Bekker, *Theophanes Continuatus,* p. 386.

37. George the Monk, *Chronicon,* p. 855.

38. Bekker, *Theophanes Continuatus,* p. 425.

39. Leo Diac., p. 7, l. 3. Constantine Gongyles and his eunuch brother, Anastasios, served at court in the mid-tenth century. The life of St. Basil the Younger talks about two brothers, identified as the Gongyles brothers, who were retired court eunuchs. This life also features Samonas, a eunuch who served from approximately 900 to 912. Vilinskii, *Zhitie sv. Vasilia Novago v russkoi literature,* p. 57, l. 16.

40. Bekker, *Theophanes Continuatus,* p. 462. 4.

41. Skyl., p. 295, l. 23.

42. Choniates, *Nicetae Choniatae Historia,* p. 505, l. 94. See note 18 above.

43. Skyl., pp. 267–270.

44. Kedrenos, *Compendium historiarum,* vol. 2, p. 365, l. 12; Skyl., p. 272, l. 79.

45. Leo Diac., pp. 81–82; Kedrenos, *Compendium historiarum,* vol. 2, pp. 365–366; Skyl., p. 272, l. 83.

46. Leo Diac., p. 106–107. Byzantine sources use the archaic term "Scythian" for all steppe nomads including the Kievan Russians. This particular text refers to John Tzimiskes's wars against the Kievan Russians.

47. Leo Diac., p. 103; Scyl., pp. 282, 287, l. 87.

48. Guilland, *Recherches,* 1. p. 220, n. 77; Scyl., p. 320, l. 26; Kedrenos, *Compendium historiarum,* vol. 2, p. 424; letter nos. 1 and 6 to John the Ostiarios, the nephew of Leo, in Leo, metropolitan of Synada, *Correspondence.*

49. Skyl., p. 389, l. 54; Kedrenos, *Compendium historiarum,* vol. 2, p. 503, l. 16.

50. Mark Whittow, *The Making of Byzantium, 600–1025* (Berkeley, 1996), p. 376 and n. 37.

51. Skyl., p. 370, l. 30.

52. Skyl., p. 432, l. 91.

53. Skyl., p. 438, l. 60.

54. Skyl., p. 402, l. 6.

55. Skyl., p. 464, ll. 14, 28.

56. Skyl., p. 472, l. 30.

57. Skyl., p. 409, l. 83.

58. Skyl., p. 478, l. 90; p. 479, l. 6; p. 493, l. 80.

59. Nikephoros Bryennios, *Histoire,* bk. 4, ch. 31, p. 301, ll. 23–24.

60. Nikephoros Bryennios, *Histoire,* bk. 4, ch. 32, l. 12. The meaning of "Klu, klu" is un-

clear. Du Cange, *Glossarium,* suggests that it refers to the dribbling manner of the eunuch's urination. I am inclined to discard this suggestion, since urinary tract problems are characteristic only of fully castrated eunuchs.

61. Nikephoros Bryennios, *Histoire,* bk. 4, ch. 38. One of the earliest identifiable members of the wealthy, noble Palaiologos family, George was a supporter of the Komnenoi.

62. Nikephoros Bryennios, *Histoire,* bk. 4, ch. 40.

63. Anna Komnene, *Alexiade,* bk. 11, ch. 10, l. 7.

64. Choniates, *Nicetae Choniatae Historia,* p. 245, l. 85.

65. Choniates, *Nicetae Choniatae Historia,* p. 318, l. 26.

66. Choniates, *Nicetae Choniatae Historia,* p. 461, l. 26.

CHAPTER 7

1. André Grabar, *Christian Iconography: A Study of the Origins* (Princeton, 1986), p. 79.

2. "Testamentum Adae," p. 1317.

3. Theodore Studites, *Oration VI. On the Holy Angels,* p. 730.

4. Cyril Mango, *Byzantium, the Empire of New Rome* (London, 1980), pp. 151–158.

5. Cyril Mango, "St Michael and Attis," *Deltion* 12 (1984): 45.

6. Like "eunuchs," the term "angels" is an omnibus term that includes several subgroups.

7. Niketas Pectoratos, *Opuscules et lettres [par] Nicétas Stethatos,* pp. 301–365.

8. Choniates, *Nicetae Choniatae Historia,* p. 540, l. 87. The groves contained trees that the navy hoped to harvest for ship masts. The imperial eunuchs would not let them be cut because they were considered sacred.

9. The better text is in Preger, *Scriptores,* p. 86. It is also in *Scriptores Originum Constantinopolitanorum* in the Bonn Corpus, in connection with the pseudo-Kodinus. There is a detailed discussion of these texts in Dagron, *Constantinople imaginaire,* p. 21.

10. George P. Majeska, *Russian Travelers to Constantinople in the Fourteenth and Fifteenth Centuries* (Washington, D.C., 1984). See also discussion in Dagron, *Constantinople imaginaire.*

11. Victor Saxer, "Jalons pour servir à l'histoire du culte de l'archange Saint Michel en Orient jusqu'à l'iconoclasme," in *Noscere sancta: Miscellanea in memoria di A. Amore O. F. M.* (Rome, 1985), pp. 357–426. See also *ODB,* s.v. "Michael, archangel and saint."

12. Its cult center was at Pessinous, near Germia. The Sangarios River flows in a loop around Germia and was sacred to the Cybele and personified in its mythology. Mango suggests that these sites were transferred to St. Michael. Mango, "St. Michael and Attis," pp. 54–55.

13. In the life of St. Basil the Younger, it appears in descriptions of angels or heavenly plants or structures. It appears to suggest the change from an earthly nature to a heavenly one. Vilinskii, *Zhitie sv. Vasiliia Novago v russkoi literature.*

14. Preger, *Scriptores,* pp. 85–87.

15. Symeon Metaphrastes, Vita of St. Sampson, p. 283. See chapter 4, note 48 above.

16. "Moses did not know that the skin of his face shone because he had been talking with God" (Ex. 34:29 NOAB). "And while he [Jesus] was praying, the appearance of his face changed, and his clothes became dazzling white" (Luke 9:29 NOAB).

17. Van den Ven, *La vie ancienne de S. Syméon Stylite le Jeune,* p. 127, l. 31. The anonymous author is considered to be contemporary with Symeon, who died in 592.

18. Stephanos Efthymiadis, ed. and trans., *The Life of the Patriarch Tarasios by Ignatios the Deacon,* par. 421, ll. 29–37 (translation on p. 201). See also Talbot, "Women's Space," p. 117.

19. Symeon Metaphrastes, *Passio* of St. Anthimios, col. 180.

20. Symeon Metaphrastes, Vita of St. Aberchios, p. 1213.

21. Symeon Metaphrastes, Vita of St. Daniel the Stylite, p. 988.

22. Nikephoros, *The Life of Saint Andrew the Fool,* vol. 2, p. 77, l. 962. See also Sara Murray, *A Study of the Life of Andreas: The Fool for the Sake of Christ* (Borna-Leipzig, 1910), pp. 85–106.

23. Mango, *Byzantium, The Empire of New Rome,* p. 155.

24. Delelaye, Vita of St. Paul the Younger of Latros, ch. 31, p. 141, l. 15. The saint died in 955; the life was written by a monk of Latros. Kazhdan thinks it was written in the tenth century.

25. Vilinskii, *Zhitie sv. Vasiliia Novago v russkoi literature,* p. 158.

26. Fourmy and Leroy, "La vie de S. Philarète," p. 163, l. 25. The life written by his grandson about thirty years after saint's death in 792.

27. *Vision* of St. Kosmas, beginning p. 86, l. 188. The story is from the tenth century. Kosmas was *koitonites* of the emperor Alexander (r. 912–913) and became a monk after the emperor's death. A partial translation is in Mango, *Byzantium, The Empire of New Rome,* p. 152.

28. Greenfield, *The Life of Lazaros of Mt. Galesion,* pp. 297–298, 301. The events date to the eleventh century.

29. Vita of Niphon of Constantiana, p. 44, l. 24; p. 53, l. 33; p. 62, l. 18.

30. Nikephoros, *The Life of Saint Andrew the Fool,* vol. 2, p. 291, l. 4211 ff.

31. Rydén observes that while this version has four eunuchs, the church historians offer a version featuring a single youth with a towel. Nikephoros, *The Life of Saint Andrew the Fool,* vol. 2, p. 356, n. 7.

32. On representations of angelic hierarchies, see Jean Danielou, *The Angels and Their Mission,* trans. David Heiman (Westminster, Md., 1956), p. 86. Among Byzantine authors, see Glykas, *Michaelis Glycae Annales,* pp. 144–153; and Theodore Studites, *Oration VI. On the Holy Angels,* pp. 730–746.

33. The most obvious example is the image of the Virgin flanked by a pair of angels. Grabar, *Christian Iconography,* p. 79. Angels are also depicted as "night watchmen" who guard souls from evil forces during sleep. Danielou, *The Angels and Their Mission,* p. 106.

34. In Byzantium it was believed that asexuality produced the best servants, since eunuchs could not have sons who might threaten the emperor's hegemony. At the same time, their asexual status made them uniquely qualified to become surrogates of imperial power. This asexuality, as well as its benefits for a master, needs exploration.

35. On "virgins who do not walk to the king" and angels who guard tombs in expectation of the Second Coming, see Danielou, *The Angels and their Mission,* pp. 101, 106.

36. Shaun Marmon, "Eunuchs of the Prophet: Space, Time and Gender in Islamic Society" (Ph.D. diss., Princeton University, 1990).

37. "Basil the *patrikios* and prefect of the holy bedchamber wrapped the emperor Constantine's body for burial as was customary," Skyl., p. 179, l. 73. See also Sokrates Scholasticus, *Hermiae Sozomeni Historia ecclesiastica,* p. 690; Bekker, *Theophanes Continuatus,* p. 406.

38. An excellent early example is in Sokrates Scholasticus, *Hermiae Sozomeni Historia ecclesiastica,* p. 690. See also Moran, "Byzantine Castrati."

39. Gleason, "The Semiotics of Gender," pp. 389–417.

40. Vita of Niphon of Constantiana, p. 44, l. 24. The life is set in the early fourth century. The manuscript, at least its long version, is twelfth century or later. Kazhdan dated the life itself to the tenth century or later.

41. Vita of Niphon of Constantiana, p. 44, l. 24.

42. Vita of Niphon of Constantiana, p. 53, l. 33.

43. Vita of Niphon of Constantiana, p. 62, l. 18.

44. Kenneth Snipes, "An Unedited Treatise of Michael Psellos on the Iconography of Angels and on the Religious Festivals Celebrated on Each Day of the Week," *Gonimos: Neoplatonic and Byzantine Studies Presented to Leendert G. Westerink at 75*, ed. John Duffy and John Peradotto (Buffalo, N.Y., 1988), pp. 189–205.

45. Mango, "St. Michael and Attis," p. 39.

46. Marmon, *Eunuchs and Sacred Boundaries*, pp. 84–92.

47. Betz, *Greek Magical Papyri*, p. 5.

48. Thomas Wiedemann, *Adults and Children in the Roman Empire* (New Haven, 1989), pp. 178, 180–181, on the magical powers of children in the Roman Empire and the idea that eunuchs and monks were forever cast in the role of prepubescent boys.

49. Lucian of Samosata, "The Eunuch," in *Lucian*, vol. 5, pp. 329–345; quotation from p. 336, ch. 6.

50. St. Basil, *The Letters*, no. 115, l. 24.

51. Claudius Claudianus, *Claudian*, trans. Maurice Platnauer, 2 vols. (1922; reprint, Cambridge, Mass., 1956), vol. 1, p. 148, l. 125.

52. Eunapios of Sardis, *FHG*, vol. 4, frag. 66, 68, 69.

53. Ammianus Marcellinus, *Ammianus Marcellinus*, vol. 2, p. 358, ch. 17; vol. 2, p. 582, ch. 3.

54. Skylitzes Continuatus, *He synecheia tes Chronographias tou Ioannou Skylitse*, p. 155, l. 18. This text is thought to be a reworking of Attaleiates, *Historia*.

55. Nikephoros, *The Life of Saint Andrew the Fool*, vol. 2, p. 145, l. 1973. Rydén comments that "the eunuchs are, of course, the two angels, one good and one evil, that since early Christian times had been believed to accompany every human being" (vol. 2, p. 327, n. 6).

56. Gautier, "Le *De daemonibus* du pseudo-Psellos," p. 165, l. 480.

57. Preger, *Scriptores*, ch. 11, pp. 88–90. This is the source of the following two paragraphs of paraphrase.

58. Skyl., p. 395, l. 84.

59. Skyl., p. 395, l. 1. Drafted as emperor, Romanos had the choice of setting aside his wife to marry the empress Zoe or being blinded. After his murder, Zoe remarried with clerical approval.

60. A. Kazhdan, "Byzantine Hagiography and Sex in the Fifth to Twelfth Centuries," *DOP* 44 (1990): 142.

61. Symeon Metaphrastes, Vita of St. Sampson, p. 238.

62. For example, Michael the eunuch, who attended Alexios Komnenos at his death. Anna Komnene, *Alexiade*, vol. 3, p. 236.

63. The action in this life, a fourteenth-century rewrite of an earlier life, is set in the ninth century during the reign of Leo VI. Vita of Euphrosyna, p. 870, ch. 24, ll. 16–20.

64. Theodore Studites, *Oration VI. On the Holy Angels,* col. 738.

65. Preger, *Scriptores,* p. 87, ch. 10, l. 14.

66. On angels as created beings, see Photios I, *Homiliae,* col. 254.

67. Halkin found these ideas long ago in a set of unedited texts. See François Halkin, *Inédits Byzantins D'Ochrida, Candie et Moscou* (Brussels, 1963), p. 139: "The angels are the servants of the creator on earth," and "After the ascension they guarded the disciples, breaking the bonds of Peter, guarding Paul safe upon land and sea, acting as a mediator (μεσιτεύοντὲ) to the faith of Cornelius and bringing justice to Herod."

CHAPTER 8

1. Currently we must rely on J. J. Reiske, ed. and trans., *Constantini Porphyrogeniti imperatoris De ceremoniis aulae byzantinae,* 2 vols. (Bonn, 1829–30); hereafter cited as *De cer.* The text and commentary is also in *PG* 112. A newer edition of chapters 1–83 with commentary and French translation is in A. Vogt, ed., *Constantine VII Porphyrogénète, Le livre des cérémonies,* 4 vols. (Paris, 1935–1939); hereafter cited as *De cer.,* ed. Vogt. Dagron and his associates are working on a new edition, and Ann Moffatt has prepared an English translation that is in press.

2. The preferred text of the *Kletorologion* is in Oikonomidès, *Listes de préséance byzantines des IXe et Xe siècles* (Paris, 1972).

3. Marmon, *Eunuchs and Sacred Boundaries,* pp. 55–61, 79–92.

4. Marmon, *Eunuchs and Sacred Boundaries,* pp. 45–53.

5. Marmon, *Eunuchs and Sacred Boundaries,* pp. 79–92.

6. Foucault, *The History of Sexuality,* vol. 2, p. 157.

7. This problem is outlined in Dagron, *Empereur et prêtre,* p. 18.

8. Dagron, *Empereur et prêtre,* pp. 112–113, divides the city into three realms: imperial institution, society, and the patriarchate. He stresses the separation between the emperor and the society.

9. The relationship of eunuchs to the empress and the women's quarters in the palace is seen only dimly in the sources. We can get a general impression from the insights suggested by Herrin, *Women in Purple,* pp. 17–19, 58, 66, 77–82, 92–94, 107–112, 241; James, *Empresses and Power,* pp. 6, 51, 89; and Garland, *Byzantine Empresses,* pp. 5, 77, 137, 139, and 261 n83. Their inferences are based largely on scattered references in the *De cer.,* Theophanes the Confessor, and Leo Grammaticus.

10. *De cer.,* bk. 1, ch. 50, p. 257, l. 15. She is described as the empress's "lady of honor." *ODB,* s.v. "Zoste Patrikia."

11. Oikonomidès, *Listes de préséance,* pp. 134, 329. The one exception I have found is the eunuch Gregory, who is mentioned as the *eparch* of Constantinople in 652, when Pope Martin was brought to the city and imprisoned. *PBE,* Gregorios 149.

12. This can also be seen in the *PBE,* which goes to great lengths to preserve the distinction between "title" and "office."

13. Oikonomidès, *Listes de préséance,* presents five *taktika,* including that of Philotheos. The section of Philotheos that deals with eunuchs at court is on p. 125, commentary on p. 300. For a discussion of the offices and titles of eunuchs, see also Guilland, *Recherches,* which includes a series of articles written about eunuchs (vol. 1, pp. 165–381).

14. This designation was very old, and functionally the *praepositos* seems to have been replaced by the *parakoimomenos* (παρακοιμώμενος), "one who sleeps beside the bed," in the

eighth century, when we have examples of the terms being used interchangeably. The term *praepositos* is used later for a ceremonial office as an honorific title. Guilland, *Recherches,* vol. 2, p. 203. There is some discussion about whether there were one or two *praepositoi;* the *De ceremoniis* suggests the possibility of two *praepositoi* serving simultaneously. *De cer.* ed. Vogt, p. 107, l. 23.

15. The *epi tes katastaseos,* chief of presentations or master of ceremonies, appears twice in Oikonomedès's edition of the *taktikon* of Uspenskii (Oikonomedès, *Listes de préséance,* p. 57, l. 25 and p. 59, l. 17) and again in the *Kletorologion* of Philotheos (p. 109, l. 7) with a staff of subordinate titles (p. 125, ll. 8–12). Oikonomedès suggests that the lesser titles may be largely honorific. In Philotheos, the title *epi tes katastaseos* does not appear in the section on offices reserved to eunuchs, and it may well have been a honorific held by a bearded man.

16. Oikonomidès, *Listes de préséance,* p. 306; Guilland, *Recherches,* vol. 2, p. 198.

17. Guilland, *Recherches,* vol. 2, p. 266.

18. Guilland, *Recherches,* vol. 2, p. 203.

19. This space was not sacred in a strictly religious sense but was specially charged and protected from the intrusion of outsiders who represented transgression or pollution.

20. For example, the emperor had a special *cubiculum* at the Church of the Virgin at Blachernai, and also in the Daphne Palace near the Church of St. Stephen. For locations of other *cubicula,* both inside and outside the palace complex, see *De cer.,* bk. 1, ch. 1, pt. 26, p. 32, l. 21; bk. 1, ch. 9, pt. 4, p. 62, l. 11; bk. 1, ch. 9, pt. 5, p. 63, l. 20; bk. 1, ch. 10, pt. 8, p. 84, l. 20; bk. 1, ch. 17, pt. 2, p. 100, l. 21; bk. 1, ch. 17, pt. 4, p. 104, l. 17; bk. 1, ch. 18, pt. 1, p. 109, l. 23; bk. 1, ch. 23, pt. 1, p. 129, l. 9; bk. 1, ch. 23, pt. 4, p. 132, l. 13; bk. 1, ch. 23, pt. 5, p. 134, l. 14; bk. 1, ch. 23, pt. 6, p. 136, l. 13; bk. 1, ch. 25, pt. 140, l. 18; bk. 1, ch. 26, pt. 2, p. 145, ll. 2, 22; bk. 1, ch. 30, pt. 6, p. 169, l. 2; bk. 1, ch. 37, pt. 1, p. 187, l. 9; bk. 1, ch. 37, pt. 2, p. 189, ll. 21–22; and bk. 1, ch. 37, pt. 2, p. 191, l. 7.

21. There were both eunuch and bearded *protospatharioi.*

22. Dressers, or *vestiarioi,* could be eunuchs or bearded men.

23. *De cer.,* bk. 1, ch. 9, p. 63, l. 10, specifies that the emperor was escorted by members of the *cubiculum.*

24. *De cer.,* bk. 1, ch. 10, p. 78, l. 13.

25. The role of the *spatharokandidatoi* is unclear. The *spatharioi* were both eunuchs and bearded men, organized into different units; the *patrikioi* included eunuchs and bearded men.

26. *De cer.,* bk. 1, ch. 11, p. 87, l. 6.

27. *De cer.,* bk. 1, ch. 14, p. 92, l. 1.

28. *De cer.,* bk. 1, ch. 17, p. 100, l. 16.

29. *De cer.,* bk. 1, ch. 21, p. 122, l. 24.

30. *De cer.,* bk. 1, ch. 67, p. 30, l. 17.

31. *De cer.,* bk. 2, ch. 12, p. 552, l. 17.

32. Other references support the proposition that eunuchs provided a barrier between the emperor and the ordinary world. When the emperor left in a procession to adore the wood of the True Cross, he was accompanied only by his *cubiculum. De cer.,* bk. 1, ch. 22, p. 125, l. 22. At ceremonial receptions in the palace, the *koubikoularioi* entered and stood to the left and the right of the throne, "as is customary." *De cer.,* bk. 1, ch. 24, p. 138, l. 8. When the emperor went to Hagia Sophia he was accompanied by his *koubikoularioi. De cer.,* bk. 1, ch. 28, p. 157, l. 8. On the occasion of the Feast of the Annunciation to the Holy Virgin, the em-

peror arrived at a ceremonial dinner in his honor and "at this time the *koubikoularioi* did not encircle the emperor." The implication is that they usually did. *De cer.*, bk. 1, ch. 30, p. 170, l. 3. At Palm Sunday services in the *khrysotriklinos* of the Great Palace, the emperor sat "surrounded, as is customary, by his *koubikoularioi.*" *De cer.*, bk. 1, ch. 32, p. 172, l. 1.

33. This is a paraphrase of Arethas's third oration. In Jenkins, Mango, and Laourdas, *Nine Orations of Arethas from Cod. Marc. Gr. 524*, p. 6. The oration is dated to May 4, 902.

34. *De cer.*, bk. 1, ch. 27, p. 149, ll. 16–21; *De cer.*, ed. Vogt, p. 138.

35. This was the third-ranking title available to bearded men in the ninth century.

36. This is illustrated by the ceremonies for promotion to *magistros.* The candidate was escorted to the throne and prostrated himself on the step. He then adored and kissed the feet of the emperor who, because it was a feast day, was standing. Having kissed the emperor's feet, the *magistros* stood while a *praepositos* handed the ceremonial tunic and belt to the emperor. The emperor then gave them directly to the new *magistros,* who kissed the emperor's hands while taking the tunic and belt. The *praepositos* then took the regalia and led the *magistros* into the winter *consistorium,* where he dressed him. The *praepositos* then led the *magistros* to the *ciborium,* where the emperor was standing. The *magistros* prostrated himself again, kissed the emperor's feet, got up, and gave thanks. *De cer.*, bk. 1, ch. 46, p. 232, l. 18.

37. These are eunuchs who carried ceremonial weapons and were assigned to the *cubiculum.*

38. *Magistros* is a high rank awarded to a few bearded men in the ninth century.

39. On the Feast of the Ascension, the emperor also gave his high dignitaries gold and silver crosses with his own hand. *De cer.*, bk. 1, ch. 19, p. 115, l. 11.

40. On the Feast of the Pentecost, after an elaborate reception, the emperor prepared to take communion. "The emperor takes a purse from the *praepositos* and gives it to the patriarch." *De cer.*, bk. 1, ch. 9, p. 68, l. 20. The same thing took place on the second day of Holy Week. *De cer.*, bk. 1, ch. 10, p. 76, l. 23. We find it again in *De cer.*, bk. 1, ch. 27, p. 151, l. 8 and ch. 35, p. 182, l. 8.

41. *De cer.*, bk. 1, ch. 32, p. 172, l. 2.

42. The *orphanotrophos* supervised the imperial orphanages. *De cer.*, bk. 1, ch. 32, p. 172, l. 2.

43. On the day of the festival and procession of Christ, the *domestikos* (supervisor, administrator) of the schools places a book in the emperor's own hand. The emperor passes the book to the *praepositos,* who passes it to a *koubikoularios. De cer.*, bk. 1, ch. 23, p. 131, l. 23. On this occasion the treasurer indicates who is to receive purses of gold from the emperor. These are given to the *praepositos,* who hands them to the emperor for distribution. *De cer.*, bk. 1, ch. 23, p. 135, l. 7.

44. One of many examples of this is in *De cer.*, bk. 1, ch. 1, p. 7, l. 21.

45. See, for example, *De cer.*, bk. 1, ch. 14, p. 94, l. 13.

46. The golden *triklinos* or *khrysotriklinos* was a hall in the Great Palace, probably built at the end of the sixth century. A domed octagon lit by sixteen windows, the *khrysotriklinos* was the site of ceremonial receptions, especially at Easter. The throne, decorated with a mosaic of the enthroned Christ, was in the apse of *the khrysotriklinos.* See *ODB,* s.v. "*Chrysotriklinos* of Justinian."

47. *De cer.*, bk. 2, ch. 13, p. 558, l. 3.

48. *De cer.*, bk. 1, ch. 10, p. 81, l. 18.

49. *De cer.*, bk. 1, ch. 35, p. 135, l. 20.

50. Nikephoros, *The Life of Saint Andrew the Fool,* vol. 2, pp. 53–59.

51. These rituals are described in *De cer.,* bk. 1, ch. 37, pt. 1, p. 187.

52. *De cer.,* bk. 1, ch. 38, pt. 2, p. 193, l. 2; Elisabeth Piltz, "Middle Period Court Costume," in Henry Maguire, ed., *Byzantine Court Culture from 829 to 1204* (Washington, D. C., 1997), pp. 39–40.

53. This is a problematic sentence, given that normally no one but the emperor wore purple.

54. *De cer.,* bk. 1, ch. 18, p. 109, ll. 2–4.

55. *De cer.,* bk. 1, ch 97.

56. *ODB,* s.v. "*De ceremoniis,*" gives this date for chapter 97 of the *De ceremoniis,* where this description is found.

57. The head of a group of middle-level imperial officials and the count of the stable.

58. *De cer.,* bk. 2, ch. 15, p. 584, ll. 1–10.

59. Liudprand, bishop of Cremona, *Die Werke,* p. 154, l. 20.

60. The *komes* was a high honorary title in the ninth century.

61. *De cer.,* bk. 1, ch. 23, p. 131, l. 9.

62. *De cer.,* bk. 1, ch. 24, p. 138, l. 17.

63. *De cer.,* bk. 1, ch. 26, p. 147, l. 13.

64. *De cer.,* bk. 1, ch. 43, p. 224, l. 4; bk. 1, ch. 44, p. 227, l. 5.

65. *De cer.,* bk. 1, ch. 50, p. 257, l. 15.

66. *De cer.,* bk. 1, ch. 51, p. 262, l. 16.

67. In the sixth century a visiting monk was escorted into the emperor Justinian's presence by a eunuch. The monk is reported to have seen a demon sitting on the throne. Prokopios, *Anecdota,* 12, l. 26. The very pure *hegumen,* Niketas, sent before him eunuchs carrying torches. Leontius, bishop of Neapolis, *Vie de Syméon le Fou,* p. 119, l. 25. Shortly after 927 the eunuch *protovestiarios* Theophanes escorted Maria, granddaughter of Niketas Magistros and Romanos, when she was married by proxy to Tsar Peter. Bekker, *Theophanes Continuatus,* p. 413. It is hard to discern the actual hierarchies in these tales other than that the people are important and that the escorts are all eunuchs.

68. Noret, *Vitae,* ch. 28, p. 156, l. 13.

69. Greenfield, *The Life of Lazaros of Mt. Galesion,* pp. 247–248.

70. *De cer.,* bk. 2, ch. 25, p. 624.

71. The chronicles imply that there is only one *praepositus sacri cubiculi* at court, but the *De ceremoniis* often mentions two. This may reflect periods when empresses or co-emperors had separate households. See note 14 above.

72. This is a small room believed to have opened off the *khystotriklinos.* It is not clear which St. Theodore is connected with this *oratorium,* since none of the saints listed in Halkin can be connected with the site. See Dagron, *Empereur et prêtre,* p. 224.

73. Du Cange, *Glossarium,* says that this is a Phrygian garment. A *praepositus sacri cubiculi* wearing his golden robe is mentioned in the Vita of St. Sampson. That vita is dated to the tenth century because it is one of Symeon Metaphrastes's rewrites. Symeon Metaphrastes, Vita of St. Sampson, p. 283.

74. This insight comes from Herrin, *Women in Purple,* pp. 17–19.

75. Oikonomidès, *Lists de préséance,* p. 179.

76. *De cer.,* bk. 1, ch. 52, p. 263, l. 10.

77. The one exception seems to be the eunuch Gregorios in 652. *PBE,* Gregorios 149.

CHAPTER 9

1. Herrin, *Women in Purple,* pp. 17, 58, 163; Garland, *Byzantine Empresses,* pp. 5, 261 n83.

2. S. Miers and I. Kopytoff, eds., *Slavery in Africa: Historical and Anthropological Perspectives* (Madison, Wisc., 1977), pp. 22–49, 205–257; Edward Reynolds, *Stand the Storm: A History of the Atlantic Slave Trade* (London, 1989), pp. 9–12.

3. Morris, *Monks and Laymen,* p. 59.

4. Prokopios, *Wars,* bk. 3, ch. 11, l. 18.

5. Prokopios, *Wars,* bk. 4, ch. 22, l. 1.

6. This historical eunuch named Euphratas should not be confused with the fictional Euphratas associated with Constantine the Great in chapter 4.

7. Prokopios, *Wars,* bk. 8, ch. 4, l. 1; *Anecdota,* ch. 29, l. 12.

8. There was a long legal tradition that denied eunuchs the right of adoption. The Justinian Code (*CIC*) says that those who cannot procreate, like eunuchs, cannot adopt (*CIC,* Institutes vol. 1, XI). The code did, however, allow eunuchs to make wills (*CIC,* vol. 2, XXII, no. 5). The *Ecloga,* a law code issued in 741 by Leo III and Constantine V, divides eunuchs into three classes: *spadones,* who were born without sexual capabilities or desires, *thlibiai,* whose testicles had been crushed, and *kastratoi,* whose testicles had been removed. The code does not allow *thlibiai* or *kastratoi* to adopt, since they have no possibility of ever procreating children. *Spadones,* however, were permitted to adopt on the ground that, since they suffered from a disease, they might be cured. (Zachariä, *Ecloga privata aucta,* bk. 4, p. 399.) Somewhat later, as we enter the period when eunuchs were increasingly integrated into conceptions of social normality, the emperor Leo VI (r. 886–912) passed legislation designed to allow eunuchs to adopt (*Law Code of Leo the Wise,* ch. 26, p. 484). He argues that men who have lost their genitalia should not be further punished by legislation that denies them the right to adopt children.

9. Theophanes the Confessor, *Theophanis chronographia,* p. 473, l. 19; p. 474, l. 22; p. 475, l. 20. Page reference numbers also on pp. 649–653 of the Mango and Scott edition. Their careers are summarized in *PBE,* Staurakios 1; and *PBE,* Aetios 1.

10. Herrin, *Women in Purple,* pp. 92–94, 107–112; Garland, *Byzantine Empresses,* p. 72; James, *Empresses and Power,* p. 89.

11. Much primary material on Samonas is in Rydén, "The Portrait of the Arab Samonas." Rydén notes that Samonas is treated positively in Karliln-Hayter, Vita of Euthymios, patriarch, and negatively in the chronicles. This may reflect the negative attitude of the chroniclers toward the Macedonian dynasty. While this may be true, the treatment of the eunuch Samonas exemplifies the way in which a eunuch identified with, and the perfect servant of, an emperor could become the target of criticism that was really directed at the emperor. It also illustrates the extremes that characterize writings about eunuchs.

12. Leo Grammaticus, p. 282, l. 22.

13. *ODB,* s.v. "Constantine of Rhodes."

14. Vilinskii, *Zhitie sv. Vasiliia Novago v russkoi literature,* pt. 2, p. 57.

15. See note 11 above.

16. Leo of Synada, *The Correspondence of Leo, Metropolitan of Synada and Syncellus.*

17. *Narratio* of St. Metrios.

18. Bekker, *Theophanes Continuatus,* pp. 713–714.

19. Nicholas I Mystikos, *Letters: Nicholas I, Patriarch of Constantinople,* letter 47.

20. Skyl., pp. 370–374.

21. Psellos, *Chron.,* bk. 3, ch. 19.

22. Skyl., p. 390, l.77.

23. Skyl., p. 395, l. 4.

24. Skyl., p. 400, l. 26.

25. Skyl., p. 406, l. 6.

26. Psellos, *Chron.,* bk. 5, ch. 11.

27. Skylitzes believed that John and George fell when Michael V took over the throne. (Skyl., p. 416, l. 76) Psellos, however, gives us an account in which John survived the early months of Michael's reign. Psellos does not say what happened to George (Psellos, *Chron.,* bk. 5, ch. 11.)

28. Skyl., p. 400, l. 29.

29. Skyl., p. 394, l. 62.

30. Skyl., p. 392, l. 22. This illustrates the importance of eunuchs in the political dynamics around effective imperial women. Garland, *Byzantine Empresses,* p. 139; Herrin, *Women in Purple,* p. 256.

31. Psellos, *Chron.,* bk. 5, ch. 43.

32. Skyl., p. 393, l. 48.

CONCLUSION

1. Romanos's illegitimate son Basil was castrated but became prominent. Leo Diac., p. 46, l. 19.

2. *Defense of Eunuchs,* p. 319, l. 15 through 323, l. 6; p. 325, l. 15.

3. *Defense of Eunuchs,* p. 291, l. 19.

4. *Defense of Eunuchs,* p. 291, l. 23.

5. *Defense of Eunuchs,* p. 291, ll. 13–14.

6. *Defense of Eunuchs,* p. 299, ll. 3–23.

7. *Defense of Eunuchs,* p. 301, l. 18.

8. *Defense of Eunuchs,* p. 303, l. 16.

9. *Defense of Eunuchs,* p. 303, l. 22.

10. *Defense of Eunuchs,* p. 305, l. 17.

11. *Defense of Eunuchs,* p. 307, l. 15.

12. *Defense of Eunuchs,* p. 309, l. 5.

13. *Defense of Eunuchs,* p. 309, l. 11

14. *Defense of Eunuchs,* p. 311, ll. 24–27.

15. *Defense of Eunuchs,* p. 313, ll. 4–14.

16. *Defense of Eunuchs,* p. 315, ll. 12–23.

17. *Defense of Eunuchs,* p. 323, l. 7.

18. *Defense of Eunuchs,* p. 325, l. 20.

19. *Defense of Eunuchs,* p. 329, l. 9 through p. 331, l. 6.

20. Gautier, *Theophylacte d'Achrida,* vol. 1, p. 367, poem 13.

21. Gautier, preface, *Theophylacte d'Achrida,* vol. 1, p. 289.

22. Ninth- and tenth-century examples include the eunuch Theoktistos, who ran the government with the empress Theodora during the minority of Michael III (Bekker, *Theophanes Continuatus,* p. 148, l. 11); the eunuch Constantine, who was on the council of the empress Zoe during the minority of Constantine VII (Skyl., p. 201, l. 34); and Basil Lekapenos who, though officially ruling jointly with the youthful Basil II, was in charge during the early part of Basil's reign (Skyl., p. 314, l. 56).

23. Vita of Euphrosyna, pp. 861–877.

24. Rosenqvist, *The Life of St. Irene Abbess of Chrysobalanton,* ch. 12. The editor points to the mediation by the eunuch Cyril. We are told that the eunuch's name was Cyril but the saint's sister is nameless.

25. Symeon Metaphrastes, Vita of St. John the Almsgiver, p. 936.

26. Angeliki E. Laiou, *Gender, Society and Economic Life in Byzantium* (Brookfield, Vt., 1992), p. 249.

27. Spyros Stavrakas, "The Byzantine Provincial Elites: A Study in Social Relationships during the Ninth and Tenth Centuries" (Ph.D. diss., University of Chicago, 1978), pp. 110–122, argues for the role of eunuchs as intermediaries between court and provincial aristocracy in the ninth and tenth centuries.

28. Psellos, *Chron.,* bk. 1, ch. 3.

29. See especially Skyl., p. 389, l. 54; p. 400, l. 48.

30. *Defense of Eunuchs,* p. 317, l. 22.

31. J. Noret, ed., *Vitae duae antiquae sancti Athanasii Athonitae,* vita A, ch. 10; vita B, ch. 4.

32. See F. Dvornik, *Byzantine Missions among the Slavs* (New Brunswick, N.J., 1970), pp. 39–63; also F. Halkin, "Trois dates précisées," pp. 11–14.

33. Kosmas became a monk after the emperor Alexander's death. A translation of parts of the vision is in Mango, *Byzantium, The Empire of New Rome,* pp. 151–155. See also Henry Maguire, "The Heavenly Court," in Henry Maguire, ed., *Byzantine Court Culture from 829 to 1204* (Washington, D.C., 1997), pp. 247–258; Herrin, *Women in Purple,* p. 19.

34. Vision of St. Kosmas, p. 112, l. 52. For a discussion of this text, see Mango, "The Invisible World of Good and Evil," in his *Byzantium, The Empire of New Rome,* p. 153.

35. Noret, *Vitae duae antiquae sancti Athanasii Athonitae,* vita B, p. 156, ch. 28, l. 13.

36. Grabar, *Christian Iconography,* p. 79; and Jean Danielou, *The Angels and Their Mission,* p. 101.

37. Greenfield, *The Life of Lazaros of Mt. Galesion,* p. 247.

38. Vita of Niphon Constantiana, p. 62, l. 18.

39. The best-known cases of confusion between eunuchs, angels, and young boys, discussed earlier, are in Preger, *Scriptores,* p. 86. A study of this text is in Dagron, *Constantinople imaginaire,* pp. 200–202, 230, 285, 292. The Skylitzes example is in Skyl., p. 395, l. 83. The nuance in Skylitzes is that the eunuch is found in a heavenly vision that relates to sexual sin and, while context implies an angelic messenger, the topic is too earthy for angelic intervention.

40. Drexl, "Das Traumbuch des Patriarchen Nikephoros," p. 105, l. 97. The *oneirokritika* (dream books), handbooks used in the interpretation of dreams, contain scant but interesting information about eunuchs. Traditionally these dream books, though anonymous, are attributed to famous individuals. The earliest we have is the *oneirokritikon* of the prophet Daniel. It tells us that "dreaming you are clad in white raiment indicates great joy for you." Naphtali Lewis, *The Interpretation of Dreams and Portents* (Toronto, 1976), p. 92. Our other dream books are later, probably dating from the ninth to the thirteenth century. The *oneirokritikon* of Achmet tells us that "if someone dreams that he had anal intercourse with a eunuch he knows, he will entrust both his wealth and secrets to that eunuch; but if the eunuch was a stranger, he will do good to his enemy," and "if someone dreams that he had sex with a eunuch or a young male acquaintance he will entrust his secret to that man and do him good; but if he dreams that he forcibly submitted to sex with that man, the secret will be held up to shame." Drexl, *Achmetis Oneirocriticon*, pp. 121, 134. Finally, the *oneirokritikon* of the patriarch Germanos tells us that "to see a eunuch is good luck." Drexl, "Das Traumbuch des Patriarchen Nikephoros," p. 436.

41. Romano, *Timarione / Pseudo-Luciano*, p. 79, l. 815.

42. The emperor Theophilos (r. 829–842) was the last of the iconoclastic emperors.

43. St. Hippolytus, "Commentarii in Danielum," *PG* 10, col. 33, ch. 3–5.

44. *Passio* of Eleutherios the Martyr, p. 323, ch. 3. Eleutherios was martyred under Maximian.

45. *Passio* of Eleutherios the Martyr, ch. 3.

46. *Passio* of Eleutherios the Martyr, ch. 4.

47. *Passio* of Eleutherios the Martyr, ch. 5.

48. *Passio* of Eleutherios the Martyr, ch. 6.

49. Prokopios, *Wars*, bk. 6, ch. 18, l. 4.

50. Prokopios, *Wars*, bk. 8, ch. 26, l. 14.

51. Herrin, *Women in Purple*, pp. 19, 241.

BIBLIOGRAPHY

Primary Sources

Adamantius Judaeus. *Physiognomonica.* In *Scriptores physiognomonici graeci et latini,* ed. R. Foerster, 297–426. 2 vols. 1893. Reprint, Leipzig, 1994.

Aetios of Amida. *Aetii Amideni Libri medicinales,* 1–8. Ed. A. Olivieri. 2 vols. Corpus medicorum Graecorum, 8. Leipzig and Berlin, 1935–1950.

Agathias. *Agathiae Myrinaei Historiarum libri quinque.* Ed. R. Keydell. Berlin, 1967.

Alexander of Aphrodisias. *Problematum physicorum et medicorum eclogae. Libri 1–2.* In *Physici et medici graeci minores,* ed. J. L. Ideler, vol. 1: 3–80. 1841–1842. Reprint, Amsterdam, 1963.

Alexander of Tralles. *Oeuvres médicales d'Alexandre de Tralles.* Ed. F. Brunet. 4 vols. Paris, 1933–1937.

———. *Therapeutica.* In *Alexander von Tralles,* ed. T. Puschmann, vol. 1. 1878–1879. Reprint, Amsterdam, 1963.

Apophthegmata Patrum. PG 65, cols. 71–440.

Aretaeus of Cappadocia. *De causis et signis acutorum morborum.* Ed. C. Hude. Corpus medicorum Graecorum, 2. 1923. Reprint, Berlin, 1958.

———. *The Extant Works of Aretaeus the Cappadocian.* Ed. and trans. Francis Addams. 1856. Republished, Boston, 1972.

Arethas of Caesarea. *Arethae archiepiscopi Caesariensis Scripta minora.* Ed. L. G. Westerink. 2 vols. Leipzig, 1968–1972.

Aristotle. *Aristotle: Minor Works.* Trans. W. H. Hett. Cambridge, Mass., 1980.

———. *Generation of Animals.* Ed. and trans. A. L. Peck. 1953. Reprint, Cambridge, Mass., 1963.

Athanasios. Expositiones in Psalmos. *PG* 27, COLS. 59–590.

Athanasios of Emesa. *Das Novellensyntagma des Athanasios von Emesa.* Ed. Dieter Simon and S. Troianos. Frankfurt, 1989.

Athanasius, Saint. *Athanasius Werke.* Ed. H. G. Opitz, W. Schneemelcher, and M. Tetz. 3 vols. Berlin, 1934–1938.

Attaleiates, Michael. *Michaelis Attaliotae historia.* Ed. I. Bekker and W. Brunet de Presle. Bonn, 1853.

Aurelianus, Caelius. *On Acute Diseases and On Chronic Diseases.* Ed. and trans. I. E. Drabkin. Chicago, 1950.

Bakker, W. F., A. F. Van Gemert, and W. J. Aerts, eds. *Studia Byzantina et Neohellenica Neerlandica.* Leiden, 1972.

Baldwin, B., ed. and trans. *Timarion.* Detroit, 1984.

Basil, Saint. *Saint Basil, The Letters.* Ed. and trans. R. Deferrari. 4 vols. 1926–1934. Reprint, Cambridge, Mass., 1928–1962.

Basil of Seleucia. *Fragmenta in Danielem. PG* 85, cols. 1363–1382.

Baynes, N. H. "The Vita S. Danielis Stylitae." *English Historical Review* 40 (1925): 397–402.

Bekker, I., ed. *Theophanes Continuatus; Ioannes Cameniata; Symeon Magister; Georgius Monachus.* Bonn, 1838. [Also known as *Scriptores post Theophanem.*]

Betz, Hans Dieter, ed. *The Greek Magical Papyri in Translation, including the Demotic Spells.* Chicago, 1992.

Bryennios, Nikephoros. *Nikephoros Bryennios, histoire.* Ed. and trans. Paul Gautier. Brussels, 1975.

Bury, J. B. *The Imperial Administrative System in the Ninth Century, with a Revised Text of the Kletorologian of Philotheos.* 1911. Reprint, New York, 1958.

Cameron, Averil, and Judith Herrin, eds. *Constantinople in the Early Eighth Century: The Parastaseis syntomoi chronikai: Introduction, Translation, and Commentary.* Leiden, 1984.

Canard, Marius. "Deux documents arabes sur Bardas Skléros." *Studi bizantini e neoellenici* 5 (1939): 55–69.

Carras, L., ed. *Life of St. Athanasias of Aegina.* Canberra, 1984.

Cassius Dio Cocceianus. *Dio's Roman History.* Trans. E. Cary. 9 vols. Cambridge, Mass., 1970–1987.

Chariton. *Callirrhoe / Chariton.* Ed. and trans. G. P. Goold. Cambridge, Mass., 1995.

Choniates, Niketas. *Nicetae Choniatae Historia.* Ed. J. L. van Dieten. Berlin and New York, 1975.

Chrysostom, Saint John. *Homilia in Eutropium eunuchum patricium.* In *S. Joannes Chrysostomus. PG* 52, cols. 392–414.

———. *Homilia XXXV on Chapter XIV of Genesis.* In *S. Joannes Chrysostomus. PG* 58.

———. "Interpretatio in Danielem prophetam." In *S. Joannes Chrysostomus. PG* 56, cols. 194–245.

———. *S. Joannes Chrysostomus. PG* 47–64.

Claudianus, Claudius. *Claudian.* Trans. Maurice Platnauer. 2 vols. 1922. Reprint, Cambridge, Mass., 1956.

Clement of Alexandria. *Christ the Educator.* Trans. Simon Wood. Washington, D.C., 1954.

———. *Clemens Alexandrinus. Stromata.* Books 1–4. Ed. Otto Stählin and Ludwig Früchtel. Berlin, 1985.

Clugnet, L., ed. "Vie et récits de l'abbé Daniel le Scétiote." *Revue de l'Orient chrétien* 5 (1900): 49–73, 254–271, 370–406, 535–564; 6 (1901): 51–87.

Codinus, George. *Pseudo-Kodinos: Traité des offices.* Ed. J. Verpeaux. Paris, 1966.

Constantine of Rhodes. In *Anecdota graeca,* ed. P. Matranga. 2 vols. 1850. Reprint, New York, 1971.

Constantine VII Porphyrogenitus. *De administrando imperio.* Ed. G. Moravcsik, trans. R. J. H. Jenkins. 1967. Reprint, Washington, D.C., 1985.

Constas, Nicholas, ed. and trans. "Life of St. Mary/Marinos." [*BHG* 1163, 1163b, 1163e]. In *Holy Women of Byzantium: Ten Saints' Lives in English Translation,* ed. Alice-Mary Talbot, pp. 1–12. Washington, D.C., 1996.

Courtonne, Y., ed. *Lettres* [of Saint Basil]. 3 vols. Paris, 1957–1966.

Cramer, J. A., ed. *Anecdota graeca e codd. manuscriptis Bibliothecae regiae parisiensis.* 4 vols. 1839–1841. Reprint, Hildesheim, 1967.

Crisafulli, Virgil S., and John W. Nesbitt, eds. and trans. *The Miracles of St. Artemios: A Collection of Miracle Stories by an Anonymous Author of Seventh-Century Byzantium.* Leiden and New York, 1997.

Cyril of Schythopolis. *Kyrillos von Skythopolis.* Ed. Eduard Schwartz. Leipzig, 1939.

Dagron, G., and Marie Dupré la Tour, eds. *Vie et miracles de sainte Thècle: Texte grec, traduction et commentaire.* Brussels, 1978.

Daniel. *Oneirokritikon.* In Naphtali Lewis. *The Interpretation of Dreams and Portents.* New York, 1976.

Darrouzès, J., ed. and trans. *Georges et Dèmètrios Tornikès.* Paris, 1970.

Dawes, Elizabeth, and N. H. Baynes, eds. and trans. *Three Byzantine Saints: Contemporary Biographies.* Crestview, N.Y., 1996.

De alimentia. In *Physici et medici Graeci minores,* ed. J. L. Ideler. 2 vols. 1841–1842. Reprint, Amsterdam, 1963.

"De antiquitatibus Cpolitanis." *Appendix ad opera Michaelis Pselli. PG* 122, col. 1290 ff.

de Stoop, E., ed. "Onirocriticon du prophète Daniel dédié au roi Nabuchodonosor." *Revue de philologie* 33 (1909): 93–111.

Defense of Eunuchs. In Theophylactus of Ochrida. *Theophylacte d'Achrida.* Ed. and trans. P. Gautier. Vol. 1. Thessalonica, 1980–1986.

Delehaye, H., ed. "La vie de S. Daniel le stylite." *AB* 32 (1913): 121–214.

———. "La vie de S. Daniel le stylite." In *Les saints stylites,* ed. H. Delehaye, pp. 1–94. Subsidia Hagiographica, 14. Brussels, 1923.

———. "V. Nicephori." In *Monumenta latrensia hagiographica, Miletus,* 3.1: 51–157. Berlin, 1913.

———. "Vita sancti Nicephori episcopi Milesii." [*BHG* 1338] *AB* 14 (1895): 133–161.

———. "*Vita* of St. Paul the Younger of Latros." [*BHG* 1474] *AB* 11 (1892): 19–75, 136–181, *et seorsim* 19–119.

Devreese, Robert, ed. "Le Texte Grec de l'hypomnesticum de Théodore Spoudée, le supplice, l'exil et la mort des victimes illustres du Monothéisme." *AB* 53 (1935).

Dindorf, L., ed. *Chronicon Paschale.* 2 vols. Bonn, 1832.

———. *Chronographia.* [of John Malalas] Bonn, 1831.

Diodorus Siculus. *Diodorus of Sicily.* Trans. C. H. Oldfather. 12 vols. Cambridge, Mass., 1933–1967.

Diogenes, Laertius. *Lives of Eminent Philosophers.* Trans. R. D. Hicks. 2 vols. Cambridge, Mass., 1964–1965.

Dionysios the Areopagite. In *L'Univers dionysien: Structure hiérarchique du monde selon le Pseudo-Denys,* ed. René Roques, pp. 135–67. 1954. Reprint, Paris, 1983.

Drexl, Franz. "Studien zum Text des Achmet." *BZ* 33 (1933): 13–31.

Drexl, Franz, ed. *Achmetis oneirocriticon.* Leipzig, 1925.

———. *Achmets Traumbuch. Einleitung und Probe eines kritischen Texts.* Freising, 1909.

———. "Das Traumbuch des Patriarchen Germanos." *Deltion* 6.

———. "Das Traumbuch des Patriarchen Nikephoros." In *Beiträge zur Geschichte des christlichen Altertums und der Byzantinischen Literatur,* ed. A. M. Koeniger, pp. 94–118. 1922. Reprint, Amsterdam, 1969.

Doukas. *Decline and Fall of Byzantium to the Ottoman Turks.* Ed. and trans. Harry J. Magoulias. Detroit, 1975.

———. *Istoria Turco-Bizantina.* Ed. V. Crecu. With Romanian translation. Bucharest, 1958.

Efthymiadis, Stephanos, ed. and trans. *The Life of the Patriarch Tarasios by Ignatios the Deacon.* [*BHG* 1698]. Aldershot, 1998.

Epiphanios, Saint. *Epiphanius.* Ed. Karl Holl. 3 vols. 1915–1933. Reprint, Berlin, 1980–1985.

Eusebios of Caesarea. *The Ecclesiastical History.* Trans. Kirsopp Lake. 2 vols. Cambridge, Mass., 1957–1959.

———. *Histoire ecclésiastique.* Ed. Gustave Bardy. 4 vols. Paris, 1952–1971.

Featherstone, Jeffrey, and Cyril Mango, eds. and trans. "Life of St. Matrona." [*BHG* 1221] In *Holy Women of Byzantium: Ten Saints' Lives in English Translation,* ed. Alice-Mary Talbot, pp. 13–64. Washington, D.C., 1996.

Festugière, A. J., ed. and trans. *Sainte Thècle, saints Côme et Damian, saints Cyr et Jean (extraits), saint Georges.* Paris, 1971.

Foerster, Richard, ed. *Scriptores physiognomonici graeci et latini.* Leipzig, 1893.

Fourmy, M. H., and M. Leroy, eds. "La vie de S. Philarète." [*BHG* 1511z] *Byzantion* 9 (1934): 113–167.

Fragmenta historicorum graecorum. Ed. C. Müller. 5 vols. Paris, 1841–1870.

Galen. *De alimentorum.* In *Galeni De sanitate tuenda,* ed. K. Koch, G. Helmreich, C. Kalbfleisch, and O. Hartlich. Leipzing-Berlin, 1923.

———. *Hapauta. Opera omnia.* Ed. C. G. Kuhn. 20 vols. in 22. 1821–1833. Reprint, Hildesheim, 1964–1965.

———. *In Hippocratis De officina medici commentariorum.* Trans. Malcolm Lyons. Berlin, 1963.

Gautier, Paul., ed. and trans. "Le *De daemonibus* du pseudo-Psellos." *Revue des études byzantines* 38 (1980): 105–194.

———. *Theophylacte d'Achrida.* Vol. 1. *Discours, traités, poésies.* Vol. 2. *Lettres.* Thessalonica, 1980–1986.

George the Monk [Georgius, Monachus, Hamartolos]. *Chronicon.* Ed. C. de Boor. 2 vols. 1904. Reprint, Stuttgart, 1978.

Georgios, ho Eleusios. *Vie de Théodore de Sykéon.* [*BHG* 1748]. Ed. A. J. Festugière. Brussels, 1970.

Germanos I, patriarch of Constantinople. *PG* 98, cols. 39–454.

Glykas, Michael. *Michaelis Glycae Annales.* Ed. I. Bekker. Bonn, 1836.

Goar, J. *Euchologion sive Rituale Graecorum.* 1730. Reprint, Graz, 1960.

Greenfield, Richard, trans. *The Life of Lazaros of Mt. Galesion: An Eleventh-Century Pillar Saint.* Washington, D.C., 2000.

Gregory of Nazianzos. *Discours.* Ed. M.-A. Calvet-Sabati, J. Mossay, C. Moreschini, and P. Gallay. 8 vols. Paris, 1978–1995.

———. "Gregorii theologi vulgo Nazianzeni, archipiscopi Constantinopolitani, Opera quai ex stant omnia." *PG* 35–38.

———. "Laudatio Athanasios." [*BHG* 186]. *PG* 35, cols. 1081–1128.

Grivec, F., and F. Tomsic, eds. *Constantinus et Methodius Thessalonicenses: Fontes.* Zagreb, 1960.

Halkin, François, ed. *Inédits byzantins d'Ochrida, Candie et Moscow.* Subsidia Hagiographica, 38. Brussels, 1963.

———. "L'Empereur Constantin converti par Euphrates." *AB* 78 (1960): 5–17.

———. "Les deux derniers chapitres de la Nouvelle Vie de Constantin." *AB* 77 (1959): 370–372.

———. *Novum Auctarium. Bibliotheca hagiographica Graeca.* Subsidia Hagiographica, 65. Brussels, 1984.

———. "V. SS. Constantini, Cyrilli et Methodii." *Byzantion* 24 (1954): 11–14.

———. "Une Nouvelle vie de Constantin dans un légendier de Patmos." *AB* 77 (1959): 63–107.

Halkin, François, ed. and trans. *Hagiologie byzantine: Textes inédits publiés en grec et traduits en français.* Subsidia Hagiographica, 71. Brussels, 1986.

Hartman, Louis F., and Alexander A. Di Lella, eds. *The Book of Daniel.* In *The Anchor Bible,* ed. W. F. Albright and D. N. Freedman, vol. 23. New York, 1978.

Heikel, I. A., et al., eds. *Eusebius Werke.* 9 vols. Leipzig and Berlin, 1902–1956.

Hippocrates. *Hippocrates.* Trans. W. H. S. Jones. 8 vols. Cambridge, Mass., 1967–1995.

Hippolytus, Antipope. *Refutatio omnium haeresium.* Ed. P. Wendland. Hildesheim and New York, 1977.

Hippolytus. "Commentarii in Danielem." *PG* 10, cols. 637–697.

———. *Philosophumena, or The Refutation of All Heresies.* Trans. F. Legge. 2 vols. New York, 1921.

Ideler, Julius L., ed. *Physici et medici Graeci minores.* 2 vols. 1841–1842. Reprint, Amsterdam, 1963.

Jeffreys, Elizabeth, ed. and trans. *Digenis Akritis: The Grottaferrata and Escorial Versions.* Cambridge, 1998.

Jenkins, Romilly J. H., Cyril A. Mango, and Vasileios Laourdas. "Nine Orations of Arethas from Cod. Marc. Gr. 524." In Romilly J. H. Jenkins, *Studies on Byzantine History of the Ninth and Tenth Centuries.* London, 1970.

Jerome, Saint. "Adversus Jovinianum." Ed. J. P. Migne. *PL* 23.

———. *Commentarius in Danielem.* In *Corpus Christianorum,* ser. lat., vol. 75A.

———. *Opera. Corpus Christianorum, ser. lat.* Vols. 72–79. Turnholt, 1958–62.

John Droungarios. *Catena.* In *Scriptorum veterum nova collectio,* ed. Angelo Mai, vol. 1.2: 1–56. Rome, 1825–1838.

John of Damascus. *Joannis damascini, monachi, et presbyteri Hieroslymitani. Opera omnia exstant. PG* 94–96.

Karlin-Hayter, Patricia. ed. *Vita Euthymii patriarchae CP.* [*BHG* 651–52]. Brussels, 1970. First published in *Byzantion* 25–27 (1955–1957): 8–152.

Kedrenos, Georgios. *Compendium historiarum.* Ed. I. Bekker. 2 vols. Bonn, 1838–1839.

Kinnamos, John. *Deeds of John and Manuel Comnenus.* Trans. Charles M. Brand. New York, 1976.

———. *Joannis Cinnami Epitome rerum ab Ioanne et Alexio Comnenis gestarum.* Ed. Augustus Meineke. Bonn, 1836.

Komnene, Anna. *Alexiade (règne de l'empereur Alexis I Comnène, 1081–1118).* Ed. B. Leib. 4 vols. Paris, 1937–1976.

Lampros, S., ed. "Bardas the Monk." *Neos Hellenomnemon* 21 (1927): 136–141.

———. *Excerptorum Constantini De natura animalium libri duo: Aristophanis Historiae animalium epitome, subiunctis Aeliani, Timothei aliorumque eclogis.* Berlin, 1885.

———. "Leo of Synnada." *Neos Hellenomnemon* 20 (1926): 324–342.

———, ed. "Theodore of Nicaea." *Neos Hellenomnemon* 16 (1922): 476–477.

Lamza, Lucian, ed. *Patriarch Germanos I. von Konstantinopel (715–730).* [*BHG* 697]. Würzburg, 1975.

Laurent, V., ed. "Jean VII le Grammairien (837–43)." *Catholicisme* 6 (1964): 513–515.

Law Code of Leo the Wise. PG 107.

Lemerle, Paul, A. Guillou, Denis Papachryssanthou, and N. Svoronos, eds. *Actes de Lavra.* 4 vols. Paris, 1970–1982.

Lemerle, Paul. *Les plus anciens recueils des miracles de Saint-Démétrius et la pénétration des Slaves dans les Balkans.* 2 vols. Paris, 1979–1981.

Leo the Deacon [Diaconus]. *Leonis diaconi Caloënsis Historiae libri decem.* Ed. C. B. Hase. Bonn, 1828.

Leo Grammaticus. *Leonis grammatici chronographia.* Ed. I. Bekker. Bonn, 1842.

Leo the Physician. *Conspectus medicinae.* In *Anecdota medica graeca,* ed. F. Z. Ermerins, 79–221. 1840. Reprint, Amsterdam, 1963.

———. *Epitome on the Nature of Man.* Ed. and trans. R. Renehan. In *Corpus medicorum Graecae* 10.4. Berlin, 1969.

Leo, metropolitan of Synada. *The Correspondence of Leo, Metropolitan of Synada and Syncellus.* Ed. and trans. Martha Pollard Vinson. Washington, D.C, 1985.

Leontius, bishop of Neapolis. *Vie de Syméon le Fou (et) Vie de Jean de Chypre.* [*BHG* 1677]. Ed. A. J. Festugière. Paris, 1974.

Liudprand, bishop of Cremona. *Die Werke Liudprands von Cremona.* Ed. J. Bekker. In *MGH SRG* 41. 1915. Reprint, Hannover, 1977.

Lucian of Samosata. *Lucian.* Ed. and trans. A. M. Harmon, K. Kilburn, and M. D. Macleod. 8 vols. Cambridge, Mass, 1968–1979.

Macler, F., ed. and trans. "L'Apocalypse arabe de Daniel, publiée, traduite et annotée." *Revue de l'histoire des religions* 49 (1904): 265–292.

Magie, David, trans. *The Scriptores historiae Augustae.* 3 vols. Cambridge, Mass., 1921–1932.

Malalas, John. *The Chronicle of John Malalas.* Trans. Elizabeth Jeffreys, Michael Jeffreys, Roger Scott, and Brian Coke. Melbourne, 1986.

Marcellinus, Ammianus. *Ammianus Marcellinus.* Ed. and trans. John C. Rolfe. 3 vols. 1935–39. Reprint, Cambridge, Mass., 1956–1958.

Mavrogordato, John, ed. *Digenes Akrites.* Oxford, 1963.

Meletios the Monk. *On the Constitution of Man.* In *Anecdota Graeca e codd. Manuscriptis Bibliothecarum Oxoniensium,* ed. J. A. Cramer, 3: 1–157. 1836. Reprint, Amsterdam, 1963.

Meletios the Monk. *Meletii Tractatus De Natura Hominis. PG* 64, cols. 1025–1310.

Moschos, John. *PG* 87, vol. 3, cols. 2851–3112.

Narratio of St. Metrios. [*BHG* 2272]. *AASS, Propylaeum, Synaxarium Ecclesiae Constantinopolitanae* (Nov. 1902): 721–724.

Nikephoros. *The Life of Saint Andrew the Fool.* Ed. and trans. Lennart Rydén. 2 vols. Uppsala, 1995.

———. Vita of St. Andrew Salos. *AASS* (May, vol. 6, 1688): 4*–102*.

Nicholas I Mystikos. *Letters: Nicholas I, Patriarch of Constantinople.* Trans. R. Jenkins and L. Westerink. Washington, D.C., 1981.

Niketas Magistros. *Lettres d'un exilé (928–946).* Ed. L. G. Westerink. Paris, 1973.

Niketas Paphlagonis. *Vita* of St. Ignatios, Archbishop of Constantinople. [*BHG* 817]. *PG* 105, cols. 487–574.

Niketas Pectoratos. *Opuscules et lettres [par] Nicétas Stethatos.* Ed. and trans. J. Darrouzès. Paris, 1961.

Noailles, P., and A. Dain, eds. and trans. *Les novelles de Léon VI, le Sage.* Paris, 1944.

Noret, J., ed. *Vitae duae antiquae sancti Athanasii Athonitae.* [*BHG* 187–188b]. Turnhout, 1982.

Oberhelman, S. M., trans. *The Oneirocriticon of Achmet: A Medieval Greek and Arabic Treatise on the Interpretation of Dreams.* Lubbock, Tex., 1991.

Oikonomidès, Nicholas, ed. *Kletorologion.* In *Les Listes de préséance byzantines des IXe et Xe siècles,* ed. Nicholas Oikonomidès. Paris, 1972.

———. *Les listes de préséance byzantines des IXe et Xe siècles.* Paris, 1972.

Opitz, H. G., ed. "Die Vita Constantine des Codex Angelicus 22." *Byzantion* 9 (1934): 545–590.

Oribasios. *Collectionum medicarum reliquae.* Ed. I. Raeder. 4 vols. 1928–1933. Reprint, Amsterdam, 1964.

Origen. *Commentary on Ezekiel. PG* 13, cols. 699–704.

Palladios. *Dialogue on the Life of St. John Chrysostom.* Ed. R. T. Meyer. New York, 1985.

Pantoleon, deacon at Constantinople. *Miracles* [of the archangel Michael]. [*BHG* 1285–1288b]. *PG* 140, cols. 573–92.

Papachryssanthou, D., ed. "Un Confesseur de second Iconoclasme, la vie du Patrice Niketas (+836)." *Travaux et mémoires* 3 (1968): 309–351.

———. *Actes du Prôtaton.* 2 vols. Paris, 1975.

———. *Actes de Xénophon.* Paris, 1986.

Papadopoulos-Kerameus, A., ed. "V. Patriarch Germanus." [*BHG* 697] In *Maurokhordateios Bibiothēkē. Anekdota Hellēnika,* 3–17. Constantinople, 1884.

———. "Vita Paulus et Ioannes." [*BHG* 1476] In *Analekta Hierosolymitikes stachyologias.* Vol. 5, pp. 368–383. Moscow, 1898.

———. "Bios kai thaumata tou hosiou patros Hēmōn Eustratiou." In *Analekta Hierosolymitikes stachyologias.* Vol. 4, pp. 367–400, and vol. 5, pp. 408–410. Moscow, 1897–1898.

Passio Andrew in Chrisi. [*BHG* 111, 112]. *AASS* (Oct., vol. 8, 1873): 135–149.

Passio Artemios. [*BHG* 169–174]. *PG* 96, cols. 1252–1320.

Passio of Eleutherios the Martyr. [*BHG* 572]. *AASS* (Aug., vol. 1, 1733): 321–326; in 3d. ed., 322–327.

Passio of St. Eugenia, with Basilla, Protas and Hyacinthus. [*BHG* 608]. *PG* 116, cols. 609–652.

Paton, W. R., ed and trans. *The Greek Anthology.* 5 vols. Cambridge, Mass., 1956–1960.

Paul of Aegina. *Chirurgie.* Ed. and trans. René Briau. Paris, 1860.

———. *Surgery.* In *Paulus Aegineta,* ed. J. L. Heiberg. 2 vols. Corpus medicorum Graecorum, 9, 1–2. Leipzig, 1921–1924.

Petit, L., ed. "Vie de saint Athanase l'Athonite." [*BHG* 188]. *AB* 25 (1906): 12–87.

Philostratus, Flavius. *The Life of Apollonius of Tyana, the Epistles of Apollonius and the Treatise of Eusebius.* Trans. F. C. Conybeare. 2 vols. Cambridge, Mass., 1912–1950.

Photios I, Patriarch. *Homiliae. PG* 101.

———. *Homiliai.* Ed. B. Laourdas. Thessalonica, 1959.

———. *The Homilies of Photius, Patriarch of Constantinople.* Ed. and trans. C. Mango. Washington, D.C., 1958.

———. *Photii Patriarchae Constantinopolitani Epistulae; et, Amphilochia.* Ed. B. Laourdas and L. G. Westerink. 6 vols. Leipzig, 1983–1988.

———. *Photii Patriarchae Lexicon.* Ed. C. Theodoridis. Vol. 1. New York and Berlin, 1982.

Pliny the Elder. *Pliny: Natural History.* Trans. H. Rackham. 10 vols. Cambridge, Mass., 1960–1968.

Pirgî Rabbi 'Elîêzer. Ed. Miguel Péreg Fernández. Valencia, 1984.

Preger, Theodore, ed. *Scriptores originum Constantinopolitanarum.* 2 vols. 1901–1907. Reprint, New York, 1975.

Prokopios. *Procopii Caesariensis opera omnia.* Ed. Jacobus Haury and G. Wirth. 4 vols. Leipzig, 1962–1963.

Psellos, Michael. *Chronographie; où, Histoire d'un siècle de Byzance (976–1077).* Ed. E. Renauld. 2 vols. 1926–28. Reprint, Paris, 1967.

———. *De legum nominibus de legum et legalium definitionium latini nominibus. PG* 122.

———. *De omnifaria doctrina.* Ed. L. G. Westerink. Utrecht, 1948.

———. *Fourteen Byzantine Rulers: The Chronographia of Michael Psellus.* Trans. E. R. A. Sewter. Baltimore, 1966. Reprint, New York, 1982.

———. *Michaelis Pselli Scripta minora.* Ed. Eduard Kurtz and Franz Drexl. 2 vols. Milan, 1936–41.

Psellos, Michael [Pseudo-Psellos]. *De daemonum operatione.* Ed. J. F. Boissonade. 1838. Reprint, Amsterdam, 1964.

Rahlfs, A., ed. *Septuaginta.* Stuttgart, 1952.

Reardon, B. P., ed. and trans. *Collected Ancient Greek Novels.* Berkeley, 1989.

Rhalles, G. A., and M. Potles, eds. *Syntagma ton theion kai hieron kanonon.* 6 vols. 1852–1859. Reprint, Athens, 1966.

Romano, Roberto, ed. and trans. *Timarione / Pseudo-Luciano, testo critico, introduzione, traduzione, commentario e lessico.* Naples, 1974.

Rosenqvist, Jan Olof, ed. and trans. *The Life of St. Irene Abbess of Chrysobalanton: A Critical Edition with Introduction, Translation, Notes and Indices.* [*BHG* 952]. Uppsala, 1986.

Sathas, C. N., ed. *Documents inédits relatifs à l'histoire de la Grèce au Moyen âge.* 1880–1890. Reprint, Athens, 1972.

Scheltema, H. J., N. Van der Wal, and D. Holwerda, eds. *Basilicorum libri LX.* Groningen, 1953–1988.

Sextus, Pythagoreus. *The Sentences of Sextus.* Ed. Richard Edwards and Robert Wild. Chico, Calif., 1981.

Sextus, Pythagoreus. *The Sentences of Sextus: A Contribution to the History of Christian Ethics.* Ed. Henry Chadwick. Cambridge, 1959.

Simeo Sethus. *Simeonis Sethi Syntagma de alimentorum facultatibus.* Ed. Bernhard Langkavel. Leipzig, 1868.

Simokattes, Theophylaktos. *The History of Theophylact Simocatta.* Trans. Michael Whitby and Mary Whitby. Oxford, 1986.

Skylitzes Continuatus. *He synecheia tes Chronographias tou Ioannou Skylitse (Ioannes Skylitzes Continuatus).* Ed. E. Th. Tsolakes. Thessalonica, 1968.

Skylitzes, John. *Ioannes Scylitzes: Synopsis historiarum.* Ed. H. Thurn. New York, 1973.

Sokrates Scholasticus. *Socratis Scholastici, Hermiae Sozomeni Historia ecclesiastica. PG* 67, cols. 29–842.

Soranos of Ephesus. *Caelius Aurelianus, Gynaecia: Fragments of a Latin version of Soranus' Gynaecia from a Thirteenth Century Manuscript.* Ed. Miriam Drabkin and Israel Drabkin. Baltimore, 1951.

———. *Gynecology.* Trans. Owsei Temkin. Baltimore, 1956.

———. *Maladies des femmes / Soranos d'Ephèse.* Ed. Paul Burguière, Danielle Gourevitch, and Yves Malinas. 3 vols. Paris, 1988–94.

———. *Sorani Gynaeciorum libri IV, De signis fracturarum, De fasciis, Vita Hippocratis secundum Soranum.* Ed. John Ilberg. Berlin, 1927.

Sozomenos. *Histoire ecclésiastique.* Ed. J. Bidez, and trans. A. J. Festugière. 2 vols. Paris, 1983–1996.

Symeon Metaphrastes. *Commentarius* on the Passion of the Prophet Daniel. [*BHG* 485]. *PG* 115, cols. 371–404.

———. *Passio* of St. Anthimios. [*BHG* 135]. *PG* 115, cols. 172–84.

———. *Passio* of Saints Indes and Domna. [*BHG* 823]. *PG* 116, cols. 1037–1081.

———. *Passio* of St. Lucian. [*BHG* 997]. *PG* 114, cols. 397–416.

———. *Opera Omnia. PG* 114–116.

———. Vita of St. Aberchios. [*BHG* 4]. *PG* 115, cols. 1212–1248.

———. Vita of St. Clement of Ancyra. [*BHG* 353]. *PG* 114, cols. 816–893.

———. Vita of St. Daniel the Stylite. [*BHG* 490]. *PG* 116, cols. 969–1037.

———. Vita of St. Euthymios. [*BHG* 649]. *PG* 114, cols. 596–733.

———. Vita of Ioannikios. [*BHG* 937]. *PG* 116, cols. 36–92.

———. Vita of St. John the Abbot. [*BHG* 937]. *PG* 116, cols. 36–92.

———. Vita of St. John the Almsgiver. [*BHG* 888]. *PG* 114, cols. 896–965.

———. Vita of John Chrysostom. [*BHG* 875]. *PG* 114, cols. 1045–1209.

———. Vita of St. Kyriakos the Anchorite. [*BHG* 464]. *PG* 115, cols. 920–944.

———. Vita of St. Melania. [*BHG* 1242]. *PG* 116, cols. 753–793.

———. *Vita* S. Prophetae Danielis. *PG* 115, cols. 371–403.

———. Vita of St. Sampson. [*BHG* 1615]. *PG* 115, cols. 277–308.

———. Vita of St. Theodosios Coenobiarcha. [*BHG* 1778]. *PG* 114, cols. 469–553.

———. Vita of St. Theophanes. [*BHG* 1789]. *PG* 115, cols. 9–29.

———. Vita of Theodora Alexandrina. [*BHG* 1730]. *PG* 115, cols. 665–689.

Tabari. *The Ancient Kingdoms.* Ed. and trans. Moshe Perlmann. Albany, N.Y., 1987.

———. *Les prophètes et les rois de Salomon à la chute des Sassanides.* Trans. Hermann Zotenberg. Paris, 1984.

Talbot, Alice-Mary, ed. *Holy Women of Byzantium.* Washington, D.C., 1996.

"Testamentum adae." Fragment 3. In *Patrologia syriaca,* ed. R. Gaffin, J. Parisot, F. Nau, and M. Kmoskó. 1 vol. in 3. Paris, 1894–1926.

Theodore of Kyzikos. "Epistolai ek tou Biennaiou kodikos phil. gr. 342." Ed. S. Lampros. *Neos Hellenomnemon* 19 (1925): 269–296; 20 (1926): 31–46, 139–157.

———. *Lettres.* In *Epistoliers byzantins du Xe siècle,* ed. J. Darrouzès, pp. 317–341. Paris, 1960.

Theodore Studites. *Oration VI. On the Holy Angels. PG* 99.

———. *Parva Catechesis.* Ed. E. Auvray. Paris, 1891.

Theodoret of Cyrrhus. "Interpretatio in Danielem." *PG* 81, cols. 1256–1546.

Theophanes the Confessor. *The Chronicle of Theophanes Confessor: Byzantine and Near Eastern History,* A.D. 284–813. Ed. and trans. Cyril Mango and Roger Scott. Oxford, 1997.

———. *Theophanis chronographia.* Ed. C. de Boor. 2 vols. 1883–1885. Reprint, Hildesheim, 1963.

Theophilos Protospatharios. *Peri tes tou anthropou kataskeues biblio E. De corporis humani fabrica libri V.* Ed. W. A. Greenhill. Oxford, 1842.

Theophylactos of Ohrid. *Theophylactus bulgariai archiepiscopus. PG* 123–126.

Thomas, John, and Angela Constantinides Hero, eds. *Byzantine Monastic Foundation Documents.* Washington, D.C., 2000. Available on the World Wide Web from Dumbarton Oaks at www.doaks.org.

Towner, W. Sibley. *Daniel.* Atlanta, 1984.

Vita of Anna Euphemianos. [*BHG* 2027]. *AASS, Propylaeum, Synaxarium ecclesiae Constantinopolitanae* (Nov. 1902): 174–178.

Vita of Athanasia Aegina. [*BHG* 180]. *De sancta Athanasia vidua ac hegumena in aegina insula. AASS* (Aug., vol. 3, 1737): 170–175.

Vita of Blasios of Amorion. [*BHG* 278]. *AASS* (Nov., vol. 4, 1925): 657–669.

Vitae of Eugenius et Maria eius filia. [*BHG* 614]. *PG* 115, cols. 348–353.

Vita of Euphrosyna. [*BHG* 627]. *AB* 2 (1883). *AASS* (Nov., vol. 3, 1910): 861–877.

Vita of Ioannikios. [*BHG* 935]. *AASS* (Nov., vol 2, part 1, 1894): 332–435.

Vita of John of Damascus. [*BHG* 884]. *PG* 94, cols. 429–490.

Vita of Luke the Stylite. [*BHG* 2239]. In *Les saints stylites,* ed. H. Delehaye, pp. 195–237. Subsidia Hagiographica, 14. 1923. Reprint, Brussels, 1962.

Vitae of Martyrs from Thrace. *AASS, Propylaeum, Synaxarium ecclesiae Constantinopolitanae* (Nov. 1902): 414–416.

Vita of Methodios. [*BHG* 1278]. *PG* 100, cols. 1243–1262.

Vita of Nikephoros I, Patriarch. "Vita of Nicephorus I, Patriarch." [*BHG* 1335]. *AASS* (March, vol. 2, 1668): 704–726; 3d ed.: 901–919.

Vita of Niketas David Paphlagon. *PG* 105, cols. 16–581.

Vita of Niketas of the Medikion. [*BHG* 1341]. *AASS* (April, vol. 1, 1675): xxii–xxxii; 3d ed.: xviii–xxvii.

Vita of Nilus. [*BHG* 1370]. *AASS* (Sept., vol. 7, 1760): 282–342.

Vita of Niphon of Constantiana. [*BHG* 1371z]. In *Materialien zur Geschichte der byzantinisch-slavischen Literatur und Sprache*, ed. A. V. Rystenko and P. O. Potapow, pp. 17–186. Odessa, 1928.

Vita of Stephen Sabaita. [*BHG* 1670]. *AASS* (July, vol. 3, 1723): 531–613; 3d ed.: 504–584.

Vita of Stephen the Younger. [*BHG* 1666]. *PG* 100, cols. 1069–1186.

Vita of Theodore of Studios. [*BHG* 1754]. *PG* 99, cols. 233–328.

Vita of Theodoret of Cyrrhus. *PG* 80–84.

Vita of Theoktiste. [*BHG* 1724]. *AASS* (Nov., vol. 4, 1925): 224–233.

Vita of Thomais of Lesbos. [*BHG* 2454]. *AASS* (Nov., vol. 4, 1925): 234–246.

van den Gheyn, J., ed. "Acta Theogini episcopi beteliae." [*BHG* 1786]. *AB* 10 (1891): 73–113.

———. *Acta graeca SS. Davidis, Symeonis et Georgii Mitylenae ininsula Lesbo. AB* 18 (1899): 209–259.

Van den Ven, Paul, ed. *La vie ancienne de S. Syméon Stylite le Jeune.* [*BHG* 1689] 2 vols. Brussels, 1962–1970.

Vasiliev, A., ed. "Zhitie Filareta Milostivogo." [*BHG* 1512] *Izvestiia Russkago Arkheologicheskogo Instituta v Konstantinopole* 5 (1900): 64–86.

Vasilievskii, A., and P. Nikitin, eds. "42 Martyrs of Amorion, Constantine, Theodore and Callistos." [*BHG* 1210] *Mémoires de l'Académie imperiale de Saint-Pétersbourg*, VII, 2 (1905): 38–56.

Vilinskii, S. G., ed. *Zhitie sv. Vasiliia Novago v russkoi literature* [Life of St. Basil Younger in Russian Literature, *BHG* 263–264D]. *Zapiski Imperatorskogo novorossiiskago universiteta* 7 (Odessa, 1911): 5–346.

Vision of St. Kosmas. *AASS, Propylaeum, Synaxarium Ecclesiae Constantinopolitanae* (Nov. 1902): 107–114

Vivian, Tim, ed. and trans. *Journeying into God. Seven Early Monastic Lives.* Minneapolis, 1996.

von Gebhardt, Oscar, and E. von Dobschütz, eds. *Die Akten der Edessenischen Bekenner Gurjas, Samonas und Abibos.* Leipzig, 1911.

Zachariä von Lingenthal, K. E., ed. *Ecloga privata aucta: Epanagoge aucta, Ecloga ad Prochiron mutata, Synopsis minor.* Athens, 1931.

Zepos, J., and P. Zepos, eds. *Jus graecoromanum.* 8 vols. 1931. Reprint, Aalen, 1962.

Zonaras, Joannes. *Ioannes Zonaras: Epitome historiarum.* Ed. M. Pinder and M. Büttner-Wobst. 3 vols. Bonn, 1841–1897.

———. *Ioannis Zonarae Epitome historiarum.* Ed. L. Dindorf. 6 vols. in 4. Leipzig, 1868–1875.

Zosimos. *Histoire nouvelle.* Ed. François Paschaud. 3 vols. in 5. Paris, 1979.

Secondary Works Consulted

Abramson, Paul R., and Steven D. Pinkerton, eds. *Sexual Nature / Sexual Culture.* Chicago, 1995.

Ahmed, Leila. *Women and Gender in Islam.* New Haven, 1992.

Al-Azmeh, Aziz. "Barbarians in Arab Eyes." *Past and Present* 134 (1992): 3–18.

Anderson, Mary. *Hidden Power: The Palace Eunuchs of Imperial China.* Buffalo, N.Y., 1990.

Anson, J. "The Female Transvestite in Early Monasticism: The Origin and Development of a Motif." *Viator* 5 (1974): 1–32.

Archer, L. J., Susan Fischer, and Maria Wyke, eds. *Women in Ancient Societies: An Illusion of the Night.* London, 1994.

Asher-Greve, Julia M. "Mesopotamian Conceptions of the Gendered Body." In *Gender and the Body in the Ancient Mediterranean,* ed. Maria Wyke, pp. 8–37. Oxford, 1998.

Ayalon, David. *Eunuchs, Caliphs and Sultans.* Jerusalem, 1999.

———. *Outsiders in the Lands of Islam: Mamluks, Mongols, and Eunuchs.* London, 1988.

Bakker, W. F., A. F. Van Gemert, and W. J. Aerts, eds. *Studia Byzantina et Neohellenica Neerlandica.* Leiden, 1972.

Baldwin, Barry. *Studies in Late Roman and Byzantine History, Literature and Language.* Amsterdam, 1984.

Barkaï, Ron. *Les infortunes de Dinah: Le livre de la génération. La gynécologie juive au Moyen-Age.* Paris, 1991.

Barnes, Timothy. *Athanasius and Constantius: Theology and Politics in the Constantinian Empire.* Cambridge, Mass., 1993.

———. *Constantine and Eusebius.* Cambridge, Mass., 1981.

Bassi, Karen. *Acting Like Men. Gender, Drama and Nostalgia in Ancient Greece.* Ann Arbor, Mich., 1998.

Bates, Don, ed. *Knowledge and the Scholarly Medical Traditions.* Cambridge, 1995.

Bauer, Walter. "Matth. 19,12 und die alten Christen." In *Neutestamentliche Studien Georg Heirici,* 235–244. Leipzig, 1914.

Beard, Mary. "The Roman and the Foreign: The Cult of the 'Great Mother' in Imperial Rome." In *Shamanism, History and the State,* ed. Nicholas Thomas and Caroline Humphrey, pp. 164–190. Ann Arbor, 1994.

Beaucamp, Joelle. *La transmission du patrimoine: Byzance et l'aire méditerranéenne.* Paris, 1998.

Beck, Hans Georg, "Der Byzantinische 'ministerpräsident.'" *BZ* 48 (1955): 309–338.

———. *Byzantinisches Erotikon: Orthodoxie, Literatur, Gesellschaft.* Munich, 1984.

Belting, H., and G. Cavallo. *Die Bibel des Niketas.* Wiesbaden, 1979.

Bersani, Leo. *Homos.* Cambridge, Mass., 1995.

Bertocchi, P. "Eunuco l'Etiope." *Bibliotheca sanctorum* 5 (1964): col. 228.9

Bleye, Rudi C. *The Geography of Perversion: Male-to-Male Sexual Behavior outside the West and the Ethnographic Imagination, 1750–1918.* New York, 1995.

Blinzler, Josef. "Εἰσὶν εὐνοῦχοι. Zur Auslegung von Mt. 19, 12." *Zeitschrift für die Neutestamentliche Wissenschaft* 48 (1957): 254–270.

Blok, Josine, and Peter Mason, eds. *Sexual Asymmetry: Studies in Ancient Society.* Amsterdam, 1987.

Blumenfeld-Kosinski, Renate, and Timea Szell, eds. *Images of Sainthood in Medieval Europe.* Ithaca, 1991.

Boak, A., and J. Dunlap. "The Grand Chamberlain Narses." In *Two Studies in Later Roman and Byzantine Administration,* ed. A. Boak and J. Dunlap. New York, 1924.

Boswell, John. *Christianity, Social Tolerance, and Homosexuality: Gay People in Western Europe from the Beginning of the Christian Era to the Fourteenth Century.* Chicago, 1981.

———. *The Kindness of Strangers: The Abandonment of Children in Western Europe from Late Antiquity to the Renaissance.* New York, 1988.

———. *Same-Sex Unions in Premodern Europe.* New York, 1994.

Boulhol, Pascal. *Les héritiers de Melchisedech. Famille et sainteté dans l'hagiographie antique II–VI siecle.* In press.

Boulhol, Pascal, and Isabelle Cochelin. "La réhabilitation de l'eunuque dans l'hagiographie antique (IIe—VIe siècles)." In *Memoriam sanctorum venerantes: Miscellanea in onore de Monsignor Victor Saxer,* pp. 49–73. Vatican, 1992.

Bowersock, G. W. *Hellenism in Late Antiquity.* Ann Arbor, Mich., 1990.

Bowersock, G. W., Peter Brown, and Oleg Grabar, eds. *Late Antiquity: A Guide to the Post Classical World.* Cambridge, Mass., 1999.

Bremmer, Jan, and Herman Roodenbert, eds. *A Cultural History of Gesture.* Cambridge, Mass, 1991.

Brettell, Caroline B., and Carolyn F. Sargent, eds. *Gender in Cross-Cultural Perspective.* Englewood Cliffs, N.J., 1993.

Brock, Sebastian P., and Susan Ashbrook Harvey. *Holy Women of the Syrian Orient.* Berkeley, 1987.

Brokkaar, W. G. "Basil Lekapenus." In *Studia Byzantina et Neohellenica Neerlandica,* ed. W. F. Bakker, A. F. Van Gemert, and W. J. Aerts, pp. 199–235. Leiden, 1972.

Brooks, E. W. "The Sources of Theophanes and the Syriac Chroniclers." *BZ* 15 (1906): 578–587.

Brower, Gary. "Ambivalent Bodies: Making Christian Eunuchs." Ph.D. diss., Duke University, 1996.

Brown, Peter. *The World of Late Antiquity,* A.D. 150–750. New York, 1976.

———. *The Cult of the Saints: Its Rise and Function in Latin Christianity.* Chicago, 1981.

———. *Society and the Holy in Late Antiquity.* Berkeley, 1982.

———. *The Body and Society: Men, Women and Sexual Renunciation in Early Christianity.* New York, 1988.

———. *Power and Persuasion in Late Antiquity: Towards a Christian Empire.* Madison, 1988.

———. "Bodies and Minds: Sexuality and Renunciation in Early Antiquity." In *Before Sexuality: The Construction of Erotic Experience in the Ancient Greek World,* ed. David Halperin, John J. Winkler, and Froma I. Zeitlin, pp. 479–493. Princeton, 1990.

———. *Authority and the Sacred: Aspects of the Christianisation of the Roman World.* Cambridge, 1995.

Browning, Robert. *Medieval and Modern Greek.* London, 1969.

———. *Studies on Byzantine History, Literature and Education.* London, 1977.

———. "An Unpublished Funeral Oration on Anna Comnena." In *Studies on Byzantine History, Literature and Education.* London, 1977.

———. *The Byzantine Empire.* New York, 1980.

Brubaker, Leslie, ed. *Byzantium in the Ninth Century: Dead or Alive?* Brookfield, Vt., 1998.

Bullough, Vern L. *Sexual Variance in Society and History.* Chicago, 1976.

Bullough, Vern L., and Bonnie Bullough. *The Subordinate Sex: A History of Attitudes toward Women.* Urbana, 1976.

Bullough, Vern L., and James A. Brundage, eds. *Handbook of Medieval Sexuality.* New York, 1996.

———. *Sexual Practices and the Medieval Church.* Buffalo, 1982.

Burkert, Walter. *Structure and History in Greek Mythology and Ritual.* Berkeley, 1979.

Bury, J. B. "The Ceremonial Book of Constantine Porphyrogennetus." *English Historical Review* 22 (1907): 209–227, 417–439.

———. "The Great Palace." *BZ* 21 (1910): 210–225.

———. *History of the Later Roman Empire from the Death of Theodosius I to the Death of Justinian.* 2 vols. New York, 1958.

Butler, Judith. *Gender Trouble: Feminism and the Subversion of Identity.* New York, 1990.

Bynum, Caroline Walker. *Holy Feast and Holy Fast: The Religious Significance of Food to Medieval Women.* Berkeley, 1987.

Bynum, Caroline Walker, Steven Harrell, and Paula Richman, eds. *Gender and Religion: On the Complexity of Symbols.* Boston, 1986.

Cadden, Joan. *Meanings of Sex Difference in the Middle Ages: Medicine, Science, and Culture.* Cambridge, 1993.

Cahen, Claude. *Pre-Ottoman Turkey.* London, 1968.

Cameron, Alan. *Claudian: Poetry and Propaganda at the Court of Honorius.* Oxford, 1970.

———. *The Greek Anthology from Meleager to Planudes.* Oxford, 1993.

Cameron, Averil. *Procopius and the Sixth Century.* Berkeley, 1983.

———. *The Later Roman Empire.* Cambridge, Mass., 1993.

———. "Sacred and Profane Love: Thoughts on Byzantine Gender." In *Women, Men and Eunuchs: Gender in Byzantium,* ed. Liz James, pp. 1–23. London, 1997.

Canard, M. "Deux documents arabes sur Bardas Skléros." In *Atti del v congresso internazionale di studi bizantini, 1,* 55–69. Nendeln, 1939.

Cannadine, David, and Simon Price, eds. *Rituals of Royalty: Power and Ceremonial in Traditional Societies.* Cambridge, 1992.

Cantarella, Eva. *Pandora's Daughters: The Role and Status of Women in Greek and Roman Antiquity.* Trans. Maureen B. Fant. Baltimore, 1987.

———. *Bisexuality in the Ancient World.* Trans. Cormac Ó. Cuilleanáin. New Haven, 1992.

Caplan, Patricia, ed. *The Cultural Construction of Sexuality.* London, 1987.

Carpenter, Edward. *Intermediate Types among Primitive Folk.* London, 1914.

Cavallaro, M. Adele. "Intorno ai rapporti tra cariche statalie cariche ecclesiastiche nel basso imperio: Nota storico-epigrafiche sul cubiculariato." *Athenaeum* 50 (1972): 158–175.

Cavallo, Guglielmo. *The Byzantines.* Chicago, 1997.

Cavarnos, Constantine. *Byzantine Thought and Art: A Collection of Essays.* Belmont, Mass., 1980.

Chantraine, Pierre. *Dictionnaire étymologique de la langue Grecque. Histoire des mots.* 4 vols. Paris, 1968–1980.

Charanis, Peter. "Imperial Coronation in Byzantium: Some New Evidence." *Byzantina* 8 (1976): 37–46.

Chatzidakis, Manolis, and André Grabar. *Byzantine and Early Medieval Painting.* New York, 1965.

Cheynet, Jean-Claude. *Pouvoir et contestations à Byzance (963–1210).* Paris, 1990.

Cheynet, Jean-Claude, Cécile Morrisson, and Werner Seibt, eds. *Sceaux byzantins de la Collection Henri Seyrig.* Paris, 1991.

Clark, Gillian. *Women in the Ancient World.* Oxford, 1989.

———. *Women in Late Antiquity: Pagan and Christian Lifestyles.* Oxford, 1994.

———. *This Female Man of God: Women and Spiritual Power in the Patristic Age,* A.D. 350–450. London, 1995.

Cohen, David. "Review Article: Sex, Gender, and Sexuality in Ancient Greece." *Classical Philology* 87 (1992): 145–160.

Collier, Jane, and Sylvia Yanagisako. *Gender and Kinship: Essays Towards a Unified Analysis.* Stanford, 1988.

Cooper, Kate. *The Virgin and the Bride: Idealized Womanhood in Late Antiquity.* Cambridge, Mass., 1996.

Dagron, Gilbert. *Constantinople imaginaire, études sur le recueil des "Patria."* Paris, 1984.

———. *Empereur et prêtre: Étude sur le "Césaropapisme" byzantin.* Paris, 1996.

Daniel, G. "Esséniens et Eunuques (Matthieu 19, 10–12)." *Revue de Qumran* 6 (1968): 353–390.

"Daniel." In *Dictionnaire d'archéologie chrétienne et de liturgie,* ed. Henri Leclercq and Fernand Cabrol, vol. 4, pt. 1-d, pp. 221–247. Paris, 1907–1945.

Danielou, Jean. *The Angels and Their Mission.* Trans. David Heiman. Westminster, Md., 1956.

Darrouzès, J. *Epistoliers byzantins du Xe siècle.* Paris, 1960.

———. *Recherches sur les ophphikia de l'église byzantine.* Paris, 1970.

———. *Littérature et histoire des textes byzantins.* London, 1972.

Davids, Adelbert, ed. *The Empress Theophano: Byzantium and the West at the Turn of the First Millenium.* Cambridge, 1995.

de Laurentis, Theresa. *Technologies of Gender.* Bloomington, Ind., 1987.

de Meester, Placidus, ed. *De Monachico statu iuxta disciplinam Byzantinam: Statuta selectis fontibus et comentariis instructa.* Vatican, 1942.

Dean-Jones, Lesley Ann. "The Cultural Construct of the Female Body in Classical Greek Science." In *Women's History and Ancient History,* ed. Sarah B. Pomeroy. Chapel Hill, N.C., 1991.

Dean-Jones, Lesley Ann. *Women's Bodies in Classical Greek Science.* Oxford, 1994.

del Valle, Teresa, ed. *Gendered Anthropology.* London, 1993.

Delehaye, H. *Les Saints Stylites.* Brussels and Paris, 1923.

———. "Les recueils antiques de miracles des saints." *AB* 43 (1925): 5–73.

———. *Études su le légendier romain.* Subsidia Hagiographica, 23. Brussels, 1936.

Diehl, Charles. "De la signification du titre de proèdre à Byzance." *Mélanges offerts à m. Gustave Schlumberger, membre de l'Insitut, à l'occasion du quatre-vingtième anniversaire de sa naissance,* vol. 1, pp. 105–17. Paris, 1924.

———. *Byzantium: Greatness and Decline.* New Brunswick, N.J., 1957.

Dirks, Nicholas B., Geoff Eley, and Sherry B. Ortner, eds. *Culture / Power / History: A Reader in Contemporary Social Theory.* Princeton, 1994.

Dorfman, Ralph I., and Reginald A. Shipley. *Androgens.* New York, 1956.

Douglas, Mary. *Purity and Danger: An Analysis of the Concepts of Pollution and Taboo.* London, 1979.

Dover, K. J. *Greek Homosexuality.* New York, 1989.

Drew-Bear, Thomas. "Un Eunuque armenien en Cappadoce." *Epigraphica anatolica* 4 (1984): 139–149.

Du Cange, Charles. *Glossarium ad scriptores mediae et infimae Graecitatis.* 1688, 1793. Reprint, Graz, 1958.

Duberman, Martin, Martha Vicinus, and George Chauncey, Jr., eds. *Hidden from History: Reclaiming the Gay and Lesbian Past.* New York, 1990.

DuBois, Page. *Sowing the Body: Psychoanalysis and Ancient Representations of Women.* Chicago, 1988.

Ducellier, Alain. *Byzance et le monde orthodoxe.* Paris, 1986.

Duffy, John. "Byzantine Medicine in the Sixth and Seventh Centuries." *DOP* 38 (1984): 21–28.

Duffy, John, and John Peradotto, eds. *Gonimos: Neoplatonic and Byzantine Studies Presented to Leendert G. Westerink at 75.* Buffalo, N.Y., 1988.

Dunn, A. W. *A Handlist of the Byzantine Lead Seals and Tokens.* Birmingham, 1983.

Durling, R. *A Dictionary of Medical Terms in Galen.* Leiden, 1993.

Dvornik, Francis. *Les légendes de Constantin et de Méthode vues de Byzance.* Prague, 1933.

———. *Byzantine Missions among the Slavs: SS. Constantine-Cyril and Methodius.* New Brunswick, N.J., 1970.

Ebersolt, J. "Sur les fonctions et dignités du Vestiarium Byzantin." *Mélanges Charles Diehl,* vol. 1, pp. 81–89. Paris, 1930.

Edelman, Lee. *Homographesis: Essays in Gay Literature and Cultural Theory.* New York, 1994.

Eftychiades, A. *The Practice of Byzantine Medical Science and Its Social Application according to Relative Orders.* Athens, 1983.

Englestein, Laura. *Castration and the Heavenly Kingdom: A Russian Folktale.* Ithaca, N.Y., 1999.

Epstein, Julia. "Either/Or—Neither/Both: Sexual Ambiguity and the Ideology of Gender." *Genders* 7 (1990): 99–142.

Epstein, Julia, and Kristina Straub, eds. *Body Guards: The Cultural Politics of Gender Ambiguity.* New York, 1991.

Faraone, Christopher A. "Binding and Burying the Forces of Evil: The Defensive Use of 'Voodoo Dolls' in Ancient Greece." *Classical Antiquity* 10, no. 2 (1991): 165–220.

Farmer, Sharon, and Carol Pasternak, eds. *Difference and Genders in the Middle Ages.* Minneapolis, 2002.

Fausto-Sterling, Anne. *Myths of Gender: Biological Theories about Men and Women.* New York, 1992.

———. *Sexing the Body: Gender Politics and the Construction of Sexuality.* New York, 2000.

Ferguson, Kathy E. *The Man Question: Visions of Subjectivity in Feminist Theory.* Berkeley, 1993.

Filoramo, Giovanni. *A History of Gnosticism.* Trans. Anthony Alcock. Oxford, 1992.

Finet, A. "Les anges gardiens du Babylonien." In *Anges et démons: Actes du colloque de Liège et de Louvain-la-Neuve, 25–26 novembre 1987,* ed. J. Ries, pp. 37–52. Louvain, 1989.

Fischer, Benno. *Daniel und seine drei Gefährten im Talmud und Midrasch.* Temesvar, 1906.

Flint, Valerie I. J. *The Rise of Magic in Early Medieval Europe.* Princeton, 1991.

Foucault, Michel. *The History of Sexuality.* Vol. 1, *An Introduction.* Vol. 2, *The Use of Pleasure.* Vol. 3, *The Care of the Self.* New York, 1978–1990.

Fowden, Garth. *The Egyptian Hermes: A Historical Approach to the Late Pagan Mind.* Princeton, 1986.

———. *Empire to Commonwealth: Consequences of Monotheism in Late Antiquity.* Princeton, 1993.

Frend, W. H. C. "The Roman Empire in Eastern and Western Historiography." *Proceedings of the Cambridge Philological Society* 194, n.s. 14 (1968): 19–32.

Frisk, Hjalmar. *Griechisches etymologisches Wörterbuch.* Heidelberg, 1960.

Frye, R. N. "The Charisma of Kingship in Ancient Iran." *Iranica Antiqua* 4 (1964): 36–54.

Gaiffier, B. de. "Palatins et eunuques dans quelques documents hagiographiques." *AB* 65 (1957): 17–46.

Garland, Lynda. *Byzantine Empresses: Women and Power in Byzantium, 527–1204.* London, 1997.

Geertz, Clifford. *Local Knowledge: Further Essays in Interpretive Anthropology.* New York, 1983.

Ghirshman, R. *Iran from the Earliest Times to the Islamic Conquest.* Middlesex, 1954.

Gilles, Pierre. *The Antiquities of Constantinople.* Trans. John Ball. 1729. Reprint, New York, 1988.

Gilligan, Carol. *In a Different Voice.* Cambridge, Mass., 1982.

Gleason, Maud W. "The Semiotics of Gender: Physiognomy and Self-Fashioning in the Second Century C.E." In *Before Sexuality: The Construction of Erotic Experience in the Ancient Greek World,* ed. David M. Halperin, John J. Winkler, and Froma I. Zeitlin, pp. 389–417. Princeton, 1990.

———. *Making Men: Sophists and Self-Presentation in Ancient Rome.* Princeton, 1995.

Glykatzi-Ahrweiler, Hélène. *Recherches sur l'administration de l'empire byzantin aux IXe–XI siècles.* Athens and Paris, 1960.

———. *Byzance et la mer, la marine de guerre, la politique et les institutions maritimes de Byzance aux VIIe–XVe siècles.* Paris, 1966.

Gordon, Linda. "On "Difference." *Genders* 10 (1991): 91–111.

Grabar, André. *Christian Iconography: A Study of the Origins.* Princeton, 1986.

Grabar, André, and M. Manoussacas, eds. *L'Illustration du manuscrit de Skylitzès de la Bibliothèque Nationale de Madrid.* Venice, 1979.

Graef, Hilda. "The Spiritual Director in the Thought of Symeon the New Theologian." In *Kyriakon: Festschrift Johannes Quasten,* ed. Patrick Granfield and Josef Jungmann, vol. 2, pp. 609–614. Munster, 1970.

Granfield, Patrick, and Josef Jungmann, eds. *Kyriakon: Festschrift Johannes Quasten.* 2 vols. Munster, 1970.

Grant, Mark. *Galen on Food and Diet.* London, 2000.

Guilland, Rodolphe. "Les eunuques dans l'empire byzantine: Étude de titulature et de prosopographie byzantines." *Etudes byzantines* 1 (1943): 197–238.

———. "Fonctions et dignités des eunuques." *Études byzantines* 2 (1945): 185–225, 3 (1945): 179–214.

———. "Études de titulature byzantine; les titres auliques réservés aux eunuques." *Revue des études byzantines* 12 (1954): 50–84, 14 (1956): 122–157.

———. "Études sur l'histoire administrative de l'empire byzantine: Les titres auliques des eunuques. Le protospathaire." *Byzantion* 25–27 (1955–57): 649–695.

———. "Le sébastophore." *Revue des études byzantines* 21 (1963): 203–205.

———. *Recherches sur les institutions byzantines.* 2 vols. Amsterdam, 1967.

Gundert, Beate. "Parts and Their Roles in Hippocratic Medicine." *Isis* 83 (1992): 453–465.

Guyot, Peter. *Eunuchen als Sklaven und Freigelassene in der griechisch-römischen Antike.* Stuttgart, 1980.

Hackel, Sergei. *The Byzantine Saint.* London, 1981.

Haldon, J. F. "On the Structuralist Approach to the Social History of Byzantium." *Byzantinoslavica* 42 (1981): 203–211.

———. *Byzantine Praetorians: An Administrative, Institutional, and Social Survey of the Opsikion and Tagmata, c. 500–900.* Bonn, 1984.

———. *Byzantium in the Seventh Century.* Cambridge, 1997.

Halkin, F. "Trois dates précisées grâce au Synaxaire." *Byzantion* 24 (1954): 11–14.

Hallett, Judith P., and Marilyn Skinner, eds. *Roman Sexualities.* Princeton, 1997.

Halperin, David M. *One Hundred Years of Homosexuality and Other Essays on Greek Love.* London, 1990.

Halperin, David M., John J. Winkler, and Froma I. Zeitlin, eds. *Before Sexuality: The Construction of Erotic Experience in the Ancient Greek World.* Princeton, 1990.

Hamilton, Janet, and Bernard Hamilton, eds. and trans. *Christian Dualist Heresies in the Byzantine World, c. 650–c. 1405.* Manchester, 1998.

Handbuch der klassischen Altertums-Wissenschaft. 9 vols. Munich, 1886.

Hanson, Ann Ellis. "The Origins of Female Nature." *Helios* 19 (1992): 31–71.

Harries, Jill, and Ian Wood, eds. *The Theodosian Code.* Ithaca, N.Y., 1993.

Helck, Wolfgang, and Eberhard Otto. *Lexikon de Ägyptologie.* 7 vols. Wiesbaden, 1972–1992.

Helly, Dorothy, and Susan Reverby, eds. *Gendered Domains: Rethinking Public and Private in Women's History.* Ithaca, N.Y., 1992.

Hendy, Michael F. *The Economy, Fiscal Administration and Coinage in Byzantium.* Northhampton, 1989.

Herdt, Gilbert, ed. *Third Sex, Third Gender: Beyond Sexual Dimorphism in Culture and History.* New York, 1994.

Herrin, Judith. *The Formation of Christendom.* Princeton, 1987.

———. "Ideas of Charity, Realities of Welfare: The Philanthropic Activity of the Byzantine Church." In *Church and People in Byzantium,* ed. Rosemary Morris, pp. 151–64. Birmingham, 1990.

———. "Byzance: Le palais et la ville." *Byzantion* 61 (1991): 213–230.

———. "Public and Private Forms of Religious Commitment among Byzantine Women." In *Women in Ancient Societies: An Illusion of the Night,* ed. L. J. Archer, Susan Fischer, and Maria Wyke, pp. 181–203. London, 1994.

———. *Women in Purple: Rulers of Medieval Byzantium.* London, 2001.

Hill, Robert. "Chrysostom as Old Testament Commentator." *Prudentia* 20 (1988): 44–56.

Hinsch, Bret. *Passions of the Cut Sleeve: The Male Homosexual Tradition in China.* Berkeley, 1990.

Holum, Kenneth G. *Theodosian Empresses: Women and Imperial Dominion in Late Antiquity.* Berkeley, 1982.

Hopkins, M. Keith. "Eunuchs in Politics in the Later Roman Empire." *Proceedings of the Cambridge Philological Society* 189 (1963): 62–80.

———. *Conquerors and Slaves.* Cambridge, 1978.

Hubner, H. "Zolibat in Qumran?" *New Testament Studies* 17 (1970): 153–167.

Humphreys, S. C. *The Family, Women and Death: Comparative Studies.* 2d ed. Ann Arbor, 1993.

Hunger, Herbert. *Die hochsprachliche profane Literatur der Byzantiner.* Munich, 1978.

Hussey, Joan M. *Church and Learning in the Byzantine Empire, 867–1185.* 1937. Reprint, New York, 1963.

———. *The Orthodox Church in the Byzantine Empire.* Oxford, 1986.

Jacobs, SueEllen, and Christine Roberts. "Sex, Sexuality, Gender, and Gender Variance." In *Gender and Anthropology: Critical Reviews for Research and Teaching*, ed. Sandra Morgen, pp. 438–462. Washington, D.C., 1989.

Jacquart, Danielle, and Claude Thomasset. *Sexuality and Medicine in the Middle Ages.* Trans. Matthew Adamson. Princeton, 1988.

Jakobson, R. *Selected Writings.* The Hague, 1962.

James, Liz. *Empresses and Power in Early Byzantium.* London, 2001.

James, Liz, ed. *Women, Men and Eunuchs: Gender in Byzantium.* London, 1997.

———. *Denial and Desire in Byzantium.* Aldershot, 1999.

Jantzen, Grace M. *Power, Gender, and Christian Mysticism.* Cambridge, 1995.

Jay, Jennifer W. "Castration and Medical Images of Eunuchs in Traditional China." In *Cultural Perspectives in the History of Science in East Asia*, ed. Sik Kim and Francesca Bray. Seoul, 1999.

Jeffreys, Elizabeth. "The Later Greek Verse Romances: A Survey." In *Byzantine Papers*, ed. Elizabeth Jeffreys, Michael Jeffreys, and Ann Moffatt, pp. 116–127. Canberra, 1981.

Jenkins, Romilly J. H. "The Flight of Samonas." In *Studies on Byzantine History of the Ninth and Tenth Centuries.* London, 1970. First published in *Speculum* 23 (1948): 217–35.

———. *Studies on Byzantine History of the Ninth and Tenth Centuries.* London, 1970.

Jones, C. P. *Culture and Society in Lucian.* Cambridge, Mass., 1986.

Kadish, Gerald E. "Eunuchs in Ancient Egypt?" In *Studies in Honor of J. A. Wilson*, ed. G. E. Kadish. Chicago, 1969.

Kaegi, Walter Emil, Jr. *Byzantium and the Decline of Rome.* Princeton, 1968.

———. *Byzantium and the Early Islamic Conquests.* Cambridge, 1993.

Karlin-Hayter, Patricia. "L'Adieu à l'empereur." *Byzantion* 61 (1991): 112–147.

Kazhdan, Alexander. "Hermitic, Cenobitic and Secular Ideals in Byzantine Hagiography of the Ninth Century." *Greek Orthodox Theological Review* 30, no. 4 (1985): 473–487.

———. "'Constantin imaginaire': Byzantine Legends of the Ninth Century about Constantine the Great." *Byzantion* 57 (1987): 196–250.

———. "Byzantine Hagiography and Sex in the Fifth through Twelfth Centuries." *DOP* 40 (1990): 131–143.

———. *Authors and Texts in Byzantium.* Aldershot, 1993.

Kazhdan, Alexander, and Ann Wharton Epstein. *Change in Byzantine Culture in the Eleventh and Twelfth Centuries.* Berkeley, 1985.

Kazhdan, Alexander, and Giles Constable. *People and Power in Byzantium: An Introduction to Modern Byzantine Studies.* Washington, D.C., 1982.

Kazhdan, Alexander, and Michael McCormick. "The Social World of the Byzantine Court." In *Byzantine Court Culture from 829 to 120*, ed. Henry Maguire, pp. 167–197. Washington, D.C., 1997.

Kazhdan, Alexander, and Simon Franklin. *Studies on Byzantine Literature of the Eleventh and Twelfth Centuries.* Cambridge, 1984.

Keddie, Nikki, and Beth Baron. *Shifting Boundaries: Women and Gender in Middle Eastern History.* New Haven, 1991.

Kee, Howard Clark. *Miracle in the Early Christian World: A Study in Sociohistorical Method.* New Haven, 1983.

Kelly, J. N. D. *Early Christian Creeds.* 3d ed. New York, 1972.

Keuls, Eva C. *The Reign of the Phallus: Sexual Politics in Ancient Athens.* Berkeley, 1985.

Kinsman, Gary. "'Homosexuality' Historically Reconsidered Challenges Heterosexual Hegemony." *Journal of Historical Sociology* 4 (1991): 91–111.

Kitzinger, Ernst. *Byzantine Art in the Making: Main Lines of Stylistic Development in Mediterranean Art, Third–Seventh Century.* Cambridge, Mass., 1977.

Klibansky, R. *The Continuity of Platonic Tradition during the Middle Ages.* London, 1958.

Koder, Johannes. "Fresh Vegetables for the Capital." In *Constantinople and Its Hinterland: Papers from the Twenty-Seventh Spring Symposium of Byzantine Studies,* pp. 49–56. Oxford, 1993.

Koder, Johannes. *Der Lebensraum der Byzantiner: Historisch-geographischer Abriss ihres mittelalterlichen Staates in östlichen Mittelmeerraum.* Graz, 1984.

———. *Gemüse in Byzanz: Die Versorgung Konstantinopels mit Frischgemüse im Lichte der Geoponika.* Vienna, 1993.

Kolias, G. *Léon Choerosphactès, magistre, proconsul et patrice.* Athens, 1939.

Koloski-Ostrow, Ann, and Claire Lyons, eds. *Naked Truths: Women, Sexuality, and Gender in Classical Art and Archaeology.* London, 1997.

Koukoules, Phaidon I. *Byzantinon bios kai politismos.* 6 vols. in 7. Athens, 1948–1957.

Kramer, Stephen A. "Emperors and Aristocrats in Byzantium, 976–1081." Ph.D. diss., Harvard University, 1983.

Krautheimer, Richard. *Three Christian Capitals: Topographical Politics. Rome, Constantinople, Milan.* Berkeley, 1983.

Krumbacher, Karl. *Geschichte der byzantinischen litterature.* Handbuch der Klassischen Altertums-Wissenschaft, 9.1. Munich, 1891.

Kuefler, Mathew S. "Castration and Eunuchism in the Middle Ages." In *Handbook of Medieval Sexuality,* ed. Vern L. Bullough and James A. Brundage, pp. 279–306. New York, 1996.

———. *The Manly Eunuch: Masculinity, Gender Ambiguity, and Christian Ideology in Late Antiquity.* Chicago, 2001.

Kuhrt, Amélie. *The Ancient Near East, c. 3000–330 B.C.E.* 2 vols. London, 1995.

Lagrange, M. J. "Attis et le Christianisme." *Revue biblique,* n.s., 16 (1919): 419–80.

Laiou, Angeliki E. *Gender, Society and Economic Life in Byzantium.* Brookfield, Vt., 1992.

Lamphere, Louise, and Michelle Rosaldo. *Women, Culture, and Society.* Stanford, 1974.

Laqueur, Thomas. *Making Sex: Body and Gender from the Greeks to Freud.* Cambridge, Mass., 1990.

Lascaratos, J., and A. Kostakopoulos. "Operations on Hermaphrodites and Castration in Byzantine Times (324–1453)." *Urologia internationalis* 58, no. 4 (1997): 232–235.

Laurent, V. *Les bulles métriques dans la sigillographie byzantine.* Athens, 1932.

———. *La Collection C. Orghidan. Documents de sigillographie byzantin.* Paris, 1952.

———. "Byzance et Antioche." *Mélanges de l'Université Saint-Joseph* 38 (1962): 221–254.

———. *Le corpus des sceaux de l'Empire byzantin.* Vols. 2 and 5. Paris, 1963, 1981.

Leclercq, Henri. "Castration." In *Dictionnaire d'archéologie chrétienne,* vol. 2, pt. 2. cols. 2369–72. Paris, 1910.

Leclercq, Henri, and Fernand Cabrol, eds. *Dictionnaire d'archéologie chrétienne et de liturgie.* 15 vols. in 30. Paris, 1907–1945.

Lefkowitz, Mary R., and Maureen B. Fant, eds. *Women's Life in Greece and Rome: A Source Book in Translation.* Baltimore, 1993.

Leitner, Helmut. *Bibliography to the Ancient Medical Authors.* Bern, 1973.

Lemerle, Paul. *Prolégomènes à une édition critique et commentée des "Conseils et Récets" de Kekaumenos.* Brussels, 1960.

———. *Le premier humanisme byzantin; notes et remarques sur l'enseignement et culture à Byzance des origines au Xe siècle.* Paris, 1971.

Lemerle, Paul, André Guillou, Nicolas Svoronos, and Denise Papachryssanthou, eds. *Actes de Lavra.* Paris, 1970–1982.

Leonardo, Micaela di. *Gender at the Crossroads of Knowledge.* Berkeley, 1991.

Lepori, N. G. *Sex Differentiation, Hermaphroditism and Intersexuality in Vertebrates, including Man.* Padua, 1980.

Levin, Eve. *Sex and Society in the World of the Orthodox Slavs, 900–1700.* Ithaca, N.Y., 1989.

Levy, Howard S. *The Lotus Lovers: A Complete History of the Curious Erotic Custom of Footbinding in China.* Buffalo, N.Y., 1991.

Lewis, Bernard. *Race and Slavery in the Middle East: An Historical Enquiry.* New York, 1990.

Lewis, Naphtali. *The Interpretation of Dreams and Portents.* New York, 1976.

Lieu, Samuel N. C., and Dominic Montserrat, eds., *Constantine: History, Historiography and Legend.* London and New York, 1998.

Lloyd, G. E. *Greek Science after Aristotle.* New York, 1973.

Long, Jacqueline Flint. "Claudian's 'In Eutropium': Artistry and Practicability in Slandering a Eunuch." Ph.D. diss., Columbia University, 1989.

———. *Claudian's In Eutropium, or, How, When, and Why to Slander a Eunuch.* Chapel Hill, N.C., 1996.

Loraux, Nicole. *The Experiences of Tiresias: The Feminine and the Greek Man.* Trans. Paula Wissing. Princeton, 1995.

Luck, Georg. *Arcana Mundi: Magic and the Occult in the Greek and Roman Worlds.* Baltimore, 1985.

Lybyer, Albert. *The Government of the Ottoman Empire in the Time of Suleiman the Magnificent.* Cambridge, Mass., 1913.

Maas, Ernst. "Eunuchos und Verwandtes." *Rheinisches Museum für Philologie* 74 (1925): 432–76.

Maas, Michael. *John Lydus and the Roman Past: Antiquarianism and Politics in the Age of Justinian.* London and New York, 1992.

MacCormack, Carol, and Marilyn Strathern. *Nature, Culture, and Gender.* Cambridge, 1980.

MacCormack, Sabine. *Art and Ceremony in Late Antiquity.* Berkeley, 1981.

MacMullen, Ramsay. "Roman Attitudes to Greek Love. *Historia* 31 (1982): 484–502.

———. "What Difference Did Christianity Make?" *Historia* 35 (1986): 322–343.

———. *Christianity and Paganism in the Fourth to Eighth Centuries.* New Haven, 1997.

Macrides, Ruth. "The Byzantine Godfather." *Byzantine and Modern Greek Studies* 11 (1987): 139–162.

Magdalino, Paul. *Tradition and Transformation in Medieval Byzantium.* Aldershot, 1991.

———. *The Empire of Manuel I Komnenos, 1143–1180.* Cambridge, 1993.

Magdalino, Paul, and Robert Nelson. "The Emperor in Byzantine Art of the Twelfth Century." *Byzantinische Forshungen* 8 (1982): 123–183. Reprinted in Paul Magdalino, *Tradition and Transformation in Medieval Byzantium.* Aldershot, 1991.

Magoulias, Harry J. *Byzantine Christianity: Emperor, Church, and the West.* Chicago, 1970.

Maguire, Henry. *Art and Eloquence in Byzantium.* Princeton, 1981.

———. "The Heavenly Court." In *Byzantine Court Culture from 829 to 1204,* ed. Henry Maguire, pp. 247–258. Washington, D.C., 1997.

Maguire, Henry, ed. *Byzantine Court Culture from 829 to 1204.* Washington, D.C., 1997.

Majeska, George P. "A Medallion of the Prophet Daniel in the Dumbarton Oaks Collection." *DOP* 28 (1974): 361–67.

———. *Russian Travelers to Constantinople in the Fourteenth and Fifteenth Centuries.* Washington, D.C., 1984.

Mango, Cyril. "The Date of Cod. Vat. Reg. Gr. I and the Macedonian Renaissance." *Acta ad Archaeologiam et artium historiam pertinentia* 4 (1969): 122–126.

———. "On the History of the *Templon* and the Martyrion of St. Artemios at Constantinople." *Zograf* 10 (1979): 40–43.

———. *Byzantium, the Empire of New Rome.* London, 1980.

———. *Byzantium and Its Image: History and Culture of the Byzantine Empire and Its Heritage.* London, 1984.

———. "St. Michael and Attis." *Deltion* 12 (1984): 39–62.

———. "Diabolus Byzantinus." *DOP* 46 (1992): 215–223.

Mango, Cyril, and I. Sevcenko. "A New Manuscript of the *De ceremoniis.*" *DOP* 14 (1960): 247–249.

Marava-Chatzenikolaou, Anna. *Recherches sur la vie des esclaves dans le monde byzantin.* Athens, 1950.

Markopoulos, A., ed. *Konstantinos [VII] ha Porphyrogennetos kai he epoche tou.* Athens, 1989.

Markus, Robert. *The End of Ancient Christianity.* Cambridge, 1990.

Marmon, Shaun E. "The Eunuchs of the Prophet: Space, Time and Gender in Islamic Society." Ph.D. diss., Princeton University, 1990.

———. *Eunuchs and Sacred Boundaries in Islamic Society.* Oxford, 1995.

Martindale, J. R., A. H. M. Jones, and J. Morris. *The Prosopography of the Later Roman Empire.* 2 vols. Cambridge, 1971–1980.

Mathews, Thomas F. *The Clash of the Gods: A Reinterpretation of Early Christian Art.* Princeton, 1993.

McCormick, Michael. "Analyzing Imperial Ceremonies." *Jahrbuch der österreichischen Byzantinistik* 35 (1985): 1–20.

———. *Eternal Victory: Triumphal Leadership in Late Antiquity, Byzantium, and the Early Medieval West.* Cambridge, 1986.

Meinardus, O. "The Beardless Patriarch: St. Germanus." *Makedonika* 13 (1973): 178–186.

Meyendorff, John. *Le millénaire du Mont Athos, 963–1963: Études et mélanges.* 2 vols. Chevetogne, 1963–1964.

———. *Byzantine Theology: Historical Trends and Doctrinal Themes.* New York, 1979.

———. *Byzantium and the Rise of Russia: A Study of Byzantino-Russian Relations in the Fourteenth Century.* Crestwood, N.Y., 1989.

Meyer, Marvin, and Richard Smith, eds. *Ancient Christian Magic: Coptic Texts of Ritual Power.* New York, 1994.

Meyer, Philipp. *Die Haupturkunden für die Geschichte der Athosklöster: Grösstentheils zum ersten Male.* 1894. Reprint, Amsterdam, 1965.

Miers, S., and I. Kopytoff, eds. *Slavery in Africa: Historical and Anthropological Perspectives.* Madison, Wisc., 1977.

Miller, Barbara Diane, ed. *Sex and Gender Hierarchies.* Cambridge, 1993.

Miller, Barnet. *The Palace School of Muhammad the Conqueror.* New York, 1973.

Miniatura della Bibbia co. Vat. Regin. greco I e del Salterio co. Vat. Palat. greco 381. Collezione palaeografica Vaticana, 1. Milan, 1905.

Mitamura, T. *Chinese Eunuchs: The Structure of Intimate Politics.* Rutland, Vt., 1970.

Moffatt, Ann. "The Byzantine Child." *Social Research* 53 (1986): 705–723.

Mohrmann, Christine. "'Tertium genus,' Les relations judaisme, antiquité, christianisme reflète dans la langue des chretiens." In *Études sur le latin des chrétiens.* Vol. 4, pp. 195–210. Rome, 1965.

Money, John. *Sex Errors of the Body: Dilemmas, Education, Counseling.* Baltimore, 1968.

———. *Social Constructionism, Feminism, and Sexosophical History.* New York, 1995.

Money, John, and Anke A. Ehrhardt. *Man and Woman, Boy and Girl: The Differentiation and Dimorphism of Gender Identity from Conception to Maturity.* Baltimore, 1972.

Moore, Henrietta. *Feminism and Anthropology.* Cambridge and Oxford, 1986.

Moran, Neil. *Singers in Late Byzantine and Slavonic Painting.* Leiden, 1986.

———. "Monasteries for Eunuchs, 890–1078." Paper presented at the Conference on Byzantine Monasticism, Toronto, 2001.

———. "Byzantine Castrati." Forthcoming in *Plainsong and Medieval Music,* 2002.

Morgen, Sandra, ed. *Gender and Anthropology: Critical Reviews for Research and Teaching.* Washington, D.C., 1989.

Morris, Rosemary. "The Political Saint of the Eleventh Century." In *The Byzantine Saint,* ed. Sergei Hackel. London, 1981.

———. *Monks and Laymen in Byzantium, 843–1118.* Cambridge, 1995.

Morris, Rosemary, ed. *Church and People in Byzantium.* Birmingham, 1990.

Mottahedeh, Roy. *Loyalty and Leadership in an Early Islamic Society.* Princeton, 1980.

Moxnes, Halver, ed. *Constructing Early Christian Families: Family as a Social Reality and Metaphor.* London, 1997.

Mullett, M. E. "Byzantium: A Friendly Society?" *Past and Present* 118 (1988): 3–24.

Murray, Sara. *A Study of the Life of Andreas: The Fool for the Sake of Christ.* Borna-Leipzig, 1910.

Murray, Stephen O., Will Roscoe, et al. *Islamic Homosexualities: Culture, History, and Literature.* New York, 1997.

Nanda, Serena. *Neither Man nor Woman: The Hijra of India.* Belmont, Calif., 1990.

Necipoglu, Gülrü. *Architecture, Ceremonial and Power: The Topkapi Palace in the Fifteenth and Sixteenth Centuries.* Cambridge, 1991.

Nelson, Cynthia. "Public and Private Politics: Women in the Middle Eastern World." *American Ethnologist* 1, no. 3 (1974): 551–563.

Nelson, Janet. "Réflexions sur la famille impériale: À Byzance (VIIIe–Xe siècles). *Byzantion* 61 (1991): 181–212.

Nesbitt, J., and N. Oikonomidès, eds. *Catalogue of Byzantine Seals at Dumbarton Oaks and in The Fogg Museum of Art, 1.* Washington, D.C., 1991.

Nicol, Donald M. *Studies in Late Byzantine History and Prosopography.* London, 1986.

———. *The Byzantine Lady: Ten Portraits, 1250–1500.* Cambridge, 1994.

———. *The Last Centuries of Byzantium, 1261–1453.* 2d ed. Cambridge, 1995.

Nock, A. D. "Eunuchs in Ancient Religion." *Archiv für Religionswissenschaft* 23 (1925): 24–33.

Norwich, John Julius. *Byzantium: The Early Centuries.* New York, 1989.

Oberhelman, Steven. "The Interpretation of Dream-Symbols in Byzantine Oneirocritic Literature." *Byzantinoslavica* 47 (1986): 8–24.

Oehler, Klaus. "Aristotle in Byzantium." *Greek, Roman, and Byzantine Studies* 5 (1964): 133–146.

Offen, Karen. *European Feminisms, 1700–1950.* Stanford, Calif., 2000.

Oikonomidès, Nicolas. "Life and Society in Eleventh-Century Constantinople." *Südost Forschungen* 49 (1990): 1–14.

———. *Byzantium from the Ninth Century to the Fourth Crusade.* Aldershot, 1992.

Oikonomidès, Nicolas, ed. *Byzantium during the Twelfth Century.* Athens, 1991.

Ortner, Sherry B. "Is Female to Male As Nature Is to Culture?" *Feminist Studies* 1, no. 2 (1972): 5–32.

———. "Theory in Anthropology since the Sixties." *Comparative Studies in Society and History* 26 (1984): 126–166.

———. "The Virgin and the State." In *Gender in Cross-Cultural Perspective,* ed. Caroline Brettell and Carolyn Sargent, pp. 257–268. Englewood Cliffs, N.J., 1993.

Ortner, Sherry B., and Harriet Whitehead, eds. *Sexual Meanings: The Cultural Construction of Gender and Sexuality.* Cambridge, 1981.

Ostrogorsky, George. *History of the Byzantine State.* Trans. Joan Hussey. New Brunswick, N.J., 1957.

Packman, Zola Marie. "Masculine and Feminine: Use of Adjectives in the Documentary Papyri." *Bulletin of the American Society of Papyrologists* 25 (1988): 137–148.

Padel, Ruth. "Between Theory and Fiction: Reflections on Feminism and Classical Scholarship." *Gender and History* 2, no. 2 (1990): 198–211.

Padel, Ruth. *In and Out of the Mind: Greek Images of the Tragic Self.* Princeton, 1992.

Parlasca, Klaus. "Artemis Ephesia und Pseudo-men." *Anatolia* 22 (1981–1983): 255–259.

Pateman, Carol. "Feminist Critiques of the Public/Private Dichotomy." In *Feminism and Equality,* ed. Anne Phillips. New York, 1987.

Patlagean, Evelyne. "L'histoire de la femme déguisée en moine et l'évolution de la sainteté féminine à Byzance." *Studi medievali,* ser. 3, 17 (1976): 597–623.

———. *Pauvreté économique et pauvreté sociale à Byzance, 4e—7e siècles.* Paris, 1977.

———. "Chrstianisation et parentés rituelles: Le domaine de Byzance." *Annales: Économies, Sociétés, Civilisations* 33 (1978): 625–636.

———. "Sainteté et pouvoir." In *The Byzantine Saint,* ed. Georges Hackel. London, 1981.

———. "Ancient Byzantine Hagiography and Social History." In *Saints and Their Cults: Studies in Religious Sociology, Folklore and History,* ed. Stephen Wilson, pp. 101–121. Cambridge, 1983.

Peers, Glenn. *Subtle Bodies: Representing Angels in Byzantium.* Berkeley, 2001.

Peirce, Leslie P. *The Imperial Harem: Women and Sovereignty in the Ottoman Empire.* New York, 1993.

Pelikan, Jaroslav. *The Christian Tradition: A History of the Development of Doctrine.* Vol. 1, *The Emergence of the Catholic Tradition (100–600).* Vol. 2, *The Spirit of Eastern Christendom (600–1700).* Vol. 3, *The Growth of Medieval Theology (600–1300).* Chicago, 1971–1989.

Pentikäinen, P. "Angels Fallen in Love. A Comparative Study of Fallen Angels in Christian and Islamic Theology in the Seventh and Eighth Centuries." In *Byzantium and the North. Acta Byzantina Fennica* 5 (1990–1991 [1992]): 79–122.

Peschel, E. and R. "Medical Insights into the Castrati in Opera." *American Scientist* 75 (1987): 578–583.

Piltz, Elisabeth. "Middle Period Court Costume." In *Byzantine Court Culture from 829 to 1204*, ed. Henry Maguire, pp. 39–51. Washington, D.C., 1997.

Pomeroy, Sarah B. *Goddesses, Whores, Wives, and Slaves: Women in Classical Antiquity.* New York, 1976.

Pomeroy, Sarah B., ed. *Women's History and Ancient History.* Chapel Hill, N.C., 1991.

Ponthot, Joseph. "L'Angélologie dans l'apocalypse johannique." In *Anges et démons: Actes du colloque de Liège et de Louvain-la-neuve 25–26 novembre 1987*, ed. J. Ries, pp. 301–312. Louvain, 1989.

Price, S. R. F. *Rituals and Power.* Cambridge, 1984.

Ramat, Sabrina, ed. *Gender Reversals and Gender Cultures: Anthropological and Historical Perspectives.* London, 1996.

Rapp, Claudia. "Ritual Brotherhood in Byzantium." Paper presented at University of California Medieval History Seminar, 1996.

Reade, J. E. "The Neo-Assyrian Court and Army: Evidence from the Sculptures." *Iraq* 34 (1972): 87–112.

Reynolds, Edward. *Stand the Storm: A History of the Atlantic Slave Trade.* London, 1989.

Riddle, John M. *Contraception and Abortion from the Ancient World to the Renaissance.* Cambridge, Mass., 1992.

Ringrose, Kathryn M. "Living in the Shadows: Eunuchs and Gender in Byzantium." In *Third Sex, Third Gender: Beyond Sexual Dimorphism in Culture and History*, ed. Gilbert Herdt, pp. 85–110, 504–518. New York, 1994.

———. "Eunuchs as Cultural Mediators." *Byzantinische Forschungen* 23 (1996): 75–93.

———. "Language, Eunuchs, and Gender in Byzantium." Paper presented at University of California Medieval History Seminar, 1996.

———. "Reconfiguring the Prophet Daniel: Gender, Sanctity, and Castration in Byzantium." In *Difference and Genders in the Middle Ages*, ed. Sharon Farmer and Carol Pasternak. Minneapolis, 2002.

Roberts, Michael. *Poetry and the Cult of the Martyrs: The Liber Peristephanon of Prudentius.* Ann Arbor, Mich., 1993.

Roller, Lynn E. "The Ideology of the Eunuch Priest." In *Gender and the Body in the Ancient Mediterranean*, ed. Maria Wyke, pp. 118–135. Oxford, 1998.

Rosaldo, M. Z. "Women, Culture and Society: A Theoretical Overview." In *Women, Culture, and Society*, ed. M. Z. Rosaldo and L. Lamphere, pp. 17–42. Stanford, 1974.

Roscoe, Will. *The Zuni Man-Woman.* Albuquerque, N.M., 1991.

Rosser, John. "Theophilus 'the Unlucky' (829–842): A Study of the Tragic and Brilliant Reign of Byzantium's Last Iconoclastic Emperor." Ph.D. diss., Rutgers University, 1972.

Rouselle, Aline. *Porneia: On Desire and the Body in Antiquity.* Trans. Felicia Pheasant. Oxford, 1988. First published as *Porneia: De la maitrise du corps à la privation sensorielle, IIe–IVe siècles de l'ère Chrétienne.* Paris, 1983.

Rousseau, Philip. *Basil of Caesarea.* Berkeley, 1994.

———. "'Learned Women' and the Development of a Christian Culture in Late Antiquity." *Symbolae Osloenses* 79 (1995): 116–147.

Runciman, S. *The Emperor Romanus Lecapenus and His Reign: A Study of Tenth-Century Byzantium.* 1929. Reprint, Cambridge, 1988.

Rydén, Lennart. "The Date of the Life of Andreas Salos." *DOP* 32 (1978): 127–155.

———. "The Portrait of the Arab Samonas in Byzantine Literature." *Graeco-Arabica* 3 (1984): 101–108.

Sahlins, Marshal. *Historical Metaphors and Mythical Realities: Structure in the Early History of the Sandwich Islands Kingdom.* Ann Arbor, Mich, 1981.

———. *How "Natives" Think, about Captain Cook, for Example.* Chicago, 1995.

Sakkelion, I., ed. "Romanos Lecapenus." *Deltion* 1 (1883–1884): 657–666; 2 (1885): 38–48, 385–409.

———. "Nicholas Mysticus." *Deltion* 3 (1890–1892): 108–116.

Salisbury, Joyce. *Medieval Sexuality: A Research Guide.* New York, 1990.

Sanday, Peggy, and Ruth Goodenough. *Beyond the Second Sex: New Directions in the Anthropology of Gender.* Philadelphia, 1990.

Sanders, G. M. "Gallos." *Reallexikon für Antike und Christentum,* ed. T. Klauser et al., vol. 8, cols. 984–1034. Stuttgart, 1969–1972.

Sanders, Paula. "Gendering the Ungendered Body: Hermaphrodites in Medieval Islamic Law." In *Shifting Boundaries: Women and Gender in Middle Eastern History,* ed. Nikki Keddie and Beth Baron. New Haven, 1991.

Saxer, Victor. "Jalons pour servir à l'histoire du culte de l'archange Saint Michel en Orient jusqu'à l'iconoclasme." In *Noscere sancta. Miscellanea in memoria di A. Amore O. F. M.* (+1982), pp. 375–426. Rome, 1985.

Scarborough J., ed. *Symposium on Byzantine Medicine. DOP* 38.

Scheflen, Albert, and Alice Scheflen. *Body Language and Social Order: Communication as Behavioral Control.* Englewood Cliffs, N.J., 1972.

Schlumberger, G. *Sigillographie de l'empire byzantin.* Paris, 1884.

———. *Mélanges d'archéologie byzantine.* Paris, 1895.

Schmitt, Jean-Claude. "The Rationale of Gesture in the West: Third to Thirteenth Centuries." In *A Cultural History of Gesture,* ed. Jan Bremmer and Herman Roodenburg, pp. 59–83. Ithaca, N.Y., 1992.

Scholz, Piotr. *Eunuchs and Castrati: A Cultural History.* Trans. from the German by John A. Broadwin and Shelley L. Frisch. Princeton, 2001.

Sevcenko, Ihor. *Society and Intellectual Life in Late Byzantium.* London, 1981.

———. *Ideology, Letters and Culture in the Byzantine World.* London, 1982.

Sevcenko, Nancy P. *Illustrated Manuscripts of the Metaphrastian Menologion.* Chicago, 1990.

Shboul, Ahmad M. H. "Byzantium and the Arabs: The Image of the Byzantines Mirrored in Arabic Literature." In *Byzantine Papers, Proceedings of the First Australian Byzantine Conference,* pp. 43–68. Canberra, 1981.

Simon, Bennett. *Mind and Madness in Ancient Greece.* Ithaca, N.Y., 1978.

Simon, Dieter. *Lobpreis des Eunuchen.* Munich, 1994.

Siraisi, Nancy. *Medieval and Early Renaissance Medicine: An Introduction to Knowledge and Practice.* Chicago, 1990.

Skoda, Françoise. *Médecine ancienne et métaphore: Le vocabulaire de l'anatomie et de la pathologie en grec ancien.* Paris, 1988.

Snipes, Kenneth. "An Unedited Treatise of Michael Psellos on the Iconography of Angels and on the Religious Festivals Celebrated on Each Day of the Week." In *Gonimos: Neoplatonic and Byzantine Studies Presented to Leendert G. Westerink at 75*, ed. John Duffy and John Peradotto, pp. 189–205. Buffalo, N.Y., 1988.

Sophocles, E. A. *Greek Lexicon of the Roman and Byzantine Periods.* 1914. Reprint, Hildesheim, 1992.

Souvides, A. "The Byzantine Family of Kekaumenos." *Diptycha* 4 (1986–1987): 12–27.

Spatharakis, Iohannis. "The Proskynesis in Byzantine Art." *Bulletin Antieke Beschaving* 49 (1974): 190–205.

———. *The Portrait in Byzantine Illuminated Manuscripts.* Leiden, 1976.

Spiegel, Gabrielle. "History, Historicism, and the Social Logic of the Text in the Middle Ages." *Speculum* 65 (1990): 59–86.

Stavrakas, Spyros. "The Byzantine Provincial Elites: A Study in Social Relationships during the Ninth and Tenth Centuries." Ph.D. diss., University of Chicago, 1978.

Stent, G. Carter. "Chinese Eunuchs." *Journal of the North-China Branch of the Royal Asiatic Society*, n.s., 9 (1877): 143–184.

Stock, Brian. *Myth and Science in the Twelfth Century.* Princeton, 1972.

Strunk, Oliver. *Essays on Music in the Byzantine World.* New York, 1977.

Swain, Simon. "The Reliability of Philostratus's *Lives of the Sophists.*" *Classical Antiquity* 10 (1991): 148–163.

Szemioth, A., and T. Wasilewski. "Sceaux byzantins du Musée National de Varsovie." *Studia Zródtoznawcze, Commentationes* 11 (1966): 1–38, 14 (1969): 63–69.

Talbot, Alice-Mary. "Women's Space in Byzantine Monasteries." *DOP* 52 (1998): 113–127.

Tannen, Deborah. *You Just Don't Understand: Women and Men in Conversation.* New York, 1990.

Tatic-Djuric, Mirjana. "Archanges gardiens de Porte à Decani." In *Decani et l'art byzantin au millieu de XIVe siècle*, ed. Vojislav Djuric, pp. 359–370. Belgrade, 1989.

Thomas, Garith. "Magna Mater und Attis. In *Aufsteig und Niedergang der römischen Welt*, ser. 2, vol. 17 (1989): 1500–1535.

Thomas, Nicholas, and Caroline Humphrey, eds. *Shamanism, History and the State.* Ann Arbor, Mich., 1994.

Tortzeu, Chr. Gorm. "Male and Female in Peripatetic Botany." *Classica et Mediaevalia* 42 (1991): 81–110.

Tougher, Shaun. "Monasteries for Eunuchs 1: Survey." Paper presented at the Conference on Byzantine Monasticism, Toronto, 2001.

Trautman, Donald W. *The Eunuch Logion of Matthew 19, 12: Historical and Exegetical Dimensions Related to Celibacy.* Rome, 1966.

Treadgold, Warren. *The Byzantine Revival, 780–842.* Stanford, 1988.

Trexler, Richard C. *Sex and Conquest: Gendered Violence, Political Order, and the European Conquest of the Americas.* Ithaca, N.Y., 1995.

Troianos, S. "Medical Science and Physicians in the Interpretation of the Canons of the Lawyers of the Twelfth Century." In *Byzantium in the Twelfth Century*, ed. Nicolas Oikonomidès, pp. 465–486. Athens, 1991.

Turdeanu, Émile. "Le mythe des anges déchus: Traditions littéraires de l'Europe Occidentale et Orientale." *Rivista di studi bizantini e slavi* 2 (1982): 73–117.

Van der Aalst, A. J. "The Palace and the Monastery in Byzantine Spiritual Life c. 1000." In *The Empress Theophano: Byzantium and the West at the Turn of the First Millennium*, ed. Adelbert Davids, pp. 314–336. Cambridge, 1995.

Van Gulik, R. H. *Sexual Life in Ancient China.* Leiden, 1961.

Vance, Carole, ed. *Pleasure and Danger: Exploring Female Sexuality.* London, 1989.

Vasiliev, A. "Harun ibn-Yahya and his Description of Constantinople." *Seminarium Kondakovianum* [Prague] 5 (1932): 149–63.

Vasiliev, A. "Pero Tafur . . . and His Visit to Constantinople." *Byzantion* 7 (1932): 75–122.

Verlinden, Charles. *L'esclavage dans l'Europe médiévale.* 2 vols. Bruges, 1977.

Veyne, Paul, ed. *A History of Private Life.* Vol. 1, *From Pagan Rome to Byzantium.* Trans. Arthur Goldhammer. Cambridge, Mass., 1987.

von Dobshütz, E. "Der Kammerherr Theophanes." *BZ* 10 (1901): 166–181.

von Rad, Gerhard. "Daniel and Apocalyptes." In Gerhard von Rad, *Old Testament Theology*, trans. D. Stalker, vol. 2. New York, 1962–[1965].

von Simson, Otto G. *Sacred Fortress: Byzantine Art and Statecraft in Ravenna.* Princeton, 1987.

von Staden, Heinrich. *Herophilus: The Art of Medicine in Early Alexandria.* Cambridge, 1989.

Wallace-Hadrill, D. S. *The Greek Patristic View of Nature.* New York, 1968.

Westerink, G. "Physiology and Medicine in Late Antiquity." *Janus* (1964): 168–177.

Whitehead, Harriet. "The Bow and the Burden Strap: A New Look at Institutionalized Homosexuality in Native North America." In *Sexual Meanings: The Cultural Construction of Gender and Sexuality*, ed. Sherry B. Ortner and Harriet Whitehead, pp. 80–115. Cambridge, 1981.

Whittow, Mark. *The Making of Byzantium, 600–1025.* Berkeley, 1996.

Wiedemann, Thomas, ed. *Greek and Roman Slavery.* Baltimore, 1981.

———. *Adults and Children in the Roman Empire.* New Haven, 1989.

Wikkan, Unni. *Behind Hidden Veils.* Chicago, 1982.

Williams, Craig. *Roman Homosexuality: Ideologies of Masculinity in Classical Antiquity.* New York, 1999.

Wilson, Jean D. "Sex Hormones and Sexual Behavior." In *Sexual Nature / Sexual Culture*, ed. Paul R. Abramson and Steven D. Pinkerton, pp. 121–134. Chicago, 1995.

Wilson, Robert McL. "Alimentary and Sexual Enkeratism in the Nag Hammadi text." In *La tradizione dell'enkrateia: Matrizione ontologiche e protologiche. Atti del Collquio internazionale, Milan, 20–23 Aprile, 1982*, ed. Ugo Bianchi, pp. 317–339. Rome, 1985.

Wilson, Stephen. *Saints and Their Cults: Studies in Religious Sociology, Folklore and History.* Cambridge, 1983.

Winkler, John J. "Laying Down the Law: The Oversight of Men's Sexual Behavior in Classical Athens." In *The Constraints of Desire: The Anthropology of Sex and Gender in Ancient Greece*, ed. John J. Winkler. New York, 1990.

———. "Unnatural Acts: Erotic Protocols in Artemiodoras' *Dream Analysis*." In *The Constraints of Desire: The Anthropology of Sex and Gender in Ancient Greece*, ed. John J. Winkler, pp. 17–44. London, 1990.

Wright, J. W., Jr., and Everett K. Rowson, eds. *Homeoeroticism in Classical Arabic Literature.* New York, 1997

Wyke, Maria, ed., *Gender and the Body in the Ancient Mediterranean.* Oxford, 1998.

Yannopoulos, Panayotis. *La Société profane dans l'empire byzantin des VIIe, VIIIe et IXe siècles.* Louvain, 1975.

———. "Le Couronnement de l'empereur à Byzance: Rituel et fond institutionnel." *Byzantion* 61 (1991): 71–92.

Young, William C., ed. *Sex and Internal Secretions.* Baltimore, 1961.

Zacos, G. *Byzantine Lead Seals.* Vol. 2. Bonn, 1984.

Zacos, G., and A. Veglery. *Byzantine Lead Seals.* Vol. 1. Basel, 1972.

Zito, Angela, and Tani E. Barlow, eds. *Body, Subject and Power in China.* Chicago, 1994.

INDEX